The Way
of Wisdom

New Westminster Pulpit Series

Once Saved, Always Saved

All's Well that Ends Well

Justification by Works
Sermons on James 1–3

The Way of Wisdom
Sermons on James 4–5

The Way of Wisdom

Patience in Waiting on God
Sermons on James 4–5

R.T. Kendall

Authentic
MEDIA

Authentic Media
We welcome your comments and questions.
129 Mobilization Drive, Waynesboro, GA 30830 USA authenticusa@stl.org

and 9 Holdom Avenue, Bletchley, Milton Keynes, Bucks, MK1 1QR, UK
www.authenticbooks.com

If you would like a copy of our current catalog, contact us at:
1-8MORE-BOOKS
ordersusa@stl.org

The Way of Wisdom
ISBN: 1-932805-28-1

Copyright © 2002 by R.T. Kendall
09 08 07 06 05   6 5 4 3 2 1

Published in 2005 by Authentic Media

Cover design: Paul Lewis
Interior design: WestKey Ltd, Falmouth, Cornwall

Printed in United States of America

To Bill and Rachel

Contents

Foreword

A quick glance at the average bookshelf will show that personal biographies are a growing element in the publishing world. We are in a moment where our culture has lowered its expectations on institutions and raised the value of personal stories.

It is a profoundly biographical culture in which our personal experiences count for a great deal. Our most respected documentaries and news bulletins approach global issues and current affairs from an individual perspective.

But it is also a very pragmatic world. Public life and the world of business have become driven more by what works, as opposed to what we actually believe. If it works we do it. In this market place of personal choices we are being driven by market force values where what is right is often judged by what is materially profitable.

Little wonder therefore that the twenty-first century is throwing up a serious crisis of leadership. Today popular surveys of 'the most influential people' tend to be those with high profiles and who are deemed to be successful in terms of what they own or do. Personal values and a philosophy of life based on the idea of what is true counts for little.

The difficulty is that this is rapidly influencing the Christian Church. When we discuss questions about discipleship or the ways in which Christians live, it is becoming easier to see that our models are increasingly drawn from the wider society rather than from the Bible. Wisdom has been replaced by popular consensus.

But the book of James has a great deal to say to us in our times. James is concerned primarily about precisely the things our culture is concerned about: a practical faith at work in real situations. As far as James is concerned, a faith that does not work is not worth having. Real faith is pragmatic and practical. But James has also spotted the fact that this kind of faith flows from a lifestyle which is guided by God's wisdom. So James gives us wise words to live by.

In this study of James works, R.T. Kendall takes us through a series of personal reflections on our attitudes and outlook on our relationships with

God, the Church, other people and ourselves. The *Way of Wisdom* un-
locks important principles for a contemporary Christian lifestyle which
works and which will help make sense of our faith to a waiting world.

Joel Edwards
24th November 2001

Preface

The book of James is arguably the most practical book in the whole of the New Testament. One of the things that further amazed me about James is how symmetrical and well ordered it actually is. Many good scholars have thought that James was like a string of pool pearls that broke and that the pearls were simply put back on the string without any order – that James is simply full of axioms and moralisms and witty sayings – like Proverbs. It is in fact a letter with a plan.

My own life was personally changed by preaching from the book of James. We took our time doing this, beginning in October 1979, and finishing in the late autumn of 1981. It was a great providence of God that I was led to preach through James, because no book has made such an impact on me as this one. I pray that it will do the same thing for you!

I am thrilled that Joel Edwards, Director General of the Evangelical Alliance, has written the Foreword for this volume. His well known predecessor, Clive Calver, kindly wrote the Foreword to volume one. How honoured I am to have friends like Joel and Clive. Many people thought no one could fill the shoes of Clive Calver, but how wrong they were! Joel has also been a close of mine for many years, and I am honoured that he would join me in this effort.

This volume is dedicated to Bill and Rachel Reynolds. Bill Reynolds has been the Church Secretary at Westminster Chapel for the last several years of my ministry there, and he and Rachel have been beloved friends. A book dedicated to them is certainly in order, if not overdue. God bless you dear friends.

R.T. Kendall
Westminster Chapel, London 2001
September 2001

1

Antinomianism Exposed

James 4:1–4

The fourth chapter of this general epistle of James is by far the most important chapter yet, because now James is going to apply all that he's said. In chapter 4 we see that the discussion of what comes from below – lusts – is continued, but James also picks up yet another theme that was mentioned earlier, namely that of the moral law of God. As far as James is concerned, the worst thing that could be said about a Christian is that his lifestyle is so bad that the moral law could uncover his wrongness. He knows that if you fulfill the royal law of Scripture you will do well.

The Royal Law of Scripture

'Thou shalt love thy neighbour as thyself', is the absolute guarantee of not sinning against any of the Ten Commandments. In Romans 13:8 Paul put it like this: 'Owe no man any thing, but to love one another: for he that loveth another hath fulfilled the law.' And again in Galatians 5:14: 'For all the law is fulfilled in one word, even in this; Thou shalt love thy neighbour as thyself.'

The New Testament is unanimous that it is impossible to be filled with love and break the moral law of God at the same time. If you are filled with the fruit of the Spirit, which is 'love, joy, peace, long-suffering ...' it is impossible to break the moral law. What these Jewish Christians had done – and James is appalled by it – is that they had committed murder by showing respect of persons. And this is why he begins to quote from the Ten Commandments. This is something that he ought not to have to do to a Christian.

Now when James gets to chapter 4 he spells it out. 'Ye kill, and desire to have, and cannot obtain.' James then comes to the heart of the problem. He does not bring in the moral law as the Christian code of conduct. As Paul put it: 'The law is not made for a righteous man, but for the lawless and disobedient, for the ungodly and for sinners, for unholy and profane, for murderers of fathers and murderers of mothers, for manslayers, For whoremongers, for them that defile themselves with mankind', and on and on he goes (1 Tim. 1:9–10). What James has done by bringing in the law is to show how far these Christian Jews had degenerated. The law had exposed them and the Christian ought never to be exposed by the law.

Moral Antinomians

James now has his work cut out for him because he has to convince these Jewish Christians that they have sinned. They didn't really think that being a respecter of persons was sin. These Christian Jews James was addressing prefigured a strange kind of antinomianism. They were antinomians but didn't know it. They were moral antinomians. That expression may sound like a contradiction. It's like talking about a 'hot snowball'. Moral antinomians. But that is what they were.

Antinomian simply means 'against law'. The term itself, so far as we know, never really emerged until the sixteenth century when one of Luther's ardent followers, Johann Agricola, took the position that the moral law has no place in Christian experience. His point of view became known as 'antinomianism'. This term came to be used pejoratively in church history. It is the worst thing you can call a person, in a way. It's like calling a left-winger a Communist if you really want to hurt him. Or if he's a right-winger you call him a Nazi.

There were Christians in the seventeenth century that were called antinomian. Tobias Crisp was one, a very godly man. All of Oliver Cromwell's chaplains were called antinomians because they emphasized living in the Spirit. John Cotton was called an antinomian because he refused to let sanctification be the proof of justification.

Paul himself was virtually called that. He had to defend against the claim that his own teaching encouraged people to live licentious lives. After all, Paul did say in Romans 3:28, 'We conclude that a man is justified by faith without the deeds of the law.' This sounds very antinomian. Paul's doctrine indeed gives rise to the doctrinal structures of antinomianism. However, what Paul meant – and this is often forgotten – was that the moral law has no place in Christian experience. That doesn't mean that law has no place. For Paul went on to say that 'the law of the Spirit of life in Christ Jesus hath made me free from the law of sin and death' (Rom. 8:2). Writing to the Corinthians he said, 'To them that are without law, as without law, (being not without law to God, but under the law to Christ) ...' (1 Cor. 9:21). In Galatians 6:2 he said, 'Bear ye one another's burdens, and so fulfil the law of Christ.'

Christians and the Moral Law

We as Christians are not under the moral law. We're under the law of Christ. The law of Christ is far more demanding and presents a far greater challenge to us than the moral law. This is often forgotten. And yet this matter of understanding the law is one that is not easy to grasp.

Understanding the law is not easy, but nothing is more rewarding than when one does get to the bottom of it. A fear of antinomianism even with reference to the moral law is, generally speaking, a healthy fear. Those people who are afraid of antinomianism are afraid of open immorality and licentiousness. They think that if you take away the moral law, immorality is what you're going to get.

Paul says, however, 'Walk in the Spirit, and ye shall not fulfil the lust of the flesh' (Gal. 5:16). He shows what the fruit of the Spirit is: love, that's the first. If love is there it's not possible to break any of the Ten Commandments.

Moral Law Makes us Blind

But the Spirit goes beyond the moral law – love, joy, peace, long-suffering. The law never even pretended to produce things like that. The New Testament's position is categorically against antinomianism. As Christians we are under the law of Christ. True godliness is never to be achieved by being under the moral law, which will make you a legalist, long-faced, grouchy. People who know that this is your code of ethics are not going to be impressed with you because there's no joy or peace. The law of Christ *presupposes* that one is behaving himself morally, and takes one beyond the moral law.

Here is James' point. Moral antinomianism is just as wicked and deadly and grieving to the Spirit as immoral antinomianism. I'm talking about the person who lives by the moral law so that outwardly he's clean, outwardly he's moral but inwardly he's still in rebellion to the law of Christ. A person like that doesn't really think there's anything wrong with him.

Moral antinomianism, that is, living by the moral law but rejecting the law of Christ tends to camouflage the real malady.

Moral people are the hardest in the world to convert. This is the biggest problem you have when you talk to the lost. People who are moral don't even think that they've done anything wrong. But a Christian can develop a self-righteous spirit that is ominously like the unconverted moral person. James labours to demonstrate that these Christians were really antinomians after all. Because, in the end all sin is antinomian. This is why John said that sin is lawlessness. It's breaking the law of Christ.

So moral antinomianism describes those who keep the moral law but sin against the law of Christ. They feel no guilt or shame when they commit adultery in their hearts, if in their heart there is jealousy or a grudge or hate, if they despise the poor and elevate the rich. Outwardly they're all right, and so because their orthodoxy is in place they just don't feel that they need any help.

These Jewish Christians were sound in their doctrine, and they thought that was sufficient. It is my conviction that evangelical Christianity generally is guilty of this same sin of moral antinomianism. We're smug, complacent, middle class, moral, beyond reproach. Outwardly we're proper. And many of us are articulate. But we are lifeless and irrelevant in the world. We're failures and, worst of all, we show little evidence that we're about to change.

Moral Law Hides our Ineffectiveness

This epistle is so relevant to our situation. 'From whence come wars and fightings among you?' The Greek word simply means 'quarrels'. That's the NIV translation. Evangelical Christianity generally, and nearly every congregation particularly, is known for its quarrels. Every congregation seems to have its cliques, its groups, those who aren't speaking. If that is the case you cannot expect the Spirit of God to come down. Evangelical Christianity is in a sad, melancholy state: ministers who secretly would like to leave their pulpits and go into secular work; deacons who'd prefer to stay at home but now that they're deacons they've got to go to church; sunday school teachers and Bible school teachers demoralized because so few want to come.

James comes to grips with this kind of malady. When we are not what we ought to be we always take it out on each other. When a church is not evangelistic and seeing conversions we begin to get bitter towards each other and go for one another's throats. This is why the evangelistic church is the happy church. A church not guided by the Spirit will be filled with quarreling. The church at Galatia had the same problem. Marriage, if it is not grounded in love, has the same problem – husband and wife quarrelling all the time.

Moral Law Justifies our Fighting

James shows the real cause of quarrels: your own lusts. You may not like that diagnosis. His readers may have wanted to blame outward conditions or the economic situation or one of the things we always blame when we're in trouble. When we start to go backwards and things aren't going right, we retreat from the real responsibility by homing in upon doctrine. Becoming more articulate theologically is one of the biggest cop-outs ever to come along.

A church back in my home town said, 'We're not ready to evangelize. We need to learn more. One of these days we're going to go out.' They gave themselves five years back in 1956. Now they're so dead the town doesn't even know they're there. When our evangelism is curbed we turn on each other. The real cause is your own lusts. The Greek word is *hedone*, sensual pleasure.

The Real Problem – Our Desires

The word translated 'lust' most often in the Authorised Version is a different word. This word is used in the gospel of Luke, in the parable of the sower, where there were those who never made their profession of faith. They kept hearing the word of God preached, but the word fell among thorns (8:14). These are the ones Jesus said that 'have heard, go forth, and are choked with cares and riches and pleasures of this life'. 'Pleasures' is the same word that James uses: 'lusts'.

Peter uses the word and it is translated 'pleasures'. 'They that count it pleasure to riot in the day time' (2 Peter 2:13). It means sensual pleasure. In Platonic literature the seat of this pleasure was the body. It's not a very complimentary thing to have somebody say to these Christians in the ancient world, 'Your problem is that you're living for pleasure.' We know that these Christian Jews were in trouble. They weren't winning anybody. They virtually made blasphemers out of people. They probably said, 'Yes, we have our quarrels.'

Often when there is a quarrel in the church the proposed solution is to get somebody out of the church. But the answer to the problem is usually not to throw somebody out of the church. In Philippians there was a little

problem going on and at the end of the epistle Paul says, 'I beseech
Euodias, and beseech Syntyche, that they be of the same mind in the Lord'
(4:2). Often in a marriage the husband will say, 'I just need a better wife
than you. You don't understand me. I don't deserve you. You don't
deserve me.'

Quarrels stem from desire for pleasure, sensual pleasure. Not that these
people were necessarily open adulterers or secretly reading pornography,
but here were Christians who hadn't really come to grips with themselves,
their grudges, their jealousies, their own hearts, their own lusts. They
were blaming outward conditions or blaming each other.

Paul says, 'Mortify therefore your members which are upon the earth'
and he names them: 'fornication, uncleanness' (Col. 3:5) and so forth.
'Wrath, malice, blasphemy' (v. 8). Instead of killing each other, kill these
things.

Quarrels, whether in families or in church families, in a congregation
or in your own heart, can be traced every time to our failure to set our
affections on things above, where Christ is seated on the right hand of
God (Col. 3:1). It's possible to be outwardly moral and inwardly rotten.
It's so easy to keep the moral law and hate the law of Christ. It's the case
when somebody just criticizes all the time. He doesn't realize that his own
nose is out of joint. Satan doesn't care how moral we are if he can keep us
torn up inside.

Satan turned these Jewish Christians into double agents for his own
kingdom. They had turned on each other and it had aborted the
growth of the gospel. That's what Satan wants. Churches today are
existing but losing their young people, attracting almost nobody
from outside because those within, though outwardly moral, are preoccupied with their own pleasures. We're not giving non-Christians
any tangible reason for believing.

So the root of your lusts is in your members – *melos* – the Greek word
means a limb or any part of the body. Jesus used this word in the Sermon
on the Mount. 'Ye have heard that it was said by them of old time, Thou
shalt not commit adultery' – moral law. Now what about the law of
Christ? 'But I say unto you, That whosoever looketh on a woman to lust
after her hath committed adultery with her already in his heart.' Jesus said,
'If thy right eye offend thee, pluck it out, and cast it from thee: for it is
profitable for thee that one of thy members' – *melos* – 'should perish, and
not that thy whole body should be cast into hell. And if thy right hand
offend thee, cut it off, and cast it from thee: for it is profitable for thee that
one of thy members should perish, and not that thy whole body should be
cast into hell' (Mt. 5:27–30).

Spiritually we are members of the body of Christ and spiritually we all have members within us. But we must not forget that we are members of Christ's body and as our own persons are comprised of various parts making up the whole, we have a responsibility to deal with our members that war against the mind of Christ. So if there is that area of your own life that saps you and robs you of spiritual growth you can pray around it, you can start tithing or double tithing, or come to church twice as often, but you will not grow until you cast off that member. Deal with it.

We Are Responsible for our Own Temptations

The New Testament position is that it is our job to deal with whatever militates against the supreme will of God. Paul's term is 'mortify'. Kill it. James' point is that fights and quarrels stem from unmortified members. 'Let no man say when he is tempted, I am tempted of God … but every man is tempted, when he is drawn away of his own lust, and enticed' (Jas. 1:13–14).

We are responsible for our own temptations. This is why James shows us that the chief goal in Christian living is to reduce temptation to the level of suggestion. We cannot help suggestions. But we can deal with temptation.

Three Rules to Deal with Desire

In closing, I want to suggest three rules to you for dealing with your lusts. Generally speaking, there are two sorts of lusts. One is sexual desire, and that's chiefly with the aim of physical gratification. Another kind of lust is vengeful desire. That's mostly mental gratification, a wish to get even or vindicated. I offer these three rules because they've helped me.

Rule 1: Believe You Can Resist

You must have the conviction that your lusts can be brought under control. 'There hath no temptation taken you but such as is common to man: but God is faithful, who … will with the temptation also make a way to escape, that ye may be able to bear it' (1 Cor. 10:13). When Paul says, 'Mortify your members', he is not putting before us something that cannot be done. He would not mock us like that.

Rule 2: Desire to Please Christ

When you have a desire to please Christ in such a measure that that desire becomes greater than the desire to fulfil your lusts, the suggestion may come, but you know you want to please Christ who bought you. And the desire becomes greater than the desire to be gratified on a natural level.

Rule 3: Just Say 'No'

Absolutely refuse to give mental assent to the suggestion that militates against the mind of Christ. Here's your Scripture: 'Casting down imaginations' – or reasonings – 'and every high thing that exalteth itself against the knowledge of God, and bringing into captivity every thought to the obedience of Christ' (2 Cor. 10:5). You shut off the possibility of dwelling on the thought. Believe it or not, if you do this, you reduce temptation to the level of suggestion. It works.

Our Challenge

To refuse this is to be antinomian, inwardly hostile to the supreme rule of Jesus Christ in your life. Not antinomian in the sense of outward morality or immorality, but in the refusal to let the living Christ totally reign. Our problem is antinomianism. This is the problem with the Ecumenical Movement. They are in rebellion against the law of Christ. They hide behind the social gospel to keep from dealing with their own lusts. They get exercised about preserving endangered species in the North Atlantic, but their lusts don't bother them.

The reason people are antinomians is not because of their doctrine but because of their lusts. Rather than bring their lusts under control they hide behind a doctrine that gives them a rationale for postponing obedience to Christ. Let it not be said of us. It is hard. I put before you the greatest challenge in the world. It is possible to be the winner of the Nobel Peace Prize and fail in this area.

Here's the challenge. It will be a demonstration of Christianity that this generation has not seen, where our desire to please the Lord Jesus is greater than the desire for vengeance or to fulfil our lusts, where we just refuse to think about any thought that militates against the mind of Christ. When we begin to show our love for God in that manner, the world will take notice.

2

The Glory of Unfulfilled Desire

James 4:1–4

We have had occasion to note at various times in this series that James knew the people he was talking to when he wrote this letter. Though we call it a 'general epistle' James obviously knew who his most immediate readers were. There are inferences to be drawn all the way through that show in a very real way that this is a pastoral epistle. Indeed it shows us in great detail how the Christian life is to be lived.

In commencing our study of James chapter 4 our attention is immediately drawn to the five words of verse 2: 'Ye lust, and have not.' This is an indication that James knows what was going on. He sets forward here a general description of these people. A spiritually minded man is able to make certain predictions and judgements without necessarily knowing every single fact. Paul could write to the Corinthians, 'I fear, lest by any means, as the serpent beguiled Eve through his subtlety, so your minds should be corrupted from the simplicity that is in Christ' (2 Cor. 11:3). He knew too much about the Corinthians not to give them that kind of warning. So it was here with James.

The Perceptiveness Of James

James not only had a knowledge of what was happening, but in this case more probably he was letting them know he knew what they were experiencing. It was obvious to him because when there was a disobedience to the Lord generally – and he knew this to be true – a certain thing would follow: they would be lusting but not having what they lusted after. So when James says, 'Ye lust, and have not,' he's not surprised because he knows the general principle of Scripture. 'Good

understanding giveth favour: but the way of transgressors is hard'
(Prov. 13:15).

James knew enough about them that, even if he didn't have the
specific information, he could say, 'Ye lust, and have not.' Hardly a
Sunday goes by that somebody will come to me and say, 'Did you
know that I was out there today?' or 'Did somebody tell you about me?'
And I'm forced to say, 'I'm sorry but obviously God was speaking to you.'
It could be that this is all it was, that James didn't actually know and yet he
did know.

Miserable Christians

The general spiritual state of James' readers led to more acute problems.
God has so made us, Christ has so bought us, that any rebellion toward our
Creator and our Redeemer will always backfire. Augustine said, 'Thou
hast made us for Thyself and our hearts are restless until they find their rest
in Thee.' We may add, 'Thou hast bought us for Thyself and our hearts
will be lusting and unfulfilled until they find their fulfilment in Thy will.'
This is why a Christian can be the most miserable person in the world.
I have dealt with people in the vestry who have said to me, 'I am now
unhappier than I was before I was a Christian.' This should not be all that
surprising when you understand the implications of the gospel and what it
means to believe on Christ.

When you receive Christ as Saviour you have ratified the blood of the
cross. And when that is done it means that Christ now owns you. He
begins to exercise a godly jealousy over you. You cannot live in rebellion
to the will of Christ and expect God to take no notice of that rebellion.
Paul said: 'For the love of Christ constraineth us; because we thus judge,
that if one died for all, then were all dead: And that he died for all' – why?
– 'that they which live should not henceforth live unto themselves, but
unto him which died for them, and rose again' (2 Cor. 5:14–15). Paul, a
godly man, said, 'I follow after, if that I may apprehend that for which also
I am apprehended of Christ Jesus' (Phil. 3:12). The godly man says,
'Christ died for me. He has bought me. He wouldn't own me if he didn't
have a plan for me. I want to know what that is.'

The benefits of obedience are so wonderful that they defy description.
God wants you to know his will. In short, the Christian incurs a judgement the non-Christian knows nothing of. It is called chastening. Back in
the book of Lamentations there is a question: 'Wherefore doth a living
man complain, a man for the punishment of his sins?' (3:39). The writer

to the Hebrews put it like this: 'Whom the Lord loveth he chasteneth, and scourgeth every son whom he receiveth ... if ye be without chastisement ... then are ye bastards' (12:6,8). You're not even a child of God at all if you are without chastening.

Chastening – The Hard Road To Fulfilment

The lesson for us today is to see a different kind of chastening. How is this chastening carried out? Many ways, but we must not forget the introductory lesson on chastening. There are three rules:

- Rule number one: if you're a Christian, chastening is inevitable.
- Rule number two: chastening is for our profit. So said the writer to the Hebrews. Our parents punish us partly for their own pleasure because they know others are going to wonder, 'Why is your child like that?' Sometimes parents lose their tempers with their children and they're emotionally involved. But with God there's nothing like that. God doesn't get emotionally involved. God got his satisfaction at the cross when Jesus died and God punished Jesus. 'He hath not dealt with us after our sins; nor rewarded us according to our iniquities' (Ps. 103:10). When God chastens us it's a singular kindness: he's trying to correct us.
- Rule number three: chastening is painful. 'No chastening for the present seemeth to be joyous, but grievous.' But how wonderful the results are: 'Afterward it yieldeth the peaceable fruit of righteousness unto them which are exercised thereby' (Heb. 12:11).

The first degree: internal chastening

There are degrees of chastening.

The first degree of chastening is by the surgical power of God's word. I call this 'internal chastening'. Here's the way the writer to the Hebrews put it: 'For the word of God is quick, and powerful, and sharper than any two-edged sword, piercing even to the dividing asunder of soul and spirit, and of the joints and marrow, and is a discerner of the thoughts and intents of the heart' (4:12). This chastening is normally that which is seen through the preaching of the word. It's when God speaks to you in such a way that it leaves you broken.

Do you know what it is to be broken by the preaching of the word so that you can hardly move or speak. You want to be left alone. You need to think. This is something that God does, but here is the good news: the more you are broken by God's word, the less likely it is that you will be put through severer forms of chastening. Preaching is preventive medicine as well as being a cure. This is a hint for us to take heed to God's word and avoid harsher forms of chastening. God doesn't want to chasten us in harsher ways. He only does it when he has to.

The second degree: external chastening

The second degree of chastening is by the surgical powers of providence. I call this 'external chastening.' It is a measure that God takes when preaching ceases to break us, when we don't listen to preaching. There was a time when preaching broke us but now it leaves us indifferent. 'I've heard that before.' You can talk about it in a rather academic way. The preaching isn't moving you. This is out of the preacher's hands and it's out of your hands. This is why it's external. God has no choice but to step in.

This is when things happen over which you have no control. It could be illness, a financial reverse, the loss of a friendship, the loss of your job. The surgical powers of providence are from God and are aimed to wake you up.

The third degree: withdrawal of grace

I come now to the third degree of chastening. This is by the withdrawal of certain normal Christian graces, including:

- the joy of sins forgiven
- the sense of God's presence
- peace
- the knowledge of God's will.

Here are four graces that enable you to cope. These graces partly separate the Christian from the non-Christian. The non-Christian knows nothing of the joy of sins forgiven, of the sense of God's presence or of peace or of the knowledge of God's will.

If these are taken away, you are virtually like the non-Christian. You are like any person of the world. You're as though you were never converted, save for the one thing that highly suggests that you are a Christian. 'Ye lust, and have not.' The non-Christian lusts and he has. His lusts are fulfilled. But the spiritually deficient Christian, whom I have called the 'moral antinomian', lusts and has not.

This third degree of chastening is when you are left to cope with what you are by nature. The result is that you have got your own innate weaknesses: your jealousies, your fears, your lusts, your hate, your bewilderment, the fuzzy thinking. You're left to yourself. As James puts it: 'Where envying and strife is' because this wisdom that comes from below is 'sensual' and 'devilish' – 'there is confusion and every evil work' (3:15, 16). That's the result because these graces, that enabled you to cope, that made you know that in a fresh way God was with you and loved you and that you were his child and life was wonderful, have been withdrawn and, worst of all, or shall we say best of all, you don't even get what you want. You lust and have not. Like Saul, who wanted to kill David but never succeeded, this kind of Christian has the animal-like nature and lusts of the unregenerate man but does not have what he wants. He can't even be successful at sinning.

Living With The Third Degree

These Christian Jews whom James addresses were experiencing this third degree of chastening – the withdrawal of Christian graces. It was a consequence of their moral antinomianism. They were outwardly moral, but inwardly they were hostile to the royal law of Scripture. The result for the world was that their impact on non-Christians was everything Satan could have wished for.

The tell-tale sign of God's disapproval of them was: 'Ye lust, and have not.' James says that they live so close to the world that the world is really what they want, but because God hasn't given them up they can't have it. It's the most frustrating way to live. You may even say, 'I wish I weren't a Christian.' Well, it's too late for that because you are. This is why I say sometimes, 'Stop, don't become a Christian. Wait, because once you ratify the blood of the cross you are God's for ever. And he takes seriously what he owns, namely you.'

These Christians were the most miserable people of all. Though outwardly moral, inwardly they were full of turmoil, full of lust. We may conclude that they were tempted. James said, 'Every man is tempted, when he is drawn away of his own lust' (1:14). This tells us more about them. Here were Christians who dwelt in an atmosphere charged with continuous temptation – because they preferred it. They had developed in the meantime a real allergy to godliness, godly fellowship and godly people. They knew nothing of victory. They had no sense of being on top of things and being in control of their emotions. Any suggestion of the devil just bowled them right over.

Rationalizing lust

The sad thing is that, while all this was going on, their lusting was really what they lived for. They enjoyed their lusting. They became adjusted to it. They became addicted to it. But they rationalized it. This is what always happens to a Christian when he's not what God wants him to be and yet he lusts all the time. He says, 'This is what other people really are, all these godly Christians. They just don't admit it. They're lusting just like I am.'

This is what the backslider does. He's filled with his own ways and he projects what's going on in his life upon everybody else. Misery loves company. He imputes to others what he himself feels. In the meantime, he makes sure that he seeks out those people who are like himself because he is annoyed at really godly fellowship. He can't imagine that there's anybody unlike himself.

Some people actually find Scriptures to support them in their lusts. Years ago I was counselling two different ministers at about the same time. One of these ministers, who I'm convinced was a Christian, refused to come to grips with his homosexual feelings and desires. He insisted that he was not practising, but he enjoyed the lusting. Rather than come to grips with it he said, 'The Lord has shown me that this was Paul's problem in Romans 7.' The other minister had the opposite problem – lusting after women all the time. He enjoyed that. He said, 'This is normal.' The Lord had shown him something – that that was Paul in Romans 7. The trouble is that neither of them had a clue what Paul was saying in Romans 7, but it gave them a justification for their own feelings. As Peter described some: 'Having eyes full of adultery, and that cannot cease from sin' (2 Pet. 2:14). But what James is doing here is actually to point to the undoubted glory that lies behind these unfulfilled desires.

Why is it that they lust but 'have not'? It is a case of God's over-ruling grace. It's not a case now of grace working from within. The reason they lust and have not is because God steps in and won't let them have any. It's not at all the case that they have power from within to resist. It's not like Joseph when he ran from Potiphar's wife. It is rather like the case of Lot who pitched his tent towards Sodom, and in the end he almost got burnt. He was snatched from the fire, 'hating even the garment spotted by the flesh' (Jude 23). What we have here is God in his mercy overruling, so that one lusts but has not. It is this overruling kindness that keeps one from sinning.

Overruled by grace

There are examples of this. It is frequently demonstrated in young people. Sometimes with teenagers, girls do keep their purity – perhaps because of praying mothers and fathers. There are cases where young men, boys growing up, are spared falling into sin. This is frequently demonstrated with young people, young married couples, especially in an age such as ours when temptations abound. That some younger Christians don't sin is often a case of God's overruling grace and providence. They can't really take any credit for it. They can't say, 'God enabled me.' No, God stopped it. God enabled you but not because within your will you said no. You think, 'I was spared.'

This demonstration of overruling grace can come at any age. It can come to middle-aged or older couples when the sanctity of marriage sometimes becomes trivial and unexciting. New temptations abound: when a man gets attention from a strange woman and he isn't getting that at home. Or a woman begins to get kindness from a man and she says, 'My husband hasn't appreciated me.' You begin to rationalize and you feed upon this. When a lack of spirituality sets in, the lusting of the flesh begins to abound. God steps in. The undoubted glory that lies behind unfulfilled desires is nothing but goodness and mercy in pursuit.

What James is describing is the outwardly moral but inwardly worldly Christian. The remarkable thing about a Christian like this is that he is most astonishingly kept from falling into open sin. In some cases these people are most willing. Sometimes they even try but are kept and God simply intervenes for one of four reasons:

- to spare you the sorrow of guilt. For guilt has a way of crippling your soul, crippling you emotionally and traumatizing your personality. Some never get over it.
- God steps in to spare you the sorrow of a taste of sin which engenders an even greater lust than ever. You may have said, 'I'd like to do it once.' Once will make it ten times worse.
- God intervenes because he spares you the sorrow of what it would do to your friends, maybe to your wife, to your children and to the church.
- God steps in to spare you the sorrow of becoming what Paul feared most of all, of being a castaway, of being put on the shelf and not being used.

Nothing is worse than having your lust fulfilled. God is not at the bottom of your lust. But God *is* at the bottom of your not having!

Further Degrees Of Chastening

You may want to ask, 'What if someone does fall and he's a Christian and does have his lust fulfilled? What then?' There are two further degrees of chastening.

The fourth degree: shame

The fourth degree is the shame of fulfilled lust. If the moral antinomian is not corrected in time he may well become an immoral antinomian. In other words, when God's overruling grace is not appreciated sometimes, if only to show one as an example, God allows his own to fall. This is to be seen as a severer form of chastening. In one of John Newton's letters he pointed out that God does let some of his own actually fall to show that it can happen. A lot of times the Christian will say, 'I don't think God's going to let that happen to me.' And it does. And you think, 'Surely not. I can't believe it.'

The fifth degree: destruction

There is a fifth and ultimate form of chastening. That is, being completely given over to Satan. Such a one is not fit to remain in the church. The consequence almost always is a profligate, venal lifestyle. This is what was taking place in 1 Corinthians 5:5 when Paul said there was only one thing to do, deliver him to 'Satan for the destruction of the flesh, that the spirit may be saved in the day of the Lord Jesus'. People like this frequently bring upon themselves premature, if not tragic, ends.

Hope For All

If you are in this last degree I want to say there is hope for you. This same man that Paul delivered to Satan repented, and 2 Corinthians 2 gives him some space and says to take him back, receive him. It's wonderful to know that 'if we confess our sins, He is faithful and just to forgive us our sins, and to cleanse us from all unrighteousness' (1 Jn. 1:9). Come on back. God is talking to you. Who knows what he will do with you? Spend the rest of your life living to his glory.

If you are in this fourth degree in which you have fallen into sin, confess it to God and nobody else. Make a full repentance in your heart and in your life and let God pick up the pieces.

In the third degree you lust and have not. You cannot abide in that state for ever. One of two things will happen eventually. Either you will fall into sin or you will make a full repentance and you will come back to the place that you have once known: the joy of sins forgiven, the sense of God's presence, peace and the knowledge of his will.

If I've described you and you're in the third degree, I want you to get alone with God as soon as possible and thank him for sparing you. The glory of your unfulfilled desire is God sparing you all these things. Thank him. And then say, 'Lord, you've got me now. Mind, body, heart, take me. Use me.' Say in your heart, 'Never again.'

3

Success Withheld

James 4:1–4

In the middle of verse 2 of James chapter 4 James is showing these Christian Jews what is going on in their lives. He says, 'Ye lust, and have not.' Some translate this verse: 'You desire'. I think 'lust' is truer to James' meaning, because in verse 1 the Greek word means 'sensual pleasure'. So the context should govern our translation of verse 2, which is clearly referring to lusting. And yet the marvel, the glory, is that they were kept from sinning.

Flirting With Temptation

James moves on and says another thing. 'Ye kill.' What is going on is this: there are two chief problems that all people face at the natural level. They are sexual lust and self-esteem being brought under control. James is now moving from sex to self-esteem. So he says they lust because they are flirting with temptation rather than reducing it to the level of suggestion. But not only do they lust, they kill. Killing is taking vengeance. That is, they are trying to fulfill their self-esteem by their own hands.

When he says, 'Ye kill', we are reminded of the discussion of the moral law in the second chapter of James. These Christian Jews were guilty of murder because they were sending both the rich and the poor to hell. Now James returns to that and he says, 'Ye kill', which is a very serious charge, but no more serious than that which our Lord gave in the Sermon on the Mount. According to our Lord, lusting in the heart is committing adultery. James calls them adulterers and adulteresses. And hating, according to Jesus, is committing murder. Not that these Christian Jews physically killed or were guilty of homicide in a legal way. Obviously they were not, because they lusted without actually having their lust fulfilled. Their killing is in the same way and so he goes on to say, '… and desire to have, and cannot obtain'. It's talking about what was in their hearts.

Outwardly Moral, Inwardly Rotten

These Christian Jews, like the Pharisees of Jesus' day, were moral antinomians. Outwardly they were moral, inwardly they were rotten. As Jesus put it to the Pharisees: 'Ye blind guides, which strain at a gnat, and swallow a camel. Woe unto you, scribes and Pharisees, hypocrites! for ye make clean the outside of the cup and of the platter, but within they are full of extortion and excess. Thou blind Pharisee, cleanse first that which is within the cup and platter, that the outside of them may be clean also. Woe unto you, scribes and Pharisees, hypocrites! for ye are like unto whited sepulchres, which indeed appear beautiful outward, but are within full of dead men's bones, and of all uncleanness' (Mt. 23:24–27).

But these Christian Jews had degenerated so much that they were actually being like the Pharisees. Though truly born again they had backslidden to self-righteousness. It is possible to do this and we often forget that backsliding can be like that. We tend to think of a back-slider as the one who falls into open sin. But there is a self-righteous backsliding that is just as corrupt, just as deadly. It is most difficult to get a self-righteous Christian to see himself in that manner. He is the hardest kind of Christian to reach.

I predict that when revival comes there will be as much warning over our self-righteousness as any sin that may otherwise be committed. What is killing? According to Jesus, it is hating. Who did these Christian Jews hate? The poor, for one. Yet they equally hated the rich. For by showing respect of persons you show hatred because you do that person no favour by being partial. He begins to think, if he takes you seriously, that because he's rich and he has a lot in this world and has prestige, then this will en-dear him to God. And he begins to think that God is just like the world, that he's got bargaining power with God.

It is a sad commentary to think that even the modern church has become largely a middle-class phenomenon. People coming in get the idea that because of what they are in the world this counts for something in the church. There are many of us that acquiesce in this. But that is not Christianity. Listen to Paul when he has an opportunity to address the Greek minds of Athens. He says, God 'hath appointed a day, in the which he will judge the world in righteousness by that man whom he hath ordained' (Acts 17:31). We don't find Paul saying, 'You, men of Athens, God needs your brilliant intellects. If only you were Christians. We'll make a place for you in the Christian church. We will Christianize your philosophy. With brilliant people like you it's going to do something for the faith.' That isn't the way Paul thinks. We're told that when they heard of the resurrection of the dead some mocked, others said, 'We'll talk to you again,' but Paul departed from among them.

James shows these Christian Jews that they didn't really love these rich people. There is a subtle thing to see in the translation that follows: 'Ye kill, and desire to have'. The Greek is so expressive that there's no way to fully bring out the sense of this 'desire'. The NIV says, 'You kill and you covet'. We get the word 'zeal' or 'zealot' from this word that, when used as a verb, simply wants to show a very strong feeling that drives extreme, even spiteful behaviour.

When these Christians saw a wealthy person coming along they would get emotionally involved and say, 'Do sit here. Great to have you.' It was not because they loved these people. James tells us they had this feeling of envy towards them. At the bottom of all of this outward courtesy these Christians were not thinking of what they could do for the rich but what the rich could do for them.

The picture, then, that emerges from this translation – 'Ye kill and desire to have' – is that their emotional involvement was one of sheer selfishness. They not only sent the rich and the poor to hell but continued to want their own goals achieved along their own selfish lines. These Christian Jews wanted success more than anything else in the world, success that would commend them to other Christians, so that other Christians would recognize them and say, 'Oh, you mean to tell me that you've got so-and-so coming along to your congregation.' 'Oh, yes, they want to come to us.' 'We don't have anybody like that.' They also wanted to make their non-Christian Jewish brethren feel jealous.

Here were Jews who had become Christians. They had brethren who were Jews who had not become Christians. They were being persecuted all the time for becoming Christians. They wanted so much for their brethren to see that they were successful. They wanted the world generally to see that Christianity was a force to be reckoned with. They had begun to take Christianity personally, as though it were up to them. They had made a stand for Jesus and they wanted everybody to see that they had done the right thing. They thought that success would cause everybody to stop and salute. That is carnal. In this desire to be successful they had actually sent everybody that they ran into to hell. They had simply missed the whole point of what Christian evangelism was to be. Success would make others jealous. They wanted to be able to name-drop and they wanted to notice that others were looking envious.

It's a great pity that Christianity could degenerate to this sort of thing. Christianity is essentially a heaven or hell phenomenon. If you do not believe in Jesus Christ you will die in your sins and will perish eternally in hell. It's a great pity that there would be such a thing as rivalry between congregations, and jealousy and envy between Christian churches, and a desire to have other Christians feel envious. But this was actually happening in James' own day. The saddest thing of all is that these Christian Jews wouldn't even consider the possibility that they were doing something wrong. But their desire for personal glory and prestige kept them blind to what was really happening. This is always the case when we are motivated by the wisdom that comes from below.

Nature Always Justifies Itself

Here's what happens: we grieve the Holy Spirit, almost always unconsciously. And the person still thinks he is thinking in a godly way. The possibility that he might be doing something wrong never occurs to him. He goes right on and on.

How can God reach a person like that? The amazing thing is that God was trying to reach people like that. God was simply letting them yearn for success without having it.

James therefore interjects this observation. He said earlier, 'Ye lust and have not'. Now he puts it a different way: 'Ye kill, and desire to have, but you cannot obtain.' He put before them this fact that they probably hadn't even considered. They were going on and on, really thinking that they were doing God's will. It hadn't occurred to them to stop and think to themselves, 'Why isn't this working?'

But James is trying to wake them up: to stop them lusting. What they desire they cannot obtain. Your desire for success is unfulfilled. Are you getting the rich? No. Is God blessing you? No, he's not. You cannot obtain. This Greek word for 'obtain' means 'to acquire', 'to succeed'. These Christian Jews were the most frustrated men that anybody could imagine. They couldn't even succeed at sinning.

Paul, writing to Timothy, talks about those who were 'ever learning, and never able to come to the knowledge of the truth'. He says, 'For of this sort are they which creep into houses, and lead captive silly women laden with sins, led away with divers lusts, ever learning, and never able ...' (2 Tim. 3:6–7). They couldn't even succeed in knowing anything about God.

Do you wonder why it is that you're not having the theological breakthrough, the knowledge that comes from God, the anointing whereby 'ye need not that any man teach you' (1 Jn. 2:27)? Why is it you're ever learning but never able to come to the knowledge of the truth? You're being governed by your lusts. And so with these Christian Jews. Their success was withheld no matter how hard they tried.

It's amazing how a person becomes so self-willed. As Proverbs put it: 'Filled with his own ways'. Nobody can talk to him. People tiptoe around and say, 'If only we could reach him. If we could get her to see this.' When the Spirit is grieved we lose all objectivity about ourselves. Yet the wonder of it all is that this failure to achieve success is, in fact, the best thing that could be happening to them at that moment.

As we have seen, if God keeps you from falling into sin you are spared the sorrow of guilt, of a taste of sin, of what it would do to others and of being made a castaway. We have the same principle working now. Here were those who wanted success. The worst thing that could possibly have happened to them would be for them to have succeeded in their goals. You may ask, 'Doesn't God want us to be successful?' Yes, but in his way.

Why Success Withheld Is A Blessing

There were several reasons that success withheld was a singular blessing to them.

- They were not ready for success. You could never have told them that they weren't ready, that they were ill-equipped or ill-prepared. In this connection there are two kinds of success. First, success that comes by the direct anointing of the Holy Spirit. Secondly, success that comes through one's own natural gifts, through the endowments of nature. This latter is the only kind of success the world knows. These Christian Jews were having neither kind, and it was a great mercy.
- Had they succeeded in their aims, they never would have bothered to examine themselves. Success has a way of confirming us in what we are doing at the time. But these Christians were scarcely doing anything right. Had they been successful they would have taken that success as a sign from God that they were doing everything right and they would never have looked back.

- Had they succeeded, they would have forfeited for ever the possibility of experiencing God's way of making them succeed. We cannot have it both ways: to be hostile to God and have his special blessing at the same time is impossible. You cannot love the world and have the unction of the Spirit upon your life. We read that verse in Psalm 106 verse 15 – to me it's one of the scariest verses in the Bible – 'He gave them their request; but sent leanness into their soul.' As some translations put it: 'God gave them their request but sent to them a wasting disease.' Whatever aim you may be wanting to achieve right now, whoever you are, if God lets you have what you want when your own condition is not right he's dealing with you not in mercy but in wrath and in judgement. For if he gives us what we want when we're not ready we'll never know his pre-eminent will for us.

- Had they succeeded, Christianity would never have been the same again. Consider what would have happened if they had succeeded with the rich. They were being selective in their evangelism, much the way the trend is today in medicine and in certain circles where we want to determine the kind of child that should come into the world – only an elitist type. Christianity would no longer be the Apostles' doctrine. Instead of having something to offer to the poor, Christianity would be nothing but an elitist, middle-class religion. Instead of Christianity giving no respect to persons on the basis of what they are in their works or in what they can offer, Christianity would have been regarded from then on as that which justifies the wealthy person or the person with prestige, just sanctioning a person's natural state generally. It would have been nothing but a religion of words, favouring those who already have. But God withheld success from them. Otherwise, they would have missed God's best. And they would have changed the face of Christianity.

God Has Something Better In Store

Behind their failure to achieve their goals is a merciful God doing two things. Firstly, ensuring that Christianity retained its primitive purity. Secondly, ensuring that these Christians themselves might know a success inexplicable at the natural level. God might have made them castaways, but he overruled and continued to deal with them. The withholding of success gives us every hint that God has something far better in store than the mere accomplishment of our immediate desire or goal.

If God is not giving you what you want right now, consider two things. What is he trying to tell you about yourself and your own spiritual state? And what he does have in mind for you is far better than what you're asking for. You're wanting to win the battle; God wants you to win the war. 'For the Lord God is a sun and shield: the Lord will give grace and glory: no good thing will he withhold from them that walk uprightly' (Ps. 84:11). It is better to be dealt with and not to have, than to be passed by with success.

There is one final point that James makes in this connection. He goes on to say, 'Ye fight and war, yet ye have not.' He says their problem is that they count on each other. They haven't, apparently, thought of turning to God. No, rather than ask God to pour out wisdom they're blaming each other. They say, 'You're the reason we're not having success. Here's the way you were talking at the time those people came in. You didn't present the argument right.' 'I did the best I could.' 'No, it's your fault.' 'We need to have another committee meeting.' 'We're not reaching people.' The whole time they were bickering and quarrelling with one another.

They were failures, but none was willing to admit why. They didn't turn to God, they turned on each other. This should not surprise us because when a church fails in the enterprise of evangelism it always ends up fighting and quarrelling. Yet when a church is enjoying conversions and a flow of newcomers it's a happy church. They even like the preacher!

But these evangelistic failures whom James was addressing were a frustrating lot of people. They tried everything. Nothing worked. They couldn't succeed. They couldn't sin.

God's Chastening

We have already seen the five degrees of God's chastening. The first degree is when God breaks you with his word. Always hope that that will do it and go from there. Save yourself a further sorrow. The second is when circumstances of providence cause things to happen. Things are out of your hands. The third degree is when you lust but have not. You're left to nature alone to cope and yet God just keeps you from having what you're going after. Fourth is when you do get what you want. The sorrow of guilt and the sorrow of a taste of sin and what you do to others become very acute. And the fifth degree is when God utterly abandons you to Satan.

These Christians were tottering between the third and the fourth degrees. They were utterly frustrated, they were coming short of sinning properly and they were coming short of the success that they wanted. In kindness God was trying to get them to see their folly and to know that success had been withheld from them at every level. This was their glory: they were spared sin. Yet they were denied success. God's hand couldn't have been more evident. If God deals with us like this, remember that what he has in mind is far better than what we could imagine.

4

The Silent God

James 4:1–4

The epistle of James may be said to be addressed primarily to frustrated Christians who are trying to find satisfaction at a natural level. Living the Christian life is the happiest life on earth if we submit to God's dealings with us. The unhappiest person in the world is not the non-Christian but rather the Christian who is not obedient to what God has put before him to do.

God Deals With Christians

Now we're looking at this second verse of James chapter 4 in detail. In chapter one verse two James said, 'My brethren, count it all joy when you fall into divers temptations' or 'trials'. This verse is something that we should value more and more. It is the promise that God will deal with us, and indeed it is the only hope that we might develop. Some people grow older; some grow up. James' epistle is to show us that living the Christian life is to develop so that we are not the same, being changed from glory to glory.

Reaching the third degree

God's dealings with us, or his chastening – of which, as we have seen, there are five degrees – matter in our development. God's chastening will be the only hope that we might really see him work and know that it is God at work and not a counterfeit thing.

These Christian Jews were at stage three in God's chastening. They lusted. They wanted to sin but they were kept from it. When God deals with us this way it's a sign of his kindness. He keeps us from sinning even though we are so vulnerable to it. But these Christian Jews couldn't succeed in the very thing that God himself would have wanted to see them succeed in – making an impact in the world. They ended up turning on each other, but even that didn't work. They were frustrated people.

This particular verse presents a slight difficulty in understanding the way James' mind is working. It's not translation or punctuation but verse enumeration. In the original Greek they didn't have verses or punctuation. In the Greek New Testament the punctuation has been put in by scholars who think that's the way it ought to be, but they don't always get it right. I think it would have been better if verse 3 had simply read: 'because ye ask not'. It should be read like this: 'Ye lust, and have not: ye kill, and desire to have, and cannot obtain: ye fight and war, yet ye have not'. We have a series of three 'have nots' so that when you come to this last phrase: 'because ye ask not', this ought rather to be put in a separate category. It is James' way of saying why you don't have – a simple, straightforward rationale for all of this frustration. It is simply 'because ye ask not'.

This is a very profound verse that points to some astonishing things. Why didn't they ask? Surely they did. Did James misfire when he put it like this? We have here an astonishing explanation of what besets so many of us as Christians. We may well say, 'We have asked God.' But James says we haven't.

God is jealous

We have before us here a melancholy picture of how the unhappy Christian refuses to bring God directly into his life. It shows how the backslider – moral antinomian – plays games with himself. It shows the Christian at the natural level without normal Christian graces. This verse demonstrates very boldly how jealous God is, how unyielding when he sees a rival. The very thing that the natural man hates most about God is that God is jealous.

By 'jealousy' we mean God's glory. 'I am the Lord: that is my name: and my glory will I not give to another' (Isa. 42:8). God, who will not compromise, is letting us know that either he will have his way or we will have our way. When we have our way we tend to project his will on our doings. We will not believe that God could be that far removed from us.

God is silent

This verse also gives us a rather unusual understanding of church history. For example, how many of you have wondered why God can apparently hide his face for such a long time? It's one thing to say that God hides his face for a few hours or a few days or maybe a few weeks, but the reading of church history shows that God can hide his face for generations and for centuries. Look at the Middle Ages, or the Patristic period from the first to the fourth centuries when you have just a handful of men who had anything to say. There were over one thousand years between St Augustine and Martin Luther. What was going on during this period? Not much.

Look at God's dealings with Israel in the Old Testament. Look at the barren period of the Judges, at how long they waited for a Samuel to come along and how exceedingly rare were the Elijahs and the Elishas, the Daniels. What is God doing when there is no Elijah around? Does he compromise his own standard, laying aside his jealousy and settling for the best he can get? Embodied in this phrase, 'because ye ask not', is the explanation for the long eras in God's plan of redemption when he appears not to be speaking.

I often quote the German philosopher, Feuerbach. He gave the philosophical rationale for atheism. He said that God is man's projection upon the backdrop of the universe. This is often what we do. It should cause us to hang our heads in shame when we are determined to superimpose God upon what we are doing. We say, 'Look what the Lord is doing', but God may not be in it at all. We can't bring ourselves to believe that we are in a period when he's not speaking. If God should choose to hide his face for a thousand years or pass by our own generation, can we pretend that it is otherwise? Isaiah 45:15 says, 'Verily, thou art a God that hidest thyself, O God of Israel, the Saviour.'

The Natural Reaction To Chastening

Hearing other voices

These Christians whom James was addressing were left to cope by themselves. They continued on in their lusting and in their failure generally because they did not want God to interfere. The question is, what happens when God hides his face in the way he was doing here? When the hiding of God's face is caused by our own folly we begin to hear other voices which we take as being his own word.

The pre-eminent example of this is Balaam in the Old Testament. Balaam was the popular preacher of his day. He had a gift of being able to forecast things. Balaam had such a perfect record of successes in foretelling that they knew if they could get Balaam to curse, the curse would come about. The enemies of Israel came to Balaam and asked him to curse Israel (Num. 22). When the men first came to him God said to have nothing to do with these men. But when Balaam brought the men in he didn't think he could do what God was asking. He began to pray that God would give him guidance. He began to hear other voices. Like James' readers, the temptation to personal power and prestige took hold of Balaam. He began to get a message, thinking it was God's voice.

These Christians saw a chance for prestige and for power, and by being selective in their evangelism they experienced an unconscious backfire in their own minds. James calls it being divided within double mindedness. When the jealous Spirit of God is grieved, one is stopped from hearing and knowing the high and unyielding standard of God. God sends a lying spirit in the place of the true knowledge of his will, and it can go on for generations.

An illustration of this is in two apparently conflicting Scriptures: 2 Samuel 24:1 and 1 Chronicles 21:1. Here are two descriptions of the same event. 2 Samuel 24:1 says, 'And again the anger of the Lord was kindled against Israel, and he moved David against them to say, Go, number Israel and Judah.' Here it says that God did it. 1 Chronicles 21:1 says, 'Satan stood up against Israel, and provoked David to number Israel.' What do we have here? It's the same thing with Balaam, for he was getting messages from God. 2 Samuel says, 'God says ...' Chronicles says, 'Satan said ...' It is God sending a lying spirit as described in 2 Thessalonians, 'God shall send them strong delusion, that they should believe a lie: that they all might be damned who believed not the truth' (2:11–12). God has a pre-eminent word. Believe it, or believe anything and be deceived. The sure word came to Balaam, to have nothing to do with these men, but he went right back to God and prayed for what to say to them. God does speak but we won't have it. We keep on praying. We hear voices.

Dreams that justify

What takes place then when this kind of thing is going on in heaven? Is God substituting confusion for the knowledge of his pre-eminent will? Foolish Christians are doing things their way and ascribing the entire procedure to God's will. Are Christians like this aware of what is going on? The answer is, yes and no. For example, when a Christian is lusting, hating, arguing, he's bound to know that something is truly wrong. But for him to face the fact that he is so utterly out of sorts with God is too painful for him so he seldom comes to grips with the truth. He 'asks not'.

The analogy is this. It has happened to all of us. We're in a deep sleep and the alarm clock goes off. We hear it. We know we should get up, but if we don't right away, we begin to dream that it's all right to sleep, that we don't need to get up as early as we thought. We sleep on, and often it's too late. When James says, 'Because ye ask not', he puts his finger on their refusal to come to grips with themselves. The thought of coming to God alone is so painful. It is far more pleasant to abide in their lusts and in their desire for personal power. They prefer to sleep and dream that everything is going to be all right.

Nature has a way of confirming itself and making us all feel better. This is why you can read so much literature today that is Christian, so-called, and it will make you feel better. When nature wants to confirm itself you just look into the mirror and see your face. You justify yourself and say, 'That's the best it's going to be.' The most painless act in the world is justifying ourselves. We justify our lustings, our temptations, our self-vindication, our quarrelling and our accusing each other. We impute God's will to what is apparently true to us, because that's the way we like it. We justify Feuerbach: God is man's projection on the backdrop of the universe. We say, 'Look what God is doing.'

Avoiding the issue

These Christians that James is addressing were doing what was so natural, to lust and to desire and to quarrel. There is a painful cause for this. They knew that to do what God asked, to go all the way back to God and get fresh orders, would mean that they were going to have to come to grips with their lust, their seeking of vengeance, the desire for power and blaming others. Having to deal with ourselves in that manner is not natural. It's painful.

Listen to this prayer of Ezra: 'And at the evening sacrifice I arose up from my heaviness; and having rent my garment and my mantle, I fell upon my knees, and spread out my hands unto the LORD my God.' What does he say? 'O my God, I am ashamed and blush to lift up my face to thee, my God: for our iniquities are increased over our head, and our trespass is grown up unto the heavens' (9:5, 6). That is asking God, but these Christians just couldn't pray like that. They preferred other voices that said, 'It's natural to lust. It's normal to want power.

It's quite right to say, "I'm right, you're wrong." Coming to God is precisely what they could not bring themselves to do. So James gives the explanation: 'Ye ask not.'

They knew in their hearts what God thought of their condition, but their natural inclinations deceived them and kept them dreaming. Why didn't they ask? They knew what would happen and what would be required of them: they would have to look into God's mirror and see their own hearts. You may ask, 'What was it they didn't ask for?' James tells us that right at the beginning of the epistle: 'If any of you lack wisdom, let him ask of God' (1:5). In chapter 3 verse 17 he describes the wisdom that God gives. But they had the opposite of that, the wisdom that came from below. The reason: 'Ye ask not.'

Will God Break His Silence?

Is the solution that simple? Is all we have to do to ask for wisdom? James says 'God ... giveth to all men liberally, and upbraideth not.' However there was this condition: 'But let him ask in faith, nothing wavering.' Was this saving faith? No, they had that. These were Christians. But after we've been converted there's a new level of faith that we are supposed to operate by – experiential faith, experimental faith, which is always connected to our actual conduct. As Paul put it: Christ 'died for all, that they which live should not henceforth live unto themselves' (2 Cor. 5:15). When we violate this, faith diminishes.

Learning from history

Of course, they prayed. People like this pray all the time, and get answers. Balaam got an answer – but he didn't question the source of his answer. James was kind enough to say to them, 'Ye ask ... [but] ... you ask amiss that you may consume it upon your lusts.' It was prestige these Christians were after. There was, however, one difference when you compare them to Balaam: there's no hint that God ever dealt with Balaam, but he was dealing with these Christians. So today there are churches that go on. They pray, they go on doing things, and it is amazing how much success is given to the world, to worldly churches, to worldly Christians. But these Christians weren't having that success. They were being chastened.

In kindness God is holding you back. He's trying to teach you something and to show you that what he has in mind is far better than what you could imagine.

What survives in church history, by and large, is the product of greatness, where God himself owned the ministries – this is why you hear of the peaks. You tend to think of Israel's history with Elijah and Elisha, but these men were exceedingly rare. You talk about Athanasius, Augustine. Those men were few and far between. In the early church there were dazzling successes here and there by people that you never hear of later.

Balaam's prophecy is in Numbers 24. How do you suppose it would have felt to have been around when Balaam uttered that prophecy? It would have been one of those services when everybody would say, 'I wouldn't have missed that for anything.' Dazzling prophecy. Read the gospel of Matthew. Does he refer to it? No. Mark? No. Is it in Luke, John, Acts, Paul? They refer to Balaam, but not his prophecy. We have so many things happening today that are dazzling and we're intimidated by what we're seeing. I'm sure in the Middle Ages there was a lot of noise – but God was silent.

Getting to grips with our sin

Is there hope that God will break his silence? There is when he deals with us, when he blesses us by denying the success we want so much, when we're kept from moving on to the fourth and fifth degrees of chastening. If God is dealing with us it is wonderful. Success withheld is a blessing so great that you will live to thank God, a million times over, that you didn't get what you wanted. There's only one thing to do when God begins to deal with us: come to grips with things. As Jesus put it to the church at Ephesus: 'Thou hast left thy first love. Remember therefore from whence thou art fallen, and repent, and do the first works' (Rev. 2:4–5).

You might want to hear the other voices, but if you don't go back to what God has said then you'll be deceived by a lying spirit. For God is unyielding and uncompromising. He is jealous; he will let centuries go by without speaking before he will accommodate our own belief. Yet if we wait on him and take him seriously: 'Eye hath not seen, nor ear heard, neither have entered into the heart of man, the things which God hath prepared for them that love him' (1 Cor. 2:9).

The promise of restoration

The prophet Jeremiah spoke to Israel at a time when they were in captivity in Babylon. Things were dark and the enemies of Israel were seeing success. But in a dark hour Jeremiah said, 'I will build thee, and thou shalt be built, O virgin of Israel: thou shalt again be adorned with thy tabrets, and shalt go forth in the dances of them that make merry. Thou shalt yet plant vines upon the mountains of Samaria: the planters shall plant, and shall eat them as common things. For there shall be a day, that the watchmen upon the mount Ephraim shall cry, Arise ye, and let us go up to Zion unto the LORD our God' (31:4–6).

Will God speak again? There shall be a day when he will, if he deals with us and we 'count it all joy'. There shall be a day when judgement comes down as waters and righteousness as a mighty stream (Amos 5:24). There shall be a day when the forces of hell shall be rebuked and all hypocrisy shall be uncovered. There shall be a day when the true unction of God shall come upon his servants once again – upon those who wait for him. For if we wait on him and ask for wisdom, we will receive. That's what James means. 'Ye have not, because ye ask not.' The wisdom that comes from above – when that comes there shall be a day when the silent God speaks again.

5

The Blessings of Unanswered Prayer

James 4:3

'Because ye ask not' are the last words of James we considered. Now he says, 'Ye ask, and receive not, because ye ask amiss, that ye may consume it upon your lusts.' These Christians were like Balaam, who kept on seeking for guidance although God had told him in the first place what his will was. These Christians rejected the wisdom that comes from above but kept on praying.

Prayer That Creates Problems

The problem that lies behind James' diagnosis and explanation of their condition is this: that one tends to say, 'At least I'm praying a lot.' When we think that prayer is a good and proper thing to do, we tend to think that doing it makes it right. Prayer is like any good work: we sometimes flatter ourselves for doing it. Prayer often diverts us from our real responsibility.

There are some people who judge their spiritual state by whether they have conquered this or that sin. And if they have, they become very pleased with themselves and say, 'Surely this is enough progress for now.' The one who does things like tithing, Bible reading, praying often, will sometimes say, 'I must be doing all right because I'm doing these things.' There is nothing like prayer to keep one from doing God's will or to keep a man in a backslidden condition!

Prayer that isn't sincere

These Christians whom James is addressing were doing everything wrong; being respecters of persons precipitated an unconscious backfire in their souls. It must have seemed an insult at first when James accused them of not asking. But James had one thing in mind when he wanted them to ask God; they had another thing in mind when they did ask God. James wanted to bring God utterly and completely into their lives. They wanted to manipulate God without being obedient to him. James wanted them to ask for that heavenly wisdom that is 'first pure, then peaceable, gentle, and easy to be intreated' (Jas. 3:17). But they were characterized by the wisdom that 'descendeth not from above but is earthly, sensual, devilish' (v. 15).

Had they made the heavenly wisdom their first love, their problem would have been solved. But instead they were having all kinds of problems. When we're not right with God it has an effect upon our whole lives and upon the effect we have on others. This is why Proverbs 16:7 gives us this word: 'When a man's ways please the LORD, he maketh even his enemies to be at peace with him.'

Disobedience has a way of affirming itself with a kind of peace. When the disobedient Christian undergoes the transition from grace to nature, from the spirit to the flesh, it's not only a painless transition but it seems right because nature has a way of camouflaging itself, affirming that we're doing the right thing. For example, take a person who decides deliberately to engage in some questionable conduct. Before he does it, he thinks how he might feel if he does it. But then when he does do it he says, 'That didn't make me feel like I thought I would feel at all.' Why is this? It's because nature moves in so fast, quickly affirming us in our disobedience. This is another reason Jeremiah could say, 'The heart is deceitful above all things, and desperately wicked' (Jer. 17:9).

There would be those, no doubt, who would say to James, 'Wait a minute. Surely I pray and surely I want the Lord's will.' But James asks if they are seeing their prayers answered. The obvious answer was that their prayers weren't being answered. They were complete failures. They were failures even at sinning. 'Ye lust, and have not.' They were failures in trying to reach the rich and the poor. Instead James says, 'Ye kill ... and cannot obtain.' What was the consequence of their quarrelling with each other? It wasn't working. It just kept them looking to themselves and they were frustrated.

There are other people that have the same desires and they get what they want. James' readers do it and fail. Others leave God out and are better off than ever. They do it and are more miserable than ever. I suspect it's very possible that there may have been a thousand to whom God said, 'Go to Nineveh, that great city, and cry out against it' (Jonah 1:2). There were probably a thousand that went in the opposite direction, but when

Jonah tried God prepared a wind and a fish. Jonah couldn't get away with it. Jonah was different. 'For whom the Lord loveth he chasteneth, and scourgeth every son whom he receiveth' (Heb. 12:6).

James wasn't naive. He knew that these people prayed. They were great prayers. 'Ye ask.' When James said that he was not giving them a compliment. It was rather a rebuke. They were in no condition to pray, but they did. They prayed louder and longer than ever.

Prayer that pleases the devil

Praying is something that pleases the devil when we're in the state of mind of James' readers. Their witness was null and void. They were making no impact upon the world. This is exactly the way the devil wants the church to be: paralysed. The devil, in a case like this, would never want to interfere with your prayer life. He might even make it easy and enjoyable for you, because the act of prayer offers substitutes for true obedience.

James went on to say, 'Ye ask amiss.' The Greek word translated 'amiss' in our Authorised Version is the word *kakos*, which is one of the strongest synonyms for 'sin' in the Greek language. It means 'evil', 'bad', 'wicked'. It is evil praying. Does it surprise you that praying could be wicked? The Authorised Version, by saying, 'Ye ask amiss', presents a masterpiece of British understatement.

This is the way it is when we are filled with our own ways. When we look into our own mirror we see what we want to see; when we look into God's mirror we see ourselves as we are. Isaiah had a glimpse into God's mirror and for the first time he cried out, 'Woe is me! for I am undone' (Isa. 6:5). But these Christians had very little conviction of sin.

Do you know the happiest thing that can be said about their prayers? Not their length, nor their loudness, nor their frequency, nor their eloquence. These Christians may have prayed loudly and eloquently. So did the Pharisees. The best thing that could be said about their prayers is that they were unanswered.

God's Deafness Is Kindness

Oh, the kindness of God's deafness! Think about the things you've wanted across the years that you didn't get. Or think about something you're asking for now and you're not seeing it. It could well be that God in kindness is turning a deaf ear. Look what would have happened if God had taken James' readers seriously. There are three things:

- They would have fallen into open sin. Their lusting would have brought forth sin. And that sin would have brought forth sorrow: the sorrow of guilt and a taste of deep sin which makes lusting now a thousand times worse than ever. They were spared the sorrow of hurting others and the sorrow of being made a castaway.
- They would have succeeded with the rich. And Christianity would never have had anything to say to the poor. Christianity would have become a religion of class, of good breeding and of sheer works.
- They would have remained unteachable for the rest of their lives. We know they quarrelled with one another, but if God had granted them success and given them what they wanted in that state then their divisions would have been irreparable; each would have continually said, 'I am right, you're wrong.' James knew their real motives. People like this seldom examine their real motives when they pray. They may even say, 'I want God's will.' Often because we think we want God's will, we believe that everything we're praying about is right.

These Christians might well have protested, 'I do want God's will.' People like this generally do want God's will in the smaller things. For example, in whether you ought to get this new job or a rise in pay, or whether you ought to go on this holiday, or whether you ought to go out with this girl, or date this man. It is almost impossible to get people like this to see that they don't really want God's will. They seldom know their own hearts. James knew the perversion of their praying and the perversion of their motives: 'that ye may consume it upon your lusts'.

Ignoring our insults

This Greek word *kakos* which is translated 'amiss' as an adverb is used as a verb in Acts 12:1 describing Herod the king who 'stretched forth his hands to vex certain of the church'.

What we have here is a word that means 'to offend'. When these people could ask wickedly they were trying to vex God, even if unconsciously. Isaiah puts it like this: 'Bring no more vain oblations; incense is an abomination unto me; the new moons and sabbaths, the calling of assemblies, I cannot away with; it is iniquity, even the solemn meeting. Your new moons and your appointed feasts my soul hateth: they are a trouble unto me; I am weary to bear them. And when ye spread forth your hands, I will hide mine eyes from you: yea, when ye make many prayers, I will not hear: your hands are full of blood' (Isa. 1:13–15).

The prayer that ascends to God when we really don't want to do his will is an insult. A prayer like this tries to put God into a bind and manipulate him. It's like saying, 'I don't love your glory, but I love your power.' You think, 'I don't want you to have absolute control of me, but I want my prayers to be answered because I know you can do anything.' It's the person who says, 'I don't like the God of the Bible.' But you like that God to help you out when you need him. It is tantamount to blackmail. And this is what these Christians were doing. But God wants us to love him as he is in himself and to worship him as he is revealed in holy Scripture, to love him and honour him so much that we would not change anything about him even if we could, to say, 'I love you just as you are.' God wants us to love him just as he is. How do we do this? We not only tell him but we show him by doing what he told us to do.

Jonah knew what God's will was, and when the fish ejected Jonah on dry land the first thing Jonah learned was that God's orders hadn't changed. 'Go unto Nineveh, that great city, and preach unto it the preaching that I bid thee' (Jonah. 3:2). When God touched something in our lives we didn't like it, and we rebelled against it and we went on our way. We think that in the meantime God won't come back with that. But although Jonah won the battle, God won the war. When Jonah was praying in the belly of the fish he wasn't asking for a rise in pay or a promotion or to get out of trouble. We read in Jonah 2:7: 'When my soul fainted within me I remembered the LORD.' Jonah was near to what we've learned to call the third degree of God's chastening.

The efforts of these Christians to vex God were sufficient grounds, had God so chosen, to make them irreparable castaways. How many of us are like that today? We have given God every reason to drop us but he has stayed with us and dealt with us kindly, not letting us have our way after all.

Hedonism With A Christian Facade

Not only were the prayers of these Christians ill-posed, but their motives were ill-conceived. For he says that the aim of their praying is that their lusts might be gratified. They were not thinking about God's pleasure but their own. James effectively is saying, 'Your prayer is with one aim in mind, that your pleasures may be enjoyed without hindrance.' The word translated 'lust' here is *hedonais* from which we get the word 'hedonism'.

It's used in chapter 4 verse 1: 'even of your lusts that war in your members.' Although this kind of lusting may refer to the sensual appetite (and James made it clear that these Christians indeed had to cope with this kind of temptation) it really is a word that means any kind of pleasure at a natural level as opposed to a spiritual level. It is simply talking about the one who wants to do his own thing and continues to want his own thing although he keeps praying about it. This is a hedonism with a Christian façade. There are three models of the Christian who wants to operate at the level of doing his own thing and claiming that God is approving it all the time. Their motives are not to please God but themselves, but they feel better by saying, 'Your will be done.'

An outright willingness to sin

One literally asks God that he might have his carnal desires fulfilled. A person like this is so filled with his own ways that either he regards himself as the exception or he's convinced himself that God doesn't really care about how he lives his life. It may be lusting, it may be hating. In the case of hating, a person like this takes vengeance with his own hands and feels self-appointed to be his own vindicator. This outright willingness to sin looks at God as a co-partner in his pursuits.

Regarding the kingdom of God as a medium of success

It's often put forward that God wants you to be a success in business, that failure is simply owing to your not trusting God. And God promises success to everybody. The most extreme form of this is probably TV preachers who appeal to men's pride of life to get their money. They give the impression that God is to be regarded as one that man manipulates for his own selfish ends.

Bordering on this is making merchandise of the kingdom of God. For example, those who want to see the church grow are not content for the church to grow as it promotes the honour of God, so they substitute godless methods for God's honour. It brings the world right into the church in order for the church to reach the world. Sometimes using a godless method will bring about great growth. In America there is a fifteen million-dollar glass church to prove it and a hundred other so-called Christian enterprises.

The missing note in this kind of thrust is always New Testament godliness. People like this will talk about prayer and faith. But it's always a faith that is disjointed from one's character and conduct. The

faith that James talks about in this epistle can only be increased and
built up by our obedience to Christ. In America they have a famous
faith healer who has a slogan: 'Turn your faith loose', as though
everybody has faith. 2 Thessalonians 3:2 says, 'All men have not faith.'
What the healer means is, 'Turn your faith loose by sending me your
money.' This type of pleasure is brought into the church that you
might consume it upon your lusts.

A divided mind about God's will

This may not be as serious as the first two models, but it's no less insulting
to God when you simply ask him to get you out of trouble. Or you ask
him that you might get this job with a rise in pay. It's when your heart is
not yielded to his whole will but you come to him in time of trouble.
You're still involved in this manipulation enterprise.

Saved By God's Silence

The Greek is better translated like this: 'You ask wickedly that you
might be consumed in your lusting.' The Authorised Version says
'consume it' but there's no 'it' in the Greek. For it's a Greek word here
that means 'to expend', 'to waste', 'to consume by extravagance'. The
point is, 'You ask wickedly that in your pleasures you might just waste
away.' It is the word used of the prodigal son in Luke 15:14: 'When he
had spent all, there arose a mighty famine in the land; and he began to
be in want.' What we have here is the inevitable consequence of
rebellion to God's whole will.

Do you know that lusting in pleasure is not only the greatest robber of
money in the world, but the greatest robber of your time? When you are
living in this condition, you're losing all the way around. You may even
lose your family and, if you're not stopped, your very life. It's this kind of
disobedience that causes your life to be thrown away. And you wake up
one day and you say, 'What have I done? Where have I been? Where has
the time gone?' There's no grasp of the prayer of the Psalmist: 'Teach us to
number our days, that we may apply our hearts unto wisdom' (90:12).

What was it, then, that spared these Christians from what might have
been? Only one thing: that God was dealing with them. The astonishing
thing is not their ill-posed prayers but that their prayers were not heard.
You may ask, 'Does God actually answer a wicked prayer?' The answer is
yes, he does when he's not dealing with a person. When he lets them go.

As we read in Psalm 106:15: 'He gave them their request; but sent leanness unto their soul.' This is why the Psalmist put it like this in Psalm 37: 'Fret not thyself because of evildoers, neither be thou envious against the workers of iniquity. For they shall soon be cut down like the grass, and wither as the green herb. Trust in the LORD, and do good; so shalt thou dwell in the land, and verily thou shalt be fed. Delight thyself also in the LORD; and he shall give thee the desires of thine heart' (vv. 1–4). The Psalmist could say in Psalm 27: 'One thing have I desired of the LORD, that will I seek after; that I may dwell in the house of the LORD all the days of my life, to behold the beauty of the LORD, and to enquire in his temple' (v. 4). For when all of our desires are narrowed down to one, then we begin to pray in his will. So John said, 'If we ask any thing according to his will, he heareth us' (1 Jn. 5:14). It is one thing to thank God for answered prayer, and we should, but the chances are that you will live to be even more thankful for your unanswered prayers.

6

The Worldly Christian

James 4:4

James wants to wake up these Christians who have wandered far from true obedience. Being governed by wisdom from below has basically two effects. First, it makes them act the opposite of the way a Christian is supposed to be and secondly, it has a blinding effect upon them whereby they think they're okay; they don't really come to grips with themselves. When he raises the question: 'Know ye not ...', James uses the Greek word *oidate* to shame them. It means knowledge of a well-known fact. Apparently they didn't know. Their sensual wisdom acted like an anaesthetic, rendering them impervious to pain and alarm. There was a double mindedness: they knew what they ought to do but told themselves it was okay to remain as they were.

James is appealing to their regenerate conscience. He is trying to wake them up. For there is a sense in which double mindedness is the greatest enemy to the Christian because it perpetuates an instability, frustration, confusion of mind and lack of objectivity about oneself.

Understanding God's Will

The most frequent question that any minister gets asked is: 'How can I know the will of God?' Paul said in Ephesians 5:17: 'Be ye not unwise, but understanding what the will of the Lord is.' If Paul meant what he said – and he did – it becomes a very serious indictment upon Christians who don't know God's will. As a matter of fact, we should know God's will as much as we know that we are saved. Yet double mindedness always has this two-fold subsidiary effect. It robs us of assurance of salvation and it robs us of the clear knowledge of God's will. If we are right with God we will not doubt his love or our assurance or the knowledge of his will. The chief problem with these Christians was that they were at home with this wisdom from below and couldn't bring themselves to believe that they had wandered that far.

How we should love the world

James gives this most unflattering appellation. He says, 'Ye adulterers and adulteresses'. He hasn't always addressed them like this – in chapter 1 verse 19 and in chapter 2 verse 5 he says, 'My beloved brethren'. In the Greek there's only one word. I don't know why the Authorised Version chose to say 'Ye adulterers and adulteresses'. It's the vocative case, feminine plural: 'adulteresses'. Does this mean that only women were going wrong in the church? James now addresses them as those who have committed adultery against the bridegroom. The bride has been unfaithful and he calls them 'adulteresses'. It's the way Paul described the jealousy of God in terms of the Mosaic law in Romans 7:4. He says, 'Ye also are become dead to the law by the body of Christ; that ye should be married to another, even to him who is raised from the dead, that we should bring forth fruit unto God.' This is the jealousy of the Spirit, an underlying theme of this epistle.

You may ask whether there were those in the church committing actual open adultery. No, because he says, 'Ye lust and have not.' They were moral antinomians. Outwardly they were moral but inwardly they were hostile to the law of the kingdom, which shows we are walking in the Spirit and enjoying our inheritance in the kingdom of God. These Christians were exceedingly vulnerable to sin, but only in the temptation stage. Rather than reduce temptation to the level of suggestion they enjoyed the temptation. They enjoyed their lusting.

James calls them adulteresses for three reasons. They were the bride of Christ but they were being unfaithful. They were Christians but they were double minded. They were eternally justified but were governed by temporal wisdom. James reminds them 'that friendship with the world is to be at enmity with God.' When he refers to friendship with the world he uses the Greek word *philia*. There are three Greek words for 'love': *eros* is physical love, *agape* is unselfish love, but *philia* is family love.

James is showing the incongruity of having an affection for the world, of feeling towards the world as they ought to feel for members of the family of God. The correct way to love the world is not *philia* but *agape*, the love of God. It's the word used in John 3:16: 'God so loved the world'. It's an unselfish, indiscriminate love without respect of persons. But these foolish Christians tried to love the world with *philia* love. They wanted to appeal to the non-Christian at a natural level, to endear themselves. Their folly was to be seen in the fact that nothing was going right for them.

The verb from this word *philia* means 'to kiss'. Here these foolish Christians were, trying to kiss the world and thinking that they could be God's friend, as Abraham was, at the same time. James says, in effect, 'There's no way you can have it like this because friendship with the world is to be at enmity with God.' What was it about these Christian Jews that made James talk like this to them? We've seen already how they were selective in their evangelism. But James saw that more was going on as a consequence. They began to function like the world. They forfeited their normal Christian graces. They were back to nature. They had a regenerate conscience but were functioning on unregenerate power. They lusted exactly as the non-Christian lusts except for this: the non-Christian lusts and gets what he wants.

God wants us to be different

These Christians were being kept from overt sin up to then. 'Ye lust, and have not,' James says. But in every other way they were just like the world. They liked to name-drop just like the worldly man, as if to say they were a little better because they'd been here or there or they knew this person or they'd had this success. They quarrelled just as non-Christians quarrelled. The most embarrassing indictment that the world makes of the church is that we're really no different from the world. It's embarrassing because it's so true. We who follow the New Testament shame ourselves by not obeying it. When I say that we're so much like the world I don't refer particularly to one's appearance or one's dress or even to particular things one does or doesn't do because it's in that way – and it's probably the only way – that some Christians are different from the world. But I refer to lack of self-control over one's emotions or one's pride, one's self-esteem, one's appetite generally.

So the world looks at the Christian and says, 'I've got that problem too. I don't see that you're any better off than I am.' For we are not showing the self-control and the discipline that the New Testament envisions for the Christian. The fact is that we panic in sudden disappointment as if there were no God. We name-drop just like the world. And we're vulnerable to temptation as though our minds weren't completely made up. The world can see right through us. Do you know that verse from Browning who said, 'To me faith means unbelief kept quiet, like the snake 'neath Michael's feet.' For it is our duty as Christians to show that we're on top of our enemy unbelief – and that we are different so that the world is compelled to admit it. That is when we leave the world without excuse.

God's will is for us all

James ruthlessly eliminates any exception to the rule, as he has throughout this epistle. He removes from us the luxury of saying, 'I am the exception.' If you have thought that something is wrong for anybody else but that God understands this for you this one time in this situation, you are, then and there in that moment, being governed by the 'wisdom from below'. That's exactly what the devil wants you to think. James is saying that when you are a friend of the world you are trespassing on enemy territory and this territory is under God's judgement. Do you think that because you're a Christian you have indemnity? If you walk into Sodom and Gomorrah you're going to get burnt like anybody else.

How is it that someone fancies himself to be the exception? We do it in three ways. First, by imputing to oneself more strength than is there. We say, 'I don't think anybody else could do what I'm doing but I can do it because I'm strong enough.' The second thing we do is we impute to the world less harm than is there. It shows a naive view of the nature of sin. We don't really think the world is going to damage us. And the third thing we do is we impute to God a benign disregard for true spirituality.

I want you to listen to the apostle Paul: 'Be ye not unequally yoked together with unbelievers: for what fellowship hath righteousness with unrighteousness? and what communion hath light with darkness? and what concord hath Christ with Belial? or what part hath he that believeth with an infidel? and what agreement hath the temple of God with idols? for ye are the temple of the living God; as God hath said, I will dwell in them, and walk in them; and I will be their God, and they shall be my people. Wherefore come out from among them, and be ye separate, saith the Lord, and touch not the unclean thing, and I will receive you, and will be a Father unto you, and ye shall be my sons and daughters, saith the Lord Almighty. Having therefore these promises, dearly beloved, let us cleanse ourselves from all filthiness of the flesh and spirit, perfecting holiness in the fear of God' (2 Cor. 6:14–7:1).

You will say, 'But, you know, the trouble with Christians is that they're so irrelevant, withdrawn, out of touch.' That is true in some cases. There are some who think that godliness is like living in a monastery. Wherever you have a distorted view of godliness you will almost every time have a distorted view of the doctrine of justification by faith. James isn't talking about retreat from culture, politics, recreation or the arts. And he most certainly is not talking about retreat from witnessing or from work or from being kind to the non-Christian. James is talking about the Christian who wants to be worldly. The word he uses here is a word translated simply 'will'. He says, 'Whosoever will … be a friend of the world is the enemy of God.' It is a word that simply means 'to be pleased to do', 'to be inclined to', 'to be disposed to'. You don't really have to be in the middle of Sodom and Gomorrah to get burnt or to be at enmity with God. Whoever wants to be worldly is an enemy of God.

The Worldly Christian

I want for a moment to take a look at the anatomy of the worldly Christian. See if you've ever seen anybody like this; maybe you recognize yourself. I hope not. But this is what makes him tick, the rationale that lies behind what he is:

- He values the approval of worldly people more than anyone else. He sincerely thinks that their opinions matter. He thinks that Christians are a dull lot; it's one thing to worship with them, it's another thing to enjoy them. He treasures the intellectual views of the worldly man and he wants the worldly man's approval and friendship. We can't entirely blame anybody for feeling like this, for Christians are often a dull and ill-informed lot of people. But when the worldly Christian fancies the approval of the worldly man, he feels more at home with a person like this so that he actually needs his admiration. An example of this is what is happening to the church at large when it comes to preparing men for the ministry. There has been the emergence into evangelical colleges and seminaries on both sides of the Atlantic of the need to be in touch with higher criticism of the Bible. Colleges today feel that they've got to show that they know what it's all about so that the world will say, 'Good for you. I'm glad to see that you know about that.' It's a desire for worldly approval.
- He finds more enjoyment in his worldly appetite and therefore values pleasure more than seeking the Lord's presence. He enjoys his lusting and temptation. He just wants to be able to gaze at the world. I don't say that he doesn't pray or read his Bible. As a matter of fact, the worldly Christian sometimes can be very regular in his prayer life and his Bible reading. These Christians weren't people who never prayed, as we have seen. The worldly Christian won't turn loose from enjoying

temptation. He likes worldly company whose appetites are like his own. Perhaps he won't indulge like his worldly friends, but he enjoys seeing them doing it. He enjoys sin vicariously. He doesn't want his worldly friends to think he's a fanatic, so he mixes with those who most definitely are not fanatics. Worldly Christians mix well together because they don't really like to be with the godly. They instinctively know that they are on each other's wavelength.

- The worldly Christian has persuaded himself that the effort of self-denial and Christian godliness just isn't worth it. A person like this would like to see God work, but because he hasn't seen anything extraordinary happen in his own life or in his church, he convinces himself that he never will. 'Here are those more spiritual than I am and I don't think they're any better off. If it's not working for them, why should it work for me? Why should I kill myself with discipline and self-denial?' It's exactly what Paul described in 1 Corinthians 10:7: 'The people sat down to eat and drink, and rose up to play.' For they began to think that God really wasn't going to do anything. They just gave up. Isaiah addressed this problem a long time ago: 'Why sayest thou, O Jacob, and speakest, O Israel, My way is hid from the LORD, and my judgment is passed over from my God?' (40:27).

Answering The Call

James' burden is to show true Christianity. It is not a matter of whether it works. A Christian should be obedient, tithe, hate the world and flee temptation whether God blesses him or not. He does it because it's right.

Regardless of whether there is blessing, you should obey the Lord. The way the Greek reads, the person who will be a friend of the world is rendered to be the enemy of God. Why would the worldly Christian be rendered God's enemy? For this reason: here's a man who has shown what he really is, where he gets his satisfaction. He's turned his back on the Lord although he keeps praying. As Jesus put it in Matthew 6:24: 'No man can serve two masters: for either he will hate the one, and love the other; or else he will hold to the one, and despise the other. Ye cannot serve God and mammon.' He earlier said, 'For where your treasure is, there will your heart be also' (v. 21).

James is saying to these Christians: 'You have willingly put yourself in the situation where God must treat you as though you're not a Christian. For God is no respecter of persons.' As Proverbs puts it: 'Because I have called, and ye refused; I have stretched out my hand, and no man regarded; but ye have set at naught all my counsel, and would none of my reproof: I also will laugh at your calamity; I will mock when your fear cometh' (1:24). James is saying, 'Wake up. You are leaving God with no choice but to deal with you as though you're not his. For you are a friend of the world. This means you're God's enemy.'

What exactly does it mean to be God's enemy? It means, first of all, to be subject to the same pitfalls and curses and sorrows as the ungodly. 'The way of transgressors is hard' (Prov. 13:15). And Psalm 37 tells us that the evildoer 'shall soon be cut down' (v. 2). To be God's enemy means to forfeit all of the blessings in the Bible that are promised to the godly. James is warning 'Don't expect the normal Christian graces such as the joy of sins forgiven, peace that passes understanding, the knowledge of God's guidance. You forfeit your inheritance in the kingdom of God. There will be no sweet communion.' The result as Paul put it in 1 Corinthians 3:15 is that you 'shall suffer loss'. The warning is that if you are a friend of the world you are making it so that God is left with no choice but to treat you as he does the godless. And yet there's something so tender, sweet and wonderful about everything James is saying to them right now.

They had given God every reason to treat them as an enemy, but God isn't doing it yet. How do we know that? You don't warn the enemy in the way that God is warning these that he loves. You treat an enemy with contempt, with abandonment. When it is too late God doesn't warn. And he doesn't waste a warning by giving it too late.

Here is what might have been the case with these Christians: God's irretrievable wrath had been called out on them already. I wonder if you've been trespassing on the verge of danger. You've pitched your tent towards Sodom and you might have already reached the point of no return, to be unreachable, unteachable and unusable. But it's not like that yet. That hasn't happened. 'As many as I love, I rebuke and chasten,' said Jesus (Rev. 3:19). God only rebukes, chastens and warns when there is time. There is time. That is, there is time now. Thank God for his warning. Fall on your face before him for waking you up. Do not resent the warning but trim your lamps and be ready that God might bless you because he wants to and he will.

7

The Overruling Grace of God

James 4:5

This is undoubtedly one of the most difficult verses in the New Testament, certainly the most difficult one we have in this epistle. I can give three reasons. First, we're told that the Scripture says something, but we don't know of any place in the Old Testament where we have this quotation: 'The spirit that dwelleth in us lusteth to envy.' Second, Bible scholars have been divided over whether 'spirit' here should have a capital 's' because it's the Holy Spirit or a small 's' for the spirit in man. Third, the translation of the Greek word *epipothei* as 'lusteth' is quite unfortunate.

How To Know What James Means

The problem is that in the AV this verse is poorly translated. The NIV gives three translations and the final alternative translation has got it right; most other translations miss it. Interestingly enough, the New Living Bible comes the closest. If I say that we're going to get it all straightened out I will come through to you as probably the most arrogant preacher or Bible scholar on the face of the earth! And yet I am of the opinion that there is some insight for us that will give us comfort and help us see a breakthrough.

There is one advantage that we have had, and that is that we've had fifty studies in James already so that if we've understood it up to now we really know what he's thinking.

Whose spirit?

The first rule for interpreting all Scripture is: be governed by the context. We have here introducing this fifth verse the Greek particle '*e*'. It's not even translated in the AV. It should be translated 'or'. Whenever we have the Greek particle '*e*' introducing a question it is designed to go on and ask the same thing another way. Verse 4 said, 'Ye adulterers and adulteresses, know ye not that the friendship of the world is enmity with God? Whosoever therefore will be a friend of the world is the enemy of God. Or ...' He's going to ask the same thing in a different way.

What is the context? Verse 2 tells us that these Christian Jews who were double minded couldn't even succeed at sinning. In the grave warning of verse 4 James was hoping to wake them up. James is now going to say the same thing in a different way. He says, 'Do ye think that the scripture saith in vain ...' The Greek reads like this: 'Or do you think that the scripture says in vain that the Spirit who is made to dwell in you yearns jealously?' I have translated 'spirit' here with a capital 'S', despite the AV because I am convinced it is the Holy Spirit. Calvin said, 'This is the Holy Spirit indeed.'

Which Scripture?

James is saying what we've been seeing all along, that God is dealing with these Christians and now, having shown them that they are risking having God treat them as an enemy, he puts it to them again like this: 'Do you think that the scripture says in vain ...' Now the word translated 'scripture' is *graphe*, from *grapho* which simply means the 'word that is written down'. There are other Greek words translated 'word'. But this is *graphe*, which almost always means 'scripture', 'what is written'. It is used in the New Testament to quote the Old Testament. In James 2:23 where we have: 'And the scripture was fulfilled which saith, Abraham believed God, and it was imputed unto him for righteousness', it's the word *graphe* and we know James got that from Genesis 15:6. Now he says it again: 'the scripture'.

The problem is that there is no Scripture like this in the Old Testament or in any apocryphal writing. It's not in the Septuagint. It doesn't seem to be in any extra-canonical source and I doubt that it's in some lost prophetic document. Yet James says, 'the scripture'. He says this in such a way that he thinks they'll know exactly what he means. He certainly doesn't want to get their minds off what he's just said by throwing in something wild, so he uses something that is obvious to them.

I think we can understand it like this, that James is putting in one sentence a digest or summary of Old Testament teaching that they will regard as beyond controversy: God dwells in his people by his Spirit, and God is a jealous God. Take Exodus 20:5: 'I the LORD thy God am a jealous God.' Or take Isaiah 43:1: 'I have called thee by thy name; thou art mine.' Or take the words of David in Psalm 51, 'Create in me a clean heart, O God; and renew a right spirit within me. Cast me not away from thy presence; and take not thy Holy Spirit from me' (vv. 10–11).

These Old Testament verses point to the jealousy of the Holy Spirit. 'This,' James is saying, 'is what the Scripture teaches. He has made the Spirit to dwell in us, yearning jealously, yearning with envy.' This is how James has summarized the teaching. Similarly, I could say to you that the New Testament teaches that saved people go to heaven, lost people go to hell. You can't find one verse just as I've said it. You need three or four. But it is still a true statement of Scripture.

What James has done is to bring in what is an undoubted conclusion from a variety of Old Testament Scriptures to say, 'Do you think that the Scripture says in vain that the Spirit that God has caused to dwell in us yearns with jealousy?'

When he introduces it with this Greek particle '*e*' translated 'or', he is saying in a different way what he just said in verse 4: friendship with the world is to be at enmity with God. In verse 4 he's talking about God's anger and God's wrath. In verse 5 he switches it to God's jealousy. He's doing this still to wake up these worldly Christians.

The Double Minded Christian

The reason James could ask, 'Do ye think …' is that he had become of the opinion that his readers didn't think that. Double mindedness causes us to doubt the authority of Scripture and the seriousness of God's Word and his will. And when a person is double minded he tends to forget Scripture altogether. So James is bringing them face to face with God's Word.

We can ignore doubt and try to hide

Remember that we're talking about the worldly Christian who always imputes to himself more strength than is there, who always imputes to the world less harm than is there and who imputes to God a benign disregard for godliness. James is bringing them face to face with God's jealousy love. He is possessive of us and is jealous that we do his will. James just says,

'Do you think that the Scripture has said in vain …' He's asking them whether or not they still believe in God's Word, whether they still believe it is true and whether they still believe that God is at work. It's his way of saying, 'Do you really think that you're going to get away with this?' As a pastor I often have to say to people, 'What do you think you're doing? Do you really think that God approves of that? Do you really believe that God's Word doesn't mean what it says?' This is what James is doing here.

The devil wants us to think that God will not take notice of this or that, and to minimize the seriousness of godliness. Paul says 'Know ye not that ye are the temple of God, and that the Spirit of God dwelleth in you? If any man defile the temple of God, him shall God destroy; for the temple of God is holy, which temple ye are' (1 Cor. 3:16–17). James is saying to them, 'Look what's happening to you. Can't you see that God isn't letting you have your way? What is this telling you? You can't even succeed at sin. You're making no impact on the world at all. You're doing something wrong.'

The worldly Christian tries to convince himself that God doesn't really care, isn't working. You may sometimes feel that you haven't seen God do anything lately. Listen to the Psalmist: 'He shall cover thee with his feathers, and under his wings shalt thou trust: his truth shall be thy shield and buckler' (91:4). If you don't think God is working, look how much he has kept you out of trouble to this moment.

God doesn't give up so easily

What is the explanation for this? The Holy Spirit is in you. He reflects this jealousy that we know is essential to the heart of God. That's the explanation if nothing that you want to happen in your life is happening. The very fact that you're kept and you're being spared should show you how God is in fact working overtime to keep you.

The bottom line of James 4:5 is this: you may yearn for the world, but God isn't going to give you up easily. For he's a jealous God. You may yearn for the world, but God yearns for you. The principle at work here is put like this by Nehemiah in chapter 9:15–17: Thou 'gavest them bread from heaven for their hunger, and broughtest forth water for them out of the rock for their thirst, and promisedst them that they should go in to possess the land which thou hadst sworn to give them. But they and our fathers dealt proudly, and hardened their necks, and hearkened not to thy commandments, And refused to obey, neither were mindful of thy wonders that thou didst among them; but hardened their necks, and in their rebellion appointed a captain to return to their bondage: but thou art a God ready to pardon, gracious and merciful, slow to anger, and of great kindness, and forsookest them not.'

James' readers were rebellious and worldly, but God wasn't giving them up. They may have thought that they weren't seeing him work, but he was working overtime to keep them from trouble. It was a case of overruling grace, his prevailing over their worldly bent, his setting aside their desires by his greater power and rejecting their requests by declaring them invalid. 'Ye ask amiss, that ye may consume it upon your lusts.'

God overrules by his Spirit who dwells in us. The Holy Spirit is a very sensitive person and he can be grieved, although he never leaves us utterly. Jesus said, 'He my abide with you forever' (Jn. 14:16). But when he's grieved he retreats in such a manner that leaves us as though to ourselves. When he retreats we don't feel him leave, when he departs in this manner it's an unconscious thing. The only way we know the Spirit is grieved is when we try to do something which we were previously able to do with ease. Then we find out we're having to do it in our own strength.

The Spirit Working In Us

The Spirit is sensitive and he's a person, but we need to understand that his dwelling in us is permanent and we must not underestimate this. It was God who initiated his dwelling in us. This is why James said in chapter one verse 18, 'Of his own will begat he us with the word of truth'. When James uses this word 'to dwell' it's the Greek word *katokisen* which means 'caused to dwell'. We didn't initiate conversion, the Spirit did it. 'God caused the Spirit to dwell in us,' said James. He didn't come to dwell with us because of anything we did; neither can anything we do make him utterly leave us. Hebrews 13:5 tells us: 'I will never leave thee, nor forsake thee.'

Do you know what it is to run from God and find out you couldn't do it? Jonah ran from God but he found out what the Psalmist meant in Psalm 139:7–8: 'whither shall I go from thy spirit? or whither shall I flee from thy presence? If I ascend up into heaven, thou art there: if I make my bed in hell, behold, thou art there.' His Spirit dwells in us, yearning with jealousy.

You may say, 'Doesn't the Spirit of God dwell in everybody?' There is a sense in which that is true. Paul in Acts 17:28 quoted one of the pagan poets who says, 'In him we live, and move, and have our being.' Indeed we are told that Christ upholds 'all things by the word of his power' (Heb. 1:3). You have breath by God, and if God takes it away, you're dead. In that sense God's Spirit is in every man, but not in the way James means because there is a possessiveness that is peculiar to God's elect. This is described by Jesus, talking about the Father, Son and Holy Spirit – 'we will come unto him, and make our abode with him' (Jn. 14:23). When the Spirit of Christ takes up residence, he wants sovereign control.

The Spirit is jealous

We have this Greek phrase *pros phthnon* which means 'jealously', 'with envy', 'with jealousy'. In the first five verses of the fourth chapter of James there are three different Greek words that the Authorised Version always translates 'lust.' Verse one uses *hedonais*, which means 'pleasure'. The second time it's a word that simply means 'lust' or 'desire', and the third time it is this Greek word *epipothei* which means 'earnestly desire'. James has combined this word that means 'earnestly desire' with this word that means 'jealousy' to give strength to this point.

How much does God possess us? How jealous is he? James says, 'He earnestly desires jealously.' He says it twice to show how serious God is. James is saying, 'You Christian Jews think that you can flirt with the world. Do you think the Scripture says in vain that God has caused his Spirit to dwell in us jealously, desiring jealously?' The main lesson for us to see is that the purpose of this overruling grace is not only to protect us from ourselves, and not only to protect us from forcing God to treat us like an enemy, but that the Spirit wants to teach us God's ways. That's how much God loves us. In a word, he dwells in us to help us to make the transition from the flesh to the spirit.

The transition from flesh to spirit

I don't know whether any of us have made that transition, but I'm now describing what is possibly the most painful ordeal in the world: making the transition from flesh to the spirit. God begins this transition by reaching us where we are by conversion. There's a sense in which we can say that becoming a Christian is the easiest thing in the world. Nothing is really required of anybody to become a Christian.

> *Just as I am, without one plea*
> *But that thy blood was shed for me,*
> *And that thou bidst me come to thee,*
> *O Lamb of God, I come.*

God takes you as you are and accommodates the babe in Christ in a very tender way. This accommodating protection from God is why the babe in Christ has some of his best days right at the beginning of his Christian life. One of my favourite quotes of Luther is: 'God uses sex to drive a man to marriage; ambition to drive a man to service; and fear to drive a man to faith.' A young Christian knows that God just takes care of him, answering prayer, arranging providence and supplying needs.

There comes a time when we need to make the transition from the flesh to the spirit. None of us likes to give up childhood. We are all congenitally opposed to maturity. You've seen people who just never grow up, haven't you? They've had an arrested development at some stage and they're still like children. This can happen spiritually. This is what Paul was worried about when he said the Corinthians were still carnal, still in the flesh, having to be fed with milk (1 Cor. 3:1–3).

Look how Jesus worked in John 6. At the beginning of the sixth chapter of John, Jesus, by the miracle of the loaves and the fishes, had five thousand people following him because they'd had their stomachs filled. But at the end of John 6, as he was trying to get them to make the transition from the flesh to the spirit, they all left. Jesus looked at the Twelve and said, 'Will ye also go away?' Peter answered, 'Lord, to whom shall we go? thou hast the words of eternal life' (vv. 67, 68).

God wants us to come to a maturity whereby our concerns will not simply be personal, where we're not seeking our fulfilment at a natural level. Look at the way God prepared Moses. His second forty years went to make this transition from the flesh to the spirit where his personal needs were transcended by the greater concerns of the kingdom of God. This is how Paul could describe his own situation. He said, Christ 'died for all, that they which live should not henceforth live unto themselves, but unto him which died for them, and rose again. Wherefore henceforth know we no man after the flesh: yea, though we have known Christ after the flesh, yet now henceforth know we him no more' (2 Cor. 5:15–16). But this transition presupposes suffering, and this is why the epistle of James began, 'Count it all joy when ye fall into divers temptations'.

God wants us to grow up

Here's how this transition works. God accommodates us where we are: at conversion and in early days of growth. But have you ever wondered why you woke up one day and suddenly there was a void in your life? The joy was gone and the momentum that had been carrying you through just wasn't there. It may have happened suddenly, it may have happened imperceptibly. That was God's way of saying, 'Come on. Grow up. I've got better things in mind for you.' Sometimes he hides his face. And sometimes he lets us operate at a self-defeating natural level to show us our weakness and folly.

The sad thing is that some people never do take this hint; they keep wanting to have it the old way when everything was going just right and every need was being supplied just like that. We want to have our own way when we're children. As Paul said, 'When I was a child, I spake as a child, I understood as a child, I thought as a child: but when I became a man, I put away childish things' (1 Cor. 13:11). This is why he could go on to the 'more excellent way' (1 Cor. 12:31).

As long as Paul is talking about the gifts, he's really appealing to people at a natural level. He says, 'Covet earnestly the best gifts' (1 Cor. 12:31). This is why you can have people in the charismatic movement who are so shallow. They think they're strong, but they're not. The 'more excellent way' is to become a man, and few there are that make that transition from the flesh to the spirit. Paul talks about this love whereby we are motivated entirely for the glory of God in chapter 13.

You may want to ask, 'Why does God want us to make this transition?' There's only one answer: that we might know him. All of us have our natural desires, such as ambition. But God has ambition which he calls 'jealousy'. It's an ambition for himself. We call it the kingdom of God. The Spirit dwells in us that we might participate in pleasing him. Even Christ did not please himself but learned obedience through sufferings (Heb. 5:8). So too, we enter the kingdom of God through tribulation. The goal is this: to learn to think as God thinks, to hate what God hates, to love what God loves, so that ultimately we think so much as God does that we can scarcely tell the difference between our own will and his. That is what is in store for us if we will let him rule and take control over us. This is what James envisages.

Enoch walked with God and got to know God so well that God effectively said, 'You know too much. You'd better come up here.' 'And he was not; for God took him' (Gen. 5:24). Peter was always in the flesh and for years he followed Jesus focussing on what was in it for him. There came a day when Peter could talk about being 'partakers of the divine nature, having escaped the corruption that is in the world through lust' (2 Pet. 1:4). It's wonderful that God would deal with us in such a way as to call us to that kind of living.

These Christians were being called to this transition, and at the bottom of all of their struggles was nothing but God's overruling grace, that they might take the hint that God was dealing with them. James is saying, 'Do you think that God has said it in vain?' His ways are higher than our ways and his thoughts than our thoughts (Isa. 55:9). The Spirit in us will not give up easily when we want to sin.

If we knew how much it hurt God when we sin, we wouldn't do it. If we knew how close we really were to greater blessing when we gave in to temptation, we would fall on our faces and ask God to give us a second chance. And he would. As James goes on to say, 'he giveth more grace'.

8

God's Greater Grace

James 4:6

I shall focus mainly on the first part of this verse: 'he giveth more grace'. We have seen how much God loves us. We have seen his protectiveness over us, indeed his jealousy. We have seen that he will not give us up easily although we cast our gaze to the world. We can see how much it hurts him when we sin. What James is doing is to motivate us not by fear but by love. The law motivates by fear. As Paul put it: 'The love of Christ constraineth us' (2 Cor. 5:14).

God Does Not Give Up Easily

You may ask the question, 'If God loves us so much why would his Spirit retreat and leave us, as it were, totally at a natural level where we have to cope without the normal Christian graces?' The answer is that God must be true to himself. If we gaze at the world God's going to put up a fight. Luther put it like this: 'You must know God as an enemy before you can know him as a friend.' God won't let us have our own way because he is our friend.

This is the explanation for what is going on in the lives of James' readers. They weren't able to succeed at anything. When James says, 'But he giveth more grace', it is simply a way of stating that God continues to do with us what he did when he first found us. We were saved by grace. We've been kept by grace. But James says that's not the end: 'He giveth more grace.' We have here a reaffirmation of God's electing grace and his keeping grace.

The doctrine of election has been dealt with already in this epistle. 'Of his own will begat he us with the word of truth' (1:18). It was applied in verse 5 of chapter 4: Do you think that the scripture says in vain that the Spirit which God caused to dwell in us yearns jealously. We must never forget that all participants in God's grace are enabled to be such because God took the initiative. Indeed, this initiative is apart from our works. As Paul put it: 'While we were yet sinners, Christ died for us' (Rom. 5:8).

Here were these Christians acting like worldly people, and yet we see God's keeping grace. He hasn't dropped them. This is a reaffirmation of the doctrine of justification by faith alone.

Our Need For More Grace

Despite the fact that these Christians had stooped so low, James is staying with them, showing that they're still God's own children. Instead of withdrawing grace from them, God gives more grace. Why? Not only to reaffirm his choice of us but because we need it now more than ever.

It's one thing for God to save us when we were yet sinners, before we were Christians. It is another for him to rescue us when we're not acting like Christians. We need grace more than ever now that we have cast our gaze at the world. We have here a picture of God beginning with us all over again. 'He giveth more grace.' This text is showing that God reinstitutes his calling of us. I want us to see some differences between the way God called us at the beginning and the way God comes to us as Christians.

A different call

The first difference is that originally God called us to salvation, to faith. But when he comes to us after we have become Christians it is a call to repentance. He called us originally to give us the knowledge of our eternal salvation. We call it 'justification by faith'. But he comes the second time exhorting us to Christian obedience, exhorting us to please God by what we actually do in our persons. James calls it justification by works and faith together.

God is calling these Christians to personal holiness, to new obedience. The first person, as far as I'm able to tell, who ever used the expression 'new obedience' is Martin Luther. The point is that God calls us the first time to obey the gospel and to affirm what Jesus did on the cross and this results in our eternal justification. But then he calls us to be holy and without blame before him. This is new obedience.

We get to choose

The second difference is this: when God called us the first time, calling us
to faith, we refer to it as an effectual call. And I do not mind using the
expression that it was 'irresistible'. When God comes the second time the
choice is indeed ours. The first time we make the choice as though we do
it in our own strength; we later learn the family secret, that our being able
to make that choice was nothing but the sheer grace of God. But the call
to new obedience can be resisted – and often is.

A different type of grace

The third difference is this: the first calling can be put in terms of
'prevenient grace' – that was Augustine's term – the second, to use a
Puritan term, 'experimental grace'. What I mean is this: when God came
to us the first time, presenting to us his work in Christ, we believed what
Jesus did for us. 'While we were yet sinners Christ died for us.' God 'made
him to be sin for us, who knew no sin' (2 Cor. 5:21). This is prevenient
grace. But the second time he comes to us is so that we might experience
grace as his actual power working through us.

   This word 'grace' is to be seen in three ways:

- *Saving grace* – 'By grace are ye saved through faith; and that not of
  yourselves: it is the gift of God: Not of works, lest any man should
  boast' (Eph. 2:8–9).
- *Overruling or restraining grace* – What God did with Jonah when Jonah
  went the other way. God prepared the wind and the fish. Jonah was
  kept from getting his own way. That is what James' readers were
  experiencing. They wanted to have their own way, but they
  weren't getting it.
- *Experimental grace* – This is what James has in mind when he says, 'But
  he giveth more grace.' It is a reference to God's actual power in us.
  These people had been saved and they were being kept – preserved – as
  Jonah was. But James wants them to move out of that miserable state.

Having shown that they were having such a terrible witness and having no
impact in the world, he put it like this early on: 'Wilt thou know, O vain
man, that faith without works is dead?' – that is, 'useless'. And James
concludes, 'Ye see then how that by works a man is justified, and not only
by faith' (2:20, 24). Here were these Christians who, by mixing with the
world, were having no impact on the world. They really thought that

they could achieve by saying they believed in God. They supposed that that was all that was necessary. James wants them to move on into authentic sanctification that they might know God and please him and be as Abraham was: a friend of God.

Somebody may want to ask, 'Are we talking about a second work of grace as the Wesleys put it?' The answer is no, it is not that at all. When I refer now to sanctification, James calls it 'justification by works.' It is not a crisis experience nor does it remove any, as they call it, inbred sin.

'Greater' Grace

You may want to ask the question: 'Why, when it comes to this call to new obedience, is this grace referred to in James 4:6 not effectual? Why isn't it irresistible?' It is because God deals with us in dignity, giving us opportunity to please him by our own obedience. Did not God deal with Jonah and so box him in that he was really left without any choice? Yes, and yet that is in fact the way he does deal with us when he comes and gives us more grace. But you can resist it, and Jonah could have resisted it.

This is the way God was dealing now with these Christians. It is the way he's dealing with many of us. He's boxing us in. We're looking for any way to get out. 'Surely it is not a command to self-denial. There must be another way.' But God is serious about this matter of hating the world and worldliness and ungodliness. There is no way we can rationalize and say that we can be at friendship with the world and please God at the same time. He leaves us without excuse.

So when we cast our gaze at the world the same Spirit that God caused to dwell in us yearns with jealousy. God fights hard lest we do succumb to the world, to sin, to the flesh, to the devil. God yearns in us by working overtime as he did with Jonah. This is partly what James means now: 'But he giveth more grace.'

That isn't the only thing this verse means because we must see that what has been going on up to now is really negative at best. It's simply restraining grace – God keeping us from getting our way, God not letting us have success. James wants to move on and to show the positive, that there's more to know than just the restraining grace of God.

How many of us have known almost nothing more than that? When God came to us in conversion he overruled our wills. Even with this restraining grace, he is overruling our wills. But now he wants us to receive grace, to experience something that is positive and dynamic. What is it? It is to make this transition from the flesh to the spirit, from wanting the world and wanting to be in friendship with the world, to wanting God's will only and enjoying knowing his honour only. When God offers us this grace, nothing can demonstrate ingratitude more than refusing what is offered to us.

The Greek word that is translated 'more' means 'greater'. It is the comparative form of the Greek word which means 'great'. It's an odd thing that most translations just translate it 'more'.

James might simply have said, 'He giveth great grace', as in Acts 4:33: '*Great* grace was upon them all.' That's the word, except that James uses the comparative form.

To be fair it does mean 'more', but if we leave it at that we are going to miss something that is marvellous indeed. Why would James call this 'greater grace?' The answer is, because in bestowing this grace God not only reaffirms his abiding love, showing that the grace which saves us can never be rendered invalid, but also offers his own power 'to do exceeding abundantly above all that we ask or think, according to the power that worketh in us' (Eph. 3:20). It's an invitation to experience God's own power. This is why it's called 'greater grace'.

The grace of God that brings salvation is described by Paul: 'By grace are ye saved through faith' (Eph. 2:8). But Paul goes on to say that 'we are his workmanship, created in Christ Jesus unto good works' (v. 10). James now speaks of a demonstration of God's power in and through us. It is grace that will make the world know that there is something different about us. This is why these Christians were failures. They thought their faith was sufficient, but their faith wasn't doing the job. They thought that their impact on the world would be good if they were friendly with the world. But the opposite was true. What James does now is to offer to them and to us the opportunity to experience the kind of grace that once put Christianity on the map.

That which turned the world upside down was hardly that which these Christians had going for them. At the moment God was only saving them from extinction. That's what most of church history is. What the church has experienced most throughout her history is this restraining grace, God just keeping us alive. But when James tells us that God gives greater grace it's an invitation to experience God himself and his own power. Paul, writing to the Colossians, calls it being 'partakers of the inheritance of the saints in light' (1:12).

Greater grace at work in us

Paul in the same letter to the Colossians says, 'that ye may stand perfect and complete in all the will of God' (4:12). This is what God has in mind for us. As Paul put it to the Ephesians: 'All the fulness of God' (3:19). That's what he wants us to enjoy. What James is saying, what Paul was saying, is that we might be as pliable in God's hands as these great saints were. God wants us to be in our generation what they were in theirs. What is issued before us is a call to true greatness. Yet it is a call to self-denial. It is a call to godliness but it is also a call to suffering.

Entering into greater grace

But this greater grace is not irresistible. Obviously if we're talking about irresistible grace when it comes to the call to new obedience then all Christians would be equally godly, as they already are equally righteous in God's sight through the blood of Christ. This call to receive God's greater grace is that which must be applied. And that means accepting it on the conditions on which it is offered. That means abandoning our friendship with the world and with worldly lusts. This is why James goes on to say, 'He giveth more grace. Wherefore he saith God resisteth the proud, but giveth grace unto the humble.' For this grace is the key to the highest level of reality there is, but it will only be received by hearts who yearn jealously as God does. That means that we must hate sin as God does.

If you want to know that high level of reality that has characterized the great saints, then hate sin as they did. There's no other way. You could spend seven days in prayer and fasting and be no closer to it as long as you love the world in your heart. It comes to those who want God's glory and his will and his presence more than anything.

How can it be said that it is given when it is offered upon conditions? Our first grace in conversion was given like this, wasn't it? 'For God so loved the world that he gave his only begotten Son' (Jn. 3:16) and that was on the condition of faith: 'whosoever believeth'. With this greater grace God comes to us and he gives it. When it is accepted you will never think that you did it. Jonah didn't think at all that it was anything that he did when God came the second time. There's no way we could take any credit for it because we don't deserve this offer. The paradox is that, to the one who does receive this grace that is offered, the family secret comes into play again: that God was at the bottom of it all and only a fool would turn it down.

You may want to ask, 'If it is a greater grace how is this possible? Can anything rival the grace offered to us in the gospel?' The answer is no, for throughout eternity we'll be singing this song: 'Worthy is the Lamb that was slain because he redeemed us by his blood.' Then why call this a 'greater grace?' James uses this word because, as Christ overruled our sinfulness the first time – 'Even while we were yet sinners Christ died for us' – so he does it again, overruling our worldly bent. In the gospel Christ was our substitute and there was the transaction between the Father and the Son. We are out of the picture, as it were, except that we affirm what Christ did. But it is called a 'greater grace' for because Christ has atoned for our souls by his most precious blood, we can now come to God and God affirms us. And we embark upon this new obedience. James calls it 'justification by works'.

Because Christ has atoned for our souls God can now deal with us in an immediate and direct manner, but it comes almost every time through suffering. So Paul could talk about those who could enjoy the fullness of God 'that Christ might dwell in your hearts by faith; that ye being rooted and grounded in love' and experiencing seeing God do anything even 'above all that we ask or think, according to the power that worketh in us' (Eph. 3:17, 20).

James said, 'Count it all joy when ye fall into divers temptations', because the receiving of this grace presupposes suffering. 'We must through much tribulation enter into the kingdom of God' (Acts 14:22). We're dealing here with a painful process rather than a once-for-all crisis. Sanctification is progressive rather than something that purports to remove remaining sin. For 'if we say that we have no sin, we deceive ourselves, and the truth is not in us' (1 Jn. 1:9).

To receive this grace results in such a love for God and his glory, that the one who receives it becomes what God wants him to be. John said that we show that we love him because 'we keep his commandments: and his commandments are not grievous' (1 Jn. 5:3). 'Grievous' means 'burden-some', 'demoralizing', 'unreasonable'. Paul prayed that we might 'stand perfect and complete in all the will of God' (Col. 4:12). James said, 'Let patience have her perfect work, that ye may be perfect and entire, wanting nothing' (1:3).

Would you say that Paul became what God wanted him to be? I say, yes, in the context of the circumstances and God's immediate purpose, Paul became what God wanted him to be. What about Abraham? Could Abraham have carried out the ordeal of sacrificing Isaac any better than he did? No, he did what God told him to do. James called it being justified by works. What about us? Are we as pliable in the hands of God as men like that? Why should we be content with any less than that which characterized them? I may not have Paul's intelligence or his education or his gifts, but surely I can be as pliable in the hands of God as Paul was, if I love God as he did. I can bear the thought that God might not accomplish as much in me as he did in Paul if intelligence or quality of mind or gifts have anything to do with such limitations and restrictions, but I cannot bear the thought that God could do more with me if only I were more dedicated. James says, 'He giveth more grace.' He gives greater grace that we may become what God has in mind for you and me.

9

Beginning to Grow Positively

James 4:6

James is bringing his readers along from the negative to the positive. In making the transition now, coming to the positive, he simply makes a statement we must face before we move on and begin to grow positively: 'He giveth more grace. Wherefore he saith, God resisteth the proud, but giveth grace unto the humble.'

A Better Way To Live

A way of putting James' argument is this: there's a better way to live. How many of us have known nothing really but the restraining, over-ruling grace of God? I have already said that the Greek word means 'greater grace' and I lamented the fact that most translations don't translate it that way, but somebody showed me that there is a version – the New American Standard Version says, 'He gives a greater grace.' At this point James quotes Proverbs 3:34, 'he gives grace to the humble, he resists the proud' (Septuagint rendering).

Up to now these Christians had only been growing negatively. This happens in our spiritual pilgrimage. We pick up bad habits and think that they're quite all right. Or we can pick up bad theology along the way and never move along, never really grow. You say the things you've always said, you believe what you've always believed and because you've read one or two books you just never move beyond that point – an arrested development. I say this with respect, but there are a lot of older Christians who really have not grown much over the years. The point is that we must remember it is possible to keep growing and to see things we hadn't seen before. James wants us to know that it is possible to experience more than the overruling, restraining grace of God which was the only thing going for his readers. James wants us to experience God's actual power.

Jesus said it: 'Broad is the way, that leadeth to destruction, and many there be which go in thereat: Because strait is the gate, and narrow is the way, which leadeth unto life, and few there be that find it' (Mt. 7:13–14). I suspect that it's a small percentage of Christians who see God's actual power work in a positive way.

Greater grace has conditions attached

We've seen that this greater grace has conditions attached. It's not irresistible grace, as saving grace is. If it were, then all Christians would be equally godly, equally spiritual. But the fact is some Christians are more spiritual, some grow faster, some know more than others. James wants us to realize that this greater grace is given to the humble. This is why he quotes from Proverbs 3:34: 'God resisteth the proud but giveth grace to the humble.'

Proverbs 3:34 says, 'Surely he scorneth the scorners: but he giveth grace unto the lowly.' James is quoting the Septuagint, which is the Greek translation of the Hebrew. What we have in our Authorised Version is the English translation of the Hebrew. The Greek translation of the Hebrew comes out the way James uses it. It's the same thing. He wants us to know, as we're making the transition from the flesh to the spirit, that only the humble can expect this greater grace. The literal translation from the Greek is this: 'To the proud God sets himself in opposition, to the humble he gives grace.'

I want us to see three reasons why James bothered to bring in Proverbs 3:34.

1. Facing Our Pride

The biblical method of dealing with any malady that we have, is that God deals with the problem directly. We sometimes think that if we do certain things that are right it will help a particular problem, but dealing with it indirectly is not the biblical way at all. The word translated 'humble' is the Greek word that is used in James chapter 1 verse 9 when he says that there are those of low degree that should rejoice. This word means 'low-class'. When James used the word in chapter one verse nine he contrasted the lowly with the rich. But when he comes to use it in the fourth chapter it is not contrasted with the rich but rather with the proud. This word has a double meaning. It primarily refers to one's socio-economic class, but because he can contrast it with pride we see the second meaning – an inward brokenness. James uses the word on purpose because it applies directly to his readers' situation. We're talking now about the person who is of a lowly background, and yet 'humble' means ultimately 'the one who is broken in spirit'. We must never lose sight of the primary meaning of this word or we'll miss James' purpose.

Proud outreach

He chose this word to show that there are conditions attached to this greater grace that God gives in bringing us to positive growth, because these Christian Jews had become so selective in their evangelism. To James, this was despicable: Christianity, I believe, is the only religion in the history of man to have something to offer to the poor.

In the gospel of Luke Jesus said, 'The Spirit of the Lord is upon me, because he hath anointed me to preach the gospel to the poor' (4:18). When John the Baptist queried whether or not Messiah had really come, Jesus told them to go back to John and tell him what they had heard, 'that the blind see, the lame walk, the lepers are cleansed, the deaf hear, the dead are raised, to the poor the gospel is preached' (Lk. 7:22). When James and the apostle Paul had a quarrel they finally got their differences reconciled, but James got in the last word and simply said, 'One thing, remember the poor' (Gal. 2:10).

All of us have our own emphasis. When James got word that these Christians had begun to act like this he wrote the letter; it was more than he could take. James' method, then, is to deal with this problem directly. We all admire the truly humble person. We may say that what we need to do is to imitate, as it were, humility. James isn't going to let us off that easily. He meets head-on the very problem that had rendered them powerless.

It's extraordinary how all of us want to better ourselves and in doing so we tend to despise the way we once were and unconsciously we look down on everybody else who is that way. I remember reading a book by Jilly Cooper called *Class*. She says something very interesting: that those of a particular class despise most those who are just beneath them. The aristocracy look down on the upper middle class. The upper middle class look down on the middle class. The middle class look down on the lower middle class. And the lower middle class look down on the working class. The aristocracy gets on best with the low class because they're not threatened by them. This is human nature. These Christians were poor themselves. It was ridiculous that, having been converted, they would now try to impress the rich. Their attitude toward the poor was despicable.

There is no substitute for obedience

James quotes Proverbs to deal directly with their problem, rather than concentrate on some other grace. What we often do is say, 'I need more humility. I'm going to spend more time in prayer', or 'I need to please the Lord so I'm going to start giving more.' We concentrate on some valid Christian duty that we think will deal with the other problem. But that is not the biblical way to do it; in living the Christian life there is no substitute for obedience. If there is a particular sin in your life and you're not dealing with it, all the praying in the world will not bring God's blessing upon you.

James is talking now about moving from the flesh to the spirit, and he quotes this proverb that has the double meaning showing that God gives grace to the humble. He wants them to recognize that they've got to begin there, because that's where they have transgressed. Rule number one in beginning to grow positively is to deal immediately with any known sin. Do you know of a particular sin in your life? You say, 'I'm dealing with it by praying more.' And you've been doing that for months. Has it worked? In case you wonder what I mean by 'dealing with the sin', I mean stop it permanently. You say, 'I can't.' But you can. Until you do God won't bless you. It is not until you stop it that you can even begin to make the transition.

God hates pride

Whatever our sin, God's greater grace need not be applied for unless we submit to the surgery God has in mind. You may want to ask why God resists the proud. Pride is man's attempt to rival God. Nothing is more irrational and nonsensical. Paul said, 'For who maketh thee to differ from another? and what hast thou that thou didst not receive? now if thou didst receive it, why dost thou glory, as if thou hadst not received it' (1 Cor. 4:7). There's no reason for pride. God hates it. Pride is abominable to God. That's how much God hates pride.

We have verses like this right through the Old Testament. Psalm 18:26–27: 'With the pure thou wilt shew thyself pure; and with the froward thou wilt show thyself froward. For thou wilt save the afflicted people; but will bring down high looks.' Psalm 138:6:

'Though the LORD be high, yet hath he respect unto the lowly: but the proud he knoweth afar off.' Or take Proverbs 6:17: there are things that God hates, and the first is 'a proud look'. Mary the mother of our Lord in her great prayer said, 'My soul doth magnify the Lord ... He that is mighty hath done to me great things ... He hath scattered the proud ... and exalted them of low degree' (Lk. 1:46, 49, 51, 52).

2. God's Resistance

James uses this particular proverb to show that because these Christians themselves had become proud, God had to set himself in opposition to those who were actually his own people. Their friendship with the world made them God's enemies.

God's chastening

The five degrees of God's chastening are:

- firstly, we're shattered by the word of God;
- secondly, through the providential hand of God, things just happen beyond our control;
- thirdly, the withdrawal of certain Christian graces so that we are forced to cope at a natural level;
- fourthly, he does let you have your way and you have a taste of sin;
- fifthly, God forgets you entirely and you are abandoned, which is what is meant by 'God resists the proud'.

It is one thing to know the wrath of God where he deals with us and he chastens us. Do you know what it is when God just steps in and deals with you and you know he's angry? This is why James could say, 'Count it all joy when you fall into divers temptations.' Or the writer to the Hebrews said, 'No chastening for the present seemeth to be joyous, but grievous' (Heb. 12:11).

But there's something worse than that – when God just doesn't even let you know what he's thinking. Psalm 147:17: 'Who can stand before his cold?' The worst thing that can happen to a person is for God to do nothing. Hosea 4:17: 'Ephraim is joined to idols: let him alone.' This is what is meant by 'resists'. God does nothing.

God can wait

God is not so insecure that he has to bring his vengeance upon the proud right now. He knows the proud will get what's coming to them soon enough. The worst treatment that you can ever give an enemy who used to be a friend is simply to ignore him. And so God does with the proud. God resists by, as it were, walking away from him.

That's the way you resist temptation. You resist temptation by walking away from it, not by seeing how close you can get to it. You may say, 'I did this and God didn't do a thing about it', and you may think you're so clever you got away with it. That's bad news. For it's wonderful when we're found out and God doesn't let us get away with it. But the proud look God hates. He despises it so much that he just ignores it. Look at poor King Saul. He woke up when it was too late and he said, 'I have played the fool, and have erred exceedingly' (1 Sam. 26:21). 'God is departed from me, and answereth me no more' (1 Sam. 28:15).

James' burden is: you're so friendly with the world that you're forcing God to have to treat you with contempt. 'The Spirit that he caused to dwell in us yearns with jealousy but he gives more grace.' Will we receive it? It's only given to the humble. It's not a statement of advice, it's a fact. How we react to this will determine whether we begin to grow positively.

3. Humility And Identifying With The Poor

The third and final reason why James quotes Proverbs 3:34 is to force them to identify with the very ones they despised. Now we're back to this double meaning of our word which means outwardly 'of humble class' but inwardly 'to be broken in spirit'. We may well want to pray for the grace of being inwardly broken. As David prayed in Psalm 51:17: 'The sacrifices of God are a broken spirit: a broken and a contrite heart, O God, thou wilt not despise.' These Christians would never grow until they identified with those for whom they had come to have contempt. If they were ever going to be humble they had to go back and deal with the sin that led to their falling.

This verse doesn't mean, of course, that people of humble origin are automatically recipients of this greater grace; otherwise everybody who is of humble origin – and that's most of us – would be greatly blessed spiritually. We do know that Christianity began with the poor. We know that this doesn't mean simply the poor that happened to be living in 29 AD because James just won't let us forget the poor and the humble. If we ever move away from trying to reach the poor, we never go back to them.

Token evangelism

This is the part of the epistle of James that many people don't like. When it gets on to the poor and the rich we get very nervous. The great curse of the modern church is that it has developed into a middle-class religion. The reason that Marxism moved into the third world and into the working class of Britain is because the Christian church left a gap that Marxism filled.

The working class of this country are generally untouched with the Christian message, unmoved by it. Most of our own witnessing to the working class is just token witnessing. We slip a tract in their door once in a while. It's like the Southern Baptist church in Alabama that has their one black member so they can say they're integrated. That's how many of us witness to the poor. 'We did it. We spent two hours today in the slums.' That's not the point. You can do that and never get James' message. We need not expect greater blessing until we identify with those for whom the gospel was particularly designed.

Some may question what would happen to the church if none but the poor were converted. I'd love to see what would happen. It would put us in a position of having greater blessing from God than ever. We might come to see what that verse means: 'Eye hath not seen, nor ear heard, neither have entered into the heart of man, the things which God hath prepared for them that love him' (1 Cor. 2:9). We must be gripped with this: that 'the humble' primarily means those of low-class background. And if we want to be humble we must identify with them. If we are not trying to convert them we are not humble.

Somebody is going to say, 'What about the rich, the middle class, don't they need the gospel?' I don't know how to win them, but I just know how not to: by buttering them up. That's what these Christians tried to do. What if God's elect were scattered proportionately through all classes and races of men? Do you think that the rich or the educated or the famous constitute a greater proportion of God's elect? We'd like to think that. Paul wrote to the Corinthians and he said, 'For ye see your calling, brethren, how that … not many mighty, not many noble, are called: but God hath chosen the foolish things of the world' (1 Cor. 1:26–27).

If 98 per cent of mankind deserve our attention, not the 2 per cent who are rich, why is it that the modern church has become middle class? What are we supposed to do, start knocking on doors in the slums? Maybe. But I say we could do that and miss James' point. He is calling for a spirit of self-accusation, that we will mourn our ways and understand God's ways. God isn't going to let us off easily. We may say, 'Well, let's just pray more.' Stop and think a moment. When great revival has come, look at those whom God has blessed. Look who were the converts of John Wesley, where he was really powerful. It wasn't in Oxford. It was with the coal miners. And look at the Salvation Army. God blessed them. We're fooling ourselves if we think things have changed.

The key to 'greater grace'

Whatever your sin is, you will not grow positively until you deal with it. And yet if we should submit ourselves to his ways and to his chastening ... I think of the words of the King of Nineveh when he got the message from Jonah, that in forty days Nineveh would be overthrown. The King of Nineveh said, 'Who can tell if God will turn and repent, and turn away from his fierce anger, that we perish not' (Jonah 3:9). Until you deal with sin, don't expect blessing. If all of us will take James seriously we'll then be able to move on. His next advice is 'Submit yourselves to God.' If we do that in the light of the conditions that are attached to God's greater grace, who can tell what he might do?

10

Submitting to God

James 4:7

The first half of James 4:7, 'Submit yourselves therefore to God', is James' first positive, practical step in enabling us to make the painful transition from the flesh to the spirit, from the negative to the positive. We don't have to live the Christian life knowing only the overruling grace of God. There is a better way to live. As the New American Standard Version puts it: 'He gives us a greater grace' (v. 6). But a condition to receiving this greater grace is that we do not postpone dealing with any known sin. Have we indeed come to grips with what God has clearly said to us? The most mocking thing we can do to God is to ask him for more light when we haven't walked in the light that we have. This step in submitting ourselves to God is effectual only if we have agreed with James up to now.

It is his way of showing us how to come to the point of humiliation that is required to receive this greater grace. As Peter put it, it's being 'clothed with humility' (1 Pet. 5:5).

The Command To Submit

To submit ourselves to God is a command to those who are willing to have the broken and contrite spirit that we have seen already, in the Psalm 51. David was confessing his sin to God after having been exposed for going to Bathsheba and then putting Uriah, Bathsheba's husband, at the front of the battle. Nathan the prophet had come to David. David was being dealt with by God. He prayed, 'Wash me thoroughly from mine iniquity, and cleanse me from my sin. For I acknowledge my transgressions: and my sin is ever before me. Against thee, thee only, have I sinned and done this evil in thy sight: that thou mightest be justified when thou speakest, and be clear when thou judgest' (vv. 2–4). David was dealt with while he was abandoning that sin; he now prayed for the joy of salvation to be restored (v. 12). He could say in the end, 'The sacrifices of God are a broken spirit' (v. 17). We must come to this point of humiliation, but we will not do so unless we are dealing with our own sin.

This command uses the Greek word which by itself simply means 'to subordinate'. This is the word: 'submit'. Paul used it in 1 Corinthian 15:27: 'He hath put all things under his feet.' It's the word used in Luke 2:51 where we're told that Jesus was subject to his parents. It is something we do, as though we do it without any help from God at all. We do it because it's right. We don't pray about it. It is done voluntarily and often with great struggle. It's the only way to be brought to this point of humiliation.

Submitting is not always pleasant

Look at it from a natural point of view. Do you pray about whether to go to work in the morning? You don't pray about it because it's right. It's a condition. We get up on Monday morning because we've got to, whether we feel led or not. Students know there are books they've got to read. Whether it's practising to learn the violin or to play the piano or to acquire anything, it takes diligence. How much more must we show our love to God by submitting ourselves to him? It is not passive as in regeneration; this is something we do.

You show how much you love God by doing things you don't feel like, whether it be your Bible reading or the time you spend in prayer, tithing, church attendance, witnessing, talking to people about the Lord during the week, inviting them to church. This is why Paul could say to Timothy, 'Be instant in season, out of season' (2 Tim. 4:2).

I remember some twenty years ago I was going through a particular trial and I thought to myself, 'I think I will spend more time in prayer.' I felt as though I ought to get up at five o'clock in the morning and have an extra two hours to pray. I wasn't sure whether I ought to or not so I said, 'Lord, if you really think this is a good thing would you wake me up at five o'clock.' I woke up the next morning. I was bright-eyed and bushy-tailed and I thought, 'Why am I so awake?' I looked at my watch. It was five o'clock. I thought, 'Well, isn't this wonderful? God did this.' I got up and I prayed and had a wonderful two hours. The next night I said, 'Lord, do it again.' He didn't and he never has since. I have to do it.

James is saying, 'Do it. Take the initiative.' If you don't you never will. You prove your love not by responding when he overpowers you and makes it easy, but by doing it when you don't feel like it, doing it even when everything seems to work against it.

This is the positive step. First, deal with every known sin. Now James is telling us: 'Submit yourselves … to God.' It's another way of saying, 'Stop fighting God.' These Christians had experienced God's overruling grace, but they continued to rebel. 'You lust, fight and quarrel, yet you have not. And then when you do pray you ask amiss. When are you going to learn?' says James. It seemed as though they were never going to take the hint.

God is serious about this matter of true godliness and holiness. 'The way of transgressors is hard' (Prov. 13:15). The unhappiest person in the world is the Christian who is disobedient. God in kindness has been holding on to them and not letting them have their own way. Many of us know nothing but the chastening of God! This isn't necessary if we give in and stop fighting against it. The very subsiding of the troubled waters will be more pleasant than the ordeal you have created for yourself by trying to have your own way.

Submitting to suffering and humility

There's another, more profound reason for this verse. James is saying, 'Submit to God in the light of the suffering that he has designed for you.' God's greater grace presupposes suffering.

We don't like being humiliated. The qualification for the greater grace is being humble. 'He resists the proud but gives grace to the humble.' This grace is conditional. We're to be humble rather than arrogant and proud. So because none of us is contrite by nature, it is required that we come to this point of humiliation.

Because none of us is humble by nature, there are certain things God must do to make us that way. We must be brought to humility, and the only way to be brought to it is by suffering. This brings us back to the very first thing James said. 'Count it all joy when you fall into divers trials' (1:2). This is precisely what James means now when he says 'Submit yourselves … to God' and recognize that the trial that has come your way is God's blessing, by which you can come to the point of humiliation whereby this greater grace may be received.

Repentance And Refinement

When James says, 'Submit yourselves ... to God,' he means that we must accept what he does and accept what happens as God's way of refining us and bringing us to the humble state whereby this greater grace may be received. It means to accept the trial gladly, without murmuring, persevering with dignity until it is over. While it's going on you think it's never going to end but it will, and after it's over God lets you know how you did. That, in part, is what James means by 'the crown of life' (1:12). Any secret plans you may have to get even when it's all over will only cause the trial to continue longer, until you are brought to the place where you turn it over to God.

The next rule from James in growing positively is this: bowing graciously under God's mighty hand. It is only when you do this that you will begin to experience the positive grace in your life. Jonah, still in the fish, asked God for one more chance. 'I will sacrifice unto thee with the voice of thanksgiving; I will pay that that I have vowed. Salvation is of the LORD. And the LORD spake unto the fish, and it vomited out Jonah upon the dry land. And the word of the LORD came unto Jonah the second time, saying, Arise, go unto Nineveh' (Jonah 2:9; 3:2). Jonah went, and he saw God work in a positive way.

God categorically resists the proud. He walks away from them. We're not humble by nature, but God can humble us. So James says, 'Submit yourselves ... to God.' He doesn't say, 'Submit yourself to the trial.' If you submit to the trial it may lead you to cope in your own strength. You simply recognize that the trial is from God and you submit to him. When the trial comes you just say, 'Thank you, Lord.' The great John Calvin, when he lay on his deathbed in 1564, was overheard by one of the servants to be murmuring under his breath, 'Lord, thou crushest me but that it is thy hand it is enough.' Is anything more wonderful than to know that we're in God's hands?

God can use our suffering for good

David needed humbling owing to the sin we've seen already. But here was the way David reacted. We read in 2 Samuel 12:21: 'Then said his servants unto him, What thing is this that thou hast done? thou didst fast and weep for the child, while it was alive; but when the child was dead, thou didst rise and eat bread.' This is the child that was born as a result of his sleeping with Bathsheba. 'And he said, While the child was yet alive, I fasted and wept: for I said, Who can tell whether GOD will be gracious to me, that the child may live? But now he is dead, wherefore should I fast?

can I bring him back again? I shall go to him, but he shall not return to me.' Then we read, 'David comforted Bathsheba his wife'. He had married her in the meantime. He 'went in unto her, and lay with her: and she bare a son, and he called his name Solomon: and the LORD loved him' (vv. 22–23, 24).

David was so sorry for his sin. There's no way we can justify it. But it's an extraordinary thing that we read in the genealogies (Mt. 1) in the sixth verse: 'And Jesse begat David the king; and David the king begat Solomon of her that had been the wife of Urias.' God has a way of humbling us to make us see that we're in his hands. Things can 'work together for good' (Rom. 8:28), although they don't give the remotest hint at the time that God could use them to good. Solomon, who was born from this union of David and Bathsheba, was in the bloodline of God's Messiah.

David was given the option of three punishments for another sin: numbering the people. He said 'I am in a great strait: let us fall now into the hand of the LORD; for his mercies are great: and let me not fall into the hand of man' (2 Sam. 24:14). David knew he was in God's hands. There were scars on David's life. His sin was terrible, but the amazing thing is that God could speak to Solomon in this way: 'If thou wilt walk in my ways, to keep my statutes and my commandments, as thy father David did walk …' (1 Kgs. 3:14). God can take our twisted past and works it for good. God will own our lives totally. David continued to be known as a man after God's own heart (Acts 13:22).

All of us have our scars. We all have skeletons in our closets. We wonder how God could ever get glory out of our lives. But he will if we humble ourselves and submit ourselves to him. When we come to the end of our days, in the words of an old Southern song, 'He'll understand and say well done.' All things are possible if we're in his hands. Submit yourself to God and let him take over from this day forward.

Suffering exposes our faults

There's another reason for this verse. It is through suffering that *we see ourselves as we really are*. Suffering exposes a fault in us that we could not otherwise see. It's what the hymn writer means by consuming our dross, refining our gold.

> *When through fiery trials thy pathway shall lie,*
> *My grace all-sufficient shall be thy supply;*
> *The flame shall not hurt thee: I only design*
> *Thy dross to consume, and thy gold to refine.*

This is why David could say, 'The judgments of the LORD are true and righteous altogether. More to be desired are they than gold, yea, than much fine gold: sweeter also than honey and the honeycomb. Moreover by them is thy servant warned: and in keeping of them there is great reward' (Ps. 19:9–11). Then he said, 'Who can understand his errors? cleanse thou me from secret faults' (v. 12). For suffering makes a defect in us rise to the surface, a defect that maybe others were able to see long before, but now we ourselves can see it.

What are we to do? We submit ourselves to God. We must take this sobering insight into ourselves most seriously, and thank God for showing it to us. And when we see it we deal with it, with God's help. It may be a case of making restitution. You could argue with God for twenty years, but you'll have to do it. It may mean apologizing to somebody. You may say, 'I'll die first.' You will die first then, but you'll never know this grace. It might even mean abandoning some pleasure that militates against a godly walk. You will know. This is why Paul could say, 'Let us therefore, as many as be perfect, be thus minded: and if in anything ye be otherwise minded, God shall reveal even this unto you' (Phil. 3:15).

Submit to what God has said. If he says, 'Do it', the orders will not change. When Jonah got right with God he found out that the orders were the same: 'Go', and he went. We must submit to what God shows us about ourselves and deal with the sin God's way. John said, 'This is the love of God, that we keep his commandments: and his commandments are not grievous' (1 Jn. 5:3).

Ultimate joy

Whatever we must do, whatever we must abandon in order to be brought to the point of humility, remember that the blessing far outweighs the sadness that we're already experiencing, and it far outweighs any sadness that you think you may incur because you do this or that. The devil always wants you to think that if you do this you're going to be a most unhappy person. The opposite is true: you will know the joy of the Lord. And once you know that, you wouldn't trade it for anything in the world. That will be your strength. There is nothing to compare with that.

We have now two rules from James in growing positively. Rule number one: don't postpone dealing with any known sin. Rule number two: bow graciously under the mighty hand of God. As Peter put it: 'Humble yourselves therefore under the mighty hand of God, that he may exalt you in due time' (1 Pet. 5:6). Peter also said. 'The God of all grace, who hath called us unto his eternal glory by Christ Jesus, after that ye have suffered a while' – it won't last forever – 'make you perfect, stablish, strengthen, settle you' (1 Pet. 5:10).

11

Resist the Devil

James 4:7

Having said, 'Submit yourselves to God', there is something that every Christian ought to anticipate. James puts it like this: 'Resist the devil, and he will flee from you.' James said that at this point because he knows that the moment you begin to submit yourself to God you are going to arouse the devil. As Jonathan Edwards used to put it: 'When the church is revived so is the devil.' As soon as you begin to take God's word seriously and it begins to hit you that God is wanting you to develop and grow, you are going to find opposition. For nothing is more threatening to Satan's interest than Christian obedience.

Arousing And Resisting The Devil

The devil isn't worried about your orthodoxy. That there is one God makes the devil tremble but our confession of it is not what threatens him (Jas. 2:19). It is when we show ourselves to be God's people indeed, when we abandon our friendliness with the world, the devil is threatened. His wrath is raised when we begin to make inroads into his territory by being different from the world and by witnessing to the world. It is possible to be orthodox and worldly at the same time. And that's exactly the way the devil wants to keep us.

'Let a man examine himself' (1 Cor. 11:28). When a person comes to himself and begins to follow Christ he has the biggest fight on his hands that he's ever known. Maybe some of you have begun to take James seriously and you thought that everything was going to be downhill all the way. But you've found yourself in real trouble now, because you've submitted. 'Don't be surprised', James is saying, 'if the devil is aroused.'

An obstacle course

The next practical step, then, in making this transition from the flesh to the spirit, is to anticipate the devil. He will move in at once by putting obstacles in your way, aimed to demoralize you, to shatter you, to convince you that it's not worth it. The purpose of the obstacles is to suggest that you had been doing all right before. 'You're okay. Don't worry. You know that you've been justified by faith. Your sins are forgiven. You're going to heaven. Surely that's enough.' The devil will do everything he can to keep you believing that.

How, then, does he put these obstacles in your way? What do they look like? Primarily, these obstacles take on the appearance of divine providence, the purpose being to suggest that you're okay. He would say, 'If God wanted you to be different he would make it easy for you.' Such obstacles always emerge immediately after you resolve to follow Christ fully. Another obstacle he will put in your path is to make you look at *only one side* of Christian truth: the doctrine of justification by faith alone. 'Hang onto that. Christ is your righteousness, that's enough.'

There have been many churches that have come to a standstill simply because they thought they upheld this great truth of Luther and that was what mattered. But there was no growth. Have you ever heard of German Pietism? Do you know why it emerged? Have you heard of Count Zinzendorf? We sing the hymn: 'Jesus, thy blood and righteousness'. He was a Pietist. Why? Because Lutheranism in Germany had allowed the doctrine of justification to be the thing, and worldliness crept in.

The devil wants us to have a one-sided emphasis. He will say to you, 'You're all right. You know that you're saved.' The moment you begin to obey and do what God has said in his word, you're going to find the devil giving you all kinds of trouble. Do not be surprised when there is a convergence of reasons and circumstances that add up to one thing: godliness isn't worth it. It's as if it were God's voice saying, 'You've been okay. Don't worry.'

In 1 Thessalonians 2:18 Paul said to his readers, 'We would have come unto you once and again; but Satan hindered us.' Here were circumstances that most of us would have regarded as providential, but not Paul. He said, 'Satan did it.' Most of us think that if we're going to follow God then everything is just going to work out.

In Acts 10 Cornelius was given a vision and Peter was given a vision and there was instruction just exactly where to go. It was all handed to them on a silver platter, but that isn't the way God always works. Just before Paul died he said, 'The Lord give mercy unto the house of

Onesiphorus; for he oft refreshed me, and was not ashamed of my chain: but, when he was in Rome, he sought me out very diligently, and found me' (2 Tim. 1:16–17). He had to go to a lot of trouble to find Paul. There was no vision or providential help. He kept at it. This is the way God normally works. We all know of those times when God steps in, usually at the beginning. That's the way it was at the house of Cornelius, when Christianity was in its embryonic period. But when we begin to grow we have to work, to show that we really have faith.

A prior commitment to obedience helps us resist

How do you resist the devil when there are circumstances that converge? The primary way to resist the devil is to have a prior commitment to obey the truth, regardless of the obstacles. 'To resist' means basically 'to ignore'. When we're told that 'God resisteth the proud, but giveth grace unto the humble', it means he ignores the proud. The way you must resist temptation is to ignore it. You go the opposite way. If you are held by a prior commitment to follow Christ, the devil will flee.

The devil's attack is really a wonderful opportunity. All trial is a curious mixture of God's design and the devil's attack. The devil's attack is a great opportunity for grace to function, for you to grow positively. Look at Job's ordeal. The whole thing is something God allowed to happen but the devil got in there. There are two ways to look at the cause of trial. There's the underlying cause and there's the precipitating cause. The underlying cause is God. The precipitating cause is the devil.

How you react will determine whether you begin now to grow positively in your Christian life. I've been saying that James is largely negative in chapter 4 and he now gives a positive step by saying, 'Submit yourself to God.' There is something negative about this point, 'Resist the devil', because it's a defensive measure. You never take the initiative in fighting the devil. Only a fool does that. Look at the order: submit yourself to God, resist the devil. A fundamental rule of living the Christian life is: never take the offensive in going for the devil. You might say, 'I'm going to see how close I can get to temptation to show how strong I am.' You will always get burnt.

The devil will come unexpectedly. He will come on your blind side. He never comes at a timely moment. You resist him by not listening to him. Remember this – I give this as an illustration – treat the devil as a foolish person that you ignore because you consider the source. The devil will use another person who says something to you that upsets you and your temptation will be to attack that person, but that person isn't really what's behind this, the devil is. Just refuse to take it seriously. See that the real enemy is the devil and just walk away. Paul says, 'We wrestle not against flesh and blood, but against principalities, against powers' (Eph. 6:12). If you learn to resist the devil you will have learned something that is of more value than an Oxbridge education.

The Devil's Method

The devil comes in basically two ways. We read in 2 Corinthians 11:14 how the devil comes as 'an angel of light' and in 1 Peter 5:8 where he's described as coming as 'a roaring lion ... seeking whom he may devour'.

The angel of light

This is where the devil almost always begins. The unaware are most easily caught off guard when the devil comes as an angel of light. The devil prefers to come like this, concealing his anger. He disguises himself. The last thing he wants you to see is his anger, which shows his insecurity, and shows that you are doing something right. But if he comes as an angel of light you don't even know it's the devil.

He comes as an angel of light, because if you think it is God talking you're going to listen and believe it. There are basically three ways the devil masquerades.

- Firstly, through a highly respected person. The devil can use somebody that you esteem highly.
- Secondly, he can use a one-sided emphasis of Christian doctrine. If you see only one side of the coin, such as the doctrine of imputed righteousness, he will hold that before you and say that that's all that matters.
- Thirdly, through circumstances that always seem so providential. Nothing is more providential than temptation.

How do you recognize the devil when he masquerades? You can recognize him by the lie he puts forward. Remember, everything that the devil does is embodied in the lie. As Jesus put it in John 8:44: 'When he speaketh a lie, he speaketh of his own: for he is a liar and the father of it.' A lie is always going to be the suggestion that militates against God's truth. What did the devil first say to Eve, 'Ye shall not surely die' (Gen. 3:4).

The devil will make you think that God doesn't want you to have that godly, disciplined walk.

Another way to recognize that it's the devil is that you are left with a feeling of oppression. God never oppresses us. You will say, 'But God's chastening doesn't make me feel good.' Oh, but it does. James said early on that the wisdom that comes from above is 'pure, then peaceable, gentle, and easy to be entreated' (3:17). Even when the Holy Spirit chastens us there's something good about the feeling, for you know that he cares that much. Even when the minister has to preach a hard sermon, even though you realize a feeling of being broken, you feel warmed that God cares enough to deal with you. But when the devil speaks you're left with an oppressed feeling. As James put it, 'If ye have bitter envying and strife in your hearts, glory not, lie not against the truth. This wisdom descendeth not from above, but is earthly, sensual, devilish' (4:14–15). The prior commitment to obey God is the greatest deterrent to Satan that there is. It will escort you through every trial. There's not a thing the devil can do in that case. The obstacle that he puts before you will seem as nothing. You'll wonder why you even thought it.

There is a sense in which this prior commitment is greater and stronger than prayer itself. If you've got it, that's why you want to pray. When you've got that prior commitment the devil will try to get you to hesitate. You say, 'Prayer is the right thing to do.' So you pray about it and you stall and the devil moves in. In a strange kind of way prayer will strengthen that commitment. But when you've got it, act upon it. There's a time when you don't pray, you act, and thereby show that you really have faith.

When the three Hebrew children were told to bow down to the golden image or be cast into burning, fiery furnace, they didn't say, 'Well, look, don't you think we ought to pray about this?' Oh, no. They were unanimous. They said, 'We are not careful to answer thee in this matter. If it be so our God whom we serve is able to deliver us ... but if not ... we will not serve thy gods' (Dan. 3:16–18). That's the prior commitment I'm talking about.

I've been in the ministry for many years now, and of the pastoral cases I've dealt with a high percentage found that prayer immediately preceded the sin that got them into trouble. There are countless Christians who pray about doing what God has already said not to do. Unmarried Christian couples will pray about whether they should sleep together. If you pray over what God has already said you'll get the answer you want every time. This is the devil masquerading as the angel of light.

The roaring lion

This is a different tactic of the devil. We must be wise. As Paul put it: 'We are not ignorant of his devices' (2 Cor. 2:11). We need a slightly different way to resist. When the devil comes as a roaring lion there's no masquerading. He comes in like a steam engine, a freight train. The problem in this case is that he moves in so quickly that he scares us nearly to death before we have absorbed what has happened.

A roaring lion is an animal that makes a terrifying noise to scare and disarm you, to make you think you're defeated before you really are. If you see the devil and he's roaring you might think, 'Well, that's it. Come and get me. I'm not going to fight you.' Peter says, 'Resist' (1 Pet. 5:9). Peter would not have said to resist him if he was inevitably going to devour you. The devil gets his victory as a roaring lion by making you think you've already lost. If we succumb to his roar he devours us without our putting up the slightest resistance.

This is a different tactic, but it's the same devil and he always comes with the lie, that there's nothing you can do, it's finished, it's too late, you've gone too far, you've lost. When the lion roars, the first thing is to separate the roar from the devourer. 'Your adversary the devil, as a roaring lion, walketh about, seeking whom he may devour.'

Have you ever had a situation when you were so affected emotionally by satanic activity that you were vulnerable and began to do bad things, and it wasn't until you had begun to do those things that you were sorry? You would have done anything in the world to change things if you could just move the clock back five minutes. Because the roar made you think it was too late you gave in, you began to say things and do things. That's when you were devoured.

Perhaps it's when somebody says something cutting to you. Bite your tongue and don't say anything back. You're upset. That's the lion's roar. If you lash out he devours you. Perhaps you've had a threatening bit of news and the news brings you right down. You think, 'That's it.' No, that's the lion's roar. Maybe you're in a hurry to get somewhere and you lose your keys – the lion's roar. Watch it. You haven't lost yet. You've got a headache, something happens to one of the children, they say something and you're upset – the lion's roar. The devil hasn't quite got in like you think. He's just roaring.

The sound will upset you. It's not a sin to be upset. The devil wants you to think that being upset means that you have sinned and so you should just go ahead and do anything you feel like doing now. That is when he devours you. In other words, we are affected emotionally by the lion's roar. You think the worst has happened, and you admit defeat. You blow up. It's not till you blow up that he does come in for the kill. The difference between the lion's roar and the lion's devouring is the difference between temptation and sin.

Attack is not defeat

You got upset by the lion's roar. Your feelings were involved. You reacted in a way that you wish you hadn't. That's temptation. Temptation is a sign of weakness, but it's not a sin. The devil's purpose is to tempt you. He cannot make you sin. The temptation is the roar. The sin is the devouring. There's the temptation to lose your temper but you haven't sinned until you say something. Bite your tongue and the devil's effect will be limited to upsetting you. Whenever you are upset and agitated, just say, 'This is the devil. I'm not going to let him have a victory.' Resist him and *your* victory will be sweet. When you bite your tongue or say no to whatever temptation, the devil flees. When you've got a prior commitment to please Christ, and you hold to that, the devil cannot touch you.

Our goal in the Christian life, of course, is to develop a godly habit whereby we learn not to be upset. This is the reason we must reduce temptation to the level of suggestion, so that the devil is constantly having to try a new way to get at us. The most alarming evidence of being at a standstill in your Christian development is that you are still vexed at the same old temptations. The devil had a hard time with Paul. Look how the devil had to get at Paul. He said to the Thessalonians, 'We would have come unto you once and again; but Satan hindered us.'

The way the devil had to get at Paul was to go outside himself. But with most of us the devil doesn't have to throw a fiery dart, he just blows and we fall. The great news is that the devil is resistible. When you begin to see him fleeing again and again you may know that victory in your Christian life is at hand, such as you had not dreamed of. And when we as a body of believers learn to recognize the real enemy and not take it personally when we're cast down by what is said, the devil cannot succeed: for us, victory will be at hand.

12

Defeating the Devil

James 4:7

We have seen how to resist the devil. I want us to see the possibility of victory – defeating the devil – as we look now in the main at this last part: 'He will flee from you.' When we are worldly we don't please God. When we walk in the light we do. But it is great comfort to know, as John put it: 'If our heart condemn us, God is greater than our heart' (1 Jn. 3:20). This shows his overruling grace. And yet John showed us this possibility: 'if our heart condemn us not, then have we confidence toward God' (1 Jn. 3:21). That is precisely our aim, that we might be the kind of Christians that please God.

The Position Of The Disobedient Christian

Somebody will ask, 'Is there any other kind of Christian?' The answer is, yes. Throughout church history there have been basically two ways of looking at the disobedient Christian. The most common way is simply to dismiss the problem by saying that there's no such thing as a disobedient Christian. There are those who think that if you allow for the possibility that a real Christian could be disobedient you're going to encourage this. There are those who think that the way to motivate a person who is disobedient is to make him think he's not a Christian at all. That is the wrong approach. The New Testament encourages us to say plainly that a person can be a Christian and be disobedient to God but also that God warns and chastens. Indeed, you disobey to your peril and yet you are still a Christian.

Who among us is not grateful for the patience of God? We've all been in need of this comforting doctrine to know that we are Christians. God doesn't take that from us. It's wonderful to be able to live and to know that, whatever else is true, we are his. So it's a safe way to die as well as a safe way to live.

It's this understanding that has clearly given us the breakthrough in this epistle of James. For we have seen that there is a justification by faith that saves and that gives us the assurance of heaven. But there is also a justification by words that doesn't save, but nonetheless pleases God. This is James' aim – to lead Christians to a righteousness in their persons, not that this will save them. It's not the righteousness by imputation, but it is an obedience. James is showing the folly of not living this way and giving us positive steps we may take that we might know there's a better way to live. It is not God's will that we live in the flesh, but in the spirit.

The growing Christian

Growing positively has its negative side, but the devil's attack is a wonderful way to grow. It is his fleeing from us that proves we are growing, not his attacks. Because the devil attacks a disobedient Christian. The degree to which we resist the devil and see him flee is the degree to which there may be an admission of real growth in the Christian life.

Satan's attack upon us tells us about as much of ourselves as any source of information we could think of or want. For the devil's attack is an indicator of what you really are and how you are growing. He flees because he sees he can do no good. He only attacks where we are vulnerable, where we are weak. If by playing into our vulnerability he can manage a situation of temptation, he'll just keep coming to the same place as long as he can see what upsets you, what diverts you, what makes you think twice about whether you really want to be a Christian.

Knowing oneself

But if we are wise to his devices and know his methods, we will examine ourselves and ask ourselves why it is we keep losing the battle. We could thus arm ourselves and make sure the devil doesn't achieve victory over us. The devil looks for the chink in our armour. He will not bother to attack us where we are strong. This is why the devil's attack tells us more about ourselves than it does about the devil.

In school whenever you had an examination they would say, 'This exam is going to be a learning experience for you.' I didn't always find that to be the case. But every time you're tested by the devil's attack it is a learning experience. But there's a difference between the devil's test and what it was like in school because an examination in school covers the breadth of our knowledge. We have an opportunity to show how much we know. But the devil's test is always with reference to our weakness, never our strength.

Satan's Three Major Lies

Are you being tested over the same material and you keep failing? You say, 'I just can't get the victory over that or this.' That is the devil's lie and that's exactly what he wants you to think. As long as you think that then he'll be back tomorrow morning with the same old temptation. That's the reason there are those who reach old age without any substantial growth in their Christian lives, because they believed the devil's lie over the years.

The devil is the father of liars and all that he does is against truth. There are three major lies the devil uses – probably in this order – by which he can attack us.

Lie 1: Doubting your own salvation

The first lie is this: the devil will try to get you to doubt your own salvation. If he can succeed at that, then he can put all other plans he might have had for you in abeyance. This is why it is vital, it is crucial, that a Christian know that he is saved. Nothing is more ridiculous than a Christian who is not sure he's going to heaven.

This is precisely why James never questions the salvation of his readers. Nor does Paul. Never, never, never do the writers of the New Testament want us to doubt our salvation. After all, there's no way that you can grow if you think you aren't a Christian.

This is serious. If you are not persuaded of the ground of your salvation, all your works will be selfishly motivated. Your own sanctification, for what it's worth, will be feigned and legalistic and counter-productive. Your joy will be nil, your effectiveness zero. That's exactly what the devil wants. But if it can ever become a conviction with you, you can sing:

> *My hope is built on nothing less*
> *Than Jesus' blood and righteousness;*
> *I dare not trust the sweetest frame,*

But wholly lean on Jesus' name.
On Christ, the solid Rock, I stand;
All other ground is sinking sand.

'I heard a loud voice saying in heaven, Now is come salvation, and strength, and the kingdom of our God, and the power of his Christ: for the accuser of our brethren is cast down'. How do you suppose that happened? 'They overcame him by the blood of the Lamb, and by the word of their testimony' (Rev. 12:10–11). If you doubt that, the devil can throw away all plans to defeat you because he has nipped Christian growth in the bud. But when you are persuaded that what the Lord Jesus did by his death is all that is required of you and that your trust is in him and what he did plus nothing, then the devil can never again attack you at the point of your salvation.

Lie 2: Holiness is unimportant

The second lie the devil will use to put before you is that sanctification is not all that important. It is at this point he attacks each Christian differently. He looks for our weaknesses. The devil gets a fresh computer print-out on your spiritual growth every morning. I suspect that if he keeps reading the same thing every day he will eventually not even bother to keep records. He can just take a look at you and have another go because you're not growing at all.

Why would he attack a disobedient Christian? He wants to get at you for your own sake because he doesn't like you. He hates you because you're covered by the blood of Christ. But he's got another reason which is equally important to him. That is, he wants to hurt the Christian witness in the world. Sanctification is a threat to the devil's interests. All that Satan can do to cause the Christian witness to lack credibility in the world, he will do. He wants to protect his own interests by ensuring that you are the end of the line, that there'll be no more converts if it's left up to you.

I have talked to the young people about their witnessing and making themselves spiritual parents and grandparents. For there's a greater joy than leading a person to Christ. It is seeing the person you led to Christ lead another to Christ. The devil wants to be absolutely sure that you have no spiritual offspring. If he can keep you oppressed he can ensure that, because oppressed people aren't soul winners. If he can keep you retarded in your growth he's going to do it. If he can rob you of joy and victory he will.

In this connection there are certain impediments the devil uses to abort sanctification. There are four that I will mention usually in this order (unless physiological changes solve the problem of sexual temptation, in which case you can never say you got the victory):

- sexual temptation,
- threat to your self-esteem,
- financial security,
- health.

Self-esteem, and the problems of financial security and health will stay with us as long as we live.

How do we grow in these four areas? The answer is, simply, to submit to God's dealings with us. God takes us a step at a time. We don't go from A to Z, we go from A to B to C. This is why James started out his epistle: 'count it all joy when ye fall into divers temptations'. For God allows no more than we can bear. But his method in dealing with us is to bring us face to face with the kind of trials that enable us to get victories and those victories lead to other victories. That's when we are submitting to God, constantly just submitting, not complaining. When another trial comes you say, 'Lord, let's go.' And the devil as a consequence is having to come at you in a constantly different way every time. A trial makes us face a weakness in ourselves that we didn't know was there. But apart from suffering, that weakness is not likely to be discovered. This is why chastening is necessary. This is why Paul said, 'We must through much tribulation enter into the kingdom of God' (Acts 14:22).

There are keys to victory that make the devil flee:

- Know that victory is possible if you will keep resisting. Be willing to suffer by saying no, by avoiding the temptation. This is what is meant in part by that verse in Ephesians 4:27: 'Neither give place to the devil.' Don't go where you know temptation is likely to be. It hurts when we resist in that way. But that's where the strength is. The strength is not to show how strong you are when you're tempted. The strength is anticipating what will tempt and not going there. You will surprise yourself how the devil flees when you do that.
- What about the threat to self-esteem? Two things. Refuse to judge another person's motives and refuse to vindicate yourself. If you live by those two principles you'll find great peace that you had never discovered before. Learn to live by John 5:44: 'How can ye believe, which receive honour one of another, and seek not the honour that cometh from God only?' Every time we succumb to

the devil's attack because our self-esteem is threatened it will always be because we violated John 5:44.

- What about the threat to financial security? The key here is to remember that you're bought with a price, the price being Jesus' blood. That means God owns you. If you ever take that seriously it will change the way you live. Because it is God's obligation to look after his own property. He's the one who must take care of you. Live one day at a time. 'Take ... no thought for the morrow.' Trust him. 'Sufficient to the day is the evil thereof ' (Mt. 6:34). Remember: 'My God shall supply all your need according to his riches in glory by Christ Jesus' (Phil. 4:19). God is never too late, he's never too early, he's always just on time.

- What about threats to your health? Remember Job and know that all things that come to you in the way of illness are by God's permission and that illness is not God's way of getting even with you. The devil will say, 'Here's why you're ill. God's angry.' My fellow Christians, that is not so. God wouldn't stoop to that. God got even at the cross when he punished Jesus instead. He bore our sins. This is why we can rejoice with the Psalmist: 'He hath not dealt with us after our sins; nor rewarded us according to our iniquities' (Ps. 103:10). Illness is God's way of keeping you dependent on him. He's doing you a favour to make heaven more precious and his will more central in your life.

In every condition, in sickness, in health,
In poverty's vale or abounding in wealth,
At home and abroad, on the land, on the sea,
As thy days may demand shall thy strength ever be.

Resisting the devil so that he will flee is believing God, not the devil's lies. 'Greater is he that is in you, than he that is in the world' (1 Jn. 4:4). 'This is the victory that overcometh the world, even our faith' (1 Jn. 5:4). The second lie is to say that your sanctification is not that important.

Lie 3: Needless demoralization

The third lie he puts is to demoralize you. He does this basically in three ways. First of all, by making you think you have sinned when you have only been tempted so that you'll go ahead and sin. He comes at you as a roaring lion and you're all upset. Defeating the devil, in this case, is when you refuse to give in to his roar and recognize that there is a difference between temptation and sin. If you stop and say, 'I haven't sinned yet', the devil will flee because he will see you're on to him and victory is there.

But the second way he demoralizes is this: if you have sinned he will say, 'You might as well backslide all the way now. Sin is sin, so now that you've sinned enjoy it. Or at least have another week at it because, after all, when you get right you're going to confess it all.' What the devil will do is to lead you to a place where you're in greater bondage, where repentance becomes more difficult. More damage has been done, more lives are affected and your conscience will have to live with all those extra things all your life. That way the devil has produced a chink in your armour that it's much harder to repair. Victory is this: he will flee if you confess it at once.

It could be that you're saying, 'It's no use. I'm in a situation where I'm sinning.' Stop. It will be worse if you go on. The victory comes if you will confess right now. 'If we confess our sins, he is faithful and just to forgive us our sins, and to cleanse us from all unrighteousness' (1 Jn. 1:9). This verse is not aimed at the non-Christian (although it may apply) but it is to the Christian so that he might be brought back to the situation of growing positively.

The third way the devil tries to demoralize us is to say when you're in a trial, 'This trial you are now having will never end.' If you are in this situation I've got good news for you. You're in the best position of all to grow positively. Because you are in the best situation to prove how much you do believe God. You'll never be in a situation that is more testing than that. You know God isn't going to leave you. 1 Corinthians 10:13 says, 'There hath no temptation taken you but such as is common to man.' He will 'make a way to escape, that ye may be able to bear it.' God does know how much you can bear. The devil wants you to think that it's never going to end. When the devil flees he will flee for one reason and one reason only: when he sees you are not listening to him.

Let me bring in another fundamental rule. The devil cannot even affect you unless he has grounds to do so. If you are holding a grudge, for example, toward another person, the devil doesn't have to look anywhere else. He can get to you so easily. Are you upset because of something somebody said about you? Well then, refuse to be upset. If you've got a financial problem cast your care upon God. Make it his problem. Are you worried about your health? Then remember the words of the great hymn: 'He knows the way he taketh, and I will walk with him.'

The Devil Cannot Touch Us Directly

It is a fundamental Christian fact that the devil cannot touch you directly. This is why 1 John 5:18 reads: 'But he that is begotten of God keepeth himself, and that wicked one toucheth him not.' It means that you don't have to be afraid of the devil, only the chink in your armour – be afraid of that. The devil is a bully. He can't hurt you unless you let him. Martin Luther used to say, 'The thing the devil can't stand is to be jeered at.' Listen to this line from the hymn 'A Mighty Fortress is our God':

> *And let the prince of ill*
> *Look grim as e'er he will;*
> *He harms us not a whit;*
> *For why? His doom is writ,*
> *A word shall quickly slay him.*

The Greek word means: 'he shrinks back', 'he stands fearfully aloof'. The result is so pleasant that we don't even much care that the underlying trial is over. For learning to resist the devil makes the trial virtually cease to be.

Or you may have a negative, depressing thought. It comes rushing into your mind. Have you ever noticed that you have one right after you wake up? You can hardly think about anything else all day. The devil comes right then when you're still trying to wake up. Or it can happen just as you're about to fall asleep and it will keep you awake. Or sometimes it can happen when you're feeling perfectly fine. Suddenly an evil thought grips you and your reaction is to dwell on it and everything is affected by it. You get angry with your children, angry with your boss. Everybody at work says, 'What's the matter with you today? This Christianity business is making you a fanatic.' A lot of people talk about Christians having neurotic problems. The truth is that the Christian has an enemy that the non-Christian doesn't have. The devil knows how to make us look like fools to hurt our witness.

When this evil thought comes in, say to yourself, 'This is nothing but the devil and I am not going to let him get me down.' Remember God did not put that thought there. Therefore refuse to dignify the devil's suggestion. Here's your verse: 'Casting down imaginations, and every high thing that exalteth itself against the knowledge of God, and bringing into captivity every thought to the obedience of Christ' (2 Cor. 10:5). When you cast that thought down the devil leaves. The air's clear again. It might take a minute or two when you're fighting it off, but you just say to yourself, 'I'm going to please my God by not letting the devil make me think like this and make me feel this way.' You walk the opposite way, think the opposite thought. He simply cannot do a thing to you unless you give him place to do it. He will flee and leave you alone.

One last thing: it's up to you. Don't ask God to do it for you. James says, 'You do it. Resist the devil.' In the Greek it's the imperative, a command. 'Do it!' Why would he say, 'You do it'? Because you can. James would not mock us by telling us to do what we cannot do. But you do it and it's a wonderful feeling. You begin to realize that the chink in your armour is being repaired. You're beginning to grow when you're pleasing God. According to James, it's up to you.

13

Living Close to God

James 4:8

James is now well into the process of giving us positive steps, showing us how to make the transition from living in the flesh to living in the spirit. Some will wait until glorification but those who begin to know something of it in this life are those who know God in an intimate way – the way James wants for those to whom he wrote the epistle originally and indeed for us today.

We Must Take The Initiative

The crucial thing to be seen is that we must take the initiative. We may not like this but this is the message. 'Draw nigh to God, and he will draw nigh to you.' This is not the way it was with regard to our salvation, for God took the initiative. James says so: 'Of his own will begat he us with the word of truth' (1:18). And John said so, 'We love him, because he first loved us' (1 Jn. 4:19). Jesus said so: 'Ye have not chosen me, but I have chosen you' (Jn. 15:16).

The biggest mistake people make regarding new obedience is that they want to say, 'God sought me the first time, he can do it again.' The devil will use this to keep you in a condition of paralysis. For he likes the way you are if you are at the moment basically worldly minded. If you know a little bit of theology and you know something of God's sovereign grace the devil will go for that and say, 'We know God did it the first time so let him do it again.' James knows this and he puts these commands 'Submit yourselves ... to God.' 'Resist the devil'.

'Draw nigh to God, and he will draw nigh to you' is not only a command but a high privilege to be invited to get close to God. Looking at things at the level of nature, how many people really get close to a seat of power? And yet here is an open invitation to get next to infinitude, omnipotence. It is an indiscriminate offer to all Christians, to all whose sins are washed in the blood of Christ and yet it is an invitation that can be rejected. He gives a greater grace, but it is not irresistible. For what we have before us here is a conditional promise. 'Draw nigh to God, and he will draw nigh to you.' Yet not all of God's promises are conditional. We need to realize this. There are those who want to take a simplistic view of the Bible and of theology generally and promises.

God's Unconditional Promises

We need to have some clear thinking when it comes to the promises that are in the Bible and examine Scripture in its context and look at each verse one by one. Are you aware that the promise of your final perseverance is unconditional? Jesus said, referring to 'my sheep', 'They hear my voice, and I know them, and they follow me: and I give unto them eternal life; and they shall never perish, neither shall any man pluck them out of my Father's hand' (Jn. 10:28–29). Jesus prayed in John 17:11, 12: 'Holy Father, keep through thine own name those whom thou hast given me … While I was with them in the world, I kept them in thy name: those that thou gavest me I have kept, and none of them is lost, but the son of perdition' – Judas Iscariot – 'that the scripture might be fulfilled.' Paul said to the Philippians, 'He which hath begun a good work in you will perform it until the day of Jesus Christ' (1:6). 'Who shall separate us from the love of Christ? shall tribulation, or distress, or persecution, or famine, or nakedness, or peril, or sword?' says Paul. 'I am persuaded' – are we? – 'that neither death, nor life, nor angels, nor principalities, nor powers, nor things present, nor things to come, nor height, nor depth, nor any other creature' – that means even the devil – 'shall be able to separate us from the love of God, which is in Christ Jesus our Lord' (Rom. 8:35, 38–39). There are unconditional promises. That's one of them.

Another promise is this: that the Christian's perfect righteousness before God is achieved; it is absolute. Our righteousness is not only perfect but it can never be improved upon. Paul's doctrine summed up this. 'To him that worketh not' – that means we're saved by doing nothing – 'but believeth on him that justifieth the ungodly, his faith is counted for righteousness' (Rom. 4:5). This is Paul's conviction and it is James' conviction. James never questions the salvation of his readers.

He says, 'There is a justification that saves and that is by faith. There is a justification that doesn't save, it is by works.' However, justification by works that pleases God and Abraham was an example: by his obedience he was called 'the friend of God'. And James wants that for us.

Conditional Promises

There are other promises that are conditional. One example is this: the basis for a close relationship to Jesus Christ – that's conditional. Jesus said in John 15:14–15, 'Ye are my friends, if ye do whatsoever I command you. Henceforth I call you not servants; for the servant knoweth not what his lord doeth: but I have called you friends; for all things that I have heard of my Father I have made known unto you.' Generally in Scripture the 'if clause', as we say in grammar, shows a conditional promise. 1 John 1:7 shows the basis for a close unbroken communion with God: 'If we walk in the light, as he is in the light, we have fellowship one with another, and the blood of Jesus Christ his Son cleanseth us from all sin.' You can easily detect a conditional promise by this word 'if '. However the word 'if ' is not in James 4:8. And yet the condition could not be more obvious. 'Draw nigh to God, and he will draw nigh to you', in that order.

It is not that God doesn't draw nigh to us without our having done a single thing to bring it about. Because God can draw nigh to us without our drawing nigh to him. Sometimes God surprises us by coming most unexpectedly when we feel the most unworthy. He comes near, or he just works and does something extraordinary, or he breaks through and answers prayer. Yet that doesn't prove that we ourselves are as we ought to be.

In light of Romans 8:28, the fact that something works together for good doesn't mean it was right. In fact, the implication is that it wasn't good or it wouldn't need to 'work together for good'. Our problem is that if it works together for good we say that what we did was right when it was wrong. No, *God* makes it work for good.

If God draws nigh to us when we're feeling unworthy that doesn't mean that we are right. It means God is good and kind. It is precisely because God can and sometimes does draw nigh that we are tempted to challenge him to do it again and again. But James wants to teach the Christian real maturity. We never begin to grow up until we begin to learn autonomy, that is, we know our faith is ours indeed even if nobody else believes.

We've got to learn this kind of responsibility and know that we are dependent upon God alone and not be pathologically dependent upon others. But it is possible to be pathologically dependent upon God. The one who says, 'When God moves me then I'll get on with it' exhibits the great error of the Quakers – they sit around waiting for the Spirit to move them and if the Spirit doesn't move them they just don't do anything. The trouble with that old negro spiritual, 'Every time I feel the Spirit moving in my heart I'll pray', is that most of us would never pray if we waited that long. 'Draw nigh to God.' You may not feel like it but you do it. It's God's infallible word.

Two Promises In One

There are two promises to be seen here back to back that take their fulfilment in rather opposite ways. I would have said that you ought to have 'Resist the devil, and he will flee from you. Draw nigh to God, and he will draw nigh to you' all in one verse. Because this is the way they are to be understood. Each contains a promise. 'Resist the devil and he will flee'. 'Draw nigh to God, and he will draw nigh to you.' The devil flees, God draws near.

These are infinite opposites in the universe. The greatest possible opposites of all existence and reality. 'God is light and in him is no darkness at all' (1 Jn. 1:5). But Satan is the prince of the power of darkness. And as we are to resist the devil we are to draw nigh to God. Look at it for a moment the opposite way. Draw nigh to the devil and he will draw nigh to you. Resist God and he will flee from you.

Resisting the devil

Listen to the word of Proverbs. It's a warning to anybody who hears God speak. 'Because I have called, and ye refused; I have stretched out my hand, and no man regarded; but ye have set at nought all my counsel, and would none of my reproof: I also will laugh at your calamity; I will mock when your fear cometh' (Prov. 1:24–26). The closer you get to the world and to worldliness, the closer you get to the devil. And the more you protect Satan's interests in the world, the more difficult it will be to rescue you.

One sure way to draw nigh to God is simply to get as far away as you can from the devil, from the world, from godlessness, from a secular spirit, from being where you know temptation will be. Run from that and in so doing, inadvertently as it were, you will be drawing nigh to God, and you will notice how the world loses its charm. That which seemed so important to you isn't.

Turn your eyes upon Jesus,
Look full in his wonderful face;
And the things of earth will grow strangely dim
In the light of his glory and grace.

I'm told that that was sung during World War II in London. 'The deceitfulness of riches and the lust of other things' as Luke's Gospel put it, lose their charm (Lk. 8:17). They vanish as though they had never been. Thus whether it is doing it negatively by running from the devil or doing it positively by drawing nigh to God, the promise is that he will draw nigh to you.

If you are in the devil's grip he isn't going to give you up easily when you try to break out of that mould: you will be flooded with reasons why you should stay as you are. You will have an avalanche of impediments in your way that will abort that progress that you say you're going to pursue when you're in church. Then on Monday morning you're out in the real world and every reason why you should ignore what the preacher said the day before floods your mind. James wouldn't ask you to do the impossible. May God grant that something will happen that will carry you through so you can have the break-through and you can see grace operating in your life that you didn't think was possible. It is the devil who demoralizes, never God. You can draw nigh to God. He will draw nigh to you. And you can overcome those lusts and find real freedom. You can overcome that selfish ambition and find freedom so that you can be happy with yourself. You can know God in an intimate way.

Getting close to God

Now the question is, just how close can you get to God? The answer: as close as you want to get. God is no respecter of persons. You can't buy him off. And don't say, 'It's no use for me to try to get close to God. I'll let my minister work on that. He's a little closer to God than I am. He's got a head start.' Nothing could be further from the truth. Let not your lack of usefulness or influence, let not your lack of money or power, keep you away. Let not your lack of gifts or cleverness keep you away. Don't forget that 'the gifts and calling of God are without repentance' or as some translate Romans 11:29: 'The gifts and calling of God, he never repents of.' In other words, they are irrevocable, without any conditions. A person can be called to preach or he might be a prophet or a teacher. He might have a certain gift, even a gift of the Spirit, but that has not a thing on earth to do with drawing close to God.

When we come to the end of our lives we may say we need a little more time but the answer is that God gave us enough time. We all have twenty-four hours in a day, seven days in a week. We have all the time that we need. You may say that because I spend hours in sermon preparation that counts for righteousness, that it gets me closer to God. In this connection it has nothing to do with it. What matters is how I spend my time outside that kind of preparation. What matters is what I do with temptation, what I do with the temptation to be worldly and ambitious. God himself has all the time. But we don't. What we do when we are idle tells an awful lot about us.

You can literally get as close to God as you wish. But your desire to get close to God will be gauged by how much you run the opposite way from the devil, not by how much you say to God in church, 'O Lord, I want to get so close to you.' You might feel insulted right now and say, 'I want to get as close to God as I can.' You may feel that and that might be completely sincere, but I've got to tell you how much you really want to get close to God will be gauged by what you do in the world when you're out on your own, when you're fighting temptation. That is when you show how much you want to draw nigh to God.

You can tell by how deeply you honour his Word when nobody's around or how much you pray in the quietness of a living room. Some think that living close to God means retiring into a monastery. Jesus said, 'You are my friends if you do the things that I command.' Abraham was called 'the friend of God' not because he excelled in prayer, not because he did the things that he enjoyed doing. He gave up what was most precious to him. Then he was called God's friend.

God Will Test Your Desire

You will get a chance to see how close you want to get to God. Most of us don't really want to live as close to God as we say. We're too much like the Pharisees – 'they say and do not'. If you want indeed to draw nigh to God, tell him! Ask him to show you if you mean it and he will test your desire. How will God test your alleged desire to draw close to him? Three ways:

- First, by whether you dignify the trial he allows. 'Count it all joy when ye fall into divers trials.'
- Second, by whether you deal with sin that he puts his finger on. The trial has a curious way of causing to emerge to the surface a particular sin we haven't been aware of. How you deal with that sin will tell whether you really want to draw nigh to God.
- Third, by whether you obey his Word as he makes it plain to you. Remember this verse in Luke 16:10: 'He that is faithful in the least is faithful also in much: and he that is unjust in that which is least is unjust also in much.'

This is a way of saying that God doesn't lead from A to Z. He leads from A to B, and B to C, and C to D, and so forth. That's the way God deals with us. 'One step is good enough for me.' Are you faithful in that which is least?

If you really want to draw nigh to God he will give you a test and it will come soon. You'll be up against it and you'll say, 'Ah, here's what the minister means. I'll see now whether I can do it away from the pulpit, away from the people, away from Christians. I'm alone and nobody is around me who believes like I do. Here's when I prove whether I want to draw nigh to God.' You'll get that test. That's my promise.

Drawing near to God is simply to take seriously his invitation to know him in an intimate way. When we take him seriously he will take us seriously. He will see that we really do care. Listen to what God said to Abraham in Genesis 22:12: 'Lay not thine hand upon the lad, neither do thou any thing unto him: for now I know that thou fearest God, seeing thou hast not withheld thy son, thine only son from me.' I promise you: take him seriously, he will take you seriously. Not only that, he will show you more than ever how much he loves you, how much he cares. And he will manifest himself to you at a level that you never dreamed was possible. 'Eye hath not seen, nor ear heard ...' (1 Cor. 2:9). God wants to show himself to us more than we want him to. But he won't do it unless we welcome him. As Jesus put it to that church at Laodicea, that church that had become so complacent and satisfied, saying, 'We've got it made', he said, 'As many as I love, I rebuke and chasten ... I stand at the door and knock: if any man hear my voice, and open the door, I will come in to him and will sup with him, and he with me' (Rev. 3:19, 20).

May I ask you, do you hear his voice right now? Is he speaking to you? Is God dealing with you with reference to a particular matter and you know it? Perhaps he's dealing with you by instilling a real hunger and thirst for him. Thank God for that. But you'd better nurture it because if you don't it will go away and you can never quite get it back unless he overrules. Is he instilling that? Thank God for it! Draw nigh to him. Seize the moment. Or is he convicting you of some sin in your life? Is he making you see in this moment how far you have wandered from him? Are you one of those spiritually asleep? You don't know that you've been asleep until you wake up and you see how far you have really wandered. Is God dealing with you in this moment?

Heed his Word and you can avoid needless chastening. Hear his Word: 'For as many as I love, I rebuke and chasten.' Draw nigh to him and guess what happens – he draws nigh to you and shows himself in a way you had never thought possible. That's not my promise, that's his.

14

The Nearness of God

James 4:8

I want us to take another look at this verse with particular emphasis on the second part, the conditional promise: 'he will draw nigh to you'. We saw last time that you could read it in the reverse: 'Draw nigh to the devil and he will draw nigh to you' or 'Resist God and he will resist you.' As the devil doesn't flee until he sees he's being resisted so God doesn't draw nigh until he sees that we have drawn nigh to him. These are conditional promises.

Retreating Or Holding Back

The devil retreats

From this word about the devil we may infer that the devil sees what we are thinking. You don't have to talk out loud for him to know your thoughts. If you ask me *how* or *why* the devil knows what we're thinking, I only know this, that 'we wrestle not against flesh and blood, but against principalities, against powers' (Eph. 6:12), and that we don't have to go out of our bedrooms, we don't have to open our mouths, but the devil knows exactly what we're thinking. And we can resist him mentally. He can see whether we are listening to him. We can 'cast down imaginations' (2 Cor. 10:5) without opening our mouths. When he does see that he can do no good because we're not listening to him, he flees, if only for a season, but he flees. When it comes to God drawing nigh to us this is ensured by our obedience.

God holds back

There is an important difference, however, between God drawing nigh to us and the way the devil flees. Whereas the devil can see what we're thinking and he flees, God who also sees what we are thinking doesn't draw nigh until we actually *do* what we say we will do.

James' example is Abraham. When it came to Abraham carrying out the ordeal of sacrificing Isaac you will say, 'Surely God could see Abraham's heart, that he was going to do it.' When God first said, 'Take Isaac, your only son, and offer him for a sacrifice, a burnt offering in the land of Moriah', God could see that Abraham didn't rebel. Surely that was enough for God to go ahead and draw nigh to him. But nothing happened at first. And there was no rebellion in Abraham's heart when Isaac said, 'Behold the fire and the wood: but where is the lamb for a burnt offering?' Those are some of the most heart-wrenching words in all Scripture. How Abraham could look at his only son and see him look up at his father and say, 'Where's the sacrifice?' That would have been enough for most of us to say, 'It's finished. I can't go through with it.' But Abraham wasn't rebellious. He just said, 'God will provide.'

God could see that Abraham wasn't rebellious. Why didn't God move in? God could see that Abraham knew that Isaac was, as the writer to the Hebrews put it, 'as good as dead' (11:12). For Abraham did not consider for a moment that he would back down. When he lifted up that sword he fully intended to come down upon Isaac. But, in the nick of time, God stepped in. It wasn't until that moment that God came nigh and said, 'Now I know that you love me.' You will say, 'Surely God knew before then.' Of course he did. But it's an example to show that God honours what we *do*, not what we think we are willing to do.

It Is Not Enough Just To Be Willing

All of us can be completely willing to do something, but there are times when we mean to do things most sincerely and we don't do them. Why? 'The heart is deceitful above all things, and desperately wicked: who can know it?' (Jer. 17:9). It is not that we are necessarily playing games with ourselves. We mean it when we say we want to do God's will. But until we actually carry out what God says to do he will not draw nigh to us. If we don't carry out outwardly what we promised to do inwardly, there's always something that can happen in the meantime, those hindrances. We say 'God knows that I was willing to do it but this happened and he understood that.' There's an expression we use in America – I guess we got it from you – there's many a slip between cup and lip.

How often we become inwardly, utterly willing to do what God says to do. There are not a few Christians who console themselves because they get a warm feeling in church when they respond affirmatively to the sermon. For example, a sermon may have offended some but one may say, 'It didn't offend me, I thought we needed it.' You think that because you didn't respond negatively everything is fine with you. We often take the warm response in our hearts to a sermon to mean that everything is okay. Then we go out into the real world only to realize a week or two later that nothing really happened. We didn't really change. We can feel good at church and promise God a thousand things and mean every word of it. And then that's the last we think about it.

The Roman Catholic tradition of the auricular confession does people great good. They confess and they make promises and they feel better. My background was partly Nazarene, partly Baptist, but they both have their own way of making it easy for you to feel good before you leave the service. The Nazarenes have what they call the 'altar' at the front of the church. They have an 'altar call' at the end of the service saying, 'If the sermon's touched you and you just want to come and pray about it, do.' And they pray about it and feel so much better and off they go. Southern Baptists have what they call 'rededication'. They give an invitation at the close of the service and many will be touched by the sermon and rededicate their lives and that's it.

We're no different. And yet we wonder why God hasn't drawn nigh to us. He doesn't until he *sees* our performance.

Seeking God's affirmation

The devil flees because he sees what's in our minds but God does not draw nigh until we *do* what he's asked us to do. This is why you've heard me say again and again, 'Don't pray about it, do it.' This is exactly what James means by justification by works. It's a justification that doesn't save. But it is nonetheless a righteousness that God affirms in our persons when we carry out what he told us to do.

This is a verse that is not really a reference to prayer: 'Draw nigh to God, and he will draw nigh to you.' Ninety-five per cent of people who read this verse think that it's about prayer. James wants them to enjoy the high privilege of asking and receiving. Sometimes the very people that need this word are the greatest prayers. They don't realize how far from

God they are even though they pray all the time because prayer can be a decoy of the devil to make you think all is well. It's not praying God is after, it's obedience to his Word. And praying an extra hour will not compensate for what can be dealt with in ten seconds when you do it.

It is James' conviction that drawing nigh to God is a wonderful thing. These Christians wouldn't have a clue what it is until they obey. It's James' conviction that there is a drawing nigh of God to us. And that's a wonderful thing. But we will not have a clue what it means until we carry out the obedience that God is after. I do not say that an increased prayer life is not a part of drawing nigh to God but that's not really what James means.

A real prayer life that pleases God will result not only in heart searching but in an exposure of sin. The proof that prayer is effectual is that there is conviction of sin and you deal with it. It is not then until we do this that God says, 'Now I know you love me.' It's wonderful to hear God say, 'Now I know …' (Gen. 22:12). Do not come short of that 'now I know' response that comes from God. For that is what James means: the nearness of God affirming what we do.

God Welcomes Our Obedience

What does this mean: 'He will draw nigh'? It's God's 'Now I know' response. First, it means that his Word is clear to us and we have acted upon it. How many of us long for God to speak clearly and unmistakably? God wants to do more than merely overrule in our lives all the time. 'If our heart condemn us, God is greater than our heart, and knoweth all things' (1 Jn. 3:20). That's God's overruling grace. Thank God for that. John goes on to say, 'If our heart condemn us not, then have we confidence toward God' (v. 21). That enables us to know what God is saying clearly to us.

Or to put it another way, there are two kinds of faith: saving faith but also experimental faith, the faith that is seen in Hebrews chapter 11. There are also two kinds of assurance. There is assurance of salvation but there is also the assurance when we know our obedience pleases God. The assurance of salvation is knowing that God has affirmed Christ, for it is not of works, it is what Jesus did. It is his substitutionary work and we just believe the promise. Assurance that God is pleased with us is knowing that he affirms us, our lives and how we are living. It is no small thing to know that God is pleased with our obedience.

Some think that assurance of salvation is the only thing there is in Scripture. But listen to Paul in Ephesians 5:9–10: 'For the fruit of the Spirit is in all goodness and righteousness and truth; proving what is acceptable unto the Lord.' Listen to Paul in Philippians 4:18: 'But I have all, and abound: I am full, having received of Epaphroditus the things which were sent from you, an odour of a sweet smell, a sacrifice acceptable, well pleasing to God.' Or Paul could say to the Thessalonians, 'As ye know how we exorted and comforted and charged every one of you, as a father doth his children, that ye would walk worthy of God, who hath called you unto his kingdom and glory' (2 Thess. 2:11–12).

Abraham had assurance of salvation long before God told him to sacrifice Isaac. He was called 'Friend of God'. Jesus said, in John 15:15: 'Henceforth I call you not servants; for the servant knoweth not what his Lord doeth: but I have called you friends.'

Knowing That We Please God

When God draws nigh the first thing is that it's a clear word: 'Now I know.' But the second thing it means is knowing that we do please God. Enoch had this testimony before his translation 'that he pleased God' (Heb. 11:5). Nothing is more comforting, more thrilling, more stabilising and wonderful than knowing that we please God.

Do you know what it was that really enabled Athanasius to stand alone back in the fourth century? This black theologian from North Africa stood alone for what is now an assumption in orthodoxy: the co-eternality of Jesus Christ with God the Father – that Jesus was very God of very God, very man of very man, co-equal, co-substantial, co-eternal with the Father. By the way, are you aware – this is very interesting – that when the Council met to pass on whether Athanasius was right, it looked as though everybody thought he would be voted down because Athanasius was in a minority? When the Council met at Nicea the reason it was carried was because most of those who were coming by ship got a bad wind and were delayed and on the day of the voting those who were there voted and Athanasius won. That is a fact.

They came to Athanasius once and said, 'Athanasius, the world is against you.' And he said, 'If the world is against Athanasius then Athanasius is against the world.' A lot of people call that courage, but it wasn't: it was assurance. I sometimes think that there's no such thing as courage. 'If God be for us who can be against us?' (Rom. 8:31). That's assurance. What enabled the three Hebrew children to be turned over to the fiery furnace wasn't courage, it was assurance. What enabled Daniel to open his windows and keep on praying wasn't courage, it was assurance.

When we hear God say, 'Now I know …' we can tackle the world. When God draws near we can take on lions and tigers and hypocrites and enemies of the gospel, trouble, evil circumstances. This is why Paul could say, 'Be of good cheer: for I believe God, that it shall be even as it was told me' (Acts 27:25). That wasn't courage, that was assurance.

God Gives Us External Confirmation

There's a third thing that takes place when God draws nigh in this way and that is, it is confirmed by something external and outward. What I've been saying up to now is internal. It's the inner confidence, the clear word, the knowledge that we please him. But what James means by drawing nigh to us is that we see things happen. Look what happened with Abraham. Abraham's actual obedience was by the eyes of faith. 'Faith is the substance of things hoped for, the evidence of things not seen' (Heb. 11:1). But when God draws nigh it is as though for a moment you don't need faith. You can see something happen. There comes a time when we need to see God work, as it were, at the level of nature, to see something take place so that we know by an outward combination that God is in the heavens.

The most godly person, however strong he is inwardly, still rejoices at the outward confirmation which God wants to give – but only when we're ready for it. He delays the answer to our prayers as a singular favour to us. This is why James could say, 'You have nothing. You're asking amiss and there it is.' God then gives the outward confirmation because we do need it. So when God draws nigh it means seeing him work in a coalescing of physical circumstances for which there is no natural explanation.

God Doesn't Keep Silent

The fourth thing that happens when God draws near is that he confirms his Word and his outward work by an oath which in fact thrills him even more than it thrills us. When Abraham carried out his ordeal God just couldn't keep silent. And we're told by the writer to the Hebrews what is obviously true from reading the account in Genesis 22, that God confirmed the promise by an oath (Heb. 6:17) saying, 'Surely blessing

I will bless thee, and multiplying I will multiply thee' (Heb. 6:13–14). God despatched an angel for the second time to Abraham and told him what had already been true: that he was going to bless his seed. His coming the first time was enough, but the second time only shows how pleased God was with Abraham's obedience.

God wants us to know that he does see you when you're fighting the flesh and resisting the devil. God sees you when you weep. He sees you when you're tried. We're told that when a sinner repents there's rejoicing in heaven in the presence of the angels (Lk. 15:10). So according to this, when a Christian obeys, God cannot keep silent. God wants us to pass the test and while we're taking it he can't give us the answer. We have to pass it and God waits silently to see if we will.

By the way, our Lord learned obedience through suffering (Heb. 5:8). The temptations which Jesus suffered lasted all the way to the cross. This Jesus, though he was 'in the form of God', thought it not something to be grasped, 'but made himself of no reputation … and became obedient unto death, even the death of the cross' (Phil. 2:6–8). Whereas when Abraham started to take the sword and slay his son God provided a substitute; when Jesus was on the cross they shouted out to him, 'If thou be the Son of God, come down from the cross' (Mt. 27:40). Many thought he would, and he could have, but he didn't. God went through it. There was no substitute for Jesus. He was the substitute. He was 'smitten of God, and afflicted' (Isa. 53:4) in place of us.

It's because of this that the writer to the Hebrews went on to say, 'That by two immutable things, in which it was impossible for God to lie, we might have a strong consolation, who have fled for refuge to lay hold upon the hope set before us: which hope we have as an anchor of the soul, both sure and steadfast, and which entereth into that within the veil' (Heb. 6:18–19). Because on that day when Jesus cried out, 'It is finished', God didn't keep silent. He despatched an angel to the western wall of the city of Jerusalem and 'the veil of the Temple was rent in two' (Mt. 27:51). And it's because of what Jesus did that we are able to draw near to God. James wants us to know that there is a drawing nigh of God to us. God doesn't keep silent.

God Ensures Our Usefulness

But the fifth and last thing that is meant by God drawing nigh, is that when he draws nigh it ensures our usefulness to the world. These Christians James was addressing were in a state of paralysis. They were at a standstill.

They were making an impact on nobody, trying to reach the rich but losing the rich and losing the poor at the same time. And they were the laughing stock of the world. Nobody was taking notice. When God draws nigh it has to affect others. The whole world is affected by it. But what happens when God draws nigh is that he reassures the church of what has always been true.

When the church is at a standstill and not seeing success, often the church begins to say, 'Well, what we are preaching isn't right. And maybe we're doing something wrong where our gospel is concerned.' They begin to question things. So it is often true that a church which is at a standstill begins to doubt the infallibility and inerrancy of the Bible, or the virgin birth of our Lord, or the bodily resurrection of Jesus, or the substitutionary nature of our Lord's atonement. Sometimes the church begins to doubt that there really is a heaven and a hell and, of all things, that men must be converted or they'll be damned. But when God draws nigh, the old truths that we once knew to be true are set ablaze with new power and glory.

What was at stake when God said to sacrifice Isaac, was that God wanted Abraham to see that his seed would continue by God's sovereign will, by regeneration, not procreation.

So when the church experiences God drawing nigh we shall see the same old truths preached, upheld, and know that the gates of hell shall not prevail against the church (Mt. 16:18). Which church? Rome? Canterbury? Westminster? None of these. The church that God raises up through the foolishness of preaching: converting men, women, boys and girls, one at a time. God still has the power to change the drunkard or the prostitute, the dishonest businessman, the atheist schoolteacher. Here we are in a secular age when it's an assumption now that man believes in science, evolution, chance.

Here we are set up against a secular tide that seems invincible, without hope of being reversed. How will it be reversed? When God draws nigh. When he steps in. How? By outward signs, by miracles? Perhaps. But mainly by converting men – through the foolishness of preaching, saving those that believe by regeneration, by adding to the Church one by one, week after week, until Satan's territory becomes so impoverished that the whole world is affected by it. For God made the promise, 'Thy seed shall possess the gate of his enemies; and in thy seed shall all the nations of the earth be blessed'. Why is this? 'Because thou hast obeyed my voice' (Gen. 22:17–18).

'Draw nigh to God, and he will draw nigh to you.' To whom? The world? No, to you. To the church. And then, but only then, will the world be affected by it. How could that happen? History will repeat itself again. God's eternal truth will be proclaimed. Those inside the gates of the enemy will be terrified and say one to another, 'Those that have turned the world upside down are come hither also' (Acts 17:6). Because God draws near. But not until we draw nigh to him. And we do it.

15

Return to Clear Thinking

James 4:8

These verses that we are looking at in this fourth chapter are aimed to help us to make the transition from living in the flesh to living in the Spirit and to knowing something of this nearness of God. We now turn to the last part of this verse: 'Cleanse your hands, ye sinners; and purify your hearts, ye double minded.'

What we have here is a series of imperatives: 'submit yourselves', 'resist the devil', 'draw nigh to God', and now: 'Cleanse your hands, ye sinners; and purify your hearts, ye double minded.' Calling them 'sinners' and 'double minded' is nothing new. What he is simply doing now is to move in to show how this is to be corrected. James is after basically two things. First, with respect to God's own kingdom in the world, to correct their bad witness. And second, with respect to themselves, that they might know single mindedness, peace of mind, clear thinking. We have seen all along the importance of taking James' order as he presents verses to us. We must take seriously the way he puts it. And indeed here again we can see how his mind is working. He doesn't say, 'Purify your hearts and then cleanse your hands.' He begins, 'Cleanse your hands, ye sinners and purify your hearts, ye double minded.' This order is of crucial importance for us to grasp for three reasons.

The Reputation Of Christianity

The first reason is that James wants to show the priority of the kingdom of God, not our own well-being, because James is more concerned about the reputation of Christianity in the world than he is about the individual peace of mind of every Christian. Not that God is not interested in one soul, for he is, but by thinking of millions instead of one, the one will get the benefit. And so James begins with the general kingdom of God. Jealous for the reputation of the name of God, James touches on an eternal, unchangeable principle. That is, if you put God's priorities first you're the one who will be the greatest beneficiary.

God is concerned about his name in the world. The Christian faith alone has God's name and reputation on the line. Don't worry about what people think of Allah and all of the corruption we have seen in the Islamic nations, for that is not the name of God. God is jealous for the reputation of Christians. God has not deposited his name with anyone else but only with the Lord Jesus Christ – as the voice came from heaven, whether at the baptism of Jesus or the transfiguration: 'This is my beloved Son'. We who preach the gospel uphold God's name.

When James addressed these disobedient Christians he called them 'sinners' because that's what they were. He wants everybody to know that he is calling a spade a spade, that we're not helping the reputation of Christianity by sweeping the dirt under the carpet. James lets anybody know that this is disgraceful behaviour. Today the world is confused when it looks at the church. There are various spokesmen for the church, and more often than not you find these spokesmen justifying the church for being just as it is: James doesn't talk like that. He wants us to know that it's disgraceful. Our witness is enhanced the more that we tell the truth about ourselves. We are not what we ought to be.

Take the account of Ananias and Sapphira who were struck dead by lying to the Spirit. It became something that was known everywhere. For God is jealous for his name in the world. These Christian Jews had given God a bad name. By respecting persons, becoming class-conscious and being concerned with how they looked in a society that was class-conscious, they had grieved the Spirit. In grieving the Spirit there was a backfire among themselves and they became divided in their minds. So when James says, 'Cleanse your hands, ye sinners', and then comes to 'purify your hearts, ye double minded', he begins with this general concern for the kingdom of God. But there's another reason for this order. Once our bad witness is corrected then our personal lives are benefited.

What Christianity Is About

It's amazing how many people today think that Christianity is to help you through life's problems. It is true that God will do it. But it's a subsidiary effect. It is primarily upholding the name of God that God himself is concerned about.

It is sad to say that many have given personal advantage as the best, if not the only, reason to obey the Lord. They say, 'I tithe because God will bless me if I do.' There are those churches – and I'm thinking particularly of the Southern Baptist Convention in America – who say, 'We are setting goals to win so many souls this year and God will bless us.' Here's the irony: God does bless them. The tither, even if he gives selfishly, is still blessed. There are people who want to back off from doing anything at all because they say, 'Well, I'm just not going to do it selfishly.' But even so you're the loser because there is an inherent principle here that God does honour those who honour him. Even if you serve God with the wrong motive, you're better off.

If you're a Christian and your testimony has been, 'God helped me with my problems' – fine. But you still have a defective Christianity and it can be much, much better than that. James has the priority right. First, he's thinking of the general witness of the kingdom of God; second, what it will do for you: your hearts will be purified and you will come to single mindedness.

The Danger Of Double Mindedness

And yet there's a third reason for this order, and that is that you cannot have this peace of mind, this single mindedness, when you are serving Satan's interest in the world. Here's a rule to remember. We behave a certain way because of what we believe and think, but if our obedience should turn to disobedience it in turn affects what we believe and think so that disobedience backfires, not the least result of which is a double mindedness, confusion, an absence of clear thinking.

If you want to define double mindedness James uses it in three ways. First, confusion. You didn't really know what was going on and therefore there was an instability: 'unstable in all his ways'. But it was also where there were divisions, double mindedness within the church. There were cliques, splits, people who didn't speak to others. Then, secondly, there was this division over whether they served God or tried to hold onto the world. They loved God, they loved the world. They were going to have it both ways. In the main, James referring to confusion of mind.

The cause of double mindedness

When unclear thinking emerges, James knows that he cannot deal with this question directly. It is but the symptom of something else. For the cause of double mindedness is sin. So he begins, 'Cleanse your hands, ye sinners', then you're ready to think about purifying the heart but not until sin is first dealt with. We are not in a position to purify our hearts and come to single mindedness and clearer thinking until we have washed our hands clean. If there is sin in your life, confusion will persist. This is why the order is so crucial. 'Cleanse your hands, ye sinners', then you will be able to think about that clear guidance.

Nothing is so obvious about the modern church as its confusion of mind and woolly thinking. Look at Christianity today in Britain. You've got blatant heresy at one extreme and sterile orthodoxy at the other. The effect of both is helplessness. The cause of both is sin – the failure to uphold God's name. God put it like this in Samuel: 'Be it far from me; for them that honour me I will honour, and they that despise me shall be lightly esteemed' (1 Sam. 2:30). You can't disobey God and get away with it. Neither can you obey God and get away with it because you're going to be blessed. 'Be not deceived; God is not mocked: for whatsoever a man soweth, that shall he also reap' (Gal. 6:7). One symptom of sowing to the flesh, of corruption, is always confusion.

You can see here the theological position of James. Once a person has sinned now that he is a Christian, he must get right with God not merely by faith in the blood of Christ but by doing for himself what God has already done in Christ. 'Cleanse your hands, ye sinners.' He's telling you to do that. You will say, 'Surely that's something God has already done.' You're quite right. God has done that. And not only that. We're told in Acts 15:9 that God 'put no difference between us and them, purifying their hearts by faith'.

We know from what Paul says to the Ephesians that 'Christ also loved the church, and gave himself for it that he might sanctify and cleanse it by the washing of water by the word' (5:25). In other words, these are things that are true by grace. God has done this. Jesus says, 'Ye are clean through the word which I have spoken unto you' (Jn. 15:3). But now that you have sinned, the way to get right with God is not merely to trust in the blood of Christ but to wash your own hands. Turn from that idol. Flee temptation. Then are you in a position to know single mindedness. And you purify your heart.

There are two categories of rejection of the word of God. For the non-Christian, the most effective thing in the world is the idea that God does everything for you and that you become a Christian by doing nothing. It's a humiliating thing. There are those who just won't become Christians if they find out that God's done it all. They reject that. But there's also the rejection by Christians of what James calls justification by works. There are those Christians who want to have it all by way of imputation. There is that inward hostility to actual obedience and personal holiness. There have been those who questioned James' orthodoxy because he puts the burden right on us to get right with God.

The Doctrine Of James

Yet James has laid out for us a doctrine that will preserve us against heresy and a sterile orthodoxy on the one hand and a frivolous, flippant, ungodly living on the other hand. For he wants us to see that there is that which God has done for us and that we rejoice in, but he wants us also to act and obey and get right with him by how we live our lives. He begins with the hands, the agent of doing symbolizing behaviour. He is telling us that it's an act of the will.

You may say, 'Isn't this a reversal of the order of salvation? Doesn't Paul the apostle begin with the heart?' That's true. But James is not dealing with the order of salvation, but rather with sanctification. The heart is the seat of saving faith but the will is the seat of experimental faith, of stability of mind, clear thinking. You're saved by doing nothing, by seeing that Christ has done it all. But now that you are saved you do things and this is an act of the will. James, therefore, begins with their will, because the heart that was able to see clearly in conversion is now dulled and insensitive because of disobedience.

Assurance and sanctification

Here's an aspect of the doctrine of assurance and the doctrine of sanctification that I think is interesting and also very sobering. Once our senses are dulled the same heart that is the seat of saving faith is not able to grasp things as clearly. The only place to begin then is with the hands, with behaviour, with what we are doing. So James sees these Christian Jews have disgraceful to the name of God. It seems to have begun with a class-consciousness.

Jesus said, 'I am the vine, ye are the branches' (Jn. 15:5), and the church is supposed to be all that Jesus was. Jesus went to the poor, Jesus was not a respecter of persons. Defective evangelism, or discriminate evangelism, opens the floodgates of our own lusts and our personal greed. If a congregation is not what God wants it to be then they're going to suffer. If you as an individual are not an extension of Jesus, it will backfire on you and the same heart that enabled you to see things so clearly will be dull.

These Christians had violated this basic principle. They were governed not by freedom but by the bondage of temptation. Personal greed gave way to grudges and quarrelling and gossiping. They might well want to have the clear thinking, but they had to deal first with the way they were behaving.

How does one 'cleanse his hands'? He does so first of all, by conviction. Secondly, by contrition. And thirdly, by confession – in that order. This confession is where you have become sorry for the way you've been. When you confess it to God it's not just a little ritual whereby you say, 'Lord, I've confessed it', for we're not Roman Catholics who go to confession and just take grace as a sacrament and assume it's all right. No, contrition comes second. First, conviction where you see what you've done, where the Spirit has brought things to your mind. Then you see what effect this has had and you're sorry. And then you confess it. Confessing it means you're turning from it. Once such repentance is carried out, the rest is easier. The heart which is the biblical expression for the seat of personality becomes fit to return to clear thinking and to function without the hindrances of worldly mindedness.

Assurance of salvation may subside

The heart never ceases to be the seat of saving faith. However, as worldly behaviour results in double mindedness, so does this often backfire on our own assurance of salvation. It's not that either the Christian loses his salvation or that the ground of salvation or the ground of assurance ever changes, but sin can so affect the heart that one may be confused regarding his own salvation. The ground of our salvation is Jesus and his blood shed on the cross. But if the heart becomes double minded that assurance nonetheless subsides. To put it another way, our repentance or our sanctification can never be the ground of assurance. But sanctification can have a lot to do with preparing the heart by which we see Christ clearly.

Sin jams the network by which our assurance of salvation is transmitted. It can be very serious. Take, for example, those premature deaths at Corinth when Paul says, 'Let a man examine himself' in taking the Lord's Supper. He said there were those who partook unworthily and 'for this cause many are weak and sickly among you, and many sleep' (1 Cor. 11:28–30). It's not that they partook as non-Christians but that their lifestyle so affected their spiritual senses that they were not able to discern the Lord's body in the supper.

The Results Of Having Been Disobedient

Sin removed not only purifies the heart to see Christ clearly but it also enables one to do wonderful things. This is the reason that the godly person almost always has more assurance and more effectiveness. It's not that he's more saved or justified. It's that he's got a better transmitter and he can see clearly. You may want to ask this question: 'If having come to repentance the rest is easy, why did James bother to say, "Purify the heart"?' The answer is, because the returning backslider, to use Richard Sibbes' phrase, needs to realize how distorted his thinking has become in the meantime. He needs to see that living close to the world has its negative side-effects. For the person who has lived in a worldly way and has become at home with temptation picks up extra baggage along the way.

If the person now has repented he must not assume that his repentance and his forgiveness necessarily prove he's ready to carry on without further reflecting upon himself. Because often during the period of waywardness a person becomes entrenched in a way of thinking. Even though he's now stopped his sinning and he's learned to think differently, he sometimes assumes that he is thinking clearly when, in fact, he ought to stop and think again. For if you begin to pick up assumptions while you are in a backslidden state, do not think that repentance will automatically remove those assumptions. This is why, though the worst is past if we have repented, we need to think now of the implications.

Theological implications

Disobedience can result in picking up bad theology without realizing it. What often happens when a person has fallen into sin is that he says, 'God permitted the temptation.' Any time you want to blame God for your sin that's bad theology and you need to purify your hearts.

Distorted viewpoints

Disobedience often results in a distorted picture of other people. Holding a grudge against another person often leads to exaggeration of your view of what they're thinking. It leads to suspicion. Now that you've repented, adjust your thinking. 'Purify your hearts, ye double minded.' James said: 'From whence come wars and fightings among you? Come they not hence, even of your lusts that war in your members?' False observations need correcting.

Corrupt praying

Disobedience often results in ill-posed prayer requests. 'Ye ask, and receive not, because ye ask amiss, that ye may consume it upon your lusts.' Disobedience often results in presumption of mercy. You think you can just wander right out into Satan's territory and it won't bother you one bit. But James warns, 'Ye adulterers and adulteresses, know ye not that the friendship of the world is enmity with God? Whosoever therefore will be a friend of the world is the enemy of God.'

The Results Of True Repentance

But if indeed we purify our hearts and we reassess what we think and bring it in line with 'fruits meet for repentance' (Mt. 3:8), the result is a most happy one. It's called wisdom, described in chapter 3 verse 17: 'It is first pure, then peaceable, gentle, and easy to be entreated, full of mercy and good fruits, without partiality, and without hypocrisy.' When that wisdom comes it means goodbye bitterness, vindictiveness, gossiping, confusion – and welcome back clear thinking, a sense of direction and a sense of purpose.

You as a Christian are created for good works and created with design and purpose, but if you do not continue in that which you've been created to be, namely to uphold God's name, the result will not only be scandalous but distorted thinking. And so with the church.

Jesus said, 'Abide in me, and I in you. As the branch cannot bear fruit of itself, except it abide in the vine; no more can ye, except ye abide in me' (Jn. 5:4). Abiding in the vine is to be the branch of what Jesus was. Can you imagine Jesus despising the poor, being a respecter of persons, holding a grudge or taking advantage of another person's weakness? The Psalmist put it like this: 'Who shall ascend into the hill of the LORD?

or who shall stand in his holy place? He that hath clean hands, and a pure heart; who hath not lifted up his soul unto vanity, nor sworn deceitfully. He shall receive the blessing from the LORD'. And what might that blessing be? 'Lift up your heads, O ye gates; and be ye lift up, ye everlasting doors; and the King of glory shall come in' (Ps. 24:3–5, 7). The King of glory comes in. The name of God is restored and all the world around us will be affected by this.

The reason that the church has become irrelevant is that the church has grieved God. The reason that we're not having any impact is that there's something wrong with us. God has let us abound in confusion and it will not help us to try to deal with it directly and to try to get our minds straight. We've got to begin with the way we're living, our hands, our behaviour. God demands this repentance of the church and then we can begin to think clearly. The blessing is the arrival of the King of glory. Everyone will know about it. The whole world will be affected by it.

And in the meantime when God's name is restored we get the benefit, not the least of which is this:

- a warm and a tranquil heart,
- clear thinking,
- a sense of purpose,
- the realization of being used of God.

16

The Joy of Mourning

James 4:9

This is one of those verses that, if taken out of context, gives the non-Christian reason to think that Christianity is a depressing kind of religion. Indeed, to the unspiritual or counterfeit Christian this verse is looked upon as a thing of curiosity and is never understood. We're going to look at it now in its context and see what can be an insight leading to great blessing. This verse is chiefly about repentance or, more specifically, contrition, which is a broader effect of repentance.

About Repentance And Faith

I'm bringing up a term around which no small confusion still persists. The order of salvation is not simply a theological matter, it's very pastoral. I've always been thankful to God that in my research at Oxford I dealt with an issue that had an effect upon my preaching and upon my pastoral ministry, that my research led me to face this crucial point.

There are those who say that it's just splitting a theological hair over which comes first – faith or repentance. But I answer that it is not, it is splitting a theological atom. For if we see that faith comes first, a great breakthrough follows and you understand how to know that you are a Christian and to know what God wants of you. It's not a theological but a pastoral issue, and it is what will give us an evangelistic heart.

What is meant by repentance?

The word 'repentance' comes from the Greek *metanoia* which means 'change of mind'. If we stick to the Greek etymology – 'change of mind' –

then it isn't as crucial which comes first: faith or repentance. The problem is that we have inherited a Puritan tradition that has somehow come to define repentance in a different way – as being turning from every known sin. If that is the way that repentance is going to be defined, it is absolutely crucial that we get it right in the order of salvation.

Another way of drawing this distinction to show how the Bible deals with it, is to look at the message of John the Baptist. In Matthew 3:8 John the Baptist said, 'Bring forth therefore fruits meet for repentance.' The word translated 'meet' in our Authorised Version is the Greek word *axion*. We get the word 'axiology' or an 'axiom', a 'value', a 'saying' from it. John the Baptist meant fruit that is worthy of, or due, or the equivalent value of repentance, so that he was not only calling for repentance – a change of mind – but also for fruit that is true repentance.

Don't forget that he was addressing a covenant community, Israel. In fact, he went on to say, 'Think not to say within yourselves, We have Abraham to our father: for I say unto you, that God is able of these stones to raise up children unto Abraham' (v. 9). And because John the Baptist was addressing Israel and a covenant community he could go on and talk about his brother Philip's wife whom Herod had taken over in the way he did. John the Baptist said, 'It is not lawful for you to have her' (Mt. 14:4). He not only called for repentance but also for fruits fit for repentance.

But when it comes to becoming a Christian there is no New Testament requirement that one must first turn from every known sin in order to become a Christian. The Puritans, many of them, thought that you must turn from every known sin before you could ask Christ to save you.

We are not justified by repentance

This word 'repentance' means 'change of mind'. But so many of us have assumed that repentance means turning from every known sin and have required the non-Christian to do this before he can even come to Christ. This is why I say that it's really easy to become a Christian. You look to Christ. Anybody can do that. Even so, even if we understand that the word 'repentance' simply means 'change of mind', don't forget that you are not justified by changing your mind. You're not justified by repentance. You're justified by faith alone. This insight is what Luther gave to the church, and we can be thankful for it.

Having said that, now that we are Christians God demands not only repentance but 'fruits fit for repentance', godliness. God grants us faith that he might teach us repentance. When James said, 'Draw nigh to God and he will draw nigh to you', by drawing nigh he meant turning from every known sin. But you can't begin to do it until you are a Christian. Now that we are Christians God shows us the way to live and what obedience is. May God help us as Christians to see that it is this kind of testimony and witness that can make an impact upon the world. We have a word to the non-Christian now that God saves us. We can learn to live lives that glorify Christ.

The first of the three aims of this general epistle of James is that these Christian Jews would be convicted of their sin. It is so easy for a Christian to wander so far from obedience that he doesn't even see that he's doing anything wrong. The first thing that must take place for a Christian who is in a backslidden state is to be convicted. The second aim is that there might be contrition, sorrow for sin. Finally, that there might be confession.

Conviction Of Sin And Contrition

Our confession is superfluous, meaningless, if there hasn't been contrition first. And there's no way you can be contrite unless you've first been convicted. Verse 9 of chapter 4 is an examination of contrition, this broader effect of repentance. James has been trying to show us our need. He now wants to show us that there's a place for contrition.

Why would James want us to be contrite, to mourn, to be sad, to cry? What's the value of that? His reason for wanting this is because contrition is a proof that we have been convicted. Contrition is, as it were, a seal upon our having been truly convicted. If you can be convicted about sin and not be sorry about it, one questions whether in fact you did see your sin.

All James wants to do is to ensure that we see the sin. And he's not stopping at the fact of being convicted. He says, 'Be afflicted, and mourn, and weep: let your laughter be turned to mourning, and your joy to heaviness.' Or to put it another way, James wants to ensure that we do have clear thinking.

This must be taken in context. He has just finished saying, 'Cleanse your hands, ye sinners; and purify your hearts, ye double minded.' Why then does he, right on the heels of that statement, say, 'Be afflicted, and mourn'? It's because there is this danger – and we're all prone to it in thinking that all is well simply because we have outwardly repented. That is, we've cleansed our hands, our outward behaviour has changed and we feel so good about that that we don't think about any vestige of warped thinking that might have crept in while we were in the backslidden state.

How We Think Matters

Do we realize that whenever we are friendly with the world, even if temporarily, we are prone to adopt a worldly mode of thinking? We tend to think that if we have stopped the sin that obviously our thinking is all right. But, in fact, while we were sinning we adopted a way of thinking that was alien to the mind of Christ. How you think does matter.

What happens so easily is that we change outwardly but we don't change inwardly. We assume that if our behaviour is back to normal then it is automatically true that we are bringing forth adequate fruit fit for repentance. What is so often forgotten is that intellectual habits and assumptions, which were acquired as a consequence of worldly behaviour, do not automatically disappear just because we have outwardly changed.

A partial reformation

It can happen on a broader scale. Here's an example from church history, from the Great Reformation. There was this great outward change with regard to how Christians who were affected by the Reformation looked at Rome and the Virgin Mary and purgatory and penance and the Eucharist and justification and the sacraments. But within a generation or two it was discovered that the thinking hadn't sufficiently changed. Often there was simply a Protestantizing of a way of thinking that had become normal in the Middle Ages.

It is well known that in the Middle Ages Albert the Great, who was Thomas Aquinas' teacher, discovered the writings of Aristotle. Thomas Aquinas became better known than his teacher and made Aristotelian thinking the norm for Roman Catholic theology. What happened when the Great Reformation came along is that the outward changes were made, but so many of those who kept the Reformation going still thought like Aristotle.

The Reformation largely was a Protestantizing of Aristotle so that you still had the syllogistic reasoning and the logical deductions, and it was at the bottom of Puritan thinking. The idea was that the Bible was interpreted through logic rather than comparing Scripture with Scripture.

The feeling was that if it's logical it's got to be right, when in fact that may not be the case. Most of us are affected by this and have not known why. It's so easy to want to think that being logical ensures that we're being scriptural when, in fact, a logical deduction could be alien to Scripture.

That's true at a broad level. It is equally true of an individual Christian who has wandered from the faith or from God but then reforms. Outwardly he repents and he stops sinning, broadly speaking, outwardly at least. But he doesn't realize that having been in that backslidden state he is not as reformed as he thinks. He's picked up a lot of excess baggage along the way – philosophical, political, psychological, sociological or cultural views which in fact are alien to godly thinking – and he doesn't see the connection.

James wants to ensure that any reformation that is taking place in our lives is complete, that in our hearts there is the single mindedness that puts Christ first and that we are obedient to the Word of God primarily and finally. And so in order that we will not assume that just cleansing our hands is sufficient he says, 'Be afflicted, and mourn, and weep.' Because, even though the outward change is the important thing and it's downhill thereafter, do not think that it automatically means our thinking becomes single minded. More suffering may be needed.

James wants us to see how serious God is about our obedience and that our holy living is not that which is simply outward and that our very minds are all that God wants so that we are vehicles of his grace, instruments that are meet for the Master's use. James' primary concern is the Christian witness in the world, and he was also concerned about the future of Christianity. For God knew that if these Christians weren't corrected, Christianity would have become nothing but a middle-class religion.

James' Concern About The Future Of Christianity

James was concerned about the future of Christianity. He seeks our own reformation as Christians – as individuals, as mothers, as fathers, as Christian parents. He wants our reformation to be so complete that we can hand to our children and to the next generation a Christian faith that is so devoid of error that those who go on with it will not repeat false assumptions.

If the devil cannot win the battle with regard to our outward behaviour, then he will try to slip in on our blind side and control our way of thinking lest a 'pure religion and undefiled' (Jas. 1:27) be the inheritance of the next generation. So it is important that we pass on to our children not merely the best theological insights but godly-mindedness, which is godly thinking. For our children are not likely to move beyond us, at least not at first. But if we can hand to them on a silver platter godly thinking as well as godly living, we have removed the devil by a greater distance in the next generation.

That's what James is after. That is our responsibility. We must not be concerned merely for our own witness in our own day, but if Jesus doesn't come back, what is going to happen in twenty years, forty years, sixty years? Our children deserve to have handed to them assumptions that are right, that are sound. They watch how we live and they repeat what they see. It's very sobering, isn't it? But it's true of the family. It's true of the church family. God help us to see it.

James' method is to seal conviction of sin. His first word is: 'Be afflicted'. It's a word that simply means 'endure severe hardships'. Why? One reason: lest we think that outward repentance is enough. Let me put it in another way. Maybe you have indeed been brought to a closer relationship with God. You were indulging in sinful pleasures at one time, but you're not now. You have been in the world, but you're not now. And perhaps you've noticed that your own return from your former ways did not result in the immediate breakthrough that you thought would take place. There was no chorus of angelic singing. You didn't get personal congratulations from Michael the Archangel because you stopped sinning. When you got back where you ought to be, nothing great really happened.

Perhaps you thought that once you began fighting temptation rather than enjoying it, the result would be immediate joy and great blessing. Chances are this was true to some extent, for you cannot honour God without some happy compensation. God, in kindness, does encourage us along the way with definite blessings. But for the most part you have noticed that there is still considerable conflict. There is still an inner battle and, most of all, the suffering that you've been put through has not completely subsided. There's a reason for that.

God isn't finished with you yet. There's more work to be done. There are cobwebs that need to be swept out of your mind, false assumptions that need to be corrected. You've noticed that God still puts trials before you, greater than ever perhaps. The reason he has done this is that otherwise you would have concluded that all is well and you would never have bothered to examine your own assumptions – how you regard this view or that view or how you regard this person or that person or that circumstance. James wants you to have a re-examination of how you think. Do you know what a re-examination might do for you? It might bring you to blush so that you say to yourself, 'How could I have thought like that?' But apart from the suffering that you've been through you wouldn't have bothered to think about it. 'Be afflicted', says James, because it is for your own good.

The Effects Of Suffering

Suffering in the Christian life has a two-fold effect. One, it causes sin to emerge that you didn't know was there. And two, it causes you to re-examine an assumption that you had accepted uncritically. 'Don't fight the suffering', James tells us. 'Count it all joy when you fall into diverse trials, for the trial that God has for you is to bring you to clear thinking indeed.'

> *When through fiery trials thy pathway shall lie,*
> *My grace all-sufficient shall be thy supply;*
> *The flame shall not hurt thee: I only design*
> *Thy dross to consume and thy gold to refine.*

James doesn't stop there. He says, 'Be afflicted, and mourn.' 'Mourn' simply means 'be sad'. Here is a verse that the non-Christian couldn't possibly understand. What the Christian knows, what the non-Christian does not know, is that this mourning leads to the highest level of joy that there is. It not only leads to it, but there's a certain joy in it while it is being endured. When God is chastening us and the trial is at its most fierce moment, there's a certain joy in it when you think that God's doing it.

I remember once saying to my wife, 'This is wonderful.' When I said that, if you knew what we had been going through, you would have thought there was something wrong with me. But I meant it. I said, 'I can see what God is doing. This is the only way it could happen.' It was hard, but I thought, 'God's doing it and that makes it right.' As Calvin once said, 'O God, thou crushest me but that it is thy hand, it is enough.' I believe that Jonah, with all that he was going through, must have been overwhelmed that God cared that much.

So Jesus could say to his disciples, 'Blessed are they that mourn: For they shall be comforted' (Mt. 5:4). And yet let's not underestimate that it is a real sadness. 'No chastening for the present seemeth to be joyous, but grievous', said the writer to the Hebrews (12:11). But the mourning is the means to bring us through the maze and through the confusion, the confusion of thinking that has kept us bound.

Three Reasons Why It's Good To Be Sad

Let me at a practical level give you three reasons why it's good sometimes for the Christian to be sad – sad upon the heels of having got right with God.

- First, that you might really see how your warped way of thinking has grieved God. All sin primarily is against God. David, although he had been in adultery, cried out, 'Against thee, thee only, have I sinned' (Ps. 51:4). In the case of Joseph who was almost seduced by Potiphar's wife, Joseph said, 'How can I do this great wickedness, and sin against God?' (Gen. 39:9).
- Secondly, you ought to be sad because of the effect your own assumptions have had on yourself. You're the loser. Your resources and your capabilities have been impoverished. Your own thinking is your worst enemy and your development has been at a standstill simply because the way you began to think when you were worldly resulted in, as it were, an arrested development. Those assumptions that you picked up when you were in a rebellious spirit towards God have had an effect upon you.
- There's a third reason, and that is because of the effect that this has had upon other people. Do you realize that there are those who have taken you seriously? You may have said things you don't think now. But they were believed when you said them. It is often true that we become entrenched in a position that we don't any longer want to defend but our pride makes us keep holding to the old view. You need to see the effect it has upon other people when they believe you. If you are making another person look less than perfect by little innuendos and things you say, what if people believe you? When your thinking is right you won't think like you do now but in the meantime look carefully at what you say.

'Well,' says James, 'be afflicted and mourn' and he doesn't stop there. He says, 'And weep'. The Greek literally means 'to shed tears'. Why shed tears? Because you should. Look what you've done to God and to yourself and to others. If there appears upon the scene of your heart a great sense of God, there will be a great mourning for sin. This flippancy and lightness that characterizes so many of us would go away if there were a great sense of God. Oh, the mourning that would follow. James is trying to instill this into us.

How sorry *are* you for the way you have lived? How do you feel towards God? Have you stopped to think what he thinks? How do you feel about the effect it's had upon your own thinking and how you've been impoverished and said things that you couldn't possibly believe if you thought like a godly person? How do you feel about the way you have affected others and caused them to believe and think things? How sorry are you? Do you really want the breakthrough, the peace that follows from clear thinking? 'Be afflicted, and mourn, and weep: let your laughter be turned to mourning, and your joy to heaviness.'

That is not the end. This mourning is the means to the end. For the Psalmist said, 'They that sow in tears shall reap in joy' (Ps. 126:5). 'Weeping may endure for a night, but joy cometh in the morning' (Ps. 30:5). And the Psalmist went on to say, 'Thou hast turned for me my mourning into dancing: thou hast put off my sackcloth, and girded me with gladness; To the end that my glory may sing praise to thee, and not be silent' (vv. 11–12). God wants us to be happy, but true happiness is derived only from true holiness. Holiness leads to happiness and joy. 'Weeping may endure for a night, but joy cometh in the morning.'

17

The Reconversion of the Church

James 4:9–10

We're looking at what it means to take mourning for sin seriously indeed for the particular sin that brought disgrace upon our witness. The question is, is there any value in mourning for sin?

The Value Of Mourning For Sin

Take the story of Joseph. We see the human side of Joseph when his eleven brothers came to Egypt asking for corn. Joseph gave those eleven brothers a rough time and made them eat dust before he himself finally broke down and wept. Is God making us eat dust so that it will be easy for him to forgive us? No, God only delights in seeing that we see what he sees. God is not trying to exact any payment from us for 'he hath not dealt with us after our sins; nor rewarded us according to our iniquities' (Ps. 103:10). God simply wants our repentance to be sufficient that we see what we have done. It's for our own good.

Outward change is not enough

Outward repentance, when there is a general change of behaviour, is good. The world will see that and cannot get to us with their charges of hypocrisy. And yet, according to James, the outward change is not enough. The ultimate consequence is that if we are not purified in our hearts – if there's not an inward change – then we are vulnerable to repeating the same sin.

If our repentance is sufficiently deep, we will be less likely to fall into the same sin. As a result of our friendship with the world we acquire assumptions that we don't realize need to be reassessed. If there is a remaining assumption that is wrong, there is consequently the vulnerability to fall right back into the same sin and even to do it on a grander scale.

In Luke 11 Jesus said, 'When the unclean spirit is gone out of a man, he walketh through dry places, seeking rest; and finding none, he saith, I will return unto my house whence I came out. And when he cometh, he findeth it swept and garnished. Then goeth he, and taketh to him seven other spirits more wicked than himself; and they enter in, and dwell there: and the last state of that man is worse than the first' (vv. 24–26).

Contrition safeguards against future backsliding

If we do repeat the same sin it is often the case that we're in worse shape than ever. What James is after is simply to bring about a complete reformation. It's not likely and it's not like any of us to be really sure that we won't repeat the same sin unless we are very, very sorry indeed for what we did. The depth of repentance will issue in this broader effect called contrition, and it is the best safeguard to future backsliding. For if we see the grief and the sorrow that we are put through in making our way back to God, then this alone should be a sober reminder of what's in store for us with respect to the same sin again. Peter wept bitterly because he denied the Lord; he may have made other mistakes later but he didn't make that one again.

This, then, is why James keeps on: 'Be afflicted, and mourn, and weep: let your laughter be turned to mourning'. The Greek word that is translated 'laughter' simply means 'smiling' or 'laughing' or 'grinning'. James uses this word because these Christians had had a broad grin on their faces despite what they'd done. But the world could see right through them.

The odd thing is that here were these Christian Jews who had turned Christianity from its original calling and they felt no conviction at all about this. They themselves were given the gospel because Jesus was the first ever to offer something for the poor, and now they had turned around and were trying to make Christianity into a middle-class religion. Everybody could see what they were doing. But this defective witnessing backfired on them. Their friendship with the world resulted in opening the floodgates of lust, of greed, of quarrelling with each other. And yet they went around with broad grins on their faces.

Today the world looks at the church and what does it see? We're laughing, we're smiling, we're grinning. The world is going to hell and we're just having a good time. It doesn't bother us one bit. Do you not realize that the world can see right through our superficiality, the nonsense that characterizes so much of what we do?

I remember once seeing Hans Kuhn, a controversial theologian, and another Dutch theologian being interviewed by a BBC interviewer who appeared to be a very honest man. He was putting simple questions to these two European theologians which they couldn't even answer. To Hans Kuhn he said, 'Just tell me what is the irreducible minimum of what it is to be a Christian.' Hans Kuhn stuttered around and was making no sense at all. The Dutch theologian was doing no better and the interviewer said, 'Having asked these two theologians these questions, I am more confused than ever.' And then he interviewed a Cambridge don and this man's answer was absolutely pitiful. The interviewer could see right through the shallowness and the sheer absurdity of these theological answers.

And did it bother any of these theologians? Not a bit. This is what is true on a less sophisticated level with every Christian who is divided between what he knows he ought to believe and what he ought to be like and how he actually believes and how he actually lives.

The problem that we face is that the world has a vague idea of what a Christian is supposed to be like. It puts us all on the spot. When we live in the opposite way it is absolutely destructive to the Christian witness. The modern church will disintegrate more and more until, if something doesn't happen, there'll be no Christian church left at all in Britain or in Western Europe. When the world outside laughs at us we ought to be weeping inside, not smiling. James requires that our demeanour and our countenance show an abrupt contrast to the lightness and the glibness that the world interprets as being a justification for not taking us seriously.

James Calls For A New Conversion

James asks that our 'laughter be turned ...' The Greek word means 'turned with a sense of gravity and sanctity'. What James calls for is a new conversion. A Christian often needs to have a profound change in himself outwardly and inwardly. Sometimes the restoration of a backsliding Christian can result in a more dramatic crisis than his actual initial conversion. There are those Christians who worry because they can't tell you for sure the day and the hour of their conversion. What you won't forget is the day and the hour when you are restored. We mustn't be in a theological straitjacket and have to have everything theologically categorized and slotted. What matters is that he who calls himself a Christian acts like one.

How much more wonderful when this reconversion happens on a broader scale, not merely to one individual. What would be more wonderful is when the church as a whole is reconverted. This will cause the world to take notice.

How are we to be thus reconverted? When laughter is turned to grief. The word means 'grief', 'mourning'. When the world sees through us but we laugh about it, then they laugh more. That gives them all the ammunition they need to say that we're irrelevant and making no impact. But when they see our grief they see authenticity. And for the first time they won't be laughing.

Why grief? We grieve because our witness has been brought into disgrace and because of what this witness has done to the heart of God and to ourselves. Because what we've done to others is to remove the right to lead them to Christ. For example, if you lose your temper in a super-market and then come to the cash register and invite that lady to church, it's rather embarrassing, isn't it?

These Christian Jews had alienated the poor, but in doing so they alienated the rich as well. What we ought to grieve about is how we've missed the opportunity to tell other people what they deserve to hear but will not because of ourselves. We have failed then and so, says James, there ought to be a turning from laughter to mourning, and our joy should be converted to heaviness.

One might ask how on earth the church can have joy when the world can see right through us. If another person sees your hypocrisy, how can you feel good about it? What amazes me is that the church just goes right on. We have a ready-made rationale by which we justify our priorities. We seem never to judge ourselves. We excuse ourselves and our excuse, strangely, issues in a kind of perverted joy. It is a joy we seem to get when we satisfy ourselves that we really couldn't be all that bad.

The problem with us is that having won no souls to Christ seems not to bother us any more than Hans Kuhn appeared upset that he couldn't answer. We all have our reasons, but at the end of the day we will look back and say, 'What did we do with our time?' This is why James wants us to face up to our responsibility. For if we are not witnessing for the Lord it will backfire. We are impoverished and we leave the world with an excuse. It is therefore a reconversion that every one of us needs, a conversion that means a heaviness and a sorrow.

What James is talking about here is a spirit, an attitude. This is not the kind of reconversion we want normally. We use the expression: we need to get our tank refuelled, to get our batteries recharged. We prefer the kind of conversion that will get us out of trouble, get us through a financial crisis, get the raise in pay, work it out to have the holiday, get us through this particular family crisis. We want the instant relief. That's not the conversion James has in mind. If we were to see ourselves as God sees us, the very feeling James is calling for is exactly how we would feel, a heaviness inexpressible. For a church that has been less than its calling is more likely to experience heaviness when God begins to move. If God moves upon us we will see how grieved indeed he is.

The Result Of Grieving For Sin

When Ananias and Sapphira and the whole church found out that playing games with the Holy Spirit would not be tolerated, great fear came upon all the church and upon as many as heard these things. You might have thought that that's the kind of scandal that would just finish the church. But no, we read in just three more verses that 'believers were the more added to the Lord, multitudes both of men and women' (Acts 5:14). Why? Because the world wants to see something that is authentic. When we are grieving for our sin and for the way we've lived then the world will see that there's something real about us.

So much of our joy is not a godly joy. It's mostly either a joy that comes from a natural level or just a projection of how we want to feel. But if the Spirit were to come down, the consequence would be a real horror of sin, not a rationale that we use for why we are the way we are. True revival would begin with a repentance so profound that many of us couldn't even lift our heads.

What then are we to do? James says, 'Humble yourselves'. It's the imperative word again. James won't let us get away with the idea that: 'Only God can bring revival so we'll just wait and ask him to pour out his Spirit upon us.' This is why revival tarries. We've got such a high view of the sovereignty of God that every time I hear a discussion among people about revival, usually the concluding remark is, 'Well, only God can do it.' 'Quite right.' They shake hands with each other. 'Well, may he do it someday.' James tells us to be humbled for the Word of God has already given sufficient cause to be humbled. Yet the truth is that God has already humbled us but we can't see it. Success has been withheld from us. We've been made a laughing stock but it hasn't hit us yet; we're the last to see it. James is trying to say it for us.

Yet he's not saying that this is something you can do for your own sake or for its own sake. You're not trying to manufacture humility. He says, 'Humble yourselves in the sight' that is, in the presence – 'of the Lord' because that's whom we've sinned against. He isn't requiring that we put on sackcloth and ashes for the world to see. He's not calling for a contrived penance. There are those who on Ash Wednesday get a little mark on their foreheads so they can show that they have been humbled. We can play a role, but that's a far cry from reality.

Even though our disgraceful witness is known to the world, we don't get right by making an overture to the world. Our sin is against God. When we do certain things and say certain things to the world it doesn't mean that we should go to the world now and try to make our peace, for doing that will make no impact. These Christian Jews, in any case, had become so disgraceful that there wasn't anything they could do to impress the world.

When we have made a real mess of things there's only one thing to do, and that's to turn to God. Let him handle everything. Humble yourself before the presence of the Lord. Don't try to work things out or try to nudge the arm of providence. Don't try to do what only God can do.

We are in step three with reference to James' general aim in writing this epistle. Step one is conviction of sin, step two is contrition, but now we're ready to come to step three – confession to God.

How We Should Confess

Don't confess if you're not contrite. And you can't be contrite unless you've been convicted. But if you have been convicted and you're sorry about it you're ready now to confess to God. Not to a priest or your minister. Whatever you do, don't confess to the world, for that would be casting the pearl before the swine (Mt. 7:6).

You may say, 'Well, what do I say to God?' Say what you feel. Jesus said, 'Out of the abundance of the heart the mouth speaketh' (Mt. 12:34). You cannot confess what you do not feel. Should your confession come short of what indeed ought to be confessed, all you can do is confess as much as you feel. And God will in due course convict you of yet another sin. This also will result in contrition. And when you confess, do it like a child. Don't say, 'He knows how I feel. He can see me.' Tell him. Confess every sin that you feel convicted of.

Name the place, the person, the event, the circumstance involved. Confess every sordid detail to God.

What James is really saying here is that you confess it to Jesus. Almost every time in the New Testament the word Lord is the Greek word *kyrios*, which is the common Greek word used for Jesus. What James is putting before us here is that you've got a most intimate relationship with the Lord Jesus. You tell him. He's your elder brother.

When I was a boy we used to sing a rather simple hymn:

> *Are you weary, are you heavy hearted?*
> *Tell it to Jesus, tell it to Jesus;*
> *Are you grieving over joys departed?*
> *Tell it to Jesus alone.*
> *Do the tears flow down your cheeks unbidden?*
> *Tell it to Jesus, tell it to Jesus;*
> *Have you sins that to men's eyes are hidden?*
> *Tell it to Jesus alone.*
> *Tell it to Jesus, tell it to Jesus,*
> *He is a friend that's well known;*
> *You've no other such a friend or brother,*
> *Tell it to Jesus alone.*

If you follow James' way of doing it your laughter is turned to mourning, your joy to heaviness. Then you humble yourself before the Lord Jesus and he will lift you up. And there will be real joy and a real lightness and a sense of glory. For the promise is: 'He will not always chide' (Ps. 103:9). 'If we confess our sins, he is faithful and just to forgive us our sins, and to cleanse us from all unrighteousness' (1 Jn. 1:9).

What God Does When We Confess

James uses the same word: 'Humble yourselves', as he used at the beginning of the epistle when he said, 'Let the brother of low degree rejoice in that he is exalted' (1:9). When you do humble yourself before the Lord he lifts you up.

But another thing that happens is that God will restore you to the inheritance that is yours in the kingdom of God. This also means that he will be the one to rectify your witness. You've done a lot of damage perhaps. There's not one of us who doesn't have a skeleton in his closet. There is that person we just would feel uneasy about trying to lead to the

Lord because we've let the Lord down. You leave that to him now. It is never your prerogative to do what God has promised to do. He said that 'all things work together for good to them that love God, to them who are the called according to his purpose' (Rom. 8:28).

Let him exalt you and he will vindicate you and turn things around at a visible level. The most wonderful thing is that, should this happen on a broad scale, if the church as a whole will do this, there is no way the world could be unaffected by us, by a church that is brought back to its calling.

For when the church is reconverted the world will stop laughing. When we stop laughing so will the world. When we start crying so will the world. When we are contrite the world will be. When we are convicted then we'll be in a position to take on the world and the world will be aroused by this sleeping giant called the church. And nothing shall get in our way.

18

A Touch of Greatness

James 4:10

We will take another look at this tenth verse of James chapter 4. This is another way James has of telling us how to make that painful transition from the flesh to the spirit.

When We Come To The End Of Ourselves

There is still another way to describe what is in James' mind when he makes this statement: that these Christians will come to the end of themselves, that they will have no place to go but to God. President Abraham Lincoln was once quoted as saying, 'Sometimes I'm driven to my knees with the conviction there's no place else to go.' What we have before us is a portrait of God's classic way of doing this very thing to a Christian so that he will come to the end of himself.

As Jonah put it when he was still in the belly of the fish, 'When my soul fainted within me I remembered the Lord' (Jonah 2:7). So James said, 'Let your laughter be turned to mourning, and your joy to heaviness. Humble yourselves in the sight of the Lord, and he shall lift you up.'

As we have seen, the rather sobering, if not embarrassing, thing is that these Christians that James is addressing, these Christian Jews, were finished anyway. They were doing about as much good as Jonah was when he was asleep in the sides of the ship while the world was tossed in unprecedented bewilderment. This is the thing. The Christian has a responsibility to his fellow man, to the church, to the world.

These Christians were furious. They were already humiliated but they didn't know it. James wanted them to experience inwardly what was already true of them outwardly. God with extraordinary patience was leading them to repentance. The problem was that though God wanted to use them he had to remain faithful to himself. Because here is this principle: 'God resisteth the proud, but giveth grace unto the humble.' God will not trust his power to a proud man. He will not trust his blessing to a proud church. But God will bring the same man and the same church to a state of humiliation. God had put these Christians through a humbling process by withholding success from them. As long as a person is succeeding he will never bother to reflect upon himself to see if he's doing anything wrong. This is why Dr Lloyd-Jones said that the worst thing that can happen to a man is to succeed before he's ready.

God Wants Us To Be Happy And To Succeed

James is saying, 'Look around you', to these Christians. 'Can't you see what's happening? You have lost the poor, you've lost the rich. You yourselves are divided within. And you've been filled with lust and greed.' And yet the most dazzling thought here is that God wants us to succeed. He wants us to be happy. So he says, 'Humble yourselves in the sight of the Lord, and he shall lift you up.' But is it a counterfeit success you want?

Many of us have ambitions which in their carnality are way, way short of what God has in mind. Sometimes we look at a particular situation and we say, 'All I want is for this situation to improve and I'll be happy.' But God wants more than that for you. Joseph had been betrayed by his brothers and had been falsely accused of trying to have an affair with Potiphar's wife and consequently was put in a dungeon. I suppose there was only one thing on Joseph's mind and that was to get out of there. But God had more in mind for Joseph.

Sometimes in our state of humiliation we just want the present situation to reverse. But God has something far more in mind than this immediate situation. You may want to win the battle; God wants you to win the war. 'Eye hath not seen, nor ear heard, neither have entered into the heart of man, the things which God hath prepared for them that love him' (1 Cor. 2:9).

Greatness Is By God's Design

God has true greatness in mind for every one of us. Here's your open invitation to greatness: 'Humble yourselves in the sight of the Lord, and' – see what happens – he will exalt you. God alone is great, yet he wants his people to be great and to experience greatness. Small men might have some success. Small men may even capture a seat of power, but they remain small whether they become millionaires or prime minister or president. There's no such thing as greatness by accident. It is by God's design. Greatness is owing to one thing and one thing alone: God's vindication. Men are great when God makes them great. Men are small when they try to be great.

If there's anything so incontrovertible that I could put before you it is this: that the latter half of the twentieth century has been characterized by a dearth of greatness on both sides of the Atlantic, both in church and state. Who have you seen lately [1981] that instinctively makes you think of greatness? The most scarce commodity on the horizon at the moment is not gold, minerals or oil, brains or technology; it is greatness. The source of this scarcity is the church's failure to be the salt of the earth. What did Jesus say? 'Ye are the salt of the earth: but if the salt have lost his savour, wherewith shall it be salted? It is thenceforth good for nothing, but to be cast out, and to be trodden under foot of men' (Mt. 5:13).

It is often forgotten that what Winston Churchill promised would be England's finest hour was undergirded by the fact that over half of Britain was in church and there were Christians everywhere on their knees. The last time Parliament called the nation to prayer was during World War II. Forty years later, somebody wrote to Margaret Thatcher suggesting that she called the nation to prayer and the reply came back: 'There doesn't seem to be a need for this.'

Here we are, the political leaders preoccupied with their own survival and their self-esteem, and the church is the laughing stock of this generation. It continues to go on with business as usual but only four per cent attend church, free churchmen, Catholics and Anglicans combined. There's only one thing that will change this nation, and that's when the church gets right with God – and that means us, standing in the need of prayer.

We are evangelistic failures

What do you suppose is the hardest problem when I say the church must get right? Is is liberalism? Is is modernism? Is it ecumenism? No, the heart of the problem is defective evangelism. That is precisely what was wrong with these Christian Jews. It was their failure to reach the lost of their generation that led to their falling. At the bottom of their rationale they were thinking not what Christianity could do for others, but what others could do for Christianity. They were thinking of their self-esteem, not the simple gospel. And God will not have this.

Nothing makes him angrier than when there is a perversion of the indiscriminate offer of the gospel, whether it be by theological design or sociological, economic motive. His Holy Spirit is grieved and the normal Christian graces are just gone. A silent backfire erupts. No loud explosion, only an inability to think clearly.

These Christians were in real trouble. They couldn't do anything right. But God is so jealous for his Son's witness that when it is discarded those who discard it pay for it. And yet everybody pays. For when the gospel doesn't reach man the world at large is impoverished.

A win-win situation

But when the church is true to its mission everybody wins.

Somebody told me that there was great revival in Northern Ireland under the preaching of William P. Nicholson. So many people who were involved in the revolution were converted that there was no sectarian infighting. And it is historically documented that the Wesleyan revival in England stopped a revolution like the one in France. When the church gets right with God, everybody will be affected. Let Parliament pass its laws, let trade unionists dispute with industrialists, let government call in the greatest minds and the greatest brains, but nothing will work until Britain gets right with God, and that means the church. Because God holds the destiny of every nation in his hand.

The responsibility that is ours is so sobering, and I'm talking to you. As an individual person cannot find peace until he's right with God, neither can a nation be lifted up as long as sin is excused and is justified and explained away. 'Righteousness exalteth a nation: but sin is a reproach to any people' (Prov. 14:34). England or any other country will not be great until the church is great. And the church will not be great until its top priority is soul winning.

Called Into Greatness

All the troubles that James is talking about are the consequence of defective evangelism. There's no church problem that cannot be solved overnight by continued fresh conversions: conversions to the Lord Jesus Christ. The great paradox before us is that these Christians were small by trying to be great, yet God nonetheless was calling them to greatness. But they underestimated what could happen. It's something beyond the present situation. God is calling small men to greatness.

Greatness is not feeling threatened

What is greatness? The answer is right here in this verse. First, greatness is not being threatened. 'Humble yourselves.' People are threatened because they don't humble themselves. When you humble yourself you're not threatened.

There is a play on words here in the Greek. There's more than one word that could be used, but James uses this word that by its own etymology is talking about the socio-economic class. James is calling these Christian Jews to identify with being lowly. But people cannot identify with lowliness. They're threatened by it.

You might condescend to the lowly. We all patronize and feel sorry for the lowly. That's not identification. James calls for true identification. Become like them. Be lowly like Jesus. 'The foxes have holes, and the birds of the air have nests, but the Son of Man hath not where to lay his head' (Mt. 8:20). Jesus was never threatened. But lowliness is, in fact, something that we ought quite easily to identify with because that's what we really are. We're dust. And we forget the pit from which we have been dug.

In Leviticus Moses put down this footnote, 'If a stranger sojourn with thee in your land, ye shall not vex him. But the stranger that dwelleth with you shall be unto you as one born among you, and thou shalt love him as thyself; for ye were strangers in the land of Egypt' (19:33–34). And it's repeated again in Deuteronomy 10:19: 'Love ye therefore the stranger: for ye were strangers in the land of Egypt.' Paul said to Timothy, 'We brought nothing into this world, and it is certain we can carry nothing out' (1 Tim. 6:7).

Lowly – when you are that you won't know what it is to be threatened. That's what real humility is. Greatness is not being threatened by another person. When a person is threatened he's afraid, he's defensive. To humble yourself is to take people as they are: spiritually, morally, sociologically, economically. You never think what they can do for you but what you can do for them, and that's greatness.

Greatness is not being passive

The second thing about greatness – it's not being passive. Greatness is boldly and autonomously acting upon God's imperative. He says, 'Humble yourselves.' Greatness is not waiting to be humbled, but seeing what one has to do. 'Humble yourselves' might mean doing the thing you fear or talking to that other person about the claims of Jesus Christ.

God isn't going to do any more than he's done. He's not going to supply any more grace, any more fruit of the Spirit. No more grace will be given and whatever else you do, don't pray, 'Lord, make me humble.' That's passing the buck. Greatness is humbling yourself.

What separates great men from others is that most of us wait for something to motivate us. How many of you are like that? You're waiting to be moved. But greatness is autonomy, having the integrity to see what is needed and doing it without further help.

That's the whole point in the parable of the talents. One came and said, 'Lord, thy pound hath gained ten pounds.' The second came, 'Lord, thy pound hath gained five pounds.' 'Well done.' But then came the one-talent man. This is typical of today's evangelical – still waiting on God, still scared to death that he's going to detract from the glory of God. He said, 'Lord ... I feared thee, because thou art an austere man: thou takest up that thou layedst not down, and reapest that thou didst not sow' (Lk. 19:20, 21). And so many of us are so afraid we're going to get in the flesh that God passes us by.

Jesus was not a passive person. Great men are never passive people. They are doers. There was a time when greatness would emerge from the reformed tradition. But not now. God uses the David Wilkersons, the Arthur Blessitts. I got a postcard from Arthur while he was in New Guinea carrying his cross. I don't know how many pick him to pieces, but Arthur has said, 'All I did was say, "God, give me something to do that nobody else will do." ' There'll be more people in heaven won to the Lord on a *one-to-one* basis because of Arthur Blessitt than perhaps any man in the history of the Christian church. I spent two hours with Arthur once and I knew at that moment: 'I'm in the presence of greatness.' I didn't want him to leave.

Greatness is not being self-conscious

The third thing about greatness is this: it is not being self-conscious. Small men are full of themselves. They are invariably self-conscious because they're taking their cue from others. They're motivated, they're affected, they're impressed by what others think of them. Jesus was never self-conscious. Small men live by projection. That is, they are always imagining what others will think if they do this or that, if they wear this or wear that, if they say this or say that. What will others think? Self-conscious. Smallness. Why do you suppose James said, 'Humble yourselves in the sight of the Lord'? Because greatness emerges only when you get self-conscious before God. How many of us are not at home in God's presence but feel at ease with people?

The prayer of Ezra is a prayer of greatness. He said, 'O my God, I am ashamed and blush to lift up my face to thee, my God: for our iniquities are increased over our head, and our trespass is grown up unto the heavens' (9:6). Greatness will emerge when we become self-conscious before God and unconscious of people and what they think. 'How can ye believe,' said Jesus, 'which receive honour one of another, and seek not the honour that cometh from God only?' (Jn. 5:44). When you desire nothing but God's approval, nothing else matters. That's what greatness is. It's not being threatened. It's not being passive. It's not being self-conscious. It's a case of Jesus Christ taking us over – 'and he shall lift thee up'.

Geatness Is Being Humble

Small men tend to promote themselves and they are dependent on their own resources, their own gift, their contacts and who they know. But greatness is God taking over. 'Promotion cometh neither from the east, nor from the west, nor from the south. But God is the judge: he putteth down one, and setteth up another' (Ps. 75:6–7). God exalts the one who humbles himself and who obeys without any further help. You've been given everything. But you're still waiting for something to push you. It's not going to come that way. Do it. And he will exalt you. We're talking about God's vindication.

I don't know why the Authorised Version translated this as 'he shall lift you up'. It's the same word used in 1 Peter 5:6, when the same thing is translated: 'he may exalt you'. It's God's way of telling us that greatness will be recognized. Do you have this fear that nobody will notice you? As long as that's your fear, they won't. 'He that loveth his life shall lose it; and he that hateth his life in this world shall keep it unto life eternal' (Jn. 12:25). God will exalt you when you can handle it, when it won't matter to you, but not before.

Keep in mind that James is saying this to Christians who were defective in their evangelism. You cannot possibly know your own potential until your witness for Jesus Christ. Begin by asking, 'What kind of a witness for the Lord am I?' Whoever you are, you are less than what you could be at any level until your gift as a soul winner is explored, discovered and refined.

It is only when the church fulfills her calling that she becomes 'the salt of the earth'. You may say, 'I can't.' I answer, 'You can.' Humble yourselves and the Lord will lift you up. When the church fulfills her calling she will become the salt of the earth, and when you fulfill yours you'll find yourself.

James wants you to mourn over what you've done because of what you've done to God, because of what you've done to yourself and because of what you have done to others. When you humble yourself in the sight of the Lord these three relationships are rectified because when you humble yourself you're not going to be threatened. When you humble yourself you won't be passive and it will do something for your self-image. Psychologically this is the healthiest treatment in the world. When you humble yourself in the sight of God you won't be self-conscious. And your relationship to God will be right. You will only blush before him. God will say, 'Well done.' And when he says that, that's enough, that matters.

When all of us take seriously our primary calling – winning souls – and bring men and women to church and stop saying that it can't be done, we will be seeing one person after another being converted to the Lord and those conversions will multiply and it won't be long until the world will say, 'What is this?' And we will answer, 'We've got right with God. We have obeyed.'

The most beautiful sight in the world is not the Grand Canyon or the Swiss Alps or a tropical sunset, but when somebody somewhere leads a person to Jesus. 'He that winneth souls is wise' (Prov. 11:30) because you're giving another person an entrance into heaven.

That's greatness. God wants you to succeed. But it begins by the rediscovery of our calling. When we do that and make it our top priority, everybody wins.

19

Greatness Discovered

James 4:10

This verse could be called an invitation to greatness. These Christian Jews whom James is addressing have shown themselves to be 'small men', but James invites them nonetheless to a taste of greatness.

How To Be Humble

The question that we have before us now is: 'How does one humble oneself?' The answer is that we begin to do it by accepting gladly the lot which God has designed for us. Humbling yourself is not trying to change what God has disclosed as being his will for you at the moment.

Humbling yourself means accepting God's purpose

An example of this verse which will enable us to see exactly what James means is the example of Joseph in the Old Testament. He had been betrayed by his eleven brothers and now, having been brought to Egypt, was put in a dungeon on false charges. After he was given this happy interpretation of the dream of the butler, Joseph tried to manipulate himself out of prison by bargaining with the butler who was restored to his former position. Joseph was given this interpretation and it was exactly fulfilled. And yet Joseph couldn't resist this temptation. He said, as the butler was leaving, 'Think on me when it shall be well with thee, and show kindness, I pray thee, unto me, and make mention of me unto Pharaoh' (Gen. 40:14). Joseph couldn't resist adding that personal word. Joseph needed to be humbled even further. He wanted to be out of the dungeon, but God wanted him in it.

Humbling yourself means accepting what God has designed. It means to dignify the trial he's put in your way, counting it all joy. Joseph had no choice. God has a way of making us humble ourselves. That's the first thing that is meant by humbling yourself.

Humbling yourself means refusing to vindicate yourself

The second thing is this: it is refusing to participate in your own vindication. The temptations to do so can be many and very real, so much so that the chance to vindicate yourself will look providential, as if God were handing the opportunity over to you on a silver platter. James says, 'Let no man say when he is tempted, I am tempted of God.' This equally applies to the natural desire to make yourself look good and another person look bad by taking advantage of the easy access to do so.

Humbling yourself, then, is accepting what is by design and intent God's exclusive prerogative. 'Vengeance is mine; I will repay, saith the Lord' (Rom. 12:19). Humbling yourself is believing that God is not only able to do it; it is believing that he can do it best when we refuse to take advantage of the opportunity to do it ourselves. It is absolutely refusing to compete with God's own plan to do it. It is refusing to take from him the pleasure he delights in most, executing justice. As the Psalmist put it: 'Thou hast a mighty arm: strong is thy hand, and high is thy right hand. Justice and judgment are the habitation of thy throne' (Ps. 89:13–14).

If we don't humble ourselves, God can do it for us. Joseph had two more years in the dungeon. God has a way of humiliating us that leaves events and circumstances out of our control. This matter of greatness is refusing to take advantage of the opportunity to vindicate yourself even if it's right there before your eyes.

Greatness is being unconscious of men but self-conscious only before God, and grieving over the slightest possibility that we have grieved the Holy Spirit. For greatness is placing such a high value on the esteem and honour of God that one is actually afraid to do anything that would rival God's honour. James said, 'Humble yourselves in the sight of the Lord, and he shall lift you up.'

How Greatness Is Discovered

Our part, then, is to leave it to God to do. How does God do this? How is greatness discovered? How God will do it and understanding how God goes about the matter of executing justice is to approach what is perhaps the greatest mystery of all time.

Abraham asked this question, 'Shall not the Judge of all the earth do right?' (Gen. 18:25). That is the nearest we ever get to the most perplexing question of all time: the problem of evil. Why does a just and merciful God permit suffering?

Our clue as to how God will vindicate himself (for after all, God is greatness beyond compare) is the way he vindicates his servants, who humble themselves. Because when God does it he always vindicates his servants in a way they would never have thought of. And it will do us no good to speculate how God will some day clear his name. Likewise, vengeance is his exclusive prerogative and he will clear his name in a way that the most brilliant novelist could not have construed in advance. When he does it, it will be obvious and open, but nobody will have thought of it.

Look at Joseph. He's in a dungeon, considered dead by his father, lost by his brothers, unjustly punished by Potiphar and now forgotten by the butler. As for the only person alive who could clear Joseph's name – Potiphar's wife – she wasn't talking. The consequences would have been too great for her to state the facts by this time, in any case. There appeared not the slightest hope in the world for Joseph. So with God. So far as the rational thinking of man is concerned God himself is in the dungeon. No man is able to clear his name but, as William Cowper put it:

> Blind unbelief is sure to err,
> And scan his work in vain;
> God is his own interpreter,
> And he will make it plain.

James tells us that vindication, in any case, is not only God's prerogative but also his promise. 'Humble yourselves in the sight of the Lord, and he shall lift you up.' For if greatness is being self-conscious before God and unconscious of men, James wants us equally to know that greatness will be discovered. There's no such thing as greatness that lies hidden for ever. There is nothing which God delights in more than in discovering greatness and causing everyone else to see it. But there is this one nagging problem: he will be party to no competition.

When you talk about vindication you are touching God's heart, his most sensitive nerve. Don't take from him what he lives for: the glory of his justice. If he sees anybody competing with that he backs off. He wants to do it all or he will do nothing. This should not surprise you. This is the way God deals with man at every level.

Take the way a person becomes a Christian. You will never become a Christian as long as you try to co-operate in your salvation, as long as you try to compete with the righteousness of Jesus Christ, as long as you think there's something in you that deserves attention and that there's some good work that you have done that will increase your bargaining power with God. As long as you think like that your becoming a Christian will be postponed. 'For there is none other name under heaven given among men, whereby we must be saved' (Acts 4:12). It's the name of Jesus that God has exalted. You cannot have the benefit of that name until you come to the end of yourself and admit you can do nothing. You let God do it all. And when you stand back, you see that the blood of Jesus shed on the cross is what God is after and that you can't do anything to add to that.

That is what the apostle Paul calls 'the righteousness of God revealed from faith to faith' (Rom. 1:17). This scarlet thread runs through every page of the Bible. Justice is executed at the level of the death of Jesus. That's the way men are saved but it applies equally to the execution of justice at other levels, not the least of which is this level of vindication. There is nothing we can do to bring it about. The moment you start you'll delay it.

How is greatness discovered? It's all in our text. 'Humble yourselves in the sight of the Lord, and he shall lift you up.' It is outside man. James did not say, 'Humble yourselves and you will lift yourself up.' For that is smallness, not greatness. No matter how gifted or how promising, or how seemingly inevitable that his greatness will be known, it lies outside man.

How do you suppose God lifted up Joseph? Here's a man who got off to a good start. He had a good family background, a loving father who gave him a coat of many colours. Joseph was even endowed with a special gift. He received prophecies through dreams and he could even interpret other people's dreams. The only bad thing to be said about Joseph on this is that he was rather proud of that gift and he wasn't very tactful in using it. He went to his brothers one day who were already jealous because of that coat of many colours. I don't know what would make a man do this, but he went and said to his brothers, 'I had another dream last night.' 'Well, let's hear this one.' 'You're not going to like it. I can't wait to tell you.' He said, 'We were binding sheaves in the field, and, lo, my sheaf arose, and also stood upright; and behold your sheaves stood round about, and made obeisance to my sheaf' (Gen. 37:7).

Despite that lack of tact and rather unsubtle pride, Joseph had something else going for him without which a father's love or an extraordinary gift was of no value. Joseph was in a dungeon and a forgotten man, but Stephen tells us: 'But God was with him' (Acts 7:9). My fellow Christians, that matters.

God holds the world in his hands

If it were not true that God is with us nothing else would matter but, as Paul put it: 'If God be for us, who can be against us? He that spared not his own Son, but delivered him up for us all, how shall he not with him also freely give us all things?' (Rom. 8:32). You may say, 'All right, God is with us. But wasn't God with Joseph's brothers also? They were in the covenant. How could God be with Joseph and with those who mistreated him?' The answer to that is right here in this book of James. James said, 'Know ye not that the friendship of the world is enmity with God? Whosoever therefore will be a friend of the world is the enemy of God.' The person who becomes worldly-minded and gives in to the flesh, as these eleven brothers did, sets himself up to be the object of God's justice and he will pay. But God was with Joseph, we're told. He wasn't with Potiphar or Potiphar's wife or the Pharaoh, the king of Egypt or the butler. But that didn't mean that God couldn't perform his purpose through Pharaoh. For God holds the nations in his hands.

This is why Isaiah could say that, to God, the nations are but a drop in the bucket (Isa. 40:15). Isaiah could see what seemed to be utter fantasy. 'That saith of Cyrus' – a secular man outside the tradition of God's covenant people, Cyrus, King of Assyria – 'He is my shepherd, and shall perform all my pleasure: even saying to Jerusalem, Thou shalt be built; and to the Temple, Thy foundation shall be laid' (Isa. 44:28). Or as Jeremiah put it: 'Be not afraid of the king of Babylon, of whom ye are afraid; be not afraid of him, saith the LORD: for I am with you to save you, and to deliver you from his hand' (42:11). With Nebuchadnezzar we are told that God gives the kingdom of men 'to whomsoever he will' (Dan. 4:17).

All Society Exists For God's Purposes

God has a way of bringing the most secular men and the most secular society to their knees. All society, no matter how godless, exists for God's covenant people. One evening Pharaoh, king of Egypt, went to sleep and he had a dream. He woke up. He was troubled by his dream. He realized this dream was different. But he did what he'd always done. He called in his sorcerers and magicians and asked them to interpret this dream.

No doubt these sorcerers had been eminently successful in times past. This was no trick because these sorcerers were in touch with witchcraft and evil spirits. Since the devil can give dreams, these sorcerers had easy access to the interpretation. But when God gives a dream, when God has a purpose, it is outside the bounds of evil men. 'For with God all things are possible' (Mt. 19:26). As Isaiah put it: 'My counsel shall stand, and I will do all my pleasure' (Isa. 46:10). As the Psalmist put it: 'Our God is in the heavens: he hath done whatsoever he pleased' (Ps. 115:3). The wisest magicians, the most successful sorcerers, were dumbfounded with this dream.

The butler overheard the conversations in the royal house and he got convicted of something. He came to Pharaoh and made a confession. He said, 'I do remember my faults this day. When I was in the dungeon there was with us a young man, a Hebrew, who interpreted a dream and it came out exactly like he said.' Soon, then, Pharaoh sent and called Joseph, and they brought him hastily out of the dungeon: and he shaved himself, and changed his raiment, and came in unto Pharaoh (Gen. 41:14).

The world needs your gift

All of this was happening suddenly. But God was working outside of Joseph. And yet it was Joseph's gift, after all, that was needed. So with you. God has given you a gift nobody else has. God has a purpose for you which nobody else can fulfill, but not until you humble yourself.

By this time Joseph's humiliation had done him some good. He was claiming that he had no gift at all. 'Pharaoh said unto Joseph, I have dreamed a dream, and there is none that can interpret it: and I have heard say of thee, that thou canst understand a dream to interpret it. And Joseph answered Pharaoh, saying, It is not in me' – that's the new Joseph – 'God shall give Pharaoh an answer of peace' (vv. 15–16). The old Joseph came in flaunting his gift to his brothers, making them jealous. The new Joseph said, 'It is not in me.'

God cannot use us until we are indeed nothing. We came into this world with nothing and it is certain we can carry nothing out. And that's the exhortation: humble yourself. Become what you already are. You're nothing. See it and accept it.

Joseph interpreted Pharaoh's dream, but Joseph's humiliation led him to a multiplication of graces and gifts. Added to his gift to interpret a dream was the gift of wisdom. Joseph went on to give sound counsel. You know the rest of the story. Joseph was made second only to Pharaoh in Egypt, but this exaltation was outside himself. 'Humble yourselves in the sight of the Lord, and he shall lift you up.'

God does not grant greatness or its discovery for its own sake. We are to be useful in the world. These Christian Jews whom James was addressing had become impotent in the world, and James' concern was that the world would see the authenticity of the church.

The secret of Joseph's greatness

If you want to learn the secret of Joseph's greatness you ought to know that it was not in his gift of having wise counsel to Pharaoh or in the fact that he was second in Egypt. The secret of Joseph's greatness was this: before he was ever rescued from the dungeon, he forgave his brothers. God will let you suffer until you do that, until forgiving that person is less painful than the suffering God put you through. 'We must through much tribulation enter into the kingdom of God' (Acts 14:22). Joseph entered the kingdom of God before he entered the kingdom of Pharaoh.

Jesus said, 'If ye forgive not men their trespasses, neither will your Father forgive your trespasses' (Mt. 6:15). Joseph had come to appreciate God's greater purpose in the world more than how he himself was regarded personally. Joseph could look at his brothers and say, 'Look here, you meant it for evil, God meant it for good. It's his way of preserving life. He wants you here. He wants you to have a future.' (Gen. 50:20). For greatness is seeing God's purpose in the world and devoting oneself to that, not to a personal concern.

When God brought Joseph to the place that he became enamoured with the glory of God alone, everything else seemed secondary. So we have in Genesis 45 and again in chapter 50 what I think is the most exquisite and sublime description of greatness to be found in any body of literature on the earth. 'It wasn't you that did it', said Joseph to his brothers. 'God did it. It was not you that sent me here, but God.' And that's what matters. Joseph's greatness was established because God saw in him a great heart.

One last thing. When our heart is right and exactly as God would mould it and shape it, we don't really care whether we're discovered or exalted or lifted up. Why? Because God has discovered us and when he knows, that's enough. Stephen's finest hour was when, as they were bouncing stones off his head, he said, 'Wait, I see Jesus standing at the right hand of God.' And then he bowed and prayed, 'Lord, lay not this sin to their charge' (Acts 7). How could Stephen pray that way? Because he really forgave them. That's greatness discovered. And that's what James is after. For he's been saying to us that 'the wisdom that is from above is first pure, then peaceable, gentle, and easy to be intreated, full of mercy and good fruits, without partiality, and without hypocrisy' (3:17). 'Humble yourselves in the sight of the Lord, and he shall lift you up.'

And what if your greatness is not discovered until the final hour, even at your death, even in heaven? I answer, if it is discovered then that is soon enough.

20

A Glimpse of Smallness

James 4:11a

I have given us a glimpse of greatness, that is, true greatness: how it is described and how it is discovered. It is described in the words of James 4 verse 10: 'Humble yourselves in the sight of the Lord.' The discovery of greatness is God's prerogative: 'And he shall lift you up' – he will exalt you. James invites every Christian to experience true greatness by humbling himself, by coming to terms with what he really is – nothing – that he might become what grace is designed to do, namely to make us like our Lord Jesus Christ.

Humiliation Comes Before Exaltation

Paul said to the Philippians: 'Let this mind be in you, which was also in Christ Jesus: who, being in the form of God, thought it not robbery to be equal with God: but made himself of no reputation, and took upon him the form of a servant, and was made in the likeness of men: and being found in fashion as a man, he humbled himself and became obedient unto death, even the death of the cross' (2:5–8). To the one who is humbled and who humbles himself there is the promise of exaltation. It is humiliation first, exaltation later. And only God can do the exalting. The irony of these Christian Jews is this: they were small because they were trying to be great. They tried to be great by trying to appeal to those who, to them, were great people. And so they were experiencing the pain of being abased. Not only had they become the laughing stock of the world, but they were beginning to be the laughing stock to each other. When a church becomes defective in its evangelism, everybody loses.

The Result Of Defective Evangelism

When a church is effectively engaged in the enterprise of evangelism there is a love for one another. But when a church is not true to its calling then the people in it begin to hate each other. That greatness that is promised to every believer is turned into its opposite, double mindedness.

Being a soul winner is the best cure for worldliness. A fisher of men is almost always fairly well off at the spiritual level. The Christian who isn't a soul winner is unhappy with himself. The consequence of our being evangelistic failures is instability, and this instability usually becomes apparent to everybody. To put it another way, a worldly Christian forfeits the normal Christian graces that are promised to every believer: the joy of sins forgiven, the sense of God's presence, peace, the knowledge of his will. Though the believer remains a Christian he doesn't seem like one. He even forces God to treat him like an enemy.

Thinking And Speaking Evil

James, as a consequence of that, is forced to have to say things that are beneath the kind of advice a Christian should need, on account of their smallness – advice providing us with a glimpse of that smallness: 'Speak not evil one of another, brethren.' What a pity that he had to say that. But he did. And we should have known it was coming. He talked all about the tongue back in chapter 3. They were doing everything wrong, so he has to say it again using a stronger word. The Greek for 'Speak not evil one of another' means 'to blab out'. A Christian who is living at the level of the spirit not only does not speak evil, he doesn't even think evil. This is what Paul said in 1 Corinthians 13: Love 'thinketh no evil' (v. 5). In fact, the New American Standard Version says that love 'does not take into account a wrong suffered'.

It's a bad thing to think evil. It's worse to speak evil. But to speak evil against a brother or a sister in Christ is to stoop so low and to become so small that one becomes no different from the world. It is blatant disgracefulness and beyond anything that should penetrate the realms of the Christian church. But because these Christians couldn't reach the world they had begun to blame each other.

You may ask, 'Why does a Christian speak evil of his brother?' There's only one explanation: if you speak evil of your brother or your sister you betray that there's something wrong with your relationship with Christ. Remember how Jesus put it in Matthew 25: 'Inasmuch as ye have done it

unto one of the least of these my brethren, ye have done it unto me'
(v. 40). So when you speak against your brother or your sister, you're
doing it to Jesus.

Speaking evil is never justified

There is never a justification for speaking evil against a brother or sister in
Christ. It is always wrong. Not only that, it will always be discovered and
judged by God himself sooner or later. Like greatness, smallness will
always be discovered. As Moses put it a long time ago: 'Be sure your sin
will find you out' (Num. 32:23). Jesus said, 'There is nothing covered,
that shall not be revealed; neither hid, that shall not be known. Therefore
whatsoever ye have spoken in darkness shall be heard in the light; and that
which ye have spoken in the ear in closets shall be proclaimed upon the
housetops' (Lk. 12:2–3).

It's scary, isn't it? But God calls us to greatness, the devil invites us to
smallness. When we speak evil of a brother we, in that very moment,
demonstrate to all who hear that we have accepted the devil's invitation to
smallness and join a large company of men. There may be a dearth of
greatness today; there's no dearth of smallness. But smallness has nothing
in common with our great God. And I hope and pray that these sermons
from James will inspire us to be utterly unlike those Christian Jews who
had become so bankrupt spiritually that they had to take out their
frustrations on one another.

What does it mean 'to speak evil' of another? There's a subtlety here
that we must not avoid or the verse won't even speak to us. For example,
many of us often deny that we have spoken evil against a person if we can
prove that we have spoken the truth, as if proving the veracity of what we
have said about somebody justifies saying it. We say, 'Well, I only told the
truth and the truth won't wrong anybody.' That is wrong. For the truth
can hurt sometimes more than a lie. A lie will usually die on the vine. The
truth is what hurts.

How would you like somebody to discover all that's to be known
about you and tell it? They'd be telling the truth, would they not? Is that
good or evil? I answer, it is evil. Therefore it is not only possible to speak
evil by telling the truth, normally telling the truth is the *chief* way you
speak evil against another person. What James is really after here is the
motive. Why did you tell the truth? Was it to help the person you said it
about? Was it to help the person you said it to?

Ninety-five per cent of what Job's friends said to him and about him
was true. That's why it was so hard for him to have to take. But were these

comforters better off? Was Job better off? Not only that, 95percent of what Job said back to them was true. Was he better off? Were they? In the end they all got rebuked when God came out of the whirlwind. Job got the victory when he repented in dust and ashes and prayed for his friends.

Speaking evil betrays our insecurity

What is smallness? It is the constant state of having your self-esteem threatened. It is insecurity. Speaking evil (saying something that is less than flattering about another person) is often a defence mechanism to hide our insecurity and failure to trust God. But it always backfires. Instead of *hiding* our insecurity it *betrays* our insecurity. Speaking evil against a person is a way of exalting ourselves. It's really our effort to reach out and try this art of vindicating ourselves. God doesn't like that. It's the opposite of humbling yourself. But the one who humbles himself shows that he's not threatened.

Passing judgement betrays our smallness

Smallness is the frantic state of being threatened, to refuse to identify with what we really are. We try to foster an image of what we're not. The cheapest way to do it is to say something about another person that makes that person look less than perfect. But if that person is less than perfect he's got enough problems already without your compounding them. Smallness is the constant state of being defensive, the opposite of greatness and humility. Greatness is not passivity but rather acting autonomously upon the command of Scripture: 'Humble yourselves'. Smallness is waiting for God to do it. Greatness is doing it. Smallness is to experience nothing but the overruling grace of God. It knows little of growing positively, of responding positively to the broad commandments of Scripture. Smallness is being withdrawn, sensitive, ready to attack the moment one's self-esteem is threatened. Greatness is being aggressive with respect to what Luther called 'new obedience'. Smallness is being aggressive with respect to our personal feelings. Smallness, then, is selfishness. Greatness is not being self-conscious before men but self-conscious before God. Smallness is putting self-esteem before God's honour.

The easiest thing in the world to do is to think you are honouring God by guarding your own self-esteem. Nothing is ever more providential than temptation, than the opportunity to participate in your own vindication. When you are motivated only by the glory of God your personal feelings diminish to neutrality and forgiveness becomes as easy as anything you ever experienced.

One other aspect of speaking evil is that it can be done non-verbally. I refer not merely to body language, because you can by the expression on your face convey an impression. But I also refer to what you don't say about somebody. Smallness is not only speaking evil, but it is withholding certain facts that would clarify things and set the record straight. It's withholding what you know that is good and honourable, what you know would be inconsistent with the main impression you're trying to convey. What you don't say can communicate the impression that you want another to receive without your actually saying a word. It is not the letter but the spirit, in this case, that kills. You can interpret this verse of James legalistically, as if to avoid committing a sin, and end up sinning more.

But greatness is protecting someone from a bad impression of another person. These words are in Luke 6:31: 'As ye would that men should do to you, do ye also to them likewise.' All that James is saying comes right down to this, the golden rule. James will end up this chapter with these words: 'Therefore to him that knoweth to do good, and doeth it not, to him it is sin' (v. 17).

Legalistic Christianity Puts A Ceiling On Righteousness

The Pharisees hated the Sermon on the Mount because it exposed their sin. The truth is that without the spiritual interpretation of the law the Pharisees never felt any shame over feelings of lust or over hate or personal vengeance.

The Sermon on the Mount, or what Luke calls 'the Sermon on the Plain', is the spiritual interpretation of the law. When you interpret the law as Jesus did you end up with a law much higher than that to which the Pharisees claimed to be so devoted. For the spiritual interpretation of the law convicts all of us.

The spiritual interpretation of the law is the standard set for the way life is to be lived in what Jesus called 'the kingdom of God'. If you bypass the spiritual interpretation of the law what you have is a legalistic Christianity that puts a ceiling on righteousness. Because a Christianity that limits righteousness to mere morality is not what Jesus came to show us. The Mosaic law limits a person to outward performance. It has no power to produce what Jesus taught.

The Mosaic law motivates through fear of punishment, and at best it only makes a man civil. It restrains a man from sin all right. The law can do that, but it is negative at best. It is a restraint both on the flesh and the spirit.

This is why the apostle Paul put it like this in Romans 8:3–4: 'For what the law could not do, in that it was weak through the flesh, God sending his own Son in the likeness of sinful flesh, and for sin, condemned sin in the flesh: that the righteousness of the law might be fulfilled in us, who walk not after the flesh, but after the Spirit.' Paul also said in Galatians 5:16: 'Walk in the Spirit, and ye shall not fulfil the lust of the flesh.'

The Christian knows no fear of punishment. Why? Paul said it in Romans 8:1: 'There is therefore now no condemnation to them which are in Christ Jesus.' Our motivation to be godly men and women is twofold:

- First, we're motivated because Christ has fulfilled the law and we're in Christ and we cannot be condemned.
- Secondly, we want to be godly because the Spirit motivates us to go beyond the design and purpose of the Mosaic law so that if we live in the Spirit and walk in the Spirit we do not fulfil the lust of the flesh. So when we walk in the Spirit not only is the law being kept, but we are moving beyond it, doing what the law could never do, namely to produce 'love, joy, peace, longsuffering, gentleness, goodness, faith' (Gal. 5:22). The law doesn't tell you how to forgive. It only tells you how to be moral, legally moral. The moral law bears no inner joy.

To do what James is after means great joy indeed.

'Speak not evil one of another, brethren.' That may seem negative, but it is not only positive but something that can be carried out only as a consequence of great positive growth. To refuse to speak evil and to insist on conveying only the good is to operate at the level of the Spirit. To speak evil and to say something that is less than flattering about a person or to withhold certain information is to operate at the level of nature.

True Greatness

To put it another way, not to speak evil of another, not to withhold the good, is to go right against nature. It is the hardest thing in the world to do. All of us are small men by nature. Shakespeare said, 'Some men are born great, some achieve greatness, and some have greatness thrust upon them.' But Shakespeare was talking about a different kind of greatness. We're talking now about true greatness.

No man is born great. Quite the opposite, as Paul said, 'There is none righteous, no, not one: there is none that understandeth, there is none that seeketh after God. They are all gone out of the way, they are together become unprofitable; there is none that doeth good, no, not one. Their throat is an open sepulchre; with their tongues they have used deceit; the poison of asps is under their lips: whose mouth is full of cursing and bitterness' (Rom. 3:10–14). That's what all of us are by nature.

True growth is against nature

If somebody has not been very nice to you and yet you keep giving a good impression of that person to another, that is going against nature. But if you want to speak evil and give the impression that you want to convey to bolster your self-esteem, that's the most natural thing in the world to do. There's not one of us that doesn't have the temptation several times a day to say something that's not very flattering about another person, especially if somebody's not been very nice to us.

In James chapter 1 he says, 'Let no man say when he is tempted, I am tempted of God ... but every man is tempted, when he is drawn away of his own lust' (vv. 13, 14). Lust here is not only with regard to sexual desire but to anything to fulfil satisfaction of the flesh. We are by nature threatened when someone else is admired more than we are. So if you fulfil James' admonition not to speak evil against another you are demonstrating great positive growth for which there is no natural explanation.

Revival is something for which there's no natural explanation. Let me tell you how to have a revival in your soul. When you can be loving and kind you are doing something utterly unlike nature. More than that: to refuse to speak evil of any brother or sister is fully to inherit the kingdom of God indeed. It's to know a great measure of peace, of joy, of glory, of power, of blessing. And should you refuse to speak evil when you have been the object of evil speaking, Peter says, 'The spirit of glory and of God resteth upon you' (1 Pet. 4:14).

If you ever get a taste of the spirit of glory resting upon you, not only will you be better motivated to refrain from evil speaking in the future, but you will actually learn to thank God for the very occasion and the very persons who made the spirit of glory possible. Stephen was being stoned, and he was actually saying, 'Lord, lay not this sin to their charge' (Acts 7:60). It's amazing, isn't it, that Stephen could pray that way. But do you know why he did it? Not only did he really forgive them, he was so thankful for them that he thought it would be unfair for them to be punished when they had done so much for him. Jesus prayed, 'Father, forgive them; for they know not what they do' (Lk. 23:34). I wouldn't be surprised to find the very people in heaven that nailed the nails in. And I wouldn't be surprised to find that some or all of those who stoned Stephen were converted. We know what an impact it had on Saul of Tarsus.

The less we give in to temptation that emerges at the level of nature, the more we 'experience the Spirit', to use Tozer's phrase. For the more we experience the Holy Spirit, the more we want of the Holy Spirit, until we wouldn't risk grieving the Spirit for anything in the world, as in the case of stooping so low and becoming so small as to speak evil of a brother or a sister in Christ. We mock God when we pray for revival but fail in this.

21

Smallness Discovered

James 4:11–12

At this point James carries his admonition a step further. He says that speaking against a brother or a sister in Christ shows automatically, as it were, that you've made a judgement. The awful thing is that these Christians weren't blabbing out against the world (not that that would be right) but against their brethren. James goes on: 'He that speaketh evil … and judgeth his brother' – what about him? – he 'speaketh evil of the law'. What we have here is not only a demonstration of smallness, but of self-elevation. If we speak in this way we have deemed ourselves qualified to judge. The Greek word 'to judge' is one which means 'to make a separation', 'to make a distinction'.

Putting Yourself Above The Law

It's bad enough to speak against a brother or sister but, according to James, there is something fundamentally more serious at the bottom when you judge somebody. You have in that moment put yourself on a pedestal. When you judge, according to James, you're not saying something about another person so much as you're saying a lot about yourself. You have imputed to yourself the qualification of being a judge.

You might ask, 'What's wrong with that?' In a sense there's nothing wrong with it on the condition that there's no beam in your eye. Here's the way Jesus put it: 'Thou hypocrite, first cast out the beam out of thine own eye; and then shalt thou see clearly to cast out the mote out of thy brother's eye' (Mt. 7:5). If you're judging, you have assumed you've cast out the beam. The act of judging always draws attention not to the one you're judging, but to yourself.

What Jesus said in Matthew 7:1: 'Judge not, that ye be not judged', is true partly because that's the way human nature works. Once we are on the pedestal and draw attention to ourselves, people look at us. Try it sometime. You will see it in action every time. The moment you say something to another that isn't very nice the other will spontaneously think something about you.

Jesus stated a fact of human nature but what James is saying here, apart from the fact of the way human nature works, is that the most serious thing of all is that when we play the game of judging we're speaking against the law. When you speak against the law you have bitten off more than you can chew. You've spoken against God's instrument by which sin is named and by which sin is judged. So you're not only elevating yourself above that other person, you are claiming to be qualified to put yourself above the law. And when we put ourselves above the law we have in that moment made ourselves equal with the lawgiver: God. And James said, 'There is one lawgiver' – not two – 'who is able to save and to destroy: who art thou that judgest another?'

God Is Jealous: Vindication Is His Prerogative

When we have put ourselves above the law we've made ourselves equal with the lawgiver. There are some sins that are worse than others. The book of Leviticus makes that clear. But when we begin to tamper with the role of playing God we're touching something more dangerous than wet fingers on a high voltage wire. 'I am the LORD: that is my name: and my glory will I not give to another' (Isa. 42:8). God is jealous. He says so. In fact, James alludes to it in verse 5 of this chapter. God takes seriously what is his property and we're bought with a price. God will not have anybody trying to do what is his exclusive prerogative.

The subject of vindication touches God's heart. It's his most sensitive nerve. Not only does he not want our help, he won't have it. Thus, if we speak evil of another person, if we judge another person, instead of God judging that one that we decided we'd judge, he just backs off and lets us have it all to ourselves.

It's a question of whether you want God to judge or you want to do it. If you want God to judge, don't help him. If you want to judge, God lets you get on with it. If you want to speak evil of another person, go on. If you want to put yourself above the law, go right on. If you want to play God, there won't be any thunder and lightning and you won't particularly feel that it's the worst thing you ever did. God isn't going to do a thing. At least, not then.

Forcing God to treat you as an enemy

The moment we judge another, God is turning his wrath not upon the one we are judging but upon us. If God turns his wrath on us 'eye hath not seen, nor ear heard' the sorrow that we will incur. I know what it's like to regret something that grieved the Spirit more than anything in the world. Let's find one other person who knew what it was like, in Lamentations 3: 'I am the man that hath seen affliction by the rod of his wrath. He hath led me, and brought me into darkness, but not into light. Surely against me is he turned; he turneth his hand against me all the day ... Also when I cry and shout, he shutteth out my prayer' (vv. 1–3, 8).

For the same God who wants to discover greatness also wants to discover smallness. And when he discovers it, it will be in such a way that everybody will see it and you will know your time has come. As he said in Proverbs 1: 'Ye have set at nought all my counsel, and would none of my reproof: I also will laugh at your calamity; I will mock when your fear cometh' (vv. 25–26). If greatness is there it will be discovered. If smallness is there it will be discovered.

The question is, what principle is at work when smallness is discovered? The answer is, the law of God, the Mosaic law. Here's an often overlooked but most rewarding distinction: that the Christian is under the law of liberty in so far as his eternal salvation is concerned, but when he looks to the world he forces God to treat him as an enemy. This is why James had to say 'So speak ye, and so do, as they that shall be judged by the law of liberty' (2:12). 'That's what you want, isn't it?' says James. 'Ye adulterers and adulteresses, know ye not that the friendship of the world is enmity with God? Whosoever therefore will be a friend of the world is the enemy of God' (4:4).

The Christian is not under the Mosaic law. He is under what James calls the 'law of liberty'. The Christian life, says James, is to be lived by the law of the kingdom, the royal law of Scripture: 'Thou shalt love thy neighbour as thyself ' (Mt. 19:19). It's what Paul called the 'law of Christ'. 'Bear ye one another's burdens, and so fulfil the law of Christ' (Gal. 6:2). It is the law of liberty that will save all of us, says James, because 'mercy rejoiceth against judgement' (2:13). In the end you're going to be saved. But when a Christian is friendly with the world, when you don't live by the law of the kingdom and you begin to speak evil of one another and judge one another, you force God to treat you as he does the world with whom he's at enmity.

What law do you suppose is in force between God and the world? It's the law of Moses. So said Paul to Timothy, 'The law is good, if a man use it lawfully; knowing this, that the law is not made for a righteous man, but for the lawless and disobedient, for the ungodly and for sinners, for unholy and profane, for murderers of fathers and murderers of mothers, for manslayers, for whoremongers, for them that defile themselves with mankind, for menstealers, for liars, for perjured persons, and if there be any other thing that is contrary to sound doctrine; according to the glorious gospel of the blessed God' (1 Tim. 1:8–11).

The law has various functions and I'll name three. First, to name sin. Paul said, 'I had not known lust, except the law had said, Thou shalt not covet' (Rom. 7:7). Second, to restrain sin through fear of punishment. And third, to mete out the appropriate punishment. The law is redundant for a Christian, who lives by a higher law, the law of love. James calls it the 'royal law of scripture' which always fulfils the Mosaic law. But when a Christian becomes worldly-minded he forces God in the end to treat him as an enemy.

What does it mean for God to treat a Christian as an enemy? If the Christian proceeds to stage four in the chastening of God and perhaps even to stage five, that's as far as you can go. Stages one to three relate to lusting and quarrelling and not listening to God's Word. Stage four is when a Christian gets his way and God grants him the request and sends leanness to his soul (Ps. 106:15). He falls into open sin and he gets caught and everybody sees it. Stage five is when that Christian becomes of no use to God whatsoever, what Paul called 'a castaway' (1 Cor. 9:27). This means that the law which ought never to apply to a Christian is now not only applicable but even in force.

In the Old Testament it was the duty of the priesthood to carry out certain punishments, but in the New Testament we're all priests. Because of this God himself has promised to step in. He carries out his own words. By his own hand he carries out what the Old Testament priests did by their hands. When a Christian becomes worldly, lustful, full of vengeance, he forces God to treat him like an enemy and the consequence is that God enacts judgements upon the Christian, sometimes in this life so severe, almost ruthless, that one would actually think that the person on whom the judgement is sent is not a Christian.

Treating The Law With Contempt

What does it mean to speak evil of the law, to judge the law, to treat it with contempt? That is to render it as nothing, powerless, useless. It is to say, 'God isn't going to punish this person, so I will.'

If somebody has mistreated you and you want God to get him for it, first of all remember that you're not quite sure whether that person deserves all that. Maybe you're the one that was really in the wrong. But you think you're right, don't you? If you've got vindication coming you'll get it. But just in case you don't have it coming, back off. For sooner or later the truth will be out.

God has a way of clearing the record. You can save yourself a lot of embarrassment if you won't in the meantime try to clear the record yourself. God's going to do it and everybody will see it clearly and there won't be any debate then. But if you are so anxious to be cleared and you want God to get at somebody and you say, 'God's not doing it. I don't like what's going on. God ought to get to that person. I've been treated horribly', or so you say, 'I see God has hidden himself. He isn't going to get even with this person who has done this to me so I must take into my own hands what God apparently isn't going to do', this is what I call a sin of haste. It's like the children of Israel who gave up hope that God was going to keep his word. They 'rose up to play' (Exod. 32:6). God said, 'I sware in my wrath that they should not enter into my rest' (Ps. 95:11), and they didn't.

The law says, 'I will in no way clear the guilty' (Exod. 34:7). To speak evil of the law is to say that God isn't punishing the guilty, that he's clearing this person who ought to be punished. When I judge the law I am saying, 'I will in no way clear the guilty. God is silent so I'll step in. God isn't acting so I will act.'

If you really believe that friendship with the world is enmity with God and you really believe that God should deal with this or that situation, let him do it. You'd better not do it, because if you try, God will let you. But then you'll get it from him as well.

God is no respecter of persons. We all like to think God likes us just a little more than he likes others, that we're something special. 'You don't understand me but God does. He knows I mean well.' But when you find out that God is no respecter of persons you will fear him. None of us have a head start. None of us are special in ourselves.

At the bottom of James 4:4 about being friendly with the world and having God as an enemy is a profound truth with regard to the Christian and the use of the law. The Christian is not under the law regarding his salvation or his sanctification. But the Christian who lives disgracefully by showing contempt for the law of the kingdom puts himself back under the very law that is meant to apply to the disobedient. And when a Christian puts himself back in that condition he is at the mercy of the eternal God who, according to James, 'is able to save and to destroy'. You wonder why it is that God honours obedience, that he would say, 'Draw nigh to me and I will draw nigh to you.' This is why Peter could say 'The time is come that judgement must begin at the house of God: and if it first begin at us, what shall the end be of them that obey not the gospel of God?' (1 Pet. 4:17).

What It Means To Be A Doer Of The Law

What does it mean to be a doer of the law? It means three things all at once, if you take James seriously:

* First, Christ has fulfilled the law. He is your doer. You are in Christ.
* Second, you are living by the law of the kingdom: love one another, love your neighbour as yourself. Therefore you are also keeping every one of the Ten Commandments.
* Third, if you are a doer of the law you have an abiding faith in God's exclusive prerogative to execute justice.

In a word, to speak evil of another person is to speak evil of the law, to judge the law. But a doer of the law is saying, 'I will let God do it his way, in his time, even if he postpones doing it until the final day.' For to be a doer of the law is not to care whether God vindicates you now or then. By the way, if you are fully committed to the honour that comes from God only, it doesn't make one scrap of difference when God vindicates, how he vindicates or if he does it at all. Stephen got to the place that he asked God not to do it. He said, 'Lay not this sin to their charge.' And I believe God answered that prayer. Paul said to the Corinthians: 'Therefore judge nothing before the time, until the Lord come, who both will bring to light the hidden things of darkness, and will make manifest the counsels of the hearts: and then shall every man have praise of God' (1 Cor. 4:5). Does that bother you? Do you mind having to wait that long? If it does, it shows you're still full of yourself.

Not to wait for God to vindicate is to render the law null and void and set yourself up as the one who must do what God apparently isn't going to do. Be careful about this. James says it is far better to let God have the last word. For the same God who delights in executing justice by exalting the one who humbles himself, equally delights in executing justice by abasing the one who exalts himself. That's what Jesus said: 'Everyone that exalteth himself shall be abased; and he that humbleth himself shall be exalted' (Lk. 18:14).

James says that God is able to save and to destroy. That shows what God can do with reference to eternity, but also it shows what God can do with reference to time. The Greek here shows what God has the power to do but also, according to Jesus, what he has the authority to do. For Jesus said, 'There is nothing covered, that shall not be revealed; neither hid, that shall not be known. Therefore whatsoever ye have spoken in darkness shall be heard in the light; and that which ye have spoken in the ear in closets shall be proclaimed upon the housetops. And I say unto you my friends, Be not afraid of them that kill the body, and after that have no more that they can do. But I will forewarn you whom ye shall fear: Fear him, which after he hath killed hath power to cast into hell: yea, I say unto you, Fear him' (Lk. 12:2–5).

What Happens When We Judge Another

God can equally execute justice before all in the here and now, or he can cast into hell. You may ask, 'How would God do it in the here and now? How is smallness discovered should it come out in the here and now?' The first is this: that the very act of judging another itself does it in the here and now because everybody can see you. 'Judge not, that ye be not judged.' So we who judge others disclose our smallness in that moment. It tells more about ourselves than the one that we would want to put down.

The second way it can happen in the here and now is that our smallness is discovered when greatness is set right alongside smallness. When we've been small, God has a way of making us ashamed of ourselves by the clear contrast between greatness and our smallness. The greatness of Jesus was by not saying a word, and Peter's smallness came out. 'He went out, and wept bitterly' (Mt. 26:75).

Smallness, however, is eventually discovered if it proceeds from stage three to stage four, and sometimes stage five, of God's chastening. This is the case when God lets a man have so much rope that he hangs himself. He falls into a trap or into sin that is known by everybody. And eventually if it is not caught in time he becomes a castaway in God's service.

Leave things to God to sort out – but confess first

James concludes this section by asking a rhetorical question: 'Who art thou that judgest another?' It's a question designed to help us see our smallness before it is too late. These Christians were at stage three. How many of us are at stage three? We've not made the transition from the flesh to the spirit. We're still coping as though nature is all there is and we know nothing of that sense of God. This question is designed to make us see our smallness before it is too late. But you may ask, 'What if we have sinned? What if we have judged another? What if we have spoken evil of the law? And what if we have militated against God's prerogative and rivalled him?' The answer is wonderful and simple. Confess it to God and nobody else. Say, 'God, I'm sorry. Have mercy on me.' You may say, 'Shouldn't I try to straighten out all the damage I've done?' No. Let God do that. Romans 8:28 is true.

There's another reason, though, that you shouldn't try to straighten it out. Here's where a lot of us make the mistake. We admit we are wrong. We confess it. And now we go around being a busybody after all. It is possible for a Christian to repent by coming in the front door and then going right out the back door to try to clear everything and straighten his name. If we're not careful we'll be playing God at the opposite end. It's one thing to play God by judging and speaking evil, it's another by trying to rectify everything.

To be a doer of the law indeed is fully to believe that vindication is God's exclusive prerogative. And God is the one who makes all things work together for good. I don't know how he does it, but he does. When we try to do it God backs off and leaves us to ourselves again. God wants us to know that he's alive. God is on the throne. He wants to manifest his glory. It is our task to do one thing. 'If we confess our sins, he is faithful and just to forgive us our sins, and to cleanse us from all unrighteousness' (1 Jn. 1:9). 'Against thee, thee only, have I sinned' (Ps. 51:4). To be cleansed, by the way, is enough, for that is the justice that matters.

22

Being Bored With Church

James 4:13

Now we enter into a slightly new section of our general epistle of James. The fourth chapter of James up to now has been a general description of these Christian Jews with instructions on how to make the transition from living in the flesh, which they were doing, to living in the spirit.

God's Chastening Process

James' purpose in this new section is this: he is trying to rescue these Christians from entering into stage four of this chastening of God. May I remind you what the stages are:

- Stage one is when God shatters us by his Word – to let our problem be solved by his Word successfully operating on our hearts.
- Stage two is when things outside our control happen to us that bring us to a place that hopefully will lead us to repentance.
- Stage three is when we are permitted to live as though we're not Christians and yet not have our desires fulfilled.
- Stage four is when God lets us have our way, when nothing else will work and he just gives us over to our desires.
- Stage five is when we become completely useless to God, what the apostle Paul calls 'a castaway'.

So James is trying to rescue these Christians from entering into this fourth level of chastening. His method, oddly enough, is to employ the first level, that is, God's Word. For what we have here is a last ditch effort for the Word of God to shatter. Providence didn't work, the withholding of desires didn't work, and now, before these Christian Jews are given to go right on over and fall into open sin, to have their smallness discovered and become a fact before everybody, James comes along once more with the Word and hopes that will bring about the repentance that he's after.

God Wants To Spare Us

God wants to spare us from the grief of falling openly into sin, from falling into that satanic trap when there is a public disclosure of what has always been true. The same God who takes no pleasure in the death of the wicked does not want to chasten us by extreme measures. So James tries one more time to rescue them and to bring these Christian Jews around to recognize the calling God gave them in the first place.

So he's using the Word, and may God use the Word to us because, if we reach stage three, the Word is the only thing that will work to keep us from going right on over. Are you one of those who is tottering back and forth between obeying the law and giving in to your own desires? God is trying one more time to rescue you.

At this stage James addresses certain Christians in this community. He doesn't necessarily include everybody there, because he puts it like this: 'Go to now, ye that say'. This is a rather difficult phrase for us to understand. It probably meant more in the seventeenth century than it does to us. The New American Standard Version simply puts it: 'Come now, you who say ...' The NIV: 'Now listen, you who say ...' The Greek is: 'the ones who are talking'. Those are the ones James is addressing at the moment. Perhaps not everybody was saying this. James obviously has information that some were saying, 'Today or tomorrow we will go into such a city, and continue there a year, and buy and sell, and get gain.'

The Dangers Of Procrastination

What leaks out in this first phrase in the Greek is the word which means 'now'. This is the point. James says, 'Come *now*', 'Listen *now*, you that are saying ...' because there is little time. The trouble is that these Christians were behaving as though they had all the time in the world. They had a good idea indeed what the Lord wanted, and I'm quite certain that there was nothing in this epistle that really surprised them. Not only that, chances are that they fully intended to get right with the Lord. I don't think there is a backslidden Christian anywhere who doesn't say to himself, 'I'm going to be all right. Just leave me for a while. I fully intend to do what I know God wants me to do.'

James addresses this word to those who were saying, 'And here's what we're going to do.' All of us, surely, who are Christians, know the danger of procrastinating one's personal faith in Jesus Christ. For we have no promise of tomorrow. If you're not a Christian you ought to realize that the Bible says that if you were to die in your present state, as you are, you would be eternally lost. 'For what shall it profit a man, if he shall gain the whole world, and lose his own soul' (Mk. 8:36). 'For God so loved the world, that he gave his only begotten Son, that whosoever believeth in him should not perish, but have everlasting life' (Jn. 3:16). The danger of putting off one's own salvation is beyond anybody's ability to describe. For to miss Christ is to miss heaven. To miss heaven is to miss everything.

And yet the most severe statements in the Bible are not to the world but to God's covenant people. For example, take that word in Hebrews: 'Wherefore (as the Holy Ghost saith, Today if ye will hear his voice, harden not your hearts, as in the provocation, in the day of temptation in the wilderness: when your fathers tempted me, proved me, and saw my works forty years. Wherefore I was grieved with that generation, and said, They do always err in their heart; and they have not known my ways. So I sware in my wrath, They shall not enter into my rest.) Take heed, brethren, lest there be in any of you an evil heart of unbelief ' (3:7–12).

There's that word in Proverbs: 'He that being often reproved hardeneth his neck, shall suddenly be destroyed, and that without remedy' (29:1). And then came this word: 'Harden not your hearts, as in the provocation.' 'Today' – today – 'if ye will hear his voice …' This is God's word to his own people and the most solemn word, I say, ever given as a word of warning is always to God's own. So the Psalmist went on to say, 'I sware in my wrath, they shall not enter into my rest.'

James means it when he says, 'Know ye not that the friendship of the world is enmity with God? Whosoever therefore will be a friend of the world is the enemy of God' (4:4). We may think that that doesn't mean what it says, but God means every word of that. But God doesn't give us up easily. So James has put it already: 'The spirit that God has caused to dwell in us yearns with jealousy' (v. 5). So what does he do in the meantime when he's trying to get to us? He chastens us in his hot displeasure. James is speaking for the Lord in this way through the Word, trying to shatter us. God deals with us directly and the Psalmist was afraid of God doing that: 'Neither chasten me in thy hot displeasure' (6:1).

I want you to know that there's something worse than God's hot displeasure – his cold displeasure. The Psalmist recognized this in

Psalm 147:17: 'Who can stand before his cold?' It is when God turns the cold shoulder and says, 'I also will laugh at your calamity' (1:26). It is when God lets us sin and reap to ourselves corruption. We're told in Romans 1 that God just gave them up. And there comes a time in the life of every backslider who doesn't wake up in time when God just lets him go. James is using this method of God's Word as a last resort.

To put this another way, have you ever wondered what it is like for a Christian to make the transition from the spirit to the flesh? That is exactly what was happening here. It's the most natural thing in the world. You can backslide by doing nothing.

Backsliding Begins With Talking

How many of us realize how graphically James describes the transition from the spirit to the flesh? Backsliding invariably begins with talking, verbalizing (or writing down) the suggestions that ought to have been resisted. You grieve the Spirit by what you say. 'Wherefore, my beloved brethren, let every man be swift to hear, slow to speak, slow to wrath' (1:19).

Have you ever thought about that verse: 'Be ye angry, and sin not' (Eph. 4:26)? It partly means this: you can keep from grieving the Spirit by not saying anything. That is where you exercise willpower. Don't speak. Be angry. Don't sin. When there are many words, transgression is unavoidable (Prov. 10:19). He who restrains his lips is wise.

'All right', says James. 'Come now, you that *say* ...' If only they hadn't said it. If they'd just thought it. Talking opens the floodgates of lust, of hurt, of jealousy, of self-pity, of anger. For once you verbalize something you lose control. Often you find yourself entrenched in a position you think you've got to defend because you've said it.

Taking over from God

The backsliding also begins with a certain kind of attitude, that same attitude that makes us judge one another. We're impatient that God isn't judging somebody so we judge them. Speaking evil of another person reflects an impatience with God. God just backs off and says, 'You'll never know what I would have done because you've done it.'

This attitude is brought out again in the same verse. 'Ye that say, Today or tomorrow we will go into such a city, and continue there a year, and buy and sell, and get gain.' The question of patience and impatience always has to do with time. 'Today or tomorrow.' God wasn't working fast enough for these Christians. Never mind their defective evangelism, that they had mistreated the poor, that they had been discriminate in their witnessing. But they weren't considering that. They didn't want to enter into the real cause of their malady. All they knew by now was that their prayers were unanswered. This impatience developed into defiance, into arrogance: 'Today or tomorrow' – they had all the time in the world. 'We can do it.'

It's one thing to say that today is yours, but when you say that you are suggesting that you regard time as your own commodity. To regard tomorrow as ours as well suggests that we are playing God as much as rising above the law. For it is the same evil-hearted unbelief that will make us say, 'Today or tomorrow …' When they said 'tomorrow' it was a dead giveaway that they were living at the level of nature.

Everybody knows that by nature the sun will rise in the east. They were betting that the sun would rise in the east. That's what they were living for. That's the way the natural man lives. They weren't looking at the fact that God gives us breath for every day. They said, 'Today or tomorrow we will do this.' Their attitude was that God wasn't doing anything so they would.

Defiance Leads To Self-Pity And Fantasizing

When we get this defiance we don't concentrate on it too long. We usually feel it rather unconsciously. We may at first admit a bit of anger with God's tardiness, but what happens is that a reaction formation sets in. We imagine that God is saying, 'Look, you've proved yourselves. You've waited long enough. I won't put you through any more.' What was defiance suddenly is turned to what we project upon God to say to us. The attitude of defiance becomes self-pity. Never mind the quarrelling, the bitterness, much less its cause. We begin to feel sorry for ourselves. We project the feeling that we've had enough upon God and we now call it his will. Here's the result: backsliding eventually justifies our preoccupation with things outside the church. That is exactly what Satan wants.

Unspiritual reactions and results

Never doubt this: that the devil wants you to stay at home. He wants you to retreat from anything that has to do with church. Here's a tool that the devil uses to make you feel that you're getting too involved. The more involved you get the more hurt you get. So you just back off. What these Christians decided to do was to channel their energies into something less painful – secular matters (I do not say sinful or sensual). They decided that the church was nothing but trouble. So these Christians decided that the church should no longer become their daily absorption. They reasoned this way: 'We've given a lot of time to the church but we have to live our own lives, you know. The time has come to think about our own lives, our own future, our family. We've done our part. Now let somebody else come in.'

These Christian Jews really wanted a church that would run itself without anybody half trying. They fantasized that if they could get wealthy people into the church it wouldn't have any financial problems. If they could get prestigious people into the church that would be a drawing card. Others would come along. They had wanted a church that would just go on its own.

But if there was ever a miscalculation in the history of the Christian church, here it was. For in this way of going about building a church they completely alienated the poor and lost the rich as well. And church was an unhappy place for them to be. Nothing was going right.

Backsliding Results In Justifying Our Priorities

On top of that, there was a double backfire among themselves. Something snapped inside and they couldn't even think clearly. They began to quarrel with each other and so somebody came up with the idea, 'Let's forget about church, concentrate on secular matters. We've got time. We've got our lives to live. Today or tomorrow we'll just go to this city and live there a year. That's the way to solve the problem.'

Backsliding always results in justifying our priorities. The backslider is always filled with his own way. Nothing in the world seems so right as the opportunity to make money. That's what made Eve convinced that it was all right to partake of that fruit. She saw that it was 'good for food, and pleasant to the eyes' (Gen. 3:6) and she ate. Nothing was ever the same again.

Riches and popularity

Paul said to Timothy, 'They that will be rich fall into temptation and a snare, and into many foolish and hurtful lusts, which drown men in destruction and perdition. For the love of money is the root of all evil: which while some coveted after, they have erred from the faith, and pierced themselves through with many sorrows' (1 Tim. 6:9–10). But that can happen to a minister. Many a minister gets out of the ministry because he sees he can make more money outside the ministry. It can happen to a Christian businessman. He'll say, 'The more money I make the more I can give to the church.' He convinces himself that he's actually doing this for the church.

I know a young lady who said to me, 'Dr Kendall, I won't be able to tithe for three years because I'm buying a new car and I've got to pay for that. But wait and hear what I'm going to say: God has led me to buy this car so I can bring more people to church.' We all have a way of bringing God into our decision-making process. Jesus said, 'Beware of covetousness: for a man's life consisteth not in the abundance of the things which he possesseth' (Lk. 12:15).

It's the devil's trick to make you think that if you save your life you will find it: that if you have more money you can give more to God. Or if you can be more popular you can win more souls. Or if you can be more like the world you will influence the world. But what does James say? 'Know ye not that the friendship of the world is emnity with God? Whosoever therefore will be a friend of the world is the enemy of God' (4:4). The years roll by and you begin to accumulate a little, but not as much as you think you will later. You begin to accumulate a little bit of influence, but not as much as you think you will later. You begin to be a little more popular, but not as popular as you think you will be later. All you need is just a little more time. But unexpectedly and without warning God will intervene and say, 'Thou fool, this night thy soul shall be required of thee' (Lk. 12:20).

When God steps in and exposes our smallness, what matters then? How important is that popularity? How important is money? Paul said, 'For we must all appear before the judgement seat of Christ; that every one may receive the things done in his body, according to that he hath done, whether it be good or bad' (2 Cor. 5:10). There's a little poem which is so simple, so scary:

Only one life, 'twill soon be past,
Only what's done for Christ will last.

The Psalmist said – what a wise statement – 'A day in thy courts is better than a thousand. I had rather be a doorkeeper in the house of my God, than to dwell in the tents of wickedness' (84:10).

Dignifying A Trial Of God

Another ingredient in backsliding is this. Being bored with church and with churchgoing and a decision to concentrate on things outside the church has at bottom this desire to escape the tribulation through which we must enter if we're going to experience the kingdom of God. Being bored with church is a way of rejecting the trial God puts in our path. It's a refusal to dignify God's trial. Do you know your greatest trials will be found inside the church with church people? Never mind that these Christians had brought on much of their own suffering. The truth is – regardless of the origin or the cause of their suffering here's the wonderful thing – even though they caused it, that suffering that they brought onto themselves could really be their salvation, what could rescue them from their folly. For they had an opportunity to dignify the very trial they had created.

Peter put it like this: 'It is better ... that ye suffer for well-doing, than for evil-doing' (1 Pet. 3:17). He went on to say, 'Let none of you suffer as a murderer, or as a thief, or as an evildoer, or as a busybody in other men's matters' (4:15).

But if you have suffered for that – and we all have brought on our own suffering – what do we do then? We dignify that suffering, because that can be the very tool that God can use to bring us to greater blessing. But that isn't the way these Christians were looking at things. The most natural thing in the world is to say, 'I've suffered enough.'

Some elder statesman missionary, reporting on the situation in China now, had been a missionary years ago and was talking about what's going on there today. He said that these Chinese converts years ago said to him, 'How much more do we have to suffer?' And he said, 'I had to say to them, "This is only the beginning." ' That was back in 1951 when the Cultural Revolution was just starting and Christians were being persecuted. But now all these years later those same Christians had been memorizing Scripture. Some had memorized the whole New Testament. They would take two weeks and memorize the epistle to the Hebrews. And we think we've done something great if we've memorized a verse! This is the way those Chinese Christians were looking at the Bible. They memorized it. Don't worry about Christianity in China. It's alive and well.

Blessing amidst trials – or further folly?

The one who learns to dignify God's trial cannot tell the difference between a blessing and a trial. But these Christians, James says, took matters into their own hands:

- With respect to time: 'Today or tomorrow … We have all the time in the world.' They completely lost sight of the fact that they were stewards of God's time.
- With respect to decision-making: 'We will go into such a city.' Not that they hadn't prayed about it, but they weren't getting their prayer answered. So many of us, when we're not getting our prayers answered, decide what we want to do anyway and then put a prayer just before it and say, 'Look what the Lord has done.' We precede our conclusion with a prayer. Nature not only justifies its priorities but answers its own prayers.
- They took providence into their hands. They said, 'Today or tomorrow we'll go into such a city. We'll live there a year.' They had it all figured out. James had to go on to say the obvious: 'You don't know what's going to be on tomorrow.'
- They took prosperity into their own hands. They had already decided what they were going to make: 'We'll buy and sell and get gain.' A classic example of counting your chickens before they're hatched.

You may ask, 'What makes a Christian begin to come up with this kind of thinking, this rationale?' It's the easy way out. They wanted to run from the very problem they'd created and then leave it to somebody else. We're talking about a Christian community in trouble. They wanted to solve their problems by retreating from them. James' method is to save them from the greater folly of getting their own way. Has God kept you from something and disappointed you? Thank him. For there comes a time when God's hot displeasure becomes cold, and he washes his hands and he says, 'Go on.'

They were frustrated, these Christians, because they weren't getting what they wanted and they took providence into their own hands. It's one thing to take vindication into your own hands but they weren't content with that. So James was warning them and he warns us today that we might see our folly. How? That we might accept the shattering power of his Word, not the experience that shatters. We learn basically two ways: by the Word, by experience. We save ourselves many a frightening experience if we take God's Word at face value. 'Whosoever … will be a friend of the world is the enemy of God.' 'Submit yourselves … to God.' Believe that. 'Resist the devil, and he will flee from you. Draw nigh to God, and he will draw nigh to you.' 'Humble yourselves in the sight of the Lord, and he shall lift you up.' For being shattered by the Word is better than being shattered by experience.

23

Taking Ourselves too Seriously

James 4:13–14

We are going to finish the thought that was begun in verse 13: when James had to warn these Christian Jews, who had now decided to concentrate on secular things, that they were thinking at a natural level. The opposite of going from the flesh to the spirit is making the transition from the spirit to the flesh. That is what backsliding is. In these verses we are looking at backsliding in a rather intimate way.

How The Natural Man Thinks

These Christian Jews decided to appeal to the rich and the consequence, eventually, was that they turned on each other. Coming to church was nothing but fighting. Sunday was the day they dreaded rather than the day they looked forward to. It never entered their minds to blame themselves. They just decided among themselves, 'We've had it.' Church had become too painful for them. They decided to concentrate their efforts on secular matters, things that aren't necessarily sinful or sensual, but things outside the church. At the bottom of this rationale was a rejection of suffering within the church. They took four things into their own hands: time, decision-making, providence and prosperity. That's exactly the way the natural man functions.

Natural and spiritual counsel

James counters with an undoubted fact. 'Ye know not what shall be on the morrow.' He's not putting forth a spiritual principle at all. And yet he does what he has to do, because to reach a person who is living at the level of nature you've got to begin where he is. A person like that is not likely to receive great spiritual advice, but perhaps common sense will wake him up. But we must say that it is a very sad day when godly counsel has to be underlined with truths that are even understood at a natural level.

God Wants Us To Live In The Present

By the way, to pry into tomorrow is never the Christian way, but the role of the occult, of witchcraft, of ouija boards, of fortune-telling. Unnatural forces, supernatural forces, make the promise of tomorrow and propose to give details of tomorrow. But however curious you might be about tomorrow, God isn't going to tell you. We are not to pry into tomorrow. To do that is to escape the present, and God wants us to live in the present. The only exception: if without our engineering it, God sovereignly chooses to give a prophetic word.

What God does do is to promise us grace for tomorrow. 'As thy days, so shall thy strength be' (Deut. 33:25). Sometimes God does intervene and give us a promise today that tomorrow is in his hands. As Paul once announced on the ship in the book of Acts: 'I believe God, that it shall be even as it was told me' (27:25). Jesus put it like this in the Sermon on the Mount: 'Take ... no thought for the morrow ... Sufficient unto the day is the evil thereof' (Mt. 6:34).

It takes far more grace to be willing not to know what is going to be on tomorrow than it does to know in advance precisely how everything is going to turn out. Because when you try to know in advance it is your way of escaping the need for grace and to live by faith. It's a cowardly thing to do. This is why God doesn't deal with the Christian like that. All fantasizing is carried out to avoid pain.

> *God hath not promised skies always blue,*
> *Flower strewn pathways all our lives through.*
> *God hath not promised sun without rain,*
> *Joy without sorrow, peace without pain.*
> *God hath not promised we shall not know*
> *Toil and temptation, trouble and woe.*
> *He hath not told us we shall not bear*
> *Many a burden, many a care.*
> *But God hath promised strength for the day,*
> *Rest for the labour, light for the way,*
> *Grace for the trials, help from above,*
> *Unfailing sympathy, undying love.*

Even if we knew what was going to happen tomorrow that wouldn't make us happy. Then we'd want to know what's going to happen the day after tomorrow. But knowing about the morrow would do two things. One, it would demoralize us today should tomorrow's news be bad. Then we would have a bad day today and tomorrow. But secondly, it would deprive us of tomorrow's good news which God wants us to enjoy then, when it comes, and not before.

It's at this point that James poses a question that should really be relevant only for the non-Christian. But these Christians had sunk so low that they had to have it put to them. 'What is your life?' This is a verse that is often used as an evangelistic text to the non-Christian. And quite right. But James is putting a question to Christians who have begun to take themselves very seriously. They weren't thinking that what they were proposing to do was all that bad. They were actually using the same rationale that the non-Christian uses for his decision not to be a Christian. Why is a person not a Christian? For one reason: he loves his own life too much. All of the philosophical arguments he might put up, such as the problem of evil, evolution, suffering in the world and all of this – those are just arguments he uses to bolster his basic desire to live for himself. The flesh always justifies its priorities.

We Find Ourselves When We Deny Ourselves

Jesus' teaching of the kingdom was always built upon the premise of self-denial. 'Whosoever will come after me, let him deny himself, and take up his cross, and follow me. For whosoever will save his life shall lose it; but whosoever shall lose his life for my sake and the gospel's, the same shall save it' (Mk. 8:34–35). And in John 12:24–25: 'Except a corn of wheat fall into the ground and die, it abideth alone: but if it die, it bringeth forth much fruit. He that loveth his life shall lose it; and he that hateth his life in this world shall keep it unto life eternal.'

The most ironic – but we can also say the most dazzling – truth is that we don't find ourselves until we lose or deny ourselves. We don't live until we die. Paul said to the Colossians, 'Ye are dead, and your life is hid with Christ in God' (3:3). For the man who takes himself too seriously – his love for himself, for his position, his future, his reputation, his influence, what people will think, how he will be regarded, how much loved he will be – betrays his own life. Greatness is being self-conscious before God. When we blush only before God but not before men life has a way of not mattering at all. Blushing before men betrays that we are taking ourselves too seriously. You may say, 'But wait a minute. Doesn't God want us to dignify his own creation?' The answer is, you can't really do that until you know that you are not your own and that you are bought with a price.

What is your life?

James didn't say, by the way, 'What is your soul?' but rather: 'What is your life?' God doesn't want us to lose our soul. For Jesus went on to say in the gospel of Mark, 'For what shall it profit a man, if he shall gain the whole world, and lose his own soul?' (8:36). But James is talking about our life, which is nothing in itself. It has no possibility of usefulness outside God's complete ownership. When we take ourselves too seriously it shows that we fear God isn't taking us seriously so we must do what he isn't doing, that is, we look out for ourselves. That's what happened to these Christians. 'God isn't doing what he ought to so we're going to have to do it. Today or tomorrow we'll go and live in this city, stay a year, make some money and we might go somewhere else.' They were looking out for themselves.

First of all, they had flagrantly walked upon God's exclusive prerogative to judge a man and they were speaking evil of each other. Now they were walking flagrantly upon God's exclusive promise to take care of us. Jesus tells us to consider the lilies of the field and the sparrow, how God clothes and takes care of them. How much more will he take care of us?

We are as nothing – like vapour

To all of us who take ourselves so seriously, James has this rather humbling comment about the best of us: 'For what is your life? It is even a vapour, that appeareth for a little time, and then vanisheth away.' 'Vapour' – the Greek is a word which means 'vapour', 'smoke' or 'steam', seen by a few and that but for a fleeting moment before it completely disappears. The man who takes himself seriously cannot see himself as vapour. The man who doesn't take himself seriously sees himself as vapour.

When James raised the question, 'What is your life?' he used this Greek word which means 'life', which is what God alone is by nature, as it were. Our life is by creation. God alone is life. He alone is living. He only has immortality. He is the living God. The most humbling thought that you can grasp is that you are created. At rock bottom of the soul of every man is the fantasy that we are somehow an eternal extension of the divine.

That will help you to understand natural religion. The solemn truth is that we are made, not begotten. The only human flesh that ever existed that was uncreated was the Lord Jesus Christ. In the words of Athanasius: 'He is the only begotten Son of God, begotten of the Father before all the world. God of God. Light of light. Very God of very God. Begotten not made, being of one substance with the Father by whom all things were made.' We had a beginning. But our Lord Jesus Christ had no beginning. God had no beginning. God has no ending. God knew no birth in eternity. He will know no burial in eternity. 'Even from everlasting to everlasting, thou art God' (Ps. 90:2). But God, our Creator, determined the choice, time and place of our creation. He determined our parents and the very appearance of our bodies, of our faces. If that doesn't humble you, nothing else will. You aren't God and you will never be God. You're vapour, steam, smoke.

James isn't talking about the soul because he's not dealing with our creation in God's image. He's talking about our life. He says, 'What is your life?' – your existence, as the existentialists put it – the time that exists between your birth and your death. He's not referring to eternity but to time, not to life everlasting, but to the here and now. And so he gets very personal. He says, 'What is your life?' not 'lives' so that you can just pass it to somebody else. No, he's wanting you to ask yourself this question: 'What is your life?' James answers, 'It's vapour.'

What is vapour? It is not the cause, but a subsidiary effect of a greater cause. Vapour has no energy of its own. It is aimless and without purpose. It is always localized, visible by a few. Seconds later it's gone and forgotten. Vapour has no will of its own. It is beholden to its cause and to the elements that finally result in its complete disappearance. To put it another way, that is the way your life is regarded by onlookers. It's rather humbling. Nobody takes vapour seriously unless it would be to avoid it. Nobody takes you very seriously, but if you take yourself seriously they will avoid you as one does steam or smoke.

Harnessed vapour

And yet contained in this devastating verse is the most wonderful and comforting truth: vapour becomes a cause of immense consequence when it is harnessed. Let steam escape from a furnace or from an engine or from machinery and it becomes utterly useless, but harnessed vapour will take an ocean liner across ten seas. Harnessed, vapour can put a man on the moon and send a rocket soaring to the nether regions of the universe. That's what God would do to us if we're dead, harnessed, not our own.

Do you remember the story of when D.L. Moody as a young minister heard the speaker make this statement: 'The world has yet to see what God could do with one man who was utterly, totally yielded to him'? And D.L. Moody said to himself, 'I propose to be that person.' You might think that if a person makes a statement like that, Michael the Archangel will just come right down and congratulate him and say, 'All of us up in heaven are very proud of you. That's great.' But a few days later D.L. Moody's home and tabernacle burned down and he went through the most awful suffering. And that's the thing, we all want to avoid that.

Tozer got it right. We can have as much of the Holy Spirit as we want but it's in proportion to how much we dignify the trial or how much we run from it. These Christians were running. They were just going to escape. So many of us are like the steam that escapes and is useless. The very moment we try to save our lives we're like the smoke everybody wants to avoid. It is when we see ourselves as vapour that we begin to be harnessed and useful and desirable. James says, 'Vapour appears here for a little time.' It's not a way of comparing only effect to cause, but time to eternity. Life at its longest is still short. Eternity is forever. When we live our lives with eternity in mind, everything seems different.

Planning for eternity

How do we live with eternity in mind? You make every single decision in the light of how it will appear in eternity. 'Lay up for yourselves treasures in heaven,' said Jesus, 'where neither moth nor rust doth corrupt, and where thieves do not break through nor steal: for where your treasure is, there will your heart be also' (Mt. 6:20–21). For in heaven the only thing that will matter will be the extent to which we lived for God's approval on earth. In the words of a Nazarene hymn writer – in one of his great hymns called *My Wonderful Lord*, this line: 'All the talents I have, I have laid at thy feet; thy approval shall be my reward.' Life here shall vanish away. The soul lives throughout eternity.

Four Signs Of Taking Ourselves Too Seriously

There are four signs that we are taking ourselves too seriously, and they're all right here in this text.

Too much to say

The first is when we talk too much. 'Go to now, ye that say ...' We grieve the Holy Spirit by talking. This is why James had so much to say about the tongue. 'In the multitude of words there wanteth not sin' (Prov. 10:19). As the NASV put it: 'When there are many words, transgression is unavoidable.'

Controlling events

The second way we begin to reveal we are taking ourselves too seriously is when we engage with those things over which we have no control. 'Today or tomorrow we'll do this.' Time is in God's hands. Providence is in God's hands. Satan would make us grieve the Spirit by discussing things completely out of our hands. Nothing is more foolish, nothing is more counter-productive and nothing will sap your strength more, than doing this. We reveal we are taking ourselves too seriously when our future becomes our chief concern.

God has a way of taking our future from us. He can do it by calling us home right now or by giving us nothing to live for but himself. God is a ruthlessly jealous God. When anything becomes too important to us we are in great danger of losing it.

Choosing where to live

The third way that we reveal we are taking ourselves too seriously is when where we live becomes so important to us. 'Today or tomorrow we shall go to this city. We'll stay there for a year.' Evangelism, the greater glory of God, the kingdom of God, these things were replaced by the preoccupation with where they were going to live. That betrays where our heart is, that's where our treasure is. One day somebody came to Jesus and said, 'Master, I will follow thee whithersoever thou goest' and Jesus said, 'The foxes have holes, and the birds of the air have nests; but the Son of man hath not where to lay his head' and that fellow was gone (Mt. 8:20). Abraham dwelt in tents because 'he looked for a city which hath foundations, whose builder and maker is God' (Heb. 11:10). Paul said that our citizenship is in heaven.

Preoccupation with financial security

The fourth way we betray we're taking ourselves too seriously is when financial security as the ultimate concern lies behind our decisions. They said, 'We will go to a city and buy and sell and get gain.' Money lay at the bottom of all this talk. When their playing for the rich backfired they decided that they'd get rich themselves. 'The love of money is the root of all evil' (1 Tim. 6:10).

How Not To Take Ourselves Too Seriously

When may we be reasonably sure we are not taking ourselves too seriously? Only three things for this:

- First, when we 'take no thought for the morrow', when we don't try to avoid the pain of the present by escaping into tomorrow. God wants us to live in the present. When we live in his presence we're content with the present, whatever the setting may be.
- The second way we can be reasonably sure we're not taking ourselves too seriously is when we don't take other people too seriously. James says, 'What is your life?' Not 'his' or 'her' life. When Peter was told what death he would die it didn't bother him, but what did bother him was what death John was going to die. He said, 'What about this man?' The Lord said, 'That's none of your business. I'm talking to you' (Jn. 21:18–22). You tend to take other people too seriously because you take yourself too seriously.
- And third, we may be reasonably sure we are not taking ourselves too seriously when we see ourselves as a puff of vapour. How seriously should we take ourselves? When you follow the principles of the kingdom of God, you will know. I live by this verse: 'As many as be perfect, be thus minded: and if in any thing ye be otherwise minded, God shall reveal even this unto you' (Phil. 3:15). Make up your mind to be perfect: and if there is anything in you that is not perfect, trust God to reveal that to you. You will find energy that you never had, motivation unprecedented, usefulness that you never dreamed of and clarity of mind that will exceed your greatest expectations.

One last little point. People don't take us seriously because we take ourselves too seriously. This is why these Christians that James is addressing were so counter-productive. The world laughed at them. 'Do not they blaspheme that worthy name by the which ye are called?' (Jas. 2:7). If we lose ourselves we will find ourselves. That means suffering. But the reward is God's approval. And when you have God's approval you'll be useful. You'll still be vapour, but harnessed vapour.

24

Knowing the Lord's Will

James 4:15

All the problems that we have looked at, as characterized by these Christians that James originally addresses, are problems that were traceable to their own defective Christian witness. They sidestepped their own responsibility, they lost self-control. They began to take themselves too seriously. Self-pity had come in.

The Devil Sets Us Up For Destruction

When we feel sorry for ourselves we are most vulnerable to the devil. We can always think of a thousand reasons to feel sorry for ourselves. The devil moves right in like a friend. And he gives us the sympathy that we've been wanting, 'Quite right, you ought to feel like that. Nobody does appreciate you.' And he magnifies the hurt a thousand times. He will also magnify every blemish on another person. He will magnify your own blemish so that you'll feel more sorry for yourself.

So the more that hurt is magnified, the more right it seems and the more justified we feel in turning from Christian discipline, from self-discipline, from Christian service, from Christian duty. The devil is setting you up for destruction. James comes along and shows them the folly of thinking like this. For the truth is, when we begin to feel sorry for ourselves, if we're not stopped, we begin to do things we never thought we would do and, worst of all, we feel right about it. We say, 'This is God's will.'

Having dealt with the negative, James moves to the positive and says that there's a different way to look at it: 'For that ye ought to say, If the Lord will, we shall live, and do this, or that.' Having shown that our lives are but a vapour, having shown the folly of taking ourselves too seriously, he says, 'Ye ought to say …'

The Greek word here means 'anti', which is usually a negative word but here it is used as a positive word. What James means is: 'Instead you ought to think like this', 'on the other hand', 'rather'. For when you're full of self-pity you can only see things one way. But James uses a word that is normally negative to get them to see another way to consider things.

The Time To Speak

Here's an epistle that's been warning about talking, that tells us we ought to be 'slow to speak'. Now he says, 'Ye ought to say …' Why would he suddenly instruct them to speak, to talk? Because of what they had been saying. They had been vocal about their plans, what they were going to do. But they had been saying everything wrong. And now he says, 'Because you've been saying the wrong thing I want to give you the right thing to say: "If the Lord wills, we shall live, we shall do this or that." ' Our Christian confession when we're restored is always to dignify the Lord's will. When a non-Christian comes to see his need of a Saviour he is ordered in the New Testament to come out into the open and confess that Jesus Christ is Lord. When a Christian has been in a backslidden state and has been saying everything wrong he also needs to make a confession to dignify the Lord's will.

The fundamental problem, then, of these Christian Jews is that they left the Lord out. And their own testimony condemned them. In all their talking, in their inability to control their tongues, they eventually betrayed what was really wrong. They left the Lord out.

John Wesley used to say that every hour that we spend talking to one another we ought to spend praying with one another. You may say that's a bit extreme. I would only ask, how many John Wesleys have you run into lately? As for our conversation, how much of it is about the Lord? Any Christian relationship is in trouble when it takes the Lord for granted and does not preoccupy itself with him. Have you ever thought about how many relationships are actually formed because of the gospel? But that same relationship often degenerates eventually simply because the gospel that brought people together is taken for granted and it's never what keeps the relationship going.

It makes me think of a church back in the States where they began to have Bible conferences because of a newly discovered truth, and everybody was set afire with this truth. When these Christians and ministers got together all they wanted to do was talk about the Lord. We had to force ourselves to go to bed at two or three o'clock in the morning because a service was going to be at ten o'clock the next day, and all this time but we'd just been talking about the Lord. Two or three years later at the same conference, the same church, conversations had changed. The most extraordinary thing happened as the people began to talk about secular things. They still believed this newly discovered truth, but they didn't talk about it. They knew it all and they just met in a perfunctory way and they talked about other things. A year or two after that, divisions developed and hurt feelings, and yet the very thing that brought them together was this truth. When an association is formed because of the gospel, remember that having begun in the spirit, it won't be perfected in the flesh. It will go wrong and sour every time.

How much do you talk to your spouse about the gospel? Your best friend? How much conversation with each other is about the Lord? James didn't say, 'Think it', or 'Assume it'. He says, 'Ye ought to say …' Our talk must be about Christ. The simple fact is, if we let the Lord Jesus be the centre of our conversation and central to all we talk about we will save ourselves a heap of trouble. If the people that you spend a lot of time with don't want to talk about the Lord you're just with the wrong company, even if they're Christians.

An Important Distinction Concerning The Lord's Will

James comes now to an important but critical distinction. James is talking about knowing the Lord's will, not merely wanting it. Here's the subtle point: many Christians, even in a backslidden state, will claim to want the Lord's will. In twenty-six years in the ministry I have very, very rarely met a backslidden Christian who doesn't want the Lord's will.

Some of the worldliest Christians I know would claim they want the Lord's will and they don't think that they fit this passage at all because they would say, 'Well, if it's the Lord's will we shall live and do this or that.' Every Christian who has a bit of sense at all wants the Lord's will. After all, that's the position of safety. It's the law of preservation at work here. It's not spiritual grace in operation at all to want the Lord's will. As a matter of fact, most people deceive themselves because they want the Lord's will. They say, 'I couldn't be in too bad a shape because I pray for his guidance.' These Christians prayed.

They asked but asked amiss that they might consume it upon their lusts (4:3). James is putting upon us the responsibility to know *what his will is*.

To some, it may come as a surprise that you are supposed to know the Lord's will. You will find very little biblical support for your ignorance of what the Lord's will is. You'll probably go to Gideon's fleece. Gideon was a very weak man and represented a very weak faith. It was no sign of strength that he did that. The Lord simply accommodated him. Most of us are so weak that we need the continual accommodation. But that is not the spirit of the New Testament and that is not the way we are to live.

For example, the apostle Paul says in Ephesians 5:9: 'For the fruit of the Spirit is in all goodness and righteousness and truth; proving what is acceptable unto the Lord.' He goes on to say, 'Be ye not unwise, but understanding what the will of the Lord is' (v. 17). He said the same thing to the Philippians, 'I pray, that your love may abound yet more and more in knowledge and in all judgement; that ye may approve things that are excellent; that ye may be sincere and without offence till the day of Christ' (1:10). And so to the Romans, 'Be not conformed to this world: but be ye transformed by the renewing of your mind, that ye may prove what is that good, and acceptable, and perfect, will of God' (12:2). You have no excuse for not knowing the Lord's will.

We are so far removed from the level of spirituality the New Testament envisages, we are so at home in living at a natural fleshly level, that we can't conceive that there is any other way to look at things. But the New Testament shows us that godliness promises peace – peace of mind and clarity of mind, not confusion. We are hard-pressed for biblical support for the confusion that persists in not knowing the Lord's will. This is a sober word because so often what we want and what the Lord wants are two different things and we just assume that what we want is what the Lord wants. But it's so thrilling because it shows that the Lord really does care about me! That he really does have a will for me.

What if all there was to being a Christian was that the Lord saves you and then says, 'So nice to meet you. See you in heaven. Sorry I can't be with you; I've got other things to do'? It's not that way at all. Though my life is a vapour and appears but for a little time, I have a Lord who cares how that little time is spent. And I can't think of any greater sense of security than this truth: the Lord wants to enter into my life. I am bought with a price. He therefore will supply every need. 'Take no thought for your life, what ye shall eat, or what ye shall drink; nor yet for your body, what ye shall put on ... Behold the fowls of the air: for they sow not, neither do they reap ... If God so clothe the grass of the field, which today is, and tomorrow is cast into the oven, shall he not much more clothe you, O ye of little faith' (Mt. 6:25, 26, 30). You're owned by the Lord. He's got to care for you.

The Greek word here is *kyrios*, which almost always in the New Testament means Jesus. This is an important point because Christ is not an absentee watch-maker. There's a danger of deism coming into the Christian faith in evangelical dress. We forget that it's the Lord Jesus who enters into our lives. Christianity is not an impersonal fatalism. That's what the Muslims believe. We're not Christian Muslims. They say, 'Allah wills it.' No, we're talking about the Lord Jesus who has a will for me and wants me to know it. That's dynamic, alive. That's not Christianity. He doesn't want me to wait and see what happens and conclude that that's his will. That's fatalism.

What precisely is it that the Lord wills? The big things: whether we live. The little things: whether we do this or that. James moves from the general to the particular. He begins with the big thing, a matter of life and death. We ought to say, 'If the Lord will, we shall live.' This means that my own death is in his hands. Hebrews 9:27 says, 'It is appointed unto men once to die.' But James 4:15 says that Christ determines when my death comes. My very being alive is proof that I'm alive by his will.

How many times have we been close to death? Perhaps we won't know until we get to heaven but our being alive is by his will. And yet if that is why we think we're in his will then it's a very weak argument, because in so doing we are moving from the outward backwards, concluding that we must be in the Lord's will because we are alive.

A Sense Of Destiny Is Crucial

No doubt many of us are forced to this and ultimately we have to leave things in God's hands, but that's not James' point here. James wants every Christian to have a sense of purpose, a sense of destiny. I am alive but I'm not surprised I woke up this morning because when I went to bed last night I had a sense of purpose. Christ has things for me to do. I don't say, 'I'm alive, therefore I'm in his will.' I say, 'It's his will for me to live, therefore I am alive.' This is James' reasoning. It's wonderful to know that my time is in his hands. This is why it is fire in my bones. Christ is not finished with me.

He's given something for each of us to do that nobody else can do. Even in old age this conviction spells the difference between living and existing. I don't care how old you are, whether fifty or seventy or eighty,

Christ is not finished with you. You would have been called home if he had been finished with you. God does nothing without design or purpose.

Obviously this must be true or we would take the particular – that is, what we do – as being God's will. James' principle couldn't break down as he moves from the general to the particular. Surely you would not say, 'This is what I did therefore it's the Lord's will.' It's a melancholy fact that the Lord will let you get out of his will. You may have heard something about a Christian who falls or a Christian who gets into trouble and said, 'Well, that just wouldn't happen to me.' It certainly could. It is possible to get out of his will simply because you reason from the outward and go backwards and say, 'This is what I'm doing so it must be the Lord's will.' It may not be and this is why James steps in to say, 'If the Lord wills we will do this or that.'

This is why a sense of destiny is crucial to every Christian. It's what makes a great leader in the realm of common grace. There was a particular ex-Prime Minister who was being interviewed. They were talking about Winston Churchill and this Prime Minister said, 'The thing about Winston was he always had a sense of destiny.' Very sharply the interviewer picked that up and looked at him and said, 'Do you have a sense of destiny?' And he said, 'No, I never did.' This is the problem with leaders today. But saddest of all is when it's lacking in Christians in their service to the Lord.

It's the weak Christian who has to be told what to do. He's got to be told to witness, to tithe, to resist temptation and deny the flesh. But if we catch the fever, then we're motivated like the patriarchs. We respond. Abraham went out not knowing whither he went, but he obeyed. That is what God is after with us. Therefore, with regard to the particular we should know the Lord's will. This or that. There must be a sense of godly purpose in all that we do. We're told by the writer to the Hebrews: 'By faith Noah, being warned of God of things not seen as yet, moved with fear, prepared an ark to the saving of his house' (11:7).

We're not talking about a 'leap of faith' as the existentialists call it. Nothing is more aimless and without purpose than existential philosophy. Rather, it's knowing the Lord so well that you know his will. It's like a husband and wife when they know each other so well they know what the other is thinking. We're the bride of Christ. What pleases a husband or wife most is when the other does something for that one without even being told. He or she just knows. We're talking about the highest level of freedom. The patriarchs moved in freedom. The law came in because Israel had to be told what to do. Christ wants his people to know him so well that they don't wait to be told every move. They know what to do.

How To Know What Pleases God

You may want to ask, 'How can I know the Lord so well that I know what pleases him?' I'll put three questions to you:

- First question: how much time do you give him? You get to know a person by how much time you spend with him. How much actual time do you spend in prayer every day? I mean when you stop and you put everything aside. If you're spending five or ten minutes a day you're not really getting to know him. But if you're spending a half hour or an hour you're beginning to know him. And you just know what pleases him.
- Second question: how much do you talk about him? Have you met any fanatics lately? They just want to talk about the Lord all the time. I haven't. Who do you talk about mostly? You tell how much another means to you by how much you talk about them. How much do you talk to your spouse or your flatmate about the Lord?
- Third question: how much do you resist temptation? Sexual lust – until you conquer that, whoever you are, you will not grow. What about concern for your self-esteem? Christ will not be formed in you until you are obsessed with his honour. How much are you giving in to self-pity? When you do these things you're grieving the Spirit. You can't know the Lord's will. Knowing him so well that you know his will depends on how much time you give him, how much you talk about him, and how much you resist temptation.

You may want to ask the question: how can I know this or that is God's will? My answer is: Please God in all your ways and then be at liberty in your decision-making. St Augustine said it first. Love God then do what you please. God will spare you from major mistakes if you live like this. I don't say you won't make mistakes, but such mistakes will not be sin and I doubt that they will be major mistakes. The Christian makes mistakes, even the one who lives at the level of the spirit. But they are almost always errors in judgement, owing partly to our own stupidity over which we have little control. They're not serious mistakes. They may seem so, but if you live by Psalm 84:11: 'The LORD God is a sun and shield: the LORD will give grace and glory: no good thing will he withhold from them that walk uprightly.' If you live by that you'll be all right.

Sometimes a mistake made by error in judgement will turn out to be God's gracious overruling. You may be disappointed at the job you didn't get, that you didn't get a husband or wife. You might get disappointed if you do! But give it a little time and you may be thankful later that God overruled. You see, what James is talking about is not error in judgement but this arrogance of assuming God's will. These Christians thought they could do what they wanted to when, in fact, they were living in flagrant disobedience. But love God and please him in all your ways, then do what you please. 'Delight thyself also in the LORD; and he shall give thee the desires of thine heart' (Ps. 37:4). 'No good thing will he withhold from them that walk uprightly' (Ps. 84:11).

25

Seeing our own Sin

James 4:16

This General epistle of James can be safely called a study in the subtleties of backsliding. All of us have been backsliders at one time or another, and not all backsliding is as bad as it could be perhaps. But even though 'all things work together for good' (Rom. 8:28) – and that includes backsliding – we will still be sorry for it.

James had dealt with several aspects of backsliding – the lack of tongue control, the problem of lust and the problem of our self-esteem. But now he says, 'Ye rejoice in your boastings.' For that's the way this verse begins: 'But now ...' James had to warn them in chapter 4 verse 4: 'Ye adulterers and adulteresses, know ye not that the friendship of the world is enmity with God? Whosoever therefore will be a friend of the world will be the enemy of God.'

Our Obedience Matters

How can you be God's enemy if you are a Christian? Because when you cast your gaze to the world you force God to treat you as one who is disobedient. Our obedience matters. How could these Christians go so far in their backsliding that the very things they've done wrong in their backsliding they now justify by bragging about them? The irony of backsliding is that the further one goes wrong, the more right it seems. You would think it would be the other way around. Common sense tells us that blatant disobedience is self-revealing. We say: give a person enough rope and he'll hang himself. It's common sense to the Christian in his right mind that such blatant disobedience is wrong but when we're in the process of backsliding we're not in our right mind. We're told of the prodigal son: 'He came to himself' (Lk. 15:17) and then he got back on the right path.

Sometimes the process of bringing someone to see himself can be most painful indeed. When we're fully awakened we blush that we could think what we thought, that we could say what we said, that we did what we did. Looking back we say, 'Surely I should have known better.' But when we're involved with an idea that Satan has put into our mind he will give you every reason to feel more sorry for yourself and justify this decision.

Pride Takes Over When We Backslide

These Christian Jews had gone so far that James now says, 'But now ye rejoice in your boastings: all such rejoicing is evil.' For personal pride takes over when we are in this process of backsliding. We get in so deep that it becomes too much to admit that we could be wrong. The whole time we're justifying ourselves. The backslider always tries to make two wrongs make a right. Then he gets the third wrong, then the fourth.

This can happen on a smaller scale. Even the Christian who, generally speaking, is not in a bad state, can fall into a satanic trap. He does or says something that is wrong and rather than admit the wrong he justifies it. When we do that what we don't realize is that it wasn't quite so bad until we went that far and justified it. We should just admit to ourselves that we've made a mistake and confess it to God. Mark Twain used to say that if you keep quiet people will think you're intelligent but if you open your mouth you remove all doubt. A person can be in a backslidden state and it can be relatively secret. But these Christians had to spout off, and in doing so had to justify what they had done. 'But now,' says James, 'ye rejoice in your boastings.'

What is James' motive here? What is his rationale for saying all these things? It is to get them to see their sin. James knows he has his work cut out. Perhaps if he were right there in person he could just grab them and give them a good shake. But he has to say it. And he would love to think that maybe God would step in providentially. But sometimes God doesn't do that. He's got to say it in such a way that they would come to themselves, for their pride was working overtime. Pride blinds. We say while we're doing it, 'I don't think I'm doing that badly. Surely I couldn't have been that wrong.' So we go on to prove it.

Here were these Christians now full of self-pity. 'We'll let somebody else worry about the church. We've got gifts to make money. Why fool around with those Christians who squabble and quarrel all the time?'

They could just go on their way. At heart it was their way of revealing how seriously they took themselves and they had to justify it. How? They rejoiced.

One way of understanding church history and how various movements sprang up is that a powerful leader will get an idea and he'll get entrenched and one or two will say, 'That's a good idea.' And so he gets to feeling better about it and then he begins to amass evidence to support that idea. Before you know it he's using evidence that is irrelevant, but he's got this idea. Before you know it a new movement starts. Denominations sometimes start that way. They get entrenched into an idea. They've got to defend it. What we do is we grab a straw. A drowning man grabs for a straw and that straw always looks so good and so precious. It happens at a less sophisticated level than theological thinking. We justify everything we do. We've said it about another person; now we've got to prove it. Or we've decided that this is what we're going to do at work, our job. So we continue to prove it. Take the way we discipline our children. Most parents are too proud to say, 'I was wrong. I shouldn't have done that.'

These Christian Jews got entrenched. They had to justify the claim that they were going to go to the next town and live there for a while and they rejoiced in it. Rather than admit that we have acted immaturely or prematurely, we amass further evidence to prove that we are right. 'But now ye rejoice …' It's the Greek word that actually means 'glory'. 'Now you glory in this.' In psychology this is called reaction formation. It's repression. It's a defence mechanism whereby we deny even to ourselves how we really feel, which would make us face certain realities and demand a more mature reaction. So we don't come to grips with our real feelings. As Shakespeare put it: we protest too much. The pain of responsibility results in a feigned or contrived act.

We See Our Errors In The End

Surely it was wrong for these Christians to take time and providence into their own hands. They would see this later. We all see our error later. But in the meantime they couldn't admit to that. They acted the opposite of the way they actually felt. They said things they didn't mean. But now they got entrenched and they rejoiced. Do you ever do this? You wanted that job. 'Do you like it?' 'Oh, I love it.' You might hate it, but you're not going to admit it. Sometimes you're extra nice to a person you don't like. Why? You feel guilty that you don't like that person so you act as if you

love them. That's reaction formation. You don't really come to grips
with how you feel. James knew how they were doing. A person in a
backslidden state will deny he's unhappy. But the most miserable person
in the world is the disobedient Christian.

They rejoiced in their boastings. It's the Greek word that means
their 'presumptuous speeches', 'arrogance', 'haughtiness'. It's the
same word used in 1 John 2:16. The 'pride of life', John called it. He
said, 'Love not the world, neither the things that are in the world. If
any man love the world, the love of the Father is not in him' (v. 15).
And then he defined worldliness: 'the lust of the flesh, and the lust of
the eyes, and the pride of life'.

Speaking frankly about sin

This arrogance was the cover-up. James calls a spade a spade. 'You
rejoice in your cover-up. You know what you're saying isn't true.'
They were trying to act like the cat that swallowed the canary but they
were miserable, poor, blind, naked. Like the Laodiceans they couldn't
decide – neither cold nor hot. So James goes on. 'Such boasting,' he
says, 'is evil.' James is hoping to produce, by the help of God,
conviction of sin in these people. He has already told them once that
they've sinned. But now he uses a different word: 'evil'. It's the Greek
word *porne*, from which we get 'pornography'.

This is the eighth time he's used that word in this epistle. But this
time he says, 'What you have done is evil.' First he says, 'God cannot
be tempted with evil' (1:13) and then he says, 'You've become judges
of evil thoughts' (2:4). Then in chapter 3 verse 8 he talks about the
tongue being 'an unruly evil'. In chapter 3 verse 16 he says, 'Where
envying and strife is, there is confusion and every evil work.' Then in
chapter 4 verse 11 he uses it three times: 'Speak not evil one of
another, brethren. He that speaketh evil of his brother … speaketh evil
of the law.'

But he's gone further now. He has laid it out before them. There is
the Greek word that means 'missing the mark', and it's normally the
word used for 'sin' in the New Testament. But although James uses
these words somewhat interchangeably because he says in the next
verse, 'To him that knoweth to do good, and doeth it not, to him it is
sin', in a sense it is a stronger word. The reason is this: all Christians sin.
They all miss the mark in some sense. But to commit evil disgraces the
name of Christ indeed. He uses this strong term so that at long last they
might see that they have sinned.

Satan Alone Is The Author Of Evil

This word 'evil', I say, is probably stronger than 'sin'. And for this reason 'evil' is the word that is used to denote injustices in the world: war, crime, etc. Evil is that of which Satan alone is the author. Sin is against God, but evil is against God and man. It is possible to sin against God and still not perpetuate an evil against man. But James shows here that what these Christians had done not only was against God, but had affected human beings. 'You have misled other people', he says to them. 'You're letting the world think that Christianity is the very example that you are putting forward.' They would make the Christian faith into something it is not.

James' method is, if he can get them to see that what they have done is evil, maybe at long last they will have conviction of sin. Not that they would deny being sinners. But the problem was that they saw no serious malady in themselves. James uses the strongest term possible to convict them of the depth of sin. He's hoping that if they can see this then they will come to themselves. We all see later what we did and we think, 'How can I have done it? Why did I do it?' And so James, by using this word 'evil', hopes they'll get the hint.

We've had occasion to see the various levels of chastening. Jesus said to the church of the Laodiceans, 'As many as I love, I rebuke and chasten' (Rev. 3:19). What we have in this epistle is not only a study in the subtleties of backsliding but equally, it may be said, of how God tries to keep us from advancing to the next stage of chastening.

Doing Something About Sin

James knows if he can just succeed in getting them to see their sin then he's going to be relieved because a Christian, when he sees his sin, will do something about it. James doesn't know whether God, in his inscrutable providence, will step in. So James tries to say it as clearly as he possibly can and he uses this word 'evil'. He's pointed out their folly: 'You lust and have not.' He has warned that the friendship of the world is to be at enmity with God. He has counselled with them, 'Be afflicted, and mourn, and weep: let your laughter be turned to mourning, and your joy to heaviness.' He reminded them of the danger of quarrelling with one another, of speaking evil of one another and trying to vindicate themselves by being small. And then he quoted their speeches back to them: 'Today or tomorrow we'll go to such a city and buy and sell.' 'But now,' he says, 'you've bragged about that and you've boasted. What you've done is evil.'

These boastings were evil for four reasons.

Speaking for the Christian faith

The first is, because they were Christians and would be taken as speaking for the Christian faith, as speaking for Christianity. You may say that that's not a very good example of what a Christian is and perhaps you get fire in your bones when you see certain people on television or hear them on the radio or read about them in the newspapers. It drives you almost crazy to think that the world will say that that's what Christianity is. The problem is, when you abide in the name of Christ the world thinks that you speak for Christianity.

Here were these Christian Jews. They were examples of what Christianity is. They had abused the poor. They had decided to be selective as to who would be the next person saved. The world would regard that as meaning that Christianity is for the middle class. Sometimes a Christian can do more harm than the wicked, because the wicked man won't be taken that seriously. They'll say, 'What do you expect from a non-Christian?' But the Christian's word is more weighty. We've got a responsibility whether we like it or not. If the word leaks out from us that we're Christians, at once everything we say will be regarded against the context of Christianity.

The world has a vague idea of what a Christian is supposed to be. And so they look at you and say, 'Are you a Christian?' We confirm or deny what their anticipations and expectations are.

Speaking to other Christians

Their boastings were evil because of who they were, but also because of who heard this talk. It may have been heard by the world. But most certainly it was heard by the church or James wouldn't have known about it. These Christians, like those who had threatened to resign, let their fellow Christians know: 'We've had it up to here with all of you. We're not going to be around any more. We've got other gifts. We've got to think of our future and we're going to concentrate on secular matters. We're going to live over here. Maybe we'll do it today or maybe we'll do it tomorrow. But we won't be here much more.'

What effect do you think this would have on other Christians? Would it be good? 'No, your boastings are evil. That won't encourage the church. And after all, it's a problem of your own making', says James. 'You leave the responsibility with those who must go on with a blemished reputation and you helped cause it.' James might say, 'What about those who have to live in Jerusalem?' or wherever this Christian community was. 'Maybe they don't have the means to go to Antioch tomorrow or Samaria next week. What about them?'

Speaking to your closest friends

But there's a third reason their boastings were evil, and that's because of what they did to themselves. You can't do this and get away with it. First of all it warps your own thinking processes. Your mind becomes divided within and you can't think clearly. You won't be able to be as effective in your work if people come to you and say, 'What's the matter?'; you'll say, 'Nothing.' 'Oh, no. There's something wrong with you.' 'No, I'm fine.' But you're not the same and people can see it. You are doing injury to yourself and to them.

Speaking about God

But the fourth thing is what you've done to God, to his cause. Do you really care what happens to God's cause? These people didn't care. They said, 'We will go here. We will do this.' Self-concern, self-pity, taking themselves too seriously. The question is, what if the cause of God were up to you? Well it is! There are people you meet that no other Christians meet. If you don't witness to them they'll never be witnessed to. It's scary, isn't it?

But these people didn't care about the cause of God. When they went to the next town to live, do you think they were going to witness for the Lord there? Probably not. They'd decided that they were Christians. They were going to go to heaven. That's what mattered. Do you care about the cause of God? Jonathan Edwards once said that the one thing the devil cannot truly counterfeit is a love for God's interest in the world.

These Christians had done great damage not only to the cause of God but to the name of God. They thought that by being partial to the rich they would win the rich. And James said – I suppose if there was any unkind word in this epistle, you would talk about sticking the knife right where it hurts – 'It hasn't even worked, has it? Not only have you not won them, but they treat you like dirt.' He said, 'One other thing, do they not blaspheme that name by which you're called? All because of you. It's evil,' says James, 'what you've done.'

You may ask, 'Does God delight in his own reputation?' You'd better believe he does. He is glory. He lives for his name. And he's tied himself to this world. It's an extraordinary thought. 'For God so loved the world, that he gave his only begotten Son, that whosoever believeth in him should not perish, but have everlasting life' (Jn. 3:16). It's a thrilling thought that Christ has a will for me. But here's a sobering, thrilling thought: God has entrusted me with his reputation. How I live, what I say, matters to God.

It's a scary thing to be a Christian. It gets scarier every day. But if you're a Christian the buck stops with you. Because you matter. God's reputation is at stake in your life and your personal conduct and your language, your words. But James talks like this that they might at last see their sin. For the proof that one is a Christian is that when one sees one's sin one does something about it. Do we see our sin?

You know what breaks my heart on Sunday night is when people come by and say, 'That was great. Great preaching.' I think how few non-Christians heard it. That's what breaks my heart. When I have a bad Sunday night my consolation is that at least there weren't that many there. It's up to us. I ask, do we see our sin? What will it take to get us to move and be the church in this wicked world? 'But now ...' So James began with this verse and I end with this: But now what will we do?

26

The Folly of Unconfessed Sin

James 4:17

James' purpose in writing the letter is to produce conviction of sin. And yet in a sense it must be said that these Christians were already convicted of sin. The problem was they were not admitting to this conviction, to what they knew to be true. Conviction of sin is by degrees. Paul said this essentially in Romans 7:13 when he talked about the commandment coming so 'that sin ... might become exceeding sinful'. James wants these Christians to have deep conviction of sin.

Conviction Of Sin Is By Degrees

James is wanting to produce in them confession of sin. It is possible to be convicted without confessing. This is obviously true from Romans chapter 1 verse 20 when Paul says, 'The invisible things of him from the creation of the world are clearly seen, being understood by the things that are made, even his eternal power and Godhead; so that they are without excuse.' But being without excuse does not necessarily produce a confession. Take the account when Jesus was confronted by the Pharisees who had a woman they had found in the very act of adultery. Jesus said, 'He that is without sin among you, let him first cast a stone at her.' He stooped down and wrote on the ground. 'And they which heard it, being convicted by their own conscience, went out one by one, beginning at the eldest, even unto the last: and Jesus was left alone, and the woman standing in the midst' (Jn. 8:3–9). This didn't result in a transformation of their lives. They were convicted but it didn't produce the confession.

James is having to deal with Christians that are in this kind of situation. They were convicted and yet not to the degree that it was deep, that they were moved, that they were contrite. It was only when deep conviction resulted that they would admit the truth to themselves, to one another and to God. He's quite sure that they know they have done wrong. They know this but they have excused it. So in order to achieve this deep conviction of sin he's had to quote their own statements back to them and he's had to describe what they're going through. And now he's moving in to box them in so that there's no way out. He's concerned for their own souls. It is extraordinary how James goes to such pains. This is the way we must go about winning the lost, when we do everything we can to stop them, plead with them and say as Ezekiel did, 'Why will ye die?' (18:31). This is the way Paul was with the Galatians. He said at one time, 'My little children, of whom I travail in birth again …' (4:19) – he'd done it once. Now they're in an awful mess and he's got to come back to them. He says, 'I travail in birth again until Christ be formed in you.' Christians must have this kind of concern for fellow Christians that are overtaken in a fault. It's a delicate thing and it requires much wisdom and it requires much grace. And yet here is James delicately, convincingly, passionately, carefully, bringing them to the place where they will see it.

Looking for a breakthrough

A man convinced against his will is of the same opinion still and that will not do. James knows that. But if these Christians could come face to face with their own guilt and with the shame of what they have done and what they have repressed, what they have denied even to themselves, it would mean a great breakthrough for them personally and for the kingdom of God and the defeat of the devil. The conviction then would be a confession and the result – great joy. As Shakespeare put it, 'To thine own self be true.' They were not true to themselves; they were hypocrites.

These Christians protested loud and long. James saw right through them. He called it 'arrogance'. 'You are rejoicing in your boastings, your arrogance.' He knew that it was a cover-up for the way that they really felt. He knew what a favour he would do them if he could get them to come clean.

'Therefore to him that knoweth to do good, and doeth it not, to him it is sin.' He not only sees through them, but he has made his case so carefully that he knows they see it. 'Therefore …' It's a word you use when a natural conclusion follows. This is a conclusion he's drawing not only because of what he has said immediately before: that they have been boasting in their arrogance: but he's talking also about all that has preceded in this epistle. He's described their condition graphically.

How We Are Convicted Of Sin

The two ways that a Christian becomes convicted of sin are by the Spirit and by being confronted with the facts. By the Spirit, I mean the application of the Word. But it must be said that this kind of breakthrough presupposes a rather high degree of spirituality. Being confronted with the facts is outward, when you confront the person with the evil that has been done so that he will be boxed in and see that he is wrong.

A perfect illustration of this is the sin of David the king. He slept with another man's wife and thought that would be the end of it. But she became pregnant, so he sent for her husband who was in battle to give him a weekend off so that they could be together and then that way he would think the baby was his. They sent for Uriah, but Uriah couldn't bring himself to be with his wife whilst the battle raged and he stayed outside. David was getting a bit panicky, so he got Uriah to the front of the battle where he'd be killed, and he was (2 Sam. 11).

David was convicted of that sin, not by the direct leadership of the Spirit. The Spirit was grieved and wasn't going to communicate with David, but God sent Nathan and confronted David with the facts.

James comes as a Nathan to these Christian Jews and he is saying to them: 'Look what you have done to the poor. Look at what the world will think Christianity is. Look at your quarrelling, your lusting. God saved you from that. Now look at you. You're speaking evil of everybody. You're arguing. You're boasting. You know you're wrong.' He says, 'Therefore to him that knoweth to do good, and doeth it not, to him it is sin.'

Romans 3:23 states: 'All have sinned, and come short of the glory of God.' Anything missing the mark of God's glory is sin.

There is the problem with John Wesley's definition of sin. He said, 'Sin is the transgression of the known will of God.' In other words, it's not sin if you don't know enough. This is dangerous and misleading and suggests that ignorance is bliss and that ignorance is licence. James is saying the opposite. 'You do know. This is the problem. You cannot help but know.'

Their problem, one which recurred many times in church history, was that they said, 'I don't feel convicted by the Spirit.' Why do you suppose they thought like that? These Christians once knew this direct witness of the Spirit within, which was quite common in the first generation of the church. They knew how the Spirit could direct them and convict them. When you know something of this, it's the only way you want to be guided, because you're spoiled, as it were, for any other way of God dealing with you. It's wonderful to be guided like that. But these Christians were demanding this clear, definite word from the Spirit before they would admit to sin and confess it and they were saying, 'The Spirit hasn't shown me'. The person like that has imputed to himself the impossible. He thinks that, because the Spirit once dealt with him like that, the Spirit will continue to do that. But what he doesn't know is that the Spirit who has been grieved cannot deal like that. He retreats.

There are places the Holy Spirit will not go. There are things that, if you do them, force the Spirit to withdraw. And all the time you are wanting the conviction of the Spirit you will never get it. To get back to where he once was with an individual the Spirit uses means. He works from without. In the case of Jonah, God sent the wind and the fish. With David, Nathan came. With Simon Peter it was the crowing of a cock. If you wait for the Spirit whom you have grieved to convict you directly, you might wait a thousand years.

Nothing is more painful than having to face the fact of what you have done. Looking at what is right and what is wrong can be so painful. You want to look the other way. When you see injustice, a person who has been mistreated, you don't like to get involved. You can see how unfair it all is. This is why it's so painful to read Matthew 27: the trial of Jesus. It was so unfair. Luke 23, Mark 15. This is why people don't like preaching that gets close to the bone. They get mad at the preacher. They just don't like it. Or take a book you know will speak to you. You don't want to read it.

I remember when, some years ago, I was in a barren place in my ministry. Spiritually I was impoverished and I remember thinking, 'Maybe there's some book here on my bookshelves that will help me.' I saw Martyn Lloyd-Jones' *Sermon on the Mount*, and it had been such a blessing to me once before that I thought, 'I'll read that. No, I don't want to read that because that book is right. It will tell me.' Then I caught myself and I realized how I had become so filled with self-pity that I didn't want the truth. I just wanted something to make me feel better. I had to drive myself to read that book that time, and I'm so glad I did. When we're low spiritually we feel sorry for ourselves and we think God should give us special attention. But he uses other means so that we will face the facts and then see our sin.

James is not saying that ignorance is bliss. He says, 'You do know and if you are waiting for more convincing evidence you're not going to get it.'

James has forced them to look at what they did that was wrong. And he wants them to face what is right. The Greek word means 'good' or 'right'. The NASV translates this: 'To one who knows the right thing to do, and does not do it …' 'The right thing.'

What to do when the Spirit has departed

What is the good that one might do in a situation like this? You want to know what to do. The first big step is to admit to yourself that you are wrong. That's the opposite of repression, which produces the reaction formation, when you play games with yourself and won't even admit to yourself what you really know. When you admit that you'll feel really good inside. In Newton's words: 'pleasing grief and mournful joy'. For the first time, you can look at yourself in the mirror and look right into your own eyes. Why? You're coming to grips with the facts.

Second, admit it to God. Sin is only against God. There is a caution here. This confession means that you see the wrong to the extent that you're going to do something about it. This is why Proverbs tells us: 'He that covereth his sins shall not prosper: but whoso confesseth and forsaketh them shall have mercy' (28:13).

The question is, what if confession to God doesn't result in peace? I don't mean peace where you say, 'I've done it. Therefore it's got to be all right.' I'm talking about peace in your own heart. It's almost physical. And when you've got that peace you know it. It's wonderful. God sometimes withholds the blessing of peace until you have proved your earnestness by actual obedience. Perhaps you've promised him before. When you confessed it before you got peace but this time you don't get peace. This time God says, 'Prove it.' For that reason there's a third thing that follows in some cases.

When restitution is required

When the sin you have been confronted has been confessed but not been dealt with, then you're not always going to get peace. And so the third thing is restitution. It means putting things right. If there's any other way, God will let you off that. But if the peace is withheld I suggest this third thing: restitution. We are not talking, like some Puritans, about a special requirement for becoming a Christian. We become a Christian by looking to Christ. 'As Moses lifted up the serpent in the wilderness, even so must the Son of man be lifted up' (Jn. 3:14). In the wilderness they were saved by looking. So we are saved by looking. However, sometimes a

Christian becomes convicted of something he did before conversion or even since he's become a Christian. It could involve a sum of money, or a damaging lie. If by admitting it to yourself and admitting it to God the peace comes – fine. Forget it. Put it behind you. But if the peace doesn't come, it may mean that restitution is required.

According to James there's even a place for confessing to one another. You must be careful here, because you can do damage. One can need-lessly cause offence or bring scandal upon a Christian community. But if you've reached this stage I think you will know whether putting things right or making any confession to another person will do good or harm.

I should point out that all the tenses in this verse are in the present, in fact, four times in this very short verse. First of all: 'to him that knoweth'. Literally it should be translated 'knowing'. It's a participle. Next: 'to do' is an infinitive, present tense. Third: 'not doing' – participle, present tense. And fourth: 'to him it is sin'. The point is that knowing to do good and not doing it leaves you in a state of danger. It's an emergency. For when the Spirit is grieved, then that which grieved him must be dealt with. I'm not talking about the loss of salvation or about routinely confessing to God and pleading the blood of Christ. Sin, in this case, is not the refusing to confess to God verbally but it is not doing the good.

James says, 'Sin is' – not 'was' – 'knowing what is good and not doing it.' No amount of verbal confession to God or praying about will deal with the sin that James is referring to here. Jesus spoke of this when he said to the Pharisees, 'If ye were blind, ye should have no sin: but now ye say, We see; therefore your sin remaineth' (Jn. 9:41). James is talking about sin which the blood of Christ refuses to cleanse until one has done the good of which one knows.

People often try to pray around their real problem by confessing sin generally, by pleading the blood of Christ particularly. And yet you have to admit that it doesn't work, does it? You don't have peace. You've just done it and you've made a sacrament of it like a Roman Catholic. What is John saying? He says, 'If we walk in the light ...' It's a condition. 'If we walk in the light, as he is in the light, we have fellowship one with another, and the blood of Jesus Christ his Son cleanseth us from all sin' (1 Jn. 1:7). The blood refuses to cleanse until you have walked in the light. There are those who say, 'I'm justified by faith. The blood of Christ has washed away all my sin.' Nobody is questioning that. But that isn't what James is talking about. If he were, there would be no problem here. All these Christian Jews are going to heaven. Never mind if they despise the poor, if they have their lusts and their quarrelling. They could just say, 'The blood of Christ covers it all.' You wouldn't even need this epistle. You wouldn't even need the New Testament.

The need to put things right

Here is a truth that has almost perished from the earth. The blood of Christ refuses to cleanse this kind of sin until you've done the right and done the good. There is a sin which the blood of Christ will not cleanse. I'm not talking about your salvation. James is talking about your fellowship with God, your effectiveness as a Christian, your inheritance in the kingdom of God. Why do you suppose Jesus said, 'If ye forgive not men their trespasses, neither will your Father forgive your trespasses' (Mt. 6:15)? He's not talking about going to heaven, or else there would be almost nobody there.

Finally, James says, 'Therefore to him that knoweth to do good ...' Why is it 'to him'? Simply because it may not apply to every Christian. It is to particularize the Christian who, though like the rest of the body of Christ is justified by faith, has not dealt with a particular sin. This epistle shows us how to live the Christian life, which means to live like Jesus. And to the degree we're not like Jesus it is sin. You will say, 'We're all sinners.' Quite right. But the proof of our earnestness of wanting to be like Jesus is that we deal with sin when God draws our attention to it. Perfection is admitting our imperfections simultaneously with striving toward perfection.

This final verse of chapter 4 is not referring to general knowledge which you can do nothing about but to the specific, inescapable defect which has been brought home to you. Your confusion, your turmoil is called sin. And if you will admit it to yourself, admit it to God, walk in the light, do what he tells you, it could be painful – but the resulting peace is worth it.

27

The Danger of Accumulating Wealth

James 5:1–3

We move now into the last chapter of this general epistle of James. James returns to a subject that he introduced almost at the very beginning of the epistle. In chapter 5 verse 1 he addresses the rich: 'Go to now, ye rich men, weep and howl for your miseries that shall come upon you.' Back in chapter 1 he said, 'Let the brother of low degree rejoice in that he is exalted: But the rich, in that he is made low: because as the flower of the grass he shall pass away' (vv. 9–10).

The theme suggests strongly the kind of people he has had in mind throughout this epistle, and especially in chapter 4. For there is no doubt that anybody who had the means to say, 'Today or tomorrow we will go into such a city, and continue there a year, and buy and sell, and get gain', were those who already had a bit of money. Not everybody had the privilege of deciding where they were going to live, what they were going to do.

Now he uses the very same expression that he used in chapter 4 verse 13 for he says, 'Go to now ...' again in chapter 5 verse 1. It is perhaps better translated: 'Come now ...' The question is, why go for the rich? Isn't that being unfair? You might want to say to James, 'You're being a respecter of persons and you're going for the rich.'

The Providence In Temptation

I think I can suggest two reasons why he goes for the rich. The first is that it is a warning to anybody who wants to be rich. That includes most of us. The truth is that the problem of financial security is basic to human nature. And all of us would like to have just a little more than we've got.

The three most basic temptations in life arise from the need for: security; the desire for food, shelter and clothing, and sexual fulfilment; and that which pertains to our self-esteem.

I think it is true that more of this epistle, as we have seen, relates to the problem of sex and self-esteem. And yet I don't think there's any doubt but that James had the problem of security in mind when he said in the first chapter, 'Let no man say when he is tempted, I am tempted of God' (v. 13). For the temptation to want to be rich and to do things because money can justify it is very basic. There's nothing more 'providential' than temptation.

Back in Eden we're told that what gave Eve the final push was that she saw the tree was good for food. We can always justify what we want to do. What is more basic than the chance for financial gain? God knows I must eat, I must sleep, I must have clothes. It's so easy to believe that when there is a chance to make money it's got to be right. But it may not be. And you must be very careful about this. How subtle the temptation is to get just a little more, just to get ahead. There's nothing more serious than to make everything that happens to us providential as if it is God saying, 'All right, I've done this for you', when in fact we are being carried along by our own lust, our own insecurity, our own greed. Eve saw that it was good on the eyes, good for food and she ate (Gen. 3:6). We've been doing it ever since.

Christianity Offers Something To The Poor

The fact is that Christianity is the first enterprise ever to come along to have something to offer to the poor. But what often happens is, though Christianity is tailor-made for the poor, the poor person, when he becomes a Christian, wants to improve himself economically and socially. The gospel does this, but the problem is often that one aspires in the meantime to become middle class. This is why James talks like this, warning not only the rich but those who may want to be rich.

And yet it's a warning to those who do have a bit of money. It could be those who had the first-century equivalent of £10,000 or £100,000 in the bank. People that have a little money also have special temptations. The fact is that we're talking about real Christian people. Don't think for a minute that doesn't refer to a Christian who has some money.

The Temptations Of The Rich

We're talking about Christians in general. And it's certainly possible for a wealthy person to be a Christian. Jesus said: 'How hard is it for them that trust in riches to enter into the kingdom of God!' (Mk. 10:24). He doesn't mean it's hard for them to become a Christian. What Jesus meant by 'the kingdom of God' is coming to know God in depth, in intimacy. This is why the Lord's Prayer was given. We pray, 'Thy kingdom come' (Mt. 6:10). And then at the end of the prayer Jesus said, 'If ye forgive not men their trespasses, neither will your Father forgive your trespasses' (v. 15). He's talking about inheriting the kingdom. But the rich have a hard time with that because a special temptation to the rich is to think that the earth and all that's going on in the world matters so very much.

You may ask, 'What are the special temptations of those who have a little money?' Three things, to be specific.

- First, to trust their possessions instead of God. Jesus said, 'Take ... no thought for the morrow' (Mt. 6:34). And yet if you have a pot roast in your freezer it's not likely that you're going to pray very hard that you will have something to eat tomorrow. You can take no thought for the morrow because you're all prepared for tomorrow. That's why you're not worried about tomorrow. It has nothing to do with your faith. It's because you've already got enough. Those who have these things don't lean on God.

- The second special temptation is to see money as a harmless thing. The Bible doesn't say that money is 'the root of all evil', it says that 'the love of money is the root of all evil' (1 Tim. 6:10). It's a peculiar thing that when anybody gets his hands on a bit of money it has an odd effect upon that person. Very few people remain exactly the same when they get just a bit of money. They're the ones that cry the loudest, 'It's harmless.' James says, 'Come now, you that have got a bit of money. Weep and lament for the miseries that are coming on you.' James says, 'Your riches are corrupted, and your garments are motheaten. Your gold and silver is cankered' – tarnished.

- The third special temptation is to assume because you've got a bit of money that it ought to give you a certain right or privilege in the church. Much of the trouble these Christian Jews were having was from those who had a bit of money wanting to pull out and saying, 'We're just going to leave you all to yourselves. See how you can get on without us.' Those who have a bit of money have a temptation to use that as a threat. Then if they do stay around they want special privileges, they give but want to have a say in how things are run. Let's not be too hard on people like that. Because people who have a little money are used to doing that in the secular world. They sit on boards and committees. They know that they are there because they have learned how to handle money and they're in the habit of making decisions and dictating policy. For people like that it's a hard thing to come into the church and not exercise the same habit, to sit back and just be like everybody else. A person who has money has a different kind of ambition. In other words, people with money expect special attention. A man of God who has a bit of money is godly indeed if he can see himself as poor and wretched and naked in the sight of God. And he can be of great service to Christ. But not to warn a person like that is to be unkind to him, as these Christians had been unkind to the poor.

James Is Not A Respecter Of Persons, Especially The Rich

At the beginning of chapter 5 James now 'stands in the gap' and says what nobody had the courage or integrity to say up to now. For obviously there was a barrenness of leadership in this church. He's having to step in, much like, not a Nathan, but an Amos or a Malachi of the Old Testament. Hear what Amos says: 'Hear this, O ye that swallow up the needy, even to make the poor of the land to fail' (8:4). He went on to say, 'The LORD hath sworn by the excellency of Jacob, Surely I will never forget any of their works' (v. 7). This is Amos, the same one who had said, 'Woe to them that are at ease in Zion' (6:1). James is having to speak like this and show that he's not a respecter of persons.

It's a reminder that those Christians who have a bit of money and a bit of standing in society are really rare people. Paul had to say to the Corinthians, 'Ye see your calling, brethren, how that ... not many mighty, not many noble, are called' (1 Cor. 1:26). If you are a Christian with some intellectual or social standing or with a bit of money you're doubly lucky. For God normally doesn't even come by you. For Christianity was designed for the poor. But that isn't the way these Christians were looking at things. They felt lucky if a rich person came to church. James, Paul, the New Testament all say that it's the other way round: how grateful a person like that ought to be that God does save them.

How ridiculous that these Christians were capitalizing upon the rich. Everything was going wrong as a result of it. James is having to say now what nobody else was saying. The first thing he says is, 'Weep!' The Greek word means 'shed tears'. 'Start crying! Lament! Howl! Cry aloud!' Christian people, do we talk to the rich like that? All shall stand before God. There's a day coming, said John, that 'the kings of the earth, and the great men, and the rich men, and the chief captains, and the mighty men, and every bondman, and every free man' will hide himself 'in the dens and in the rocks of the mountains' and say 'to the mountains and rocks, Fall on us, and hide us from the face of him that sitteth on the throne, and from the wrath of the Lamb' (Rev. 6:15, 16). If we can get the rich to cry now they'll laugh then. Now they're laughing. Someday they'll howl. But get them to do it now, says James, and it will be a happy day then. This is the Christian message. This is what Isaiah said a long time ago. He said, 'Prepare ye the way of the LORD, make straight in the desert a highway for our God. Every valley shall be exalted, and every mountain and hill shall be made low: and the crooked shall be made straight, and the rough places plain: and the glory of the LORD shall be revealed, and all flesh shall see it together' (Isa. 40:3–5).

Yet another temptation for the rich is simply not to be too interested in this matter of heaven. If you've got any money at all and are able to take a holiday now and then or you're able to go out and buy a suit of clothes if you want to – you may say, 'I don't have that much', but you're all right really, aren't you? – I'll tell you something about yourself. The chances are you're not too interested in heaven. To be really interested in heaven is to be either very spiritually-minded indeed or to be so destitute that there's no place to look but up. Often to be deprived economically is God's means of making you look to heaven.

Some of the poorest people can be the most godly and the most filled with the Spirit. I could tell you stories of people I knew back in the hills of Kentucky who didn't know where their next meal was coming from but had the Shekinah glory on their faces and they didn't mind that. It's like the old Negro spirituals. So many of them were about heaven. There were blacks in the cotton fields of Alabama who didn't have anything else to look forward to.

When I was pastor of a church in Fort Lauderdale, I got to know a black minister not far from my church, an evangelical. And I came up with an idea that wasn't immensely popular. I said, 'I want you to come and preach for me on a Sunday night. You bring your people to my church and we'll have an ice cream social afterwards. I think it will be good for us.' He didn't know whether that would work or not but I got him to do it. His people came. A lot of them did. A lot of my people stayed away. He said, 'Don't worry. Some of our people wouldn't come either.'

But we had a great night. He preached on heaven and I never will forget one thing he said. He said, 'These liberals come along and they talk about having more of this world's goods.' And he cried out with the pathos of a Martin Luther King, 'Don't take heaven from me.' And he began to tell of the origins of the old Negro spirituals. 'You got shoes, I got shoes, all God's children got shoes.' Those blacks in the cotton fields didn't have shoes. They thought it was the greatest thing in the world to have a pair of shoes, so they sang, 'When I get to heaven, when I put on my shoes, I'll walk all over God's heaven.'

Money Will Not Bring Happiness

When we don't have much we look up, but God comes down. This is why James is shouting like this, showing that money is not a harmless thing. It has a way of eating in on you. He says that miseries are going to come upon you. 'Calamities' – that's the Greek word. Howl for them. Paul put it like this: 'They that will be rich' – those who want to be rich – 'fall into temptation and a snare, and into many foolish and hurtful lusts, which drown men in destruction and perdition.' That's when he went on to say, 'The love of money is the root of all evil' (1 Tim. 6:9–10). God's world is so designed that money will not bring you happiness. That's the folly of the vision of a little money. If you have a thousand pounds you want two thousand. If you have ten thousand you want twenty. If one million you want two. 'Just a little bit more and then I'll be all right.'

James doesn't merely address those who would be rich, but those who are. This ought to be a warning to us. We think that if we just have a little bit more it will solve our problem. James talked like this because these Christians had found something backfire on them: that their own money – the actual money – wasn't doing them any good. He had to say to them, 'Your riches are corrupted, and your garments'. What will money buy? What has that done for you? 'Your gold and your silver is cankered.' It was cursing them rather than blessing them. This could only happen to them because they were Christians.

If you're not a Christian and you say, 'I don't find any of this true at all', I understand that. James is talking about Christians who didn't give God what was coming to him. For, as a result of their worldliness, they had robbed God. First, they had robbed evangelism of its indiscriminate offer: they only wanted to impress the rich. Secondly, they had robbed their employees of justice and fairness. Then they had robbed God himself.

Malachi had to address the same problem of those who weren't giving their employees their right wages (Mal. 3:5). But then Malachi didn't stop there. He went on to say, 'Will a man rob God?' It fits, because worldly Christians usually are disobedient right across the board. You can get them on any point. They're lusting. They're greedy. They're quarrelling. And then you find out they're not tithing.

Most Tithers Are On Lower Incomes

Now if you are a Christian and you're wondering why you're not being blessed and why what you're not giving to God is backfiring on you, I'm telling you why. It's only because you are a Christian. It's often the case – it's extraordinary – the bulk of tithers in the Christian church are not those with higher incomes but those with lower incomes. Those with higher incomes say, 'If I just give ten or twenty pounds a week that's more than most people are giving.' You think it's the amount that matters. Don't you know that you are impoverished, that God is looking at your heart? You're saying, 'The church will get by with this.' You're robbing yourself and God is not going to bless you. This is why Malachi had decided, 'You're cursed with a curse' (3:9). And so James: 'Your riches are corrupted, and your garments are motheaten.' To the degree you do not give God what is his, you will be impoverished even at a natural level.

We all want the faith of Abraham but we don't want to tithe like Abraham. We want to wrestle with God like Jacob and prevail with God, but we don't want to tithe like Jacob. Many of you are saying, 'I'm just not convinced of tithing.' You don't want to be. Do you think that adultery became a sin after the Mosaic law or before? Do you think murder was wrong before Moses said it was wrong? And you that say, 'Well, it's going back to the law', forget that what the law did was to legalize a standard of righteousness that God had sanctioned long before. This is God's way for the church to grow.

This is the way God wants it to be. When I think of the things churches could do if everybody tithed. And the odd thing is that God has promised that the ninety per cent will go further than the hundred per cent you have yourself. This is what James means: 'Your riches are corrupted.' Let me ask you, you that are not tithing, look back over the past twelve months, are you better off? You're not. Jesus said it all: 'Lay not up for yourselves treasures upon earth, where moth and rust doth corrupt, and where thieves break through and steal: but lay up for yourselves treasures in heaven' (Mt. 6:19–20). James is simply applying a general principle to a specific situation. He says, 'You lust and have not. That's a witness against you. You're full of greed. You're quarrelling with each other. Are you better off? No, you're not.'

Now he turns to the problem of the use of money and if they are better off. No, they're corrupted. Their riches are tarnished. James comes up with a motive for why they were living like this. He says, 'You've saved up for the last days, haven't you?'

If you lust and don't deal with sexual temptation you will rob yourself. You'll be as though somebody took some strong rubber bands around your two clenched hands. You try to break loose but you can't until the rubber bands are cut. It's the same if you have a problem with your self-esteem or the use of money. You will suffer. Not only at a spiritual level are you impoverished, but at a natural level as well.

So James now, coming towards the end of this epistle, turns to this matter of money. We all know what it is to have financial pressure. Jesus said: 'Take no thought for your life, what ye shall eat, or what ye shall drink; nor yet for your body, what ye shall put on' (Mt. 6:25). He says, 'Your heavenly Father takes care of the sparrow. Aren't you better than a sparrow? Surely you are. And your heavenly Father feeds the sparrow. He's going to take care of you because not only are you a person but you're bought with the blood of Christ.'

The kind of Christianity James knows about affects the whole man, spiritually, physically, materially. He deals with your lusts, the use of the tongue, and your own security as a person. Treasures in heaven. How important are they to you? Do you know what it is to go to a teller in a bank and say, 'Withdraw everything I've got.' Someday you're going to stand before God in heaven. I don't know what it will be like, but you'll get the dividends. You'll realize that life was so short and how things seemed to have mattered so much.

The odd thing is, you don't have to wait until then to reap the benefit. It's not necessary to be poor or to be black in the cotton fields of Alabama to think about heaven, because it takes great grace to discipline yourself so that you can be spiritual. That's why it is hard for a rich man, although he didn't say it was impossible. If we will be godly indeed and give him our bodies and all that we have, oh, how he will bless us. You cannot outgive the Lord. And he will honour you. Who knows how much spiritual blessing as well will be poured out upon us because we've taken seriously that God wants his people to be happy? But that happiness will continually elude the person who lives for himself and thinks he can improve upon God's way.

28

The Oppressor – God's Enemy

James 5:1–4

This general epistle of James is a practical handbook for living the Christian life, but it is also a study in backsliding. What we have before us now is James showing one phase of backsliding. To some it might be the cause. He returns to the subject of money. Somebody has said that money, to a British evangelical in the twentieth century, is like sex in the Victorian age. Everybody thinks about it but nobody talks about it! When it comes to money we all get very nervous and quiet because this is personal. But James talks openly and freely about it and puts his finger on this malady.

God Is On The Side Of The Oppressed

Now the question is, is James against rich people? The answer is that all James does is to be no respecter of persons. And what he's doing particularly is to take sides with the oppressed, because God is always on the side of the oppressed. James started out the epistle giving a word of comfort to the person of low degree. Here in chapter 5 James is having to step in and say what nobody was saying because obviously there was a great gap of spiritual leadership.

Here we are dealing with people in this Christian church made up of Jews who had abused their money, partly because they were saving for their last days. But he says their riches are corrupted, their garments are motheaten. In other words, the money is still worth the same because tarnished gold doesn't lose its value, but it's devalued as long as it's in their hands. And in their case the hundred per cent is devalued to below ninety per cent. They have withheld from God what is his. It's as if James is saying 'You're going to be sorry. Weep now because it's coming. You might as well prepare for it.' What we have here is this double reference to God's judgement in the final day and the way things will backfire in the here and now.

Taking Obedience Lightly

There are Christians who take very lightly the matter of obedience. They say, 'I'm saved. I'm justified by faith. I'm covered by the blood of Christ. I'm going to heaven.' They think that that's all that matters. They're going to find out that God is serious about the matter of reward. The Bible does not contain idle comments. Weep and howl for the misery that is coming upon you even in this life. You're going to suffer now, but that is nothing to what you will know when the day shall declare it. You force God to treat you as an enemy. And he will do it. It's all very well saving for the last days. But it is precisely the last days you ought to be worrying about. It's a wonderful thing when a person can reach his sunset years and look back upon a godly life and a life of obedience, a life of pleasing the Lord. It ought not to be that anybody should have sorrow, but James is saying that your last days aren't going to be sweet after all.

Then he comes to the cause. The most serious charge yet. Here is a verse that tells us more about who these people were, whom they had abused and what God thinks of it. 'Behold, the hire of the labourers who have reaped down your fields, which is of you kept back by fraud, crieth: and the cries of them which have reaped are entered into the ears of the Lord of sabaoth.' James is singling out certain ones in this Christian community. Who were they that he now particularly addresses? He's addressing Christian capitalists. How do we know this? Because they were employers of men. He says to them, 'The hire – the wages – of your workers who have reaped or mowed down your fields …'

These Christians had labourers under them whom they had mistreated. They paid the salaries of certain people. We already know that they had accumulated wealth because he talks about their gold and their silver being cankered. They probably didn't do physical work. And we know that they owned real estate. He says, 'They have reaped down your fields.' We know how they partly made their money. We know from verse 13 of the previous chapter that they had enough capital to be involved in financial speculation, buying and selling and making a profit. We know that they also made money from the fields that they owned because they had people working for them who did the physical labour and brought in money for these rich landowners. So it suggests that, whatever else these Christian Jews were who had this money, they were farmers or agriculturalists, not altogether unlike the plantation owners in the south of the United States.

This sermon might have been very timely a century ago. I just wonder how much preaching there was from the first six verses of James chapter 5 by ministers of Baptist churches in Alabama back in the 1840s and the 1860s. For the fact is, the Christian faith has direct relevance for outward conditions. We evangelicals can get very nervous about any preaching that just gets slightly outside of preaching the gospel: 'Believe on the Lord Jesus Christ, and thou shalt be saved' (Acts 16:31). Of course, there have been the social gospellers who have come along and got into politics and the question of race and poverty and this is all they've talked about.

The result has been for many of us to put our backs up and say, 'We don't get into things like that.' This Christian gospel has relevance for this kind of situation, for outward physical conditions around us. If this gospel had been preached faithfully we wouldn't be having the problem we're having today. Pay day has come in the twentieth century. The cries of those who were mistreated in the last century and before went up into the ears of the Lord of hosts. All of us are affected by it.

As for these employees, what do we know about them? They were labourers. It tells us they reaped. The NIV says that they 'mowed your fields'. That shows they worked in the fields. The Greek word means 'estates' or 'farms'. One more thing. Here's where the water hits the wheel. These employees were underpaid. So James says to these Christian capitalists that the hire, or the wages, of the workers who have mowed 'your fields … you have kept back by fraud'.

It Is Honourable To Work

Everything up to now was not so bad. There's nothing wrong with the fact that these people had money. That is not a sin. There was nothing wrong with the fact that these labourers were working in the fields because work is an honourable and satisfying thing to do. Anybody who is lazy feels very guilty about it. For work makes us all feel better. The harder we work the better. But here was the problem: they were underpaid. Who can deny that the most demoralizing enterprise in the world is to work hard and not get adequate pay for it? Jesus said, 'The labourer is worthy of his hire' (Lk. 10:7). Paul repeated this (1 Tim. 5:18), and he wasn't referring merely to physical labour. For anybody who does something that is honourable, says Paul, ought to be paid for it.

The question is, what was the reaction of these labourers who had reaped down the fields? They cried. Does this surprise you? These people were human beings, created in God's image. For those of us who are not having a financial problem, who are on the end of paying others, it's so easy to say, 'They're going to be all right. They've got enough.' The common reaction when you hear about a labourer who cries and murmurs is to treat him like dirt and not be too nice to him. I remember my father, who was a labourer, quoting Senator Robert Taft many years ago, 'Let them eat beans.' This is a common reaction. Keep them in their place! And Christian capitalists, not atheist capitalists, were contributing to this.

Crying is the most natural reaction in the world when you don't have money to pay your bills, to feed your family. (Some people cry because they're too lazy to get a job and I'm not talking about people like that.) It is most demoralizing to work and have an employer hold back what is justly yours, whether it be in the cotton fields of Alabama or the coal mines in Wales. James says, 'It's been kept back by fraud.' This may refer to an agreed-upon salary. It may refer to an unfair salary to begin with.

You may have thought that Christianity shuts its eyes to this matter, that Christianity is irrelevant in today's society. But too many in this country in the last century, too many ministers, were sipping sherry with their rich parishioners. And we're reaping the results today. I have quoted that black minister in Fort Lauderdale who cried out, 'Don't take heaven from me.' Everything was being taken away from his people and the liberal ministers came along and made what is in this world all there is.

Somebody did take heaven from the blacks and from the labourers. His name was Karl Marx. He said, 'Religion is the opiate of the people.' And that caught on. You don't have new spirituals about heaven emerging from blacks today. The working class today is untouched by the Christian message. This country and the Western world at large, under the guise of the Christian faith, have failed to set the example. For what convinces those that are untouched by the gospel is not our philosophical arguments. Man come of age doesn't believe in certain epistemological assumptions of the New Testament. Why, people today don't even know about them. What would make the difference is to see living examples. You can witness, and you must, but if your life is not changed and your attitude is not different, why would anybody want to be a Christian?

Faith Must Be Combined With Works

These Christians had their faith. They were going to heaven. But James is saying, 'Your faith must be combined with works.' The relevance of the Christian faith is to be seen in terms of how we live our lives. What do you suppose people think of Christianity when a rich man who goes to church isn't nice to those who work for him? So we're reaping it today, and the consequence partly is racial strife that could have been avoided if all were paid fairly. The question of racial prejudice is inherent in this text as well, for James is addressing the question of mistreatment.

God is no respecter of persons. If you think that you're off the hook because you're not an industrialist or a capitalist, I ask you, are you offended if a Pakistani or a black man comes into your church? What about when you're on the underground? And what are your comments when you read the newspaper? How many of you are secret admirers of those who say, 'We ought to send the blacks back to Africa, the Pakistanis back to Pakistan'? You have sinned against God. And it tells, for the cries of those who have been mistreated have come into the ears of the Lord of hosts. These people are created in God's image. And we're not reaching them today. The Moslems are growing faster than the Christians in this country. This is happening because we've lost our credibility.

God Hears The Cries Of The Oppressed

Mr Businessman, are you aware that God sees everything you do? If you walk all over other people do you realize that God sees it and hears their cries? If you cut another's throat to get what you want and you say, 'The devil was defeated. I got what I wanted', the Lord sees you. If you leave somebody else demoralized by your unfair treatment God sees it. The worst miscalculation the oppressor makes is that God doesn't take any notice of this.

The biggest problem these capitalists faced was that God was listening. Because it didn't appear at the moment that God heard, they just went on. They heard the cries but they left them in a separate compartment. It didn't bother them a bit. They'd go to church on Sunday. They'd sing the hymns. They'd put money in the collection plate. They could probably pray beautiful prayers. But on Monday morning things were different. There's an old Negro spiritual that talks about having religion on Sunday but not on Monday. I wonder why those blacks thought of that?

What about you? You come to church and pray and feel good in your soul. But what about mistreating another person? They thought that they could get away with it. These Christians should have known better than that. Back in Deuteronomy Moses says, 'Thou shalt not oppress an hired servant that is poor and needy, whether he be of thy brethren' (listen) 'or of thy strangers that are in thy land within thy gates: at his day thou shalt give him his hire, neither shall the sun go down upon it; for he is poor, and setteth his heart upon it: lest he cry against thee unto the LORD, and it be sin unto thee' (24:14–15).

Robbing God

The worst miscalculation you can make is to say that the Christian faith does not relate to things. The problem, I fear, is that I'm preaching what ought to have been shouted from pulpit to pulpit a hundred years ago. Malachi said the same thing. 'I will come near to you to judgement; and I will be a swift witness against the sorcerers, the adulterers, and against false swearers, and against those that oppress the hireling in his wages, the widow and the fatherless' (3:5). It's almost a direct quote by James. And then Malachi goes on and surprise, surprise, these people weren't tithers. He says, 'You have robbed God' (v. 8).

Generally those who have the most money are not the best tithers. Those who have a little bit of money give more in proportion. But you're robbing God. It's often the case that God will bless the tither and then he begins to be blessed and doesn't tithe any more. He just gives more than others. This is what was happening and James says, 'Your gold and silver are corrupted.' Once a person reaches the stage where he's a millionaire he says, 'My goodness, if I gave a tithe that would be more than anybody else gives combined.' If God could have that money what could be done with the gospel? We wouldn't have to have special appeals for anything. Missionary societies would thrive.

Your hundred per cent is devalued to below ninety per cent. God didn't get it for the church, but you didn't get it either. You're cursed. If you don't give God what is his, you're no better off, are you? The problem is that God not only has eyes but he hears. It's James' way of saying that God is for the underdog but he's the enemy of the oppressor. Why put it like this: 'the Lord of sabaoth', the Lord of hosts? The Lord has countless armies, ten thousand times ten thousand and thousands of thousands. He can despatch a thousand angels to be at hand to take sides against the oppressor because he's going to bring judgement upon the worldly Christian, upon the Christian capitalist and, worst of all, the nation in which this abuse has spread. The cries of the last century went up and all of us are paying for it today. Abel's blood cried up from the ground and God took notice. Every abuse cries out to the Lord of hosts. What is the result? Strife, burnings, riots.

But there's something worse than that. Do you know what Amos went on to say? 'The days come, saith the Lord GOD, that I will send a famine in the land, not a famine of bread, nor a thirst for water, but of hearing the words of the LORD' (8:11). How exceedingly rare is the preaching of the undiluted gospel in Britain today. And you think God doesn't take notice of these things. We're paying for it. God stepped in. That generation may not have known how livid God was at the mistreatment toward the oppressed.

What can we do now? You say, 'This is something that's a bit late.' I say this: if the shoe fits, wear it. You've got your life to live. Don't play fast and loose with God, including your tithes. As for the warning, the good news is that God only warns when there is hope. When Sodom and Gomorrah went up in flames there's no hint they were ever warned. He just did it. But when God graces us with the dignity of being warned and there's something we can do, let's do it. Thank God that we can hear the word of the Lord in a time such as this. Let's honour the name of God by our obedience.

29

Following Jesus Indeed

James 5:4–7

One of the more interesting questions we have not addressed is, to whom exactly did this letter come, that is, who (what individual or what group of individuals) had control of the letter? Did everybody in that Jewish Christian community get the message, or how long did it take before the word got around to everybody? When the letter arrived would one person have got it? They didn't have photocopying machines to spread it to all the members of the congregation. Chances are, one person had access to it and read it publicly. It might have been an elder, it might have been some leader.

The Reader Of James' Letter

The question then is, who was present when it was read? Were all the rich that James was addressing there? Were the poor there to hear it? And were there rumours that the letter was around? Maybe some didn't want to be present on the morning it was going to be read. Would those who needed it most hear it? Or would those who needed great encouragement from it be present? It could be that if the rich Christians to whom James was talking were in control they might have tried to stop it from being heard by everybody. What we do know is that the poor had been despised.

James seems to assume that the more powerful in this Christian community will have the most immediate access to the letter. And most definitely they will hear it. Indeed in chapter 4 he says, 'You that say, Today or tomorrow we will go to this place, buy and sell ...' (v. 13) and in the end he says, 'You rich men, weep and howl' (5:1). He knows they're going to get it and they will have immediate access. The question is, would those who saw the letter first want everybody else to know that James has talked to them like that? There's the theoretical possibility that the poor would never know that James had talked to the rich as he did. This may be why James addresses these rich, class-conscious Christians in this direct manner.

As I say, the possibility existed that the poor wouldn't even hear about the letter. But just in case they would hear it, he says this to them at the beginning, 'Let the brother of low degree rejoice in that he is exalted' (1:9). But even that too could be for the rich. For it's a very powerful hint that God is on the side of the underdog. If there were a verse in this epistle that the rich and those in power would have wanted to shield from the poor it is this one in chapter 5 verse 4 when he says, 'Behold, the hire of the labourers who have reaped down your fields, which is of you kept back by fraud, crieth: and the cries of them which have reaped are entered into the ears of the Lord of sabaoth.' James is saying to them, 'Even if you don't let the poor know I've talked to you like that, understand that God hears them.

God would ensure the poor got this message

And yet having said all that, we can be sure that the poor would have got the word. There are two ways the letter would have reached the poor and James knew eventually they'd get it. One is the providential overruling grace of God. As with those who have tried to extinguish the Bible, the more this happens, the more the word of God flourishes. God has seen to it that his word stays around and alive.

But there's another possibility: that these powerful Christians to whom the letter is primarily addressed would repent and share the letter willingly with the poor – a sign of true revival breaking out. For the ungrieved Spirit of God works with the one who makes himself vulnerable. When we admit that we've been found out and God has dealt with us it has a way of breaking down barriers. During the Welsh Revival Evan Roberts stressed forgiving one another. He told of how the revival was stopped in one place because of people who wouldn't forgive each other. But when they freely and truly forgave each other, the Spirit came down. And indeed on the day of Pentecost we're told they were with one accord in one place.

But if these more influential and powerful Christians who were likely the leaders tried to keep hidden that God had rebuked them, there was no chance, no chance at all, of revival coming to that church for the Spirit would have stayed grieved. These who were mistreated had a right to know that James stepped in without any partiality whatever and rebuked those who had been so unkind.

It must have been a shock to these influential leaders that James wrote the letter at all. For the letter demonstrates that these ruthless Christians had been found out. God can do this. He did this with Jonah. Jonah thought he had executed the perfect plan. He took a trip to Tarshish, took a nap in the sides of the ship. But God even overruled the pagan superstitious casting of lots and found out Jonah.

The Backslider's Rationale

We often wonder what makes a backslider think he can get away with what he does. The rationale of every backslider is that he thinks God really won't bother to do anything about it. The Psalmist in Psalm 94 puts it like this: 'O LORD God, to whom vengeance belongeth ... shew theyself ... LORD, how long shall the wicked triumph? ... Yet they say, The LORD shall not see, neither shall the God of Jacob regard it' (vv. 1, 3, 7). Or look at Psalm 10: 'He hath said in his heart, I shall not be moved: for I shall never be in adversity. His mouth is full of cursing and deceit and fraud: under his tongue is mischief and vanity. He sitteth in the lurking places of the villages: in the secret places doth he murder the innocent: his eyes are privily set against the poor' (vv. 6–8). The same situation. Those who are put down, who have no chance of defending themselves. It goes on, 'He hath said in his heart, God hath forgotten: he hideth his face; he will never see it' (vv. 9, 11). These Christians also thought they were getting away with it. What a shock it must have been when out of the blue comes James the brother of our Lord, taking sides with the poor. God knows exactly what is going on.

And yet those backsliders had another rationale. On the one hand they say, 'God's not going to do anything about it. We'll get away with this.' But then they consoled themselves with what appeared to be God's gracious providence. They had such a good standard of living. When James said early on, 'Every good gift and every perfect gift is from above' (1:17), they liked that. They could see that God had been good to them. The providence of prosperity is often taken as a sign that we're okay.

Here was Jonah. God said, 'Go to Nineveh.' Jonah said, 'I don't think I want to do that.' He went to Tarshish and, providence of providences, there was a ship going to Tarshish. That was just wonderful for Jonah. 'God is with me. He had a ship going to Tarshish.' He got on it and he felt so good about it. The easiest thing in the world for us to do is to take providence – we always call it providence when it goes our way – as a sign God is with us.

These Christian Jews had imbibed the same theology as that of Job's comforters. Namely, prosperity is a sign of God's blessing and approval and the lack of prosperity is a sign of some secret sin and God's disapproval. Job's frustration was having to fight that common consensus. Job's friends were certain that Job had sinned. Job was sure he hadn't, but his friends had tradition on their side. That tradition has always ruled. It's the most popular theology of all, and it was ruling in James' day. The ultimate court to which these Christian Jews appealed in their refusal to come to grips with their behaviour was that God had blessed them with delicate and luxurious living. They could retort to anybody, 'Who do you suppose has blessed us? God.' That, to them, was the sign they were okay.

James acknowledges this, but he doesn't do it in exactly the way they would have liked. He says in verse 5, 'You have lived in pleasure. You have lived well.' It's a word that in the Greek means 'you have lived delicately'. But what is the source of this high living? The earth. James says, 'Ye have lived in pleasure on' – or from – 'the earth.' This was a rebuke. James would have thrilled them had he said, 'You've lived in this delicate way from heaven.' But he didn't say that. The easiest thing in the world is to conclude something is of divine origin simply because we're enjoying it and having a good time. This is why prosperity and outward blessing can be misleading and sometimes dangerous.

We Are Responsible For Our Own Temptations

James goes on, 'Ye have lived in pleasure on the earth, and have been wanton.' The Greek word means 'self-indulgent'. It means they have been given over to something by no ordinary craving or desire. This in itself was a great indictment upon them. We are responsible for our own temptations. The goal of every Christian life is to reduce temptation to the level of suggestion so that you are not governed by this feeling. But here were those who had wanton desires. To be wanton is disgraceful for any Christian. Why do things tempt you like they do? It is because you still have an appetite at the natural level that ought not to be named among those who are called to be saints. You have that strong desire because you want to have it. You are doing nothing about it. You're governed by it. And you wonder why over the years you're not growing spiritually.

But not only that, these wanton Christians indulged in a false kind of attending to their hearts. Here's how James puts it: 'Ye have lived in pleasure on the earth, and been wanton; ye have nourished your hearts.' The heart is the seat of faith, of personality. 'Keep thy heart with all diligence; for out of it are the issues of life' (Prov. 4:23). Just looking at that phrase, 'Ye have nourished your hearts', that doesn't sound too bad. The problem is that the heart is also the seat of unbelief and the seat of all that goes wrong. In fact, James says, 'You pamper your hearts. You're not being self-critical. What you're doing is amassing certain self-justifying evidence to convince you that you're okay.'

The iniquity of our selective understanding

Every backslider has two sets of evidence the whole time he's in that state. One is that you say, 'Surely God is with me. I'm not wrong.' And the other set of evidence says, 'You are wrong and you know you have grieved the Spirit.' What the backslider does is to be selective with the evidence. He can always find evidences that he couldn't be all that wrong. We can all do it. Unless God breaks through, we go on in our rebellion. He says, 'You pamper your hearts.' And for what? The 'day of slaughter'. The analogy here is like a farmer who fattens his sheep or his cattle by putting them in the best pasture just a couple of weeks before they're to be slaughtered.

James says, 'That's what's happening with you. You're pampering your hearts for the day of slaughter, which is God's judgement. It's coming. Howl, you rich men. Weep for the calamity that is coming upon you. You thought that mistreating the poor, withholding just wages, not dealing with your wanton temptation, didn't matter. But you were wrong. And God is stepping in. For God resists the proud but gives grace to the humble. Have you forgotten that?'

James has changed metaphors and reversed roles. This is very interesting from a literary point of view. James does this first of all by changing metaphors from the rust of gold, consuming the flesh as fire which was an allusion to the final day of judgement, to their delicate living making them fat for the slaughter. From rust to fat. From fire to slaughter.

But how does he reverse roles? This is even more interesting. First, he likened these Christians to fattened sheep for the slaughter, but now suddenly he turns right round and refers to those who have been mistreated as sheep slaughtered already. For he says in verse 6, 'Ye have condemned and killed the just; and he doth not resist you.' This is an obvious allusion to Isaiah 53: 'He was oppressed, and he was afflicted, yet he opened not his mouth: he is brought as a lamb to the slaughter, and as a sheep before her shearers is dumb, so he openeth not his mouth' (v. 7). 'So,' says James, 'you have slaughtered the just and he does not resist you. He openeth not his mouth.' James gives a cryptic reference to our Lord's crucifixion. Everybody knew that Jesus was not treated fairly. James is saying to these Christians, 'You're like Pontius Pilate and Herod. You've joined together and you have killed the just.' The Greek word means 'righteous' or 'innocent'.

The question is, who are the innocent that James is talking about here? It is a reference to the poor who had been brushed aside, who weren't treated with any kind of dignity because they were poor. Those coming into the assembly with the gold ring and fancy clothes were given prior treatment. It's as if James is saying, 'You've condemned and killed them. How were they sentenced and killed? They have been so ill-treated that never in a thousand years would they want to hear the gospel that you preach. The gospel of Jesus Christ has been rendered contemptible by your behaviour to the poor.' These would go to hell, because the only thing that could save them had been rendered fraudulent.

Can anything be more tragic than that? It's like a person who refuses to go to a doctor who could heal him. He is dying of disease and there's a doctor who has the treatment. But he knows something about that doctor and he says, 'I'd rather die than get well by that doctor.' This is what the poor were probably thinking: 'If these people have the only thing that can help me I would rather go to hell.

What a judgement it is upon Christianity that some would be driven to despair rather than to Christ. Is there somebody who will never be a Christian because you have lived the kind of life that is so hypocritical and so wrong that they would rather die and be lost than dignify what you believe? It's the challenge to every one of us. Even though we have the only thing that can cure the world's ills, we must live lives that will make the world want to be Christian. It's an admonition to every minister, to every deacon and to every Christian to live a life that is beyond reproach. For those who know that you're a Christian expect to see something different in you.

Suffering At The Hands Of A Fellow Christian

There's a second way to look at this verse. The innocent also included the workers in the fields, who apparently were actually Christians. These were Christians working for Christians. I say that for three reasons. First, it tells us that those in the fields cried out to God. Not only that, we're told that they are referred to as 'righteous'. But the main thing is that they did not resist. The chief difference between those workers then and workers today, generally speaking, is that those that James talks about took their ill-treatment lying down.

Today there are strikes, protests and sometimes violence. But these workers were different. They cried to the Lord of sabaoth, the Lord of hosts. They took seriously God's exclusive right to vindicate. Had they tried to vindicate themselves, God would have backed off and let them sort it out among themselves. In any case, they were defenceless. So they cried to God lying down. And James was impressed by this for the trials which some of these Christians were called on to dignify were severe beyond imagination. It's one thing to suffer at the hands of a non-Christian, but to suffer at the hands of a Christian is painful indeed.

Here was a case of Christians working for Christians and being mistreated. This problem came up in the New Testament more than once. For example, Timothy was told by Paul, 'Let as many servants as are under the yoke count their own masters worthy of all honour, that the name of God and his doctrine be not blasphemed. And they that have believing masters, let them not despise them, because they are brethren; but rather do them service, because they are faithful and beloved, partakers of the benefit' (1 Tim. 6:1–2). That was hard advice to take. But these workers were told, 'Don't resist.' Peter was addressing exactly the same thing when he said, 'Servants, be subject to your masters with all fear; not only to the good and gentle, but also to the froward', those who are not kind (1 Pet. 2:18).

How We Show We Are Following Jesus

One of the greatest trials a Christian can encounter – but it is also the cloud that is biggest with mercy that will burst upon your head – is being mistreated by another Christian. This gives you an extraordinary opportunity to be like the Lord who was mistreated by religious people. What impressed James is that those workers in the fields didn't strike back. Peter could say of Jesus, 'Who when he was reviled, reviled not again; when he suffered, he threatened not; but committed himself to him that judgeth righteously' (1 Pet. 2:23). For behaviour like this defies explanation at a natural level. It was grace and grace alone that was functioning. There are two ways, probably in this order, that show that you are following Jesus indeed. The first is that you deal with your lusts and the second is that you take ill-treatment lying down.

There is a fourth reason to believe that those who were in the fields crying out were Christians. It is that James now turns from these heartless, ruthless leaders in the church and appears to address those who had been mistreated. He says, 'Be patient therefore, brethren, unto the coming of the Lord.' He calls them 'brethren' and he says, 'Be patient therefore ...' He couldn't be saying that to those who were being fattened up for the day of slaughter.

For how long must we be patient? 'Unto the coming of the Lord.' That may have been a disappointment to them because that could mean waiting a long time. It turned out that it's been over 1900 years. Perhaps they wanted justice and vindication then. But there is no absolute promise of vindication before Jesus comes again. Any justice that takes place before Jesus comes again is when God steps in on his own.

I believe that any justice carried out before the second coming on your behalf only diminishes the trial, and might even lessen the possibility of greater treasure in heaven. So it's not necessarily good that you're vindicated. Because if you can endure it when the heat is on then there is an opportunity to inherit heavenly riches indeed. Those riches are presented to you on a silver platter. True godliness puts personal justice and personal vindication in teleological suspension. You wait until Jesus comes and you do not expect it a minute before. And you forget it and know that in the day of judgement everything will be cleared. James can only say in the meantime, 'Blessed is the man that endureth temptation: for when he is tried, he shall receive the crown of life, which the Lord hath promised' (1:12). When you've dealt with these two things: carnal desire and taking ill-treatment lying down, you are gloriously close to following Jesus indeed. He did not resist. 'Who, when he was reviled, reviled not again' (1 Pet. 2:23).

30

When the Rain is Over

James 5:7–8

We now enter the final section of the general epistle of James. James has just concluded his final attack, or strong rebuke, upon the ruthless rich who had caused the trouble in this church of Christian Jews.

James Turns From The Oppressors To The Oppressed

The rest of this epistle is not directed to these rich, prestigious, powerful Christians in the church but rather to the remnant. And he begins with those in particular who had been oppressed. A word like this coming from James must have seemed a great vindication to those godly ones in that community who had been mistreated. What a great encouragement it must have been, if only because they may have thought up to now that nobody really cared. They may have said, like the Psalmist, 'No man cares for my soul' (142:4).

It's an easy position to get in when you see things that are happening that aren't right. You see it going on and you begin to think, 'I suppose this is the way it's supposed to be.' Those who were oppressed and stood in the background might think, 'Surely this isn't Christianity, is it? Maybe it is. We don't think it is, but who are we to say?' Now James steps in.

False Guilt

Another thing is that while they were having these thoughts, wondering whether it was right that the Christian faith should be taken over by a few and the church was divided, they began to wonder if maybe they were wrong. A person can have pseudo-guilt, where you begin to think, 'How terrible of me to have thoughts like this.' And you begin to think you grieved the Lord because you had the thoughts. You see something going on that you know is wrong and you think, 'It can't be wrong or that person wouldn't do it because he's such a good person.' It's a form of false guilt. The devil can use that and even drive you to deep depression when the whole time you were not wrong to think like that.

Who was going to believe them if they had these thoughts? They were in the minority, small people without power. They were just trying to serve the Lord. But James comes in and takes over for them. So when he says, 'Be patient therefore, brethren, unto the coming of the Lord', they must have thought the Lord had already come, in a sense, because that was what they were wanting – just to know that they weren't wrong to have those thoughts. For they had seen something going on that was unjust, unfair. And for James to imply, 'Of course, this is wrong. God is going to deal with you', was a great comfort to them. But we must say that it was only a temporary respite. It was good to know that James had sanctioned them, endorsed them, but in the end they needed more than that. That's why James directs them not to himself but to the Lord and, in particular, to the Lord's coming.

When somebody says, 'Just be patient to the coming of the Lord', that could mean waiting a long time. Yet the principle to remember here is that there is no absolute promise of vindication until the final second coming. James is saying, 'Be patient therefore, brethren, in the light of all that you've been through. You've been elevated to suffer with our Lord and you've dignified the worst kind of trial. Be patient.'

The Coming Of The Lord

This reference to the coming of the Lord is to be understood in both the primary sense and the secondary sense. The primary sense refers to the physical, literal, bodily second coming of Jesus. 'Be patient ... unto the coming of the Lord.' But it's a Greek word that really means 'presence' – 'unto the presence'. It's a word often used in Greek literature when a sovereign comes in presence and with the coming you actually see the king or the queen. This is the way the second coming of Jesus is referred to many times. In the earliest church they looked for the *parousia*. It was their conviction that Jesus is coming back.

That's not the only word that is used to describe the second coming, but it was one often used. In Matthew 24 verse 3 the disciples said to Jesus,

'What shall be the sign of thy coming, and of the end of the world?' – which should be translated 'end of the age'. Or in verse 27: 'For as the lightning cometh out of the east, and shineth even unto the west; so shall also the coming' – the *parousia* – 'of the Son of man be.' And in verse 37: 'As the days of Noah were, so shall also the coming of the Son of man be.' Verse 39: 'They knew not until the flood came, and took them all away; so shall also the coming of the Son of man be.' This word translated 'coming' in James 5:7 is the translation of the Greek word *parousia*, and the primary use of it in connection with our Lord's coming refers to the physical, bodily second coming of Jesus.

But there is a secondary sense in understanding this verse that these Christians were going to hang on to if the Lord did not come bodily. So the secondary sense of this expression, 'being patient unto the coming of the Lord', is this: that James is referring to a direct, though spiritual, intervention. It is equally real. And it is equally the result of Christ's own direction. The main difference is that the Lord remains seated at the right hand of God.

This secondary use of this expression: 'Be patient ... unto the coming of the Lord', is understood two ways. First, outwardly by providence, when God just causes things to happen. This is his coming, although he stays at the right hand of God. It can also mean coming in inward power when there is a surge of power from within. It is very real.

It may be that the Lord will come in power into your heart where his presence makes him so real that it's as though he has come and you know it. He's so real that you think you could almost reach out and touch him. Then his coming might simply be that he steps into a situation. You just sit back and watch and he does it all from the right hand of God. This Greek word *parousia* is used in this way. It actually comes from a verb *pareimi* which means 'to be present' or 'to be beside'.

Paul uses this word when he addresses the church at Corinth that had that problem of incest. He says in 1 Corinthians 5:3, 'For I verily, as absent in body, but present' – the same word – 'in spirit, have judged already, as though I were present, concerning him that hath so done this deed.' Paul is saying, 'As though I were present I have done it.' That's the point. Our Lord stays at the right hand of God and yet something happens. And there is little doubt that James is letting them be encouraged to believe something like that is going to happen before the second coming to rescue them from the plight they are experiencing at the moment. The proof that he is encouraging them to believe in the secondary use of the coming of the Lord is that he gives as examples Job and Elijah, examples where the Lord does in fact step in.

What would this second meaning of the coming of the Lord mean to them or, for that matter, to anybody today? You have dignified the trial God has given you. You've not complained and you've not tried to vindicate yourself. You've just talked to the Lord about it. What would the coming of the Lord be in this case? In the case of these Christians who had been abused it could mean the containment or the subsiding of the ordeal they had been put through.

As the Psalmist put it: 'Weeping may endure for a night, but joy cometh in the morning' (Ps. 30:5). Peter put it like this: 'The God of all grace, who hath called us unto his eternal glory by Christ Jesus, after that ye have suffered a while, make you perfect, stablish, strengthen, settle you' (1 Pet. 5:10). Paul said, 'There hath no temptation' – no trial – 'taken you but such as is common to man but God … will with the trial also make a way to escape, that ye may be able to bear it' (1 Cor. 10:13). At the level of providence it would mean the end of an era. There was only so much these abused Christians could take. As the old spiritual we used to sing in the States put it: 'He knows just how much I can bear.' There comes a time when God steps in and the ordeal is over. Or at the level of the spirit it means to be changed 'from glory to glory, even as by the Spirit of the Lord' (2 Cor. 3:18).

The examples of Job and Elijah

The point is that James is encouraging them to believe that something is going to happen. He calls it the coming of the Lord and then he refers to 'the patience of Job'. We read in Job 42: 'So the LORD blessed the latter end of Job more than his beginning' (v. 12). That's the way the book of Job ended. What about Elijah? He was on the spot and he'd put the integrity of God on the line. The prophets of Baal were scoffing. Elijah said, 'Hear me, O LORD, hear me, that this people may know that thou art the LORD God, and that thou hast turned their heart back again. Then the fire of the LORD fell' (1 Kgs. 18:37–38). It was something for which there was no natural explanation. That is the line James is taking. In other words, there comes a time when God steps in.

The former and the latter rains

James uses this analogy from nature: 'Look at the husbandman, the farmer who waits for the precious fruits of the earth and has long patience for it until he receives the early and latter rain.' No farmer expects precious fruit overnight. James is saying that if that is true at the level of nature, how much more true may it be at the level of the spirit. For it is not obedience for one day or for one week that is going to see the result. A lot of Christians say, 'I went a whole day and tried to please the Lord and nothing happened.' Another says, 'I even did everything right for a whole week and I didn't feel any better.'

James is saying, 'If you want to see God work, then look at the farmer. Does he expect to plant something today and then wake up tomorrow morning and see it? Oh, no, it's quite a while that he waits.' And so he says, 'You be like that. Wait on the Lord. He will strengthen your heart.' 'They that wait upon the LORD shall renew their strength; they shall mount up with wings as eagles; they shall run, and not be weary; and they shall walk, and not faint' (Isa. 40:31).

The word actually used by James here means more than just 'to wait', however. It means 'to expect', 'to look for'. He not only waits patiently, but he's not surprised when something happens. When he sees the former rain coming the farmer thinks everything is going just right. But he knows there must be more of the latter rain coming. And then when the fruit appears he's not surprised. He expects it. That's the point James is making to these Christians. 'You wait, but in such a way that you should not be surprised when God steps in.

The patience in the case of the farmer goes beyond what James refers to as two necessary occurrences, the former rain and the latter rain. He wouldn't dream of precious fruit appearing without there first being the former rain and then the latter rain during the growing season. This was a household expression in Palestine. The former rain was in the autumn, the latter rain in the spring, and the two rains were most essential to the crops.

In Deuteronomy 11:14 it says, 'That I will give you the rain of your land in his due season, the first rain and the latter rain, that thou mayest gather in thy corn, and thy wine, and thine oil.' Jeremiah refers to it: 'Let us now fear the LORD our God, that giveth rain, both the former and the latter, in his season: he reserveth unto us the appointed weeks of the harvest' (5:24). And in Joel chapter 2 verse 23 he says, 'Be glad then, ye children of Zion, and rejoice in the LORD your God: for he hath given you the former rain moderately, and he will cause to come down for you the rain, the former rain, and the latter rain.'

Rain in Palestine is a most precious commodity. The first rain might take place for three or four weeks and that got everything started. It didn't mean that it wouldn't rain at all for the next few months, but it was most essential for the crops and for the fruit that there be this latter rain in March or April. They would want a good rain for about a month. And there was the fear many times that the latter rain wouldn't come, because if it didn't then the fruit would not swell. In fact, Zechariah speaks to a situation where they were waiting for the latter rain and it looked as if it wasn't going to come. He says in chapter 10 verse 1, 'Ask ye of the LORD rain in the time of the latter rain; so the LORD shall make bright clouds, and give them showers of rain, to every one grass in the field.'

No trial, no blessing

James' point is that what rain is to a crop or to a fruit tree at a natural level, is to dignify God's trial at a spiritual level. If there's no rain there will be no fruit. If there's no trial there will be no blessing. Rain is in God's hands. Mark Twain used to say that everybody talks about the weather but nobody does anything about it! Our Lord tells us that rain falls on the just and the unjust (Mt. 5:45), and it comes with purpose. In the days of Noah it was used to destroy the world. But it comes by God's hand and with purpose. So with the trial.

The trial is regarded by the Christian as a blessing. Because there is not going to be real blessing unless you have the trial. James' point is that as the farmer waits for two seasons of rain so every trial that God gives us has a built-in design. We're not clever enough to know all the reasons for the trial with which God graces us. Our temptation is to murmur, to ask, 'Why, Lord? This makes no sense.' But whereas the rain falls on the just and the unjust and the wicked have their trials, what do they do when they have their trials? They gripe and complain. But the Christian says, 'Thanks be to God who has given me an opportunity to grow as a result of this trial.'

If the farmer waits for the full maturation process, why shouldn't we? That's James' point and it shows why he began his epistle: 'Count it all joy when ye fall into divers temptations.' And he went on to say, 'Let patience have her perfect work, that ye may be perfect and entire, wanting nothing' (1:4). In other words, don't try to abort the trial.

It was often true in Palestine that the first rain was not so heavy. Have you ever noticed that the trial God designs for us often has two phases? The first is moderate, although it doesn't seem like it at the time. You wonder how you can go on. And then out of the blue comes the real trial and you realize you hadn't even begun. It was that way in our Lord's crucifixion. Look at all he was enduring at a physical level. They spat on him. They laughed at him. They gave him a purple robe. They were trying to agitate him so that he would defend himself and lose his cool. If our Lord had done that once, the whole plan would have been aborted by God. For it would have been sin if Jesus had reviled back. But 'he openeth not his mouth'. That was a trial. But the worst was yet to come: when abruptly he cried out, 'My God, my God, why hast thou forsaken me?' (Mt. 27:46). The second phase was the worst. The physical sufferings of Jesus didn't compare with the spiritual.

Don't expect to dignify the greater trial when you're not faithful in that which is least. When the trial comes, how you react will determine whether you qualify for the big one. But when the big one comes and you're able to endure it with dignity, James comes along and suggests to those who didn't resist, 'You're getting close to something.' James was hinting to them: 'You're enduring the latter rain now. You're in the middle of the latter rain. The Lord is about to come. The rain is nearly over.'

The second coming

Referring to the primary meaning of this term, 'coming of the Lord', our Lord gave certain signs, didn't he? He said, 'When these things begin to come to pass … your redemption draweth nigh' (Lk. 21:28). James is showing signs that you can look for to know that the trial is almost over. This is rough. The pressure is really on. You're being oppressed but you're not resisting. Of course, it's hard. But it's a wonderful sign. The Bible is full of encouragement for people like this. 'They that sow in tears shall reap in joy' (Ps. 126:5). James could say, 'Ye have heard of the patience of Job, and have seen the end of the Lord; that the Lord is very pitiful, and of tender mercy' (5:11).

'Just one more thing', says James. 'Be ye also patient; stablish your hearts: for the coming of the Lord draweth nigh.' He's saying, 'It can't be much longer now. But stablish your hearts.' He goes on to say, 'Grudge not one against another, brethren, lest ye be condemned.' Because just before the blessing the devil will find every reason why you should do something to grieve the Spirit and lose the blessing that would have been yours if you had just waited.

The Reason Behind Every Trial

It's a word that means 'stand with dignity in your hearts'. James has just said, 'You're to strengthen your heart, stablish it. Because you're being changed from glory to glory. And as an extra bonus you're going to be elevated to more grace, to a higher level of knowledge and you're going to know a sense of God and of his power that you would not have known but for this trial.'

I wish I could say to young Christians that you can know God simply by coming to church all the time and reading your Bible and praying. You ought to do those things of course. But I do you no favour to make you think that that means you're going to really grow. There's the trial. How you react to it will determine whether you know this sense of God. For your encouragement you can read the biographies of the great saints and see how they endured trial. After the trial was over – when the rain was over – they knew a sense of God that made the trial worth it all. They wouldn't take anything in the world for the trial that brought them to that place. You must wait. God's timing is what matters.

James says that it's not going to be long in their case. 'The coming of the Lord draws nigh.' As for the second coming of Jesus himself, every day brings us one step closer, one day nearer. Having said this, I think James is hinting to them to see that there is a coming of the Lord now in their situation. In fact, this Greek word that is translated 'cometh nigh', 'draweth nigh', is the word that means 'at hand'. The Lord's coming is at hand. Having the Lord at hand is what matters.

How We Dignify The Trial Is What Matters

Paul could say, 'At my first answer no man stood with me, but all men forsook me' (2 Tim. 4:16). But he said, 'The Lord stood with me' (v. 17). When you can stand tall while the pressure is on, how glad you will be when the trial is over.

Luther stood alone at the Diet of Worms in 1521. He said, 'Here I stand; I can do no other. God help me. Amen.' He was to be taken to another spot and those who tried him had promised him safety. But some of Luther's friends, through a providential accident, heard that they were going to kill him and they arranged for Luther to be kidnapped the next day as he was leaving Worms. It first appeared to be a great tragedy, but it was Luther's own friends who kidnapped him. They hid him away in Wartburg Castle, and over the next eleven months Luther translated the Bible into German and the German language was never to be the same again. It was the end of an era and Luther had a time of rest. What a joy to be able to say, as Isaiah put it, 'Lo, we have waited for him' (Isa. 25:9). Do you know what it is to go through a trial and complain the whole time? And then the trial is over and you're so ashamed.

Why, then, the trial? For the precious fruit. He will 'sanctify to thee thy deepest distress'. When the trial is over it will be as nothing. And yet there is coming a day when the rain will be over indeed. There's coming a day when we can say with the Song of Solomon, 'For, lo, the winter is past, the rain is over and gone … the time of the singing of birds is come' (2:11, 12). There's coming a day of days when all winters will be over and gone and all trials will have been dissolved.

It will be a cloudless day except for one awesome, most spectacular, most lovely cloud ever conceived by mortal eyes. John was given a premiere showing two thousand years ago. 'Behold, he cometh with clouds; and every eye shall see him, and they also which pierced him: and all kindreds of the earth shall wail because of him' (Rev. 1:7). As the prophet put it, 'They shall look upon me whom they pierced' (Zech. 12:10). Our Lord says, 'Therefore be ye also ready: for in such an hour as ye think not the Son of man cometh' (Mt. 24:44).

There's coming a day of days when this Jesus that we can now feel so near and so real we will see with these eyes. No faith will be required. It will not be through the Spirit that we sense God. All shall see him. That day may be at hand indeed. When we look at history and see what's going on surely, surely the time is at hand. John finished the book of Revelation with these words: 'He which testifieth these things saith, Surely I come quickly.' And John replied, 'Even so, come, Lord Jesus' (Rev. 22:20). 'He cometh.' Are you ready?

31

The Patience of Job

James 5:11

Carry No Grudges

Starting with verse 7 of chapter 5, James addresses these oppressed Christians in an exclusive manner. He does so by referring to the coming of the Lord. It is a reference to the second coming of Jesus. And yet we have seen that it not only has this primary reference – we must not forget that, but there is a secondary meaning of the coming of the Lord. What is that? It is that whereby the Lord remains at the right hand of God but still steps in. He did it in 70 AD when Jerusalem was destroyed. That was the coming of the Lord in judgement. And he's done it many times since.

Having encouraged these oppressed Christians to believe that the Lord will step in and it won't be much longer till they will see God at work before their eyes, what is the word to them in the meantime? Since those who have been mistreated are going to be very vulnerable to the temptation of holding a grudge toward those who have oppressed them, James says to them in verse 9, 'Grudge not one against another, brethren, lest ye be condemned.' In other words, those who have been oppressed could incur needless condemnation on themselves. They have learned that God is no respecter of persons. 'He heard your prayer and he has proved that he's no respecter of persons, but he can prove it further by condemning you if you hold a grudge. If you hold a grudge you too are in the wrong and you will be condemned.'

James is encouraging them to believe that the Lord is going to step in but warning them not to grieve the Lord at the last minute. What we have in this exhortation is just about the most encouraging thing I can think of. He has said that the one who has endured suffering without murmuring has qualified for enrolment in the school of the prophets. Even though you may never have thought yourself qualified to be a Jeremiah, or a Shadrach, a Meshach, or an Abednego, anybody who suffers unjustly but can keep quiet about it qualifies to be enrolled in the school of prophets. To be qualified to speak in the name of the Lord means that you must suffer. But you must suffer a further test and that is not only not speaking out when you're mistreated, but not even holding a grudge in your heart.

A prophet must endure affliction but also do it with patience, right to the end he must wait on the Lord. God wants the man who has no axe to grind to speak for him. He's not on a political vendetta. There's no personal issue with him. He's God's man. But in order to be a man like that – because none of us are like that by nature – we've got to be refined and brought to the place where we've got no personal issue. The last test is to endure suffering and not hold a grudge, not even to feel it in your heart. Because when you're like that, then and then only can you be the Lord's man and speak in the name of the Lord.

Here's the way Jesus put it in the Sermon on the Mount: 'Blessed are ye, when men shall revile you, and persecute you, and shall say all manner of evil against you falsely, for my sake. Rejoice and be exceeding glad: for great is your reward in heaven: for so persecuted they the prophets which were before you' (Mt. 5:11–12). It's an invitation to be elevated to the same sphere and level of knowing God that the prophets knew. That's as high as you get. And that's our invitation.

It's at this juncture that James makes a personal judgement. He doesn't do that much in this epistle but he does it again here when he says, 'Behold, we count them happy which endure.'

James Is Happy For The Oppressed

In verse 11, the Greek word literally means, 'We are happy'. James is saying, 'Behold, we are happy for you that are undergoing this.' You might find this a bit odd. Here is James addressing these oppressed Christians who have been suffering and he says, 'We're happy about you.' It's his way of saying, 'I don't feel sorry for you. We're in this together. All of those who are used of the Lord go through this.' It's so different from the way most of us think. We, who are in the ministry, when we see a new convert we become very jealous for them. We don't want to see them get discouraged. I think many ministers are very anxious for their converts to get off to a good start.

This is the way all the New Testament men speak. Listen to Paul when he comes to address the Colossians, 'I … now rejoice in my sufferings for you' (Col. 1:24). You would have thought that Paul would have written back and said, 'I'm so sorry about what you're going through.' No, he says, 'I … rejoice in my sufferings for you.' Or as he put it to the Philippians: 'It is given in the behalf of Christ, not only to believe on him, but also to suffer for his sake' (Phil. 1:29). This is why Peter said, 'But rejoice inasmuch as ye are partakers of Christ's sufferings' (1 Pet. 4:13).

It just shows how far most of us are from the way these godly men felt. We're so anxious to see Christians have prosperity. I think one of the curses of certain areas of American Christianity in particular is that they talk about 'being prospered' and knowing that God is with you by how much you make in money and how much you are feeling good about this or that. That isn't the way they talk in the Bible at all.

Suffering was the ultimate proof that you really were a child of God. The writer to the Hebrews could say, 'Whom the Lord loveth he chasteneth, and scourgeth every son whom he receiveth' (12:6). Not every Christian gets this kind of interest – or not every professing Christian. For these worldly-minded ones who had pitched their tent near Sodom and tried to get as close to the world as they could get, got this warning from James: 'If you're going to be like that you force God to treat you as an enemy' (4:4). But James recognized some – not all, but some – who had endured suffering.

Not only does it show you're the Lord's, but it means the Lord's going to use you. For when God chastens us it's not his way of getting even. He chastens us because he's not finished with us and he's got something for us to do. Our chastening is the test to see whether we will later do all right. He can't turn us loose to do what he has for us to do until we prove that we can endure hardness and, in the case of these Christians, endure that which was unfair.

James is saying to them, 'You don't have to wait until you get to heaven to see the Lord work and to see his power. The judge stands at the door but he is waiting just a bit longer to see if, now that I've come in and vindicated you, now that I've said I'm with you, now that I've affirmed you, can you still not have a trace of bitterness? Grudge not against another. Pass that test and the Lord could use you.' At this point James says, 'Ye have heard of the patience of Job.'

The Controversy About Job

It suggests by the way he puts it – 'Ye have heard' – that there was a consensus about the man Job. He was regarded as a man of patience. We don't know where they'd heard this. Perhaps in the synagogues, perhaps there was just a consensus in popular discussions, it was perhaps axiomatic to say 'the patience of Job'. But I think that James might equally have said, 'You've heard of the controversy about Job and the book of Job.' The book of Job purported a theological message that went right against the prevailing views of the rabbis. In fact, in ancient rabbinic Judaism there was the belief (much like certain American Christianity) that prosperity proves God is with you and that if you have any kind of adversity God is dealing with you, and there's some secret sin in your life. The book of Job challenges that view and really it is remarkable that the book of Job even got into the canon of Scripture. It was that controversial.

The popular consensus of ancient Judaistic theology was reflected in Job's friends, his comforters, as they're called. They came to comfort him and they saw how sad he was. If they hadn't seen how sad he was, they would have started in on him on the first day. But they saw he couldn't talk so they were polite and didn't say a word for a whole week. But it wasn't long before they started to moralize and make all kinds of comments and say, 'Now, Job, tell us the truth. We're here to help you.' I sometimes think that the old saying: 'With friends like you who needs enemies?' originates in the book of Job.

The book of Job begins with Job on top of the world. He had it made. He was rich, the greatest man in the east. Then we're told that God said to the devil, 'Hast thou considered my servant Job?' (Job 1:8). This, by the way, is a reminder to us that Satan can move no further than God lets him. God said to Satan, 'Go get him.' And Satan did. The Sabeans stole Job's oxen and his donkeys and killed his servants. Lightning burnt up sheep and servants and consumed them. Then the Chaldeans came and stole the camels and killed all the servants. One thing after another. All this was hitting Job right and left. Then a strong wind came when all of his children were together having a party at the oldest brother's house. The building collapsed and killed them all. Job lost everything: prosperity, his children. And that isn't all. Job was then afflicted with great physical pain. Then came Job's friends. They began to accuse him of some secret sin.

Job's friends were the brunt of his trial

The question is, why does James bring in Job as an illustration? Three reasons. The first is, that James sees the suffering of these oppressed Christians as an extension of Job's suffering. Job's friends became the brunt of Job's trial. The book of Job might have been wrapped up in about three or four chapters. Why does it go to forty-two chapters? The plot is all there at the beginning and at the end we see how it ends. But why these long chapters? Because Job's friends became the brunt of his suffering. That was hard on Job. But he said, 'Naked came I out of my mother's womb, and naked shall I return thither: the LORD gave, and the LORD hath taken away; blessed be the name of the LORD. In all this Job sinned not, nor charged God foolishly' (Job 1:21–22).

The physical pain was terrible. He suffered boils from the crown of his head to the soles of his feet. And it was hard. So much so that Job's wife came along and said, 'Curse God, and die.' And Job said, 'You talk like a foolish woman.' Job is all right. But what made Job's trial a trial indeed was his friends. It wasn't until they came along that Job began to see the deep recesses of his heart that he hadn't known before in their innuendoes, their snide remarks, the vast implications of their statements, their outright accusation. They insisted that Job was hiding something. They regarded themselves as agents of the Lord to get him straightened out. And Job had to listen to all this. And the thing is, Job's friends had tradition, the rabbis and popular consensus on their side.

James saw Job's suffering being repeated by these oppressed Christians who were in the minority. They were really a small remnant of the church because these ruthless social climbers, who had come into the church and wanted to turn Christianity into a middle-class religion and to change the face of Christianity, were in control. And those oppressed Christians could see something was wrong but who would listen to them? They just cried out to the Lord.

The second reason James brings in the book of Job is that Job's suffering consisted not merely in the loss of his possessions but in having to forgive those who had unjustly accused him. Job's trial suddenly took on this new twist. It was one thing to lose a possession, it was another thing to lose his family, it was another thing to have this physical pain. That's just about all that can happen to a person and still be alive. But there was something worse than that. That was having to sit there and listen to these friends talk as agents from the Lord to Job. But not only that, Job had to forgive them, to not even have a grudge against them.

These oppressed Christians were mistreated by those in this Christian synagogue. Apparently a synagogue had been taken over by Christians. There were these name-droppers who were gaining power in the church and turning it into a middle-class religion. In all probability they were even trying to take over the teaching because James has to say, 'Be not many masters.' This is why he had to warn them.

James is now having to say, 'You that are oppressed and can see how the church is being controlled by powerful, ruthless social climbers, don't even hold a grudge against them.' That was hard to do. So he brings in this man Job, who was a literal person but who also symbolized patience. The Greek word used here is not the same word for 'patience' used early on in the verse. It's a different word means 'bearing under', often translated 'enduring'. It's used by Paul in 1 Corinthians 13:7 about love: 'beareth all things … hopeth all things, endureth all things'. It's the same word the writer to the Hebrews used when he addressed Hebrew Christians: 'Call to remembrance the former days, in which, after ye were illuminated, ye endured a great fight of afflictions' (10:32). It was Jesus' word: 'He that shall endure unto the end, the same shall be saved' (Mt. 24:13).

Job was not a model of perfection

But there's something tremendously encouraging here. Job is referred to at the beginning of the book as 'perfect and upright' (1:1). This is something often overlooked about Job. The patience of Job was hardly an example of transparent perfection. This is encouraging because John said, 'His commandments are not grievous' (1 Jn. 5:3). We don't need to feel demoralized if we're not perfect. Job was not a model of perfection throughout. Before it was over Job got very discouraged indeed and showed himself to be very frail. Cursing the day of his birth isn't exactly a very godly thing to do. And he lost his temper with his friends. And then Job got just as self-righteous as they were.

Job's ordeal made him confront sin in himself. He hadn't known what was there. And that's partly the purpose of a trial: to make us see ourselves in the raw and it then puts us on trial to see what we're going to do with that now that we've found out about it. A trial will make us blush when we see how depraved, how proud, how insecure we really are, how self-centred. James saw those Christian workers out in the fields and he is saying, 'Hey, you've got something going for you. Look at Job and don't forget how it all turned out with Job. You have seen the end objective of the Lord. And you've discovered something about the Lord who is full of pity and of tender mercy.'

But Job had to come to the place that he would even forgive those friends. The forgotten line in the book of Job – you could call it the bottom line of Job – is when he prayed for his friends. 'And the LORD turned the captivity of Job, when he prayed for his friends' (Job 42:10). That's what Job had to do before he got the victory. He may have wanted to see his friends eat dust. But instead he testified, 'I abhor myself, and repent in dust and ashes' (42:6). All the time Job wanted God to deal with his friends, and here the whole time God was dealing with him.

The Timing Of The Lord

James refers to 'the end of the Lord'. It's another cryptic reference to the crucifixion of Jesus. For Jesus on the cross, 'when he was reviled, reviled not again' (1 Pet. 2:23). James is saying to these Christians in the field, 'You don't want to miss out on the ultimate blessing here: to be like Jesus.' Jesus died on the cross and he didn't get even. God punished him. 'You've already qualified to enrol in the school of the prophets', says James. 'The judge stands at the door and waits, giving you an opportunity to get a greater blessing than anything that has happened yet. Let there be no trace of bitterness. When that is true God can use you then.'

The proof that God got the victory is that Job overcame an inward grudge. He prayed for his friends. By the way, this wasn't a phoney, perfunctory prayer. For God sees the heart. Job couldn't play games with God and say, 'Lord, I've prayed for them.' But when God saw that Job really did pray for them things changed. This is why Jesus said not only to rejoice but to 'love your enemies, bless them that curse you, do good to them that hate you, and pray for them which despitefully use you' (Mt. 5:44).

But there's another reason we have this expression, 'the end of the Lord'. Not only because the Lord ended up on the cross, not only that Job in the end had to forgive as Jesus did: 'Father, forgive them: for they know not what they do' (Lk. 23:34), but, as Paul put it to the Corinthians: 'As ye are partakers of the sufferings, so shall ye be also of the consolation' (2 Cor. 1:7). So that as Jesus 'humbled himself, and became obedient unto death, even the death of the cross', God highly exalted him (Phil. 2:8–9). There is an end time of the Lord and it is this: that God eventually steps in. So James could say that he 'is very pitiful and of tender mercy.' It's the only time the Greek word for 'very pitiful' is used in the whole of the Bible. In fact, there's no frame of reference so it's hard to translate. It's two words. The first means 'many'. The second word means 'bowels', 'heart', your 'insides', the 'inner organs'. The picture is this: there comes a time when God cannot bear to see his own people suffer any more. God explodes with emotion, as it were. He's 'very pitiful', but only if his heart or insides are touched by the one being mistreated not holding a grudge. James is perhaps saying, 'Aren't you glad the Lord hasn't stepped in yet? You've got an opportunity to please the Lord in a way very few people ever do.'

The Greek word for 'tender mercy' is still not the common word used for 'mercy'. James selects a word that again shows God's emotions. Jesus used it in Luke 6:36 when he says, 'Be ye therefore merciful, as your Father also is merciful.' James is asking us to do no more than God does for us: show mercy to others, hold no grudges. As God comes to our rescue, so should we treat others that way. James is not merely talking about grace to be shown at the second coming of Jesus, but there comes a time before the end, indeed James calls it 'the end of the Lord'. It's true that if you're a friend of the world you can't do that without incurring God's hot displeasure. But if you're a friend of God's, God gets involved. James is saying, 'Be merciful like that because if you are merciful like that you can't be like that without pleasing God.'

Finally, does God show that he's pleased with us? The answer is, Job prayed for his friends and the Lord gave Job twice as much as he'd had before. 'So the LORD blessed the latter end of Job more than his beginning: for he had fourteen thousand sheep, and six thousand camels, and a thousand yoke of oxen, and a thousand she asses.' And, would you believe, Job was given a new family: 'seven sons and three daughters' (Job 42:12, 13). You just can't outdo the Lord. When you please him he often shows it. This same God who is 'slow to anger', who is 'very pitiful', will in the end step in. He wants to bless us more than we want to be blessed. He just wants to see if we love him. Job loved him. He proved it by praying for his friends.

32

Name-Dropping

James 5:12

Why did James bring in this verse at this point in time? It seems to have been brought in out of the blue, but if we understand the verse itself as it is found in the Sermon on the Mount particularly, we'll have little difficulty seeing why James brought in this verse.

James Encourages And Warns

James is encouraging these oppressed Christians to believe that the Lord will step in. 'Don't hold any grudges lest you be condemned' (5:9). He wants them to continue to grow in grace. He sees something in these Christians who had suffered: possibilities of greatness equal to the prophets of old who had spoken in the name of the Lord. The way the prophets qualified to speak in the name of the Lord was that they suffered affliction and they took it patiently. They could be devoid of being guided by personal feelings so that they could be a clear channel for the Lord to speak.

Suffering and grace

Surely by this time these suffering Christians have received all the instructions they need. What more can be expected of them if they rid themselves of any personal grudge? James says there is more, 'Above all things, my brethren, swear not, neither by heaven, neither by the earth, neither by any other oath.' 'Above all things.' This is why James has moved in. Here were some Christians who had suffered but they took their mistreatment lying down. And they had an opportunity to grow in grace in a most wonderful way.

The extraordinary thing is that there are Christians like this all over the world who haven't had special tutoring or great theological learning. But they have learned not to resist but to turn the cheek, and by doing this have brought great blessing upon themselves. James sees these Christians like that but he doesn't want them to come this far and then to have failed.

James is laying down these principles: first, 'Count it all joy when ye fall into divers temptations' (1:2). The second principle is this: don't hasten the trial along. Don't abort the trial. 'Let patience have her perfect work' (1:4). The third thing is, be careful about grudges lest you be condemned. What is left to say? He says, 'Above all else …'

We're talking about learning from God at a level that is far beyond what many Christians have experienced. It's to learn the ways of God that can only be known in the university of the Holy Ghost. It is not by grasping philosophy or becoming acquainted in the arts and the sciences. But there comes a time when, if one does indeed dignify the trial God has given, one emerges into a new area, a new sphere, a different level of learning than one ever thought possible. If the trial has been dignified, if it has been extended to last just a bit longer and there's still no murmuring, it is then, but not before, that one begins to experience this higher learning.

The pity is that so many Christians have not known this because they have complained every time they had a trial. This is why Christians can have been Christians for ten or twenty years and really not have developed a bit over those years. This is why some Christians still have the same old temptations, the same old trials. They murmur and complain in the same old way years later, simply because they have never learned to dignify the trial. If we do dignify the trial and then the trial lasts a bit longer, it is then that the learning begins to emerge. That's where these Christians were in their pilgrimage. If one begins to learn after having dignified a trial that goes on, the knowledge that is gained during that era is more precious than the very end of the trial that you had at first wanted. For the continuance of the trial begins to disappear and it's no longer a trial but the ground of great blessing such that you can't tell the difference between the blessing and the trial.

James Quotes From The Sermon On The Mount

When James says, 'Above all things … swear not', he is quoting from the Sermon on the Mount. Jesus said, 'Again, ye have heard that it hath been said by them of old time, Thou shalt not forswear thyself, but shalt perform unto the Lord thine oaths: but I say unto you, Swear not at all; neither by heaven ... nor by the earth' and so forth (Mt. 5:33–35). Why did James bring in that verse? The first thing that needs to be said is that Jesus was not quoting an Old Testament verse at all. He was simply quoting from a tradition. You need to know your Old Testament well enough to know whether Jesus is quoting from a Mosaic law as he did when he said, 'Ye have heard that it was said ... Thou shalt not commit adultery' (Mt. 5:27).

What Jesus did in that verse is simply to quote a popular rabbinic interpretation of the third commandment, 'Thou shalt not take the name of the LORD thy God in vain' (Exod. 20:7). The rabbis had reduced the third commandment to little more than the ninth commandment, 'Thou shalt not bear false witness' (v. 16). The rabbis had made the two commandments virtually the same. And if the rabbis were right, it meant one or the other must be redundant.

Did Moses get it wrong? Certainly not. The problem was this: the real meaning of the third commandment had been lost for a long, long time for so many. Here was their view that swearing, that is, affirming by an oath, was okay as long as you told the truth. The rabbis taught that the way you take the name of the Lord in vain is to swear by the name of God but not mean it when you say it, or not to tell the truth. That became the standard interpretation of the third commandment. The truth is that the third commandment doesn't mention swearing at all. Swearing simply means to affirm by an oath or to promise by an oath which may have begun *without* using gutter language. The purpose of affirming by an oath is simply to convince another of your sincerity. In order to get how you feel over to another person you appeal to a higher source, a source that will affirm you. It's not the other source you're exalting, you're simply using the other source to affirm yourself. The essence of swearing is to affirm yourself. Therefore one invoked what appeared to be the most authenticating source or name as undoubted evidence of sincerity. It was said of God in Hebrews 6:13: 'Because he could sware by no greater, he sware by himself.'

Taking God's name in vain by trying to manipulate

What, then, is taking the name of the Lord in vain? It is to manipulate God, to exploit the high name of God for a personal end. A good definition of manipulation is found in the book *Man the Manipulator* by Everett Sholstrom. He says that manipulation is 'exploiting, using and / or controlling another in self-defeating ways'. You manipulate a person when you treat another person as an object rather than a person.

When you bring in the name of God what you do is, rather than letting God be God you are involving him in that which is your concern without regard to what his will or glory is. It's the very opposite of worshipping him. It is the very opposite of adoring his name. It is taking advantage of both him and others by involving *his* name in *your* particular enterprise. Therefore to take the name of the Lord in vain doesn't have to be done by not telling the truth or by using profanity, although either of course would do that. But the essence is that you are manipulating God and using him for your own ends.

What Jesus did in the Sermon on the Mount was to refer to the common consensus of the way the third commandment was to be understood. But after Jesus did that he said, 'I say unto you ...' and he told the safest way, indeed the only way, to be sure not to take the name of the Lord God in vain – and that was not to swear at all. Don't even bring in his name, or anybody else, not even anything at the natural level.

It continues to surprise us that Jesus said that. I wonder how many of us have understood why he said it and what he meant by it. Was he saying that a Christian shouldn't take the oath in a court of law? No, he wasn't referring to anything like that at all. Jesus knew the deceitfulness of the human heart. All of us are sure that our own cause is just. We all want to affirm our sincerity and our rightness by bringing in God's name. But when we do that it is not the name of God we're jealous of. It is not the name of God we revere. When did you ever hear someone say, 'Let God be true and every man a liar' (Rom. 3:4)? We bring in God's name to affirm ourselves. Jesus is saying here that the proof that you don't want to exploit God's name is that you don't swear by his name or by any other name at all. You wouldn't ask him to lower himself by affirming you and perhaps denying another.

What lay behind the third commandment? Why did God give it to Moses to give to Israel? It was partly because the children of Israel had crossed the Red Sea and they were in the wilderness for 40 years. They were growing. There were some 600,000 of them, all claiming to be worshipping God. They were God's covenant people. When you've got that many people it isn't long until quarrels develop and one tribe or person has an axe to grind against another tribe or person. And when you had a dispute between two parties within God's covenant people, how was it to be resolved?

How do you know who is telling the truth? Or how do you know who is right? Both would claim to be right. Both pray to the same God. Both no doubt love God. Both claim God is on his side. Does it mean that one is right and the other is wrong? If so, how do you find out which it is? Or could it be that both were wrong? Could it be that both were right?

According to Jesus, you don't bring in God at all. 'Swear not at all; neither by heaven' – heaven being a euphemism for God (many would not even pronounce the name of God and so they'd use a different name) – 'nor by the earth.' Why did Jesus say it like that? Was this a new slant to the third commandment, an innovative interpretation? No, that is precisely what God meant the first time. But their hearts were too hard to perceive it. It happened with all of the commandments – they would all come up with their interpretation and make that equivalent to the truth. And it would always camouflage the real meaning.

The Ultimate Word On Vindication

If we understood what was meant by the third commandment we'd understand that the only thing Jesus could have said was what he said. We should see by now why James quoted Jesus at this point. For here is the ultimate statement of the matter of vindication. These oppressed Christians that James was now trying to supervise and bring through the crisis that they might come out on the other side victoriously, might have made the mistake of invoking God's name over against their oppressors. After all, their oppressors were Christians.

Exploiting or implicating God's name

James is saying, 'Don't put God on the spot. These who have abused you are Christians too. God is no respecter of persons and he loves them as much as he loves you.' This doesn't go down well with us, does it? We like to think that God loves us just a bit more than anybody else. Or so the devil would want me to believe. When we've been oppressed by another Christian we're quite certain that God ought to judge that other Christian and call fire down on them. Now James is saying, 'Hold it. God loves you. He loves them.' It's much like a parent where the children have come in and said, 'Look what so-and-so did or said', and the parent loves them all. James is saying, 'To you who have been suffering at the hands of Christians, if you invoke God's name, what you do is show that you've got your own feelings in mind. You're not thinking about God. You're not adoring his name.' You would be exploiting God's name for your own feelings. And if you do that, God turns on you. That's why James says, '... lest ye be condemned'. He's already said, 'If you hold a grudge you will be condemned.' Now he's saying that if you bring God into it and say, 'I'm right, you're wrong', you're condemned. This is taking us a little further along. We thought we'd learned everything if we could just deal with a grudge. But the heart is so deceitful and James keeps moving along. It's one thing to dignify the trial, it's another thing to let the trial run its full course. It's another thing not to hold a grudge, and now this.

The question is, why might these suffering Christians have wanted to imolicate God in their dealings with one another? When one gets involved in a matter like this, the temptation is immediately to say, 'May God deal with you for what you've done. I'm so sure I'm right, I'm so sure you're wrong.' There was an old saying in Israel. It went like this: 'so let the gods do to me and more also if ...' Have you ever heard anybody say, 'God strike me dead if this is not the case'? Have you done that? Don't be so foolish. Don't bring God into it. He doesn't want to be involved like that. You're thinking of yourself and not his name. Jezebel was so angry with Elijah that she said that. 'So let the gods do to me, and more also, if I make not thy life as the life of one of them by tomorrow about this time' (1 Kgs. 19:2).

Their plight might have led these suffering Christians to a different kind of bitterness than mere grudges. That is to say, 'I swear God is on my side. He showed me this. He told me this.' If you bring God in you've dishonoured him right then because you're only manipulating God. And yet, my fellow Christians, this is the easiest thing in the world to do. Obviously God was on the side of these Christians, but James nonetheless says, 'Don't bring God's name into it at all.' That was Paul's philosophy. He says, 'I judge not mine own self. For I know nothing by myself; yet am I not hereby justified: but he that judgeth me is the Lord. Therefore judge nothing before the time, until the Lord come, who both will bring to light the hidden things of darkness ...' (1 Cor. 4:3–5). Here again was a quarrel between Christians.

To put it another way, James was cautioning them not to fall into a trap like that of their oppressors, who were name-droppers. They could say, 'Look who goes to our church.' That would make everybody say, 'Well, that must mean you are something if somebody like that goes to your church.' This is happening in modern evangelistic campaigns. They bring in big names so that you can say, 'Christianity can't be so bad after all if so and so is a Christian.' Name-dropping.

Spiritual pride is as carnal as worldly pride

What was about to happen in an odd sort of way was that these suffering Christians were going to upstage the name-droppers. They were going to name-drop *God*. They could say to those ruthless, power-hungry Christians, something like 'So you've got Lord so-and-so attending your synagogue now. So you've got the Prime Minister and a member of the Cabinet. Well, guess who is with *us*. God. Top that.' James says, 'Spiritual pride is just as carnal as worldly pride.' When you bring in God's name you have brought him down to a level that is beneath him.

This sort of thing has gone on throughout the history of the Christian church. It is one way of examining church history. There are so many humorous and sad things, you don't know whether to laugh or to cry. In the nineteenth century in America as things were going westward there were revival fires burning everywhere. There were Methodists growing, Baptists growing, the Church of Christ was growing, Presbyterians. Presbyterians and Methodists would argue over Arminianism and Calvinism, Methodists and Baptists over baptism, Baptists and the Church of Christ over who was the real church. Here they were trying to win the world supposedly, but they were saying, 'We're the real church.' The Methodists would point to John Wesley and the Presbyterians to Calvin. And the Church of Christ didn't have anybody so they said, 'We're the Church of Christ. Top that one.' Baptists said, 'We can. Who did Jesus ask to baptize him? John the Baptist. We go back to then.' They were affirming themselves.

The moment one invokes the name of the Lord one violates the third commandment, whatever one's beliefs are. You force God to condemn right there on the spot. So much church history is plagued by those who became entrenched in a position. They wanted their own vindication and they brought God's name into it. 'We're the elect. We're the remnant. We're the ones preaching the truth.' Is it any wonder that revival tarries? The temptation that these Christians were vulnerable to was to manipulate God, to presume upon his name and then to claim him as the cause for all they stood for.

Over-familiarity with God's name

What about the actual name of the Lord? James says that the prophets really did speak in the name of the Lord. These prophets suffered affliction. They took it patiently. But before they could speak in the name of the Lord they had to be devoid of personal feelings, and there just aren't many people like that. We've all got our axe to grind. And God doesn't use any of us, really. James was seeing in these Christians that had suffered out in the field something unusual. He could see they were getting so close that God could trust them. It is one thing to speak in your own name, but when you claim God as the backer of your cause you're exploiting his name. You're taking advantage of the relationship.

Take, for example, members of the royal family who can't really make friends outside their own family because everybody they meet will name-drop them after that. They'll quote them. How many of you could be invited to Buckingham Palace and then keep quiet about it? And so they withdraw. The reason so many of us don't have a real intimate relationship with God is that we couldn't keep quiet about it, and so God withdraws. We're so anxious for another person to discover how godly we are and then God withdraws and we're condemned. James is literally saying, 'Leave God out of it.'

You say, 'How are they going to be vindicated?' I can tell you this: not by affirming themselves that God is on their side. If you affirm yourselves that's your reward. That's all you're going to get. God backs off and then you're condemned and you're in the same boat as those that you're wanting to deal with.

How many of us can be trusted to know God and use his name for his own sake? You say, 'Well, aren't we supposed to witness?' Here's the antinomy, these two parallel principles that are irreconcilable but both true: you must witness to the name of Jesus Christ, giving your testimony. But at the same time, how profound your knowledge of God is, is so precious and intimate that it must be kept quiet, and you won't have it unless you can keep quiet about it. If you're anxious to impress another by how close to God you are, you show how far from God you are. But that was the temptation these Christians were having to experience now. And James rushes to them and warns them to stop and to be careful. 'Above all else ...' Not many pass that test.

33

Letting God be God

James 5:12

Again my text is James 5:12. I want us to look at this most profound verse more deeply.

James Acts Like A Supervisor

What James does here in giving this final word of warning to those suffering Christians, is to quote our Lord. He moves in like a supervisor to help them along. Sometimes when we are suffering we want encouragement. But sometimes the warning will give us greater encouragement, although we do not perceive this at the moment. James has warned them about grudges, because even though they did not lash back verbally at their oppressors, if they hold a grudge God can see that. But then, having said that, James puts it like this: 'Above all things, my brethren, swear not, neither by heaven, neither by the earth, neither by any other oath.'

The Most Likely Temptation

What James did was to address the most likely temptation that people would experience under the circumstances of those suffering Christians whom he was addressing. What was that? It was to be bitter and to become self-righteous, to overstate their case by bringing in God's name. They wouldn't be doing this to be irreverent. They would not have thought perhaps that that could be taking the name of the Lord in vain. That would be the last thing they would want to do. But in doing that they would be exploiting God's name. And so strongly does James feel that he warns them, 'Above all things don't do this.'

The question that I want us to look at now is this: were they wrong to have felt that God was on their side? Is it wrong to feel God is on our side? By the expression 'on our side' I refer mainly to two Christians who have a quarrel with each other. One side would put himself against the other and each would amass friends and they would both claim to have God on their side. This is the reason for the third commandment. 'Do not take the name of the Lord thy God in vain.' Leave God out of it. This is why Jesus said, 'Don't even swear at all.'

God does not love one Christian more than another

In the case of these suffering Christians, shouldn't they have felt that God was on their side? Not necessarily. This is why we're dealing with such a profound verse. We all tend to think that if you don't agree with me and God is for me then he is against you. But that's not true because God's people are loved by God equally.

Why should we not be so certain that God is on our side? Because that would claim to know God's mind when in fact God has not disclosed what he thinks. Here were these suffering Christians who had a feeling that they had been mistreated by these oppressors who were also Christians and James was having to say, 'God loves them too.' To prejudge God's opinion would lead to the very kind of judging Jesus condemned when he said, 'Judge not, that ye be not judged' (Mt. 7:1).

James has told them not to speak evil of each other. If you speak evil of your brother and judge your brother you speak evil of the law (4:11). And we have seen that this coincides with all that Paul said, 'I judge not mine own self. For I know nothing by myself; yet am I not hereby justified: but he that judgeth me is the Lord. Therefore judge nothing before the time, until the Lord come, who both will bring to light the hidden things of darkness, and will make manifest the counsels of the hearts: and then shall every man have praise of God' (1 Cor. 4:3–5).

Wait until God acts

Until God steps in we really don't *know* what is in his mind. There are those who think they're so spiritual that they've got advance information: 'Let me tell you what God thinks about this.' That is taking the name of the Lord in vain. This happens because we all want to say that God is on our side. The truth is, God hasn't said so. This is why Paul says, 'I judge not mine own self ... judge nothing before the time.' Wait till God steps in and then you'll find out how everything is.

Swearing oaths

To swear (that is, to affirm by an oath) by heaven or by earth is tantamount to self-vindication. It is the very essence of self-righteousness. Who would have dared to stand in God's presence and claim to be right and holy and pure? We may feel that we're right but if we really were in God's presence we'd be just exactly like Isaiah who said, 'Woe is me! ... I am a man of unclean lips' (Isa. 6:5). Swearing is done for one reason and that is to affirm yourself. The temptation, then, is to become self-righteous, to become bitter at the same time.

When one does this one falls into the same malady as these oppressors, namely taking oneself too seriously. This is why James warned about grudges. It becomes painful to realize that God loves everybody the same and he is for everybody equally.

Self-righteousness

These suffering Christians now face the temptation of being carnal by being self-righteous. The same God who treats the worldly Christian like an enemy is the same God who will treat the self-righteous Christian like an enemy. The whole time we are running from the world, if we're not careful we'll run to the other extreme and become self-righteous. And God will be just as angry with that because that is just as carnal as the worldliness that we may have condemned in our efforts to draw nigh to God. These suffering Christians hadn't been worldly, but they were on the brink of becoming very self-righteous. James seems to sympathize with the problem. But he warns them in no uncertain terms.

The Promise Of Blessing

In every warning there is the promise of blessing. And in their case it is an invitation to know God at a level that is explored by an exceedingly rare number of men. That is, to qualify to speak in the name of the Lord indeed. James' method is to remove all props from under their feet, even their own claim to do right in what they were doing. In the same way that a grudge is known by God because he sees the heart, so any claim of justice that you feel is known by God. In the same way that you can refuse to strike back verbally but still hold a grudge, so in the same way you might not affirm yourself verbally but if you think it, God sees it.

What we're after here is that in the heart we won't even think it. You may say, 'God really is on my side.' What you do is project upon God what you want to be true, and that becomes something you're so involved in that you cannot tell the difference between what you think and what he might say when, in fact, he hasn't spoken. If the great apostle Paul could say, 'I judge not mine own self', where does that put us who are so certain that we are right. James wants us to renounce any claim upon God. Don't even think it. Do you really realize that if the Lord were to expose all your heart there's no way that he could vindicate you? Who among us is right all the time? Were God to expose our hearts we would cry out, 'Stop, Lord.' Nothing could be more foolish than to judge yourself. For if we saw ourselves as we really are, we wouldn't even think to judge another person.

But what if God does not vindicate us?

What James wants, then, is to teach us to adore the name of God for God's own sake. This is why Paul said, 'Let God be true, but every man a liar' (Rom. 3:4). Let God be himself. We don't know what is in his mind. Were we to know, we would blush before him. The folly of wanting to bring him in on our case! James is shouting to us to stand back and adore God himself whether or not his will or his cause coincides with our own interests. Do we love God only if he vindicates us? What if it should turn out that God should vindicate your oppressor? How would that make you feel? Will you get mad at God? Will you just pack up and say, 'I'm only for the Lord if he's for me'?

We all love God when he is with us. Who among us will praise him when he's not for our own cause? Is it the true God we love or is it the God who will vindicate us? James knows that if we don't swear at all but only adore God's name then we will stand by the Lord regardless of whose side he comes down on. The point is that we must adore the name of God and say, 'Lord, you are right. Whatever you do is right.' And then when he steps in we applaud what he does. It may turn out that we are the ones judged, but if that's what he does it's right. This way we stand above ourselves. We honour his will even in our own condemnation.

Acknowledging our own condemnation

There were certain times in the history of Christianity in this country where a man couldn't be ordained to the ministry unless he was willing to affirm the justice of God and his own condemnation. This may sound strange to us. For that's how far removed we have been from the God of the Bible who is just. The reason God said, 'Thou shalt not take my name in vain', is that we must stand back and adore him for whatever he does. As the Psalmist put it: 'Our God is in the heavens: he hath done whatsoever he hath pleased' (115:3). If we stand above ourselves then we really die and attend our own funeral.

This is the kind of suffering that we have got to go through before God can really use us. That's what Job had to learn. Job just kept affirming himself and he got angry with his comforters. He lost his temper and he got mad at God and God stepped in out of the whirlwind. Job said, 'I am vile ... I will lay mine hand upon my mouth' (40:4). As Paul put it: 'That every mouth may be stopped' (Rom. 3:19). We'd save ourselves so much trouble. This is why the trial that God puts us through is delayed. We think we've come to the end of the trial and then no, it just goes on. It helps us to see whether we really love God for what he is in himself.

God is a jealous God and he wants to be worshipped for what he is in himself alone. But we tend only to want to worship him when there is something in it for us. The kind of worship God is after requires suffering. This is what Jesus was teaching in the Sermon on the Mount and it went right across the Pharisees. It was so offensive to them and it's offensive to us. The interesting thing about Paul and that statement, 'I know nothing against myself but hereby am I not justified', is that the fact that I don't know anything against myself doesn't mean that there's not something against me. For 'the heart is deceitful above all things and desperately wicked' (Jer. 17:9). I don't want to know anything against myself. And I don't want to probe too deeply. We can all see the fault in the other person. Were God to step in and shine with that uncreated beam upon our hearts, we would hang our heads in shame. This is why we must stand back.

What if one really is right? You might say, 'What about Paul? Didn't he talk as though he was right?' Yes. For example, Paul said to the Galatians, 'If any man preach any other gospel unto you than that ye have received, let him be accursed' (1:9). He said to the Thessalonians, 'For neither at any time used we flattering words, as ye know, nor a cloak of covetousness; God is witness' (1 Thess. 2:5). And you can find other times when Paul talked like that. One never affirms oneself, but only the gospel, and that's what Paul was doing. What James meant was that these Christians could have identified their own oppression with God's name, putting both on the same level.

The Example Of Elijah

Elijah came perilously close to this. He was under the juniper tree and he said, 'It is enough; now, O LORD, take away my life' (1 Kgs. 19:4). He was really feeling sorry for himself. He said, 'I have been very jealous for the LORD God of hosts: for the children of Israel have forsaken thy covenant, thrown down thine altars, and slain thy prophets with the sword; and I, even I only, am left; and they seek my life, to take it away' (v. 10). And God just let Elijah go on. He said it again. And shortly God said, 'I have left me seven thousand in Israel, all the knees which have not bowed unto Baal' (v. 18). God has a way of putting us down. There are those who have been true to him that we are never to know about. We die hard. Elijah died hard.

Living on the brink of blessing

It's one thing to affirm the gospel (which, by the way, is the highest way we can exalt the name of God), but it is quite another matter when we hide behind the gospel when it is really our own interest at stake. James is wanting to teach these people that they really can please the Lord and they're on the brink of seeing real blessing.

This matter of hiding behind the gospel when the whole time it's our own enterprise we've got in mind is so vast that we almost hang our heads in shame. Church history is riddled with it. What has happened is that the Christian church has become divided and subdivided and every one of us says, 'God is with us.' We take the name of the Lord in vain when we do that.

Learning to keep our mouths shut

We're back to this question: what if our own cause is right? If that's true, you do not affirm yourself. You won't need to. You're in the best position to keep your mouth shut. Just let your yea be yea, your nay, nay. If one really is telling the truth, don't protest at all. Let your word be your bond. You don't need to go around raising questions. Just have the answers when you're asked: yea, yea; nay, nay. To affirm by an oath is to overclaim, to overstate. And it betrays an insecurity. It suggests that we've got a lot to worry about. The point is, if God really is with you let him say it. If you've got to say, 'God is with us', you put yourselves in the situation of the Pharisees who sound a trumpet to say, 'Look what we've done.' God backs off. No blessing comes from him.

We Should Not Claim To Know God Better Than We Do

Here is the mistake so many of us make. We read more into God's affirmation of us generally than he intends to convey. When my son or my daughter comes up to me and says, 'Daddy, can I do this?' And I look at them and smile and they run off and say, 'Mom, Dad said it was all right.' I say, 'Wait. come back here. Did I say that?' 'Ah, but you smiled.' 'Did I say that?' 'Well, no. But ...' I say, 'You're right. I didn't say that. I'm not going to say that.' We derive a false, self-serving conclusion from a positive relationship. The warning for us here is not to claim to know God better than we do. Most of us aren't nearly as spiritual as we want others to think we are.

We begin by abandoning any claim upon him. When you became a Christian did you appeal to any right that you've got that God should save you? No, you just asked for mercy. And you claimed nothing but the merit, the name, the shed blood of Christ. The only vindication you've got is the Lord Jesus Christ because he was sinless. And he is your righteousness. You've got nothing else. We never outgrow this. The substitutionary death of Christ, that's your righteousness. When we forsake any claim upon God we then show we've had a glimpse of the divine glory.

The position of true witness and worship

The fascinating irony is that the more you know God the more you will witness. It's equally true that the more you know God the more you'll keep quiet about it. For God gives himself to those who won't name-drop his name. It is then that we can be trusted with family secrets. The secret of the Lord is with them that fear him, not with those who, as soon as they get a thing from the Lord, go out and tell about it, trying to give the impression that they've got secret channels to God. God gives himself to those who will not manipulate him and exploit his name.

The happy news is that if we are suffering at this level it means that God has something for us to do. We've all got to come to the place that we rise above personal interest. Moses had to learn it. The first thing Moses thought he had to do when he left the palace in Egypt was to convince his fellow Hebrews that he was one of them. But he ended up killing an Egyptian. He wanted to convince them he was on their side and it backfired. How often we affirm ourselves and then God in kindness lets it backfire so that we will die. Moses eventually learned about God's greater glory. The time came when his personal concerns were swallowed up by the greater concern of the kingdom of God.

Those who have come to know him most intimately are those who, through suffering, learned to let God be God. To adore him without any self-concern. To praise him without any personal motive. To honour him without any self-interest. 'Let God be true and every man a liar.'

34

Afflictions

James 5:13a

We now approach the final paragraph of this general epistle of James. He begins with some questions as he comes to the last part of his letter in verses 13 and 14: 'Is any among you afflicted? Let him pray. Is any merry? Let him sing psalms. Is any sick among you? Let him call for the elders of the church; and let them pray over him, anointing him with oil in the name of the Lord.'

James' Pastoral Heart

These questions assume certain possibilities in the living of the Christian life: the possibility of being afflicted, of being merry, of being ill. Two deal with negative conditions: being afflicted and being sick. One deals with this positive condition: being merry. What James does is to raise the possibility of being in these states and then supplies an answer for what we ought to do if we find ourselves in such a state.

Here is the pastoral heart of James emerging again, perhaps as never before. Whatever else can be said about this section it is a most applicable word at any time. For any congregation at any one moment would include any of these conditions. The question is whether we have followed James' advice if we find ourselves in any one of these three states. The question of continuity emerges again. Why would James say this right here? Is James continuing to address those who have been oppressed? Perhaps so. And yet, in bringing this epistle to a close, he probably wants to bring in everybody and even the oppressors. They need a word. And so James says, 'Is any afflicted among you?' It is a word fitting to anybody who reads these lines.

Nobody Is Exempt From Affliction

It is not the first time he has used this word 'afflicted'. He used it back in verse 10 in the form of a noun. 'Take, my brethren, the prophets, who have spoken in the name of the Lord, for an example of suffering affliction, and of patience.' It's the same Greek word which comes from one word meaning 'evil', and another meaning 'enduring'. It means to endure what is adverse, evil, unfair.

All of us, when we have a particular affliction or adversity, tend to think that ours is unique. But you're not the first. For who in the world, Christian or non-Christian, is exempt from some kind of adversity? Job said, 'Man is born unto trouble' (5:7). Nobody is exempt.

The question is not, why has affliction come? The question is, how do I react to trouble? It's not the existence of trouble that tells whether you are a Christian, but it is your attitude to it that tells what kind of a person you are. But there is a fine but crucial distinction between the Christian and the non-Christian in so far as trouble is concerned. You could say the distinction lies with the origin of the trouble or, more particularly, the allocation, how it is meted out. Whereas trouble comes to everybody, only the Christian has the promise of a limitation with regard to affliction. This is why we have 1 Corinthians 10:13: 'There hath no temptation' – no trial – 'taken you but such as is common to man: but God is faithful, who will not suffer you to be tempted above that ye are able; but will with the temptation also make a way to escape, that ye may be able to bear it.'

God's intervention in affliction

This points to what I would call God's filtering chamber in heaven. It stays active twenty-four hours a day. It works perfectly and without our help. We don't know all about it now. But what we do know is that it is at work with every Christian in two ways.

First, with regard to our prayer requests. The Lord filters our requests and only lets through the requests that are best for us to have answered. Second is with regard to Satan's requests. God filters out the wicked proposals that the devil lays before him with reference to every Christian. If you sometimes feel that your afflictions are more than you can bear, why don't you ask this question: what if Satan actually got his whole way? We know from the book of Job that God lets the devil go so far and no farther. We know from the book of Job that the devil cannot come to us directly. He has to go up to heaven and God considers the various things the devil lays before him.

The devil's limited role

What if the devil got everything through that he wanted with reference to us? Do you know that the evil, the wickedness with which the devil would besiege us, if he could, is infinitely worse than anything we do experience – many, many times worse than what God finally allows to come? If the devil had his way the first thing he would do would be to kill every Christian. He wants to wipe Christianity off the face of the earth. Or if he couldn't do that he would try to destroy the credibility of every Christian witness so that nobody would take the Christian seriously.

Short of destroying us, what the devil tries to do is to demoralize us so the Christian faith loses its credibility. To demoralize means to have your spirit broken; it is extreme discouragement. It's never a good state for a Christian to be in. If the devil can bring us to extreme discouragement then he can attack us so easily. If we're always on the move and growing in grace so that the devil cannot use the same old temptations with which to bring us down, then he has a hard time defeating us. But if he can bring us to immobility so that we are full of self-pity and extreme discouragement he can just take his time, and go for us. We're sitting ducks. Paul said, 'We are troubled on every side, yet not distressed; we are perplexed, but not in despair' (2 Cor. 4:8). Paul would not let himself become demoralized.

Does God ever allow the devil to bring us so low that we are demoralized? The answer is, yes. But it doesn't follow that our discouragement is either out of our hands or God's fault, because the apostle Paul refused to let the devil get him in that condition. Our most vulnerable state ought to be the opportunity for grace to function. We are never allowed to be brought to a low estate without commensurate grace. Grace is always there if we will use it. If the devil can demoralize, we are an easy target for him. He can bring us to do the unthinkable. But it must always be said that if we do the unthinkable it is our own fault. We learn from this very epistle that falling into sin is never something for which we can blame God.

How We Should Look At Affliction

Affliction is often the devil's instrument to demoralize us, and if he wins it is our own fault. But at the same time affliction ought to be seen as that for which we can and must be truly grateful. This is why in Psalm 119:71

David could say, 'It is good for me that I have been afflicted.' Imagine saying that! Can you say what David said? Affliction is God's exclusive invitation to experience greater grace. As James put it in chapter 4: 'He giveth more grace' (v. 6).

This theme is still at work here, for there is a quality of grace that may be experienced only by this special invitation called affliction. You might admire the great saint or read the biography of a man God used or look at the stalwarts of faith in Hebrews 11, and say, 'I want to be like that.' That means you must go through the fire of affliction as these men did to get the grace they got. This is why you should be thankful for that affliction.

> *When through fiery trials thy pathway shall lie,*
> *My grace all-sufficient shall be thy supply,*
> *The flame shall not hurt thee: I only design*
> *Thy dross to consume, and thy gold to refine.*

You are gold in the sight of God. Every Christian is to God a diamond in the rough. But it's affliction that will bring you to the kind of grace that will be got no other way. So this grace is poured out that we might face the world and become a threat to the devil and make inroads on Satan's territory only by receiving the affliction with joy.

The question now is, what form may affliction take? One of two levels – the level of nature or the level of the spirit or faith. At the level of nature, affliction may take three forms. The first is that which threatens our material security: food, shelter, clothing. In a word, money, or the threat of financial reverse. Or it may take on the form of emotional or psychological insecurities. Or your human relations, being accepted by others or rejected. Your reaction when your self-esteem is threatened. It is here that marriage and family relations come in, and our children and their state of affairs. If you're a young person, it's how you're getting on with your parents, your brother, your sister, your friends at school. There's a third form of affliction at a natural level: simply, health. Illness may be a definite part of affliction.

What is affliction at the level of faith or at a spiritual level? It can be summed up one way. It is when God hides his face. All these afflictions that I've referred to at a natural level challenge faith. God can use these natural afflictions, but how we react at a spiritual level will determine whether we're growing. And yet it must be said that the hardest affliction of all to endure is when God hides his face.

The Affliction We Bring On Ourselves

Up to now we have dealt with two basic kinds of afflictions: those which Satan brings along within the bounds of God's limitations and permission, and then the affliction that can be understood as God hiding his face. The third kind of affliction is simply that which we bring on ourselves. The Psalmist dealt with that one first, in verse 67 of Psalm 119, 'Before I was afflicted I went astray: but now have I kept thy word.' In other words, there comes a time when we must honestly face up to our trouble in terms of our own disobedience. That can be an affliction at a natural level or when God hides his face. But it may be affliction that is traceable to sin.

It would be a mistake to overestimate this point, to claim that all affliction is due to sin. The book of Job was such a threat to Judaism because the popular consensus was that all suffering is a result of sin. And the book of Job refutes that. But it would also be a mistake to underestimate this aspect of Christian doctrine, because sin does lead to suffering. It's not always so easy to tell the difference between the affliction that comes within the scope of God's pleasure for us and his design and that which can be traceable to our own folly. But as a general rule you will know in your heart of hearts whether your affliction is a result of your own folly. David knew. Jonah knew. And most of us know very soon.

What if one does see that one's own affliction is because of one's own disobedience? The answer is that sometimes instant repentance can bring about an instant subsiding of the trouble. But if the affliction lingers after true repentance, the only thing that can be said then is, let God handle it because he will. 'Is any afflicted among you?' But James isn't finished. He tells us what to do. 'Let him pray.' You may have hoped for a better insight than that, for some ingenious breakthrough of knowledge. Is that the best James can do? If you're afflicted, that's what he says: 'Let him pray.'

Oh what peace we often forfeit,
O what needless pain we bear,

Why?

All because we do not carry
Everything to God in prayer.

The Greek word here literally means 'to draw near'. It's used in Hebrews 4:16: 'Let us therefore come boldly unto the throne of grace'. And in

Hebrews 7:25: 'Wherefore he is able also to save them to the uttermost that come unto God by him, seeing he ever liveth to make intercession for them.' Come to God.

Every affliction is God's design to bring you closer to himself. God gives you the affliction because he knows this much about you. Nothing else will really work. All of us are so prone to evil. As the hymn puts it: we're weak and prone to wander. We like to fancy ourselves as the type that doesn't have to have the special trial, that we can just obey the Lord from the start. That's the way we ought to be, but who among us is like that?

But here's the wonderful thing: there is no such thing as an idle affliction. Every good thing, every bad thing that happens to the Christian has meaning and purpose. James says, 'Let him pray.' Why could James say that? Because he's turning you to a wise heavenly Father who has an architectural plan in your life and you're not going to know what the plan is if you don't turn to him. This is why Paul could say to the Corinthians, 'Whether we be afflicted, it is for your consolation and salvation' (2 Cor. 1:6).

The Reason God Hides His Face

The reason, then, we turn to God is partly to discover what his plan is. When trouble comes, if we moan and groan but never turn to God, how can we ever understand what is going on? James is saying, 'If you're afflicted pray. Draw near.' James said early on in this epistle, 'Draw nigh to God, and he will draw nigh to you' (4:8). This drawing nigh was simultaneously a fleeing from the world. What an encouragement this is that James could tell us that when we are afflicted it's the time to draw nigh. Often when we're in some kind of trouble, when we're afflicted, especially when God hides his face, our most natural reaction is to say, 'God's angry with me. He doesn't want to be bothered with me.' 'No', James is saying. 'Pray. God wants you to come again and again.'

God's Call To Prayer

You say, 'Why does he hide his face from me?' God hides his face, not because he's not on speaking terms with you, but rather it's his way of saying, 'How much do your really love me?' Are you afflicted? Pray.

Draw near. It doesn't mean to do it in a perfunctory way or in a state of severe desperation. But it means to see how close you can get to God. James' choice of words here shows two things simultaneously. You're trying to see how close you can get to God and at the same time how far away from the world you can get.

Another reason for the affliction is this: that we might discover things about ourselves that we hadn't known before. You're appalled that you could react like you did. Sometimes in a self-righteous mood we say, 'That's just not me to do that. I don't know why I did it.' But it was you that did it. We blush. Affliction shows you what you really are. So what do you do when you discover this? You pray. You see how close you can get to God. You thank him for what he has shown you. It might not be very pleasant. But be thankful that you've learned this about yourself as soon as you have.

And yet there is another reason James would say, 'Is any among you afflicted? Let him pray.' God wants you to have the breakthrough, to grow, to develop. Do you think you're going to get the breakthrough by reading the newspaper or watching television? Your only hope is that God gives you the breakthrough. This is why you're going to be praying to the one who holds the breakthrough in his hands.

Looking for the breakthrough out here when it's at the throne of grace will cause you to wait indefinitely. You go to the source. You may have a natural affliction, but the breakthrough will only come at the spiritual level. God uses the natural to drive us to him, to box us in.

How we should pray

The final thing I want to raise is this: how do you pray in the light of affliction?

- First, you pray with thanksgiving. Here's the way Paul put it to the Philippians: 'Be careful for nothing; but in every thing by prayer and supplication with thanksgiving let your requests be made known unto God' (4:6). You thank God for dealing with you. You say with the Psalmist, 'It is good for me that I have been afflicted' (119:71). Thank him for loving you enough to allow this. 'Whom the Lord loveth he chasteneth' (Heb. 12:6).
- Second, in praying ask him to let the full value of the trial be your inheritance. Don't be too quick to cash in the bond. Let it grow in interest. Let it come to maturity. So when the trial comes, tell God you

want to have the ultimate benefit for which that trial is designed. Don't try to abort it and get it over with.

- Third, ask for grace to endure should the end of the trial be delayed. Don't play the hero in God's presence. Don't get a martyr complex. Say to God, 'I'm so weak I don't think I can go on. Please give me more grace to endure.' Admit your weakness. Ask for more grace. He'll give it.

- Fourth, ask him to show you how he wants you to develop. Say, 'Lord, I know you have allowed this. Show me what you want me to know about you, about myself, that I've not known before.'

- Fifth, pray for the breakthrough. God wants you to have the breakthrough more than you want it yourself. Ask him continually, but keep these other four principles in mind. The reason ultimately that James says, 'Let him pray', is that we might have the breakthrough, the light at the end of the tunnel. It may not necessarily mean the end of the affliction. But it most certainly means the end of the riddle, the end of the darkness, the end of the bewilderment, the end of the puzzle.

When the breakthrough comes it comes one of two ways. It can be a breakthrough that happens outside of you. Or it can be something that will happen inside you. If it happens outside of you, that means outward circumstances change and that resolves the matter. But what about when circumstances don't change? Then something has to happen inside you. It means that you have become master, as it were. When you're on top of the situation you could flip a coin whether the outward situation changes or you just go on, because inwardly you've got the victory. So what matters is not it but you. Not the circumstance but you. Not them but you. Not your job but you. Not your boss but you. Not your teacher, not your professor, not the person in the shop, not your enemy. Inwardly something can happen and you wouldn't take anything in the world for that.

Should the situation change first and then you feel better there's always a doubt about how strong you really are. But if God changes the situation thank him for it. He's the one that did it. His intervention is what matters. But should you get the victory despite the situation then it is a most wonderful victory indeed. 'He that ruleth his spirit' is better 'than he that taketh a city' (Prov. 16:32). Are you afflicted? Pray. Draw nigh. Don't forget about fleeing from the world and the breakthrough will come. That's why James wants to drive you to God.

35

Are You Encouraged? – Show It

James 5:13b

One cannot help but note how little space is given to this matter: 'Is any merry? Let him sing psalms.' That's all we have about being merry in this epistle of James. It's possibly because not many in this assembly that James was addressing could be said to be merry. We know that it was a church that was filled with tension between the rich and the poor, the poor being oppressed by the rich. We know that it was largely a worldly-minded church. So there isn't much to be said by James on this question of being merry. And yet, ironic as it may seem, this state of being merry is precisely what James envisages for every one of these Christians sooner or later.

Seeing Reasons To Be Merry

For that reason we can see synonyms of being merry throughout the epistle. For example, in verse 11 it is called 'the end of the Lord'. This was a reference to Job who, with all of his problems, eventually came through it. Indeed, the very epistle of James starts out with this: 'Let patience have her perfect work, that ye may be perfect and entire, wanting nothing' (1:4).

This could be called the culmination of preparation. It is when we have passed the test, as it were, and the trial is over. Not that anyone outgrows preparation, for that is not possible. None of us is ever too clever or too experienced that we don't need more preparation. Spurgeon once said, 'If I knew I had twenty-five years left to live, I would spend twenty of them in preparation.' But God would give the other five as preparation as well! What happens is, in the living of the Christian life we move from one phase of preparation to the next so that we can say with John Newton,

'I'm not what I want to be. I'm not what I ought to be. I'm not what I hope to be. But I'm not what I used to be.' Paul calls it being 'changed … from glory to glory' (2 Cor. 3:18). Every new phase or every new sense of glory is always preceded by a test or trial. But the trials don't last forever and the breakthrough does come. And each phase of glory brings greater joy.

The Joy That Comes From Within

James says, 'Is there any merry among you?' It's a very interesting Greek word here, *euthumei*. It comes from the word *thumos*, which left by itself simply means 'to boil with rage'. But when you have the little prefix *eu* in front of it, it changes the word to its opposite so that it means to boil with joy from within, 'to swell from within with cheer, with courage, with encouragement, with good spirits'. This word 'merry', in a sense, has rather bad connotations, especially in the UK. I remember shortly after we began living here I said to people, 'Why do you often say "Happy Christmas"? In America we always say "Merry Christmas".' But it was explained that 'merry' over here has come to have a slightly different meaning than it used to.

James is not talking here about being merry as brought on by spirits or strong drink, but it's a happiness from within, an encouragement, a courage springing from within. In America, various places in the south have what are called artesian wells, wells that just spring up and keep going. Jesus referred to this in John 7:38–39 when he said, 'He that believeth on me, as the scripture hath said, out of his belly shall flow rivers of living water.' By this he spoke of the Spirit, by which 'they that believe on him should receive', referring to the Holy Ghost. Its origin is from within.

Oddly enough this word 'merry' is only used by one other writer in the New Testament and that is Luke, in the book of Acts when he quotes Paul. Paul is before Felix and he says, 'After that the governor had beckoned unto him to speak, he answered, Forasmuch as I know that thou hast been of many years a judge unto this nation, I do the more cheerfully answer for myself ' (24:10). It was translated 'cheerfully'. It's used by Paul again in Acts 27 before his shipwreck: 'Wherefore sirs, be of good cheer: for I believe God, that it shall be even as it was told me' (v. 25). And the word is seen again in verse 36: 'Then were they all of good cheer, and they also took some meat.' What we have here is an inner peace in operation. It is not necessary that the outward circumstances are positive for this peace to be in operation. Indeed, here was Paul before

Felix defending the faith but, in a sense, fighting for his own life. And yet there was this peace. And so in the other two verses that Luke uses, here they were in the face of physical danger but they were 'of good cheer'.

The point is that here is a joy that defies and mocks the threatening situation. That's why Paul calls it a peace that passes understanding (Phil. 4:7). How can that be? Well, your understanding says one thing but the peace within says another. When that comes, you've really got a choice. This happened to me recently. The person who was driving me to a train said something to me just minutes before I got out of the car, something that, had I thought about it, would have made me very sad. But while he was talking I felt a peace. I realized I had the choice. The peace came simultaneously with his words. I didn't particularly have the peace before, but I had it then. It was so wonderful. I thought, 'I can dwell on what he has said or I can just let the peace be there.' That's why Paul said to the Colossians, 'Let the peace of God rule in your hearts' (3:15). You can determine whether your understanding will control how you feel or whether peace can rule.

Here James is saying, 'Is any merry? What can you do about it?' Paul referred to being sorrowful but always rejoicing (2 Cor. 6:10). We may ask, how is it possible to have such courage where the situation would suggest the opposite? The answer is, because one looks at God's side of things. Stop and think for a moment. You are living by God's promise. Paul said, 'I live by the faith of the Son of God' (Gal. 2:20). Do you know what it is to live by his promises? You go by that and there is your joy.

Consider your own salvation. Do you realize that you are eternally saved? These promises show us that we are in God, in Christ. Christ cannot be dislodged from the Father. It's wonderful to know that if you are a Christian you can never be lost, no matter what you do. I add that deliberately, not to encourage anybody to think it doesn't matter how you live the Christian life because it certainly does matter. That's what the epistle of James is all about. But the promise is there. And God does not want us to doubt our salvation. We are in Christ who cannot fall, who cannot be disenfranchised. And we're put into Christ by faith. We live by the promises.

God Takes Care Of Our Past And Our Future

Not only is our salvation secure, but even our past is owned by God. Look what an ugly past we present to him. But God says, 'Leave it to me.' 'He which hath begun a good work in you will perform it until the day of Jesus Christ' (Phil. 1:6). 'And we know that all things work together for good to them that love God' (Rom. 8:28). Because God does it. But if we try to make it work out it gets worse unless we let him have the past and say, 'Lord, I'm ashamed not only of my pre-Christian past, but of my post-conversion past.' We've all made mistakes and we've all failed and none of us has grown as we ought. But God looks at the past and says, 'Leave it to me.'

God not only takes our past on his shoulders, but he owns our future as well. Do not worry about tomorrow. God has already been there and he can say today, 'It's all right.' Here's the promise for you. It's what God said to Jehoshaphat: 'Be not afraid nor dismayed by reason of this great multitude; for the battle is not yours, but God's ... Ye shall not need to fight in this battle: set yourselves, stand ye still, and see the salvation of the LORD' (2 Chron. 20:15–17). Everybody just fell before God and worshipped.

God wants you to worship and leave tomorrow in his hands. Didn't God take you through every one of your past battles? And now you've got another he'll take you through that one. He owns your situation as his very own, because it is his. This is why we can be 'merry' despite the outward situation suggesting the opposite. But not only because of the promises of God, but because of the very presence of God. Jesus said, 'Lo, I am with you alway' (Mt. 28:20). He said that as he was ascending to the right hand of God. How can Jesus be with us when he's at the right hand of God? He said it: 'I will not leave you comfortless but I will send the promise of the Father upon you, the Holy Spirit' (Jn. 14:18; Lk. 24:49). It is the Spirit who not only brings us to these promises I've been quoting, but it's the Spirit's own witness. That is that peace that's almost physical because you can feel it.

I want to give two cautions. Caution number one: obviously one is not necessarily expected to feel very cheerful all the time. Or else there is no reason for his saying, 'Is any among you afflicted? ... Is any merry?' And though it is possible to be afflicted and be happy it's not likely one really feels merry when one's right under the affliction. This is why the writer to the Hebrews says, 'No chastening for the present seemeth to be joyous, but grievous' (Heb. 12:11). We don't need to beat ourselves into submission if we're not feeling all that cheerful. There are those who want to give you the impression that they just never have any problems. They are always wearing the mask. A lot of people preach the victorious life and you think, 'I just wish I could be like that.' But if you were to follow those preachers home and live with them every day you'd find that they have their problems too.

Constantly averting depression

The caution given by James is a definite warning against the bondage of the melancholy syndrome. Some people seem most at ease when they're sad. They're sad because they seem to think, 'If I'm not sad now I will be tomorrow so I might as well be today.' And there are those who are threatened by real joy, who don't like it. Some unconsciously look for what will make them feel bad again. The moment they feel good they begin to think, 'But I've still got this problem.' Back down to depression.

James envisages that all Christians ought to experience this joy sooner or later. He now tells us what to do when we have been moved to this phase of glory. He says, 'Is any merry? Let him sing.' We all begin to dread the feeling of being down again. Some of us are naturally prone to depression. A psychological problem can become a spiritual problem of which Satan takes advantage. It need not be a spiritual problem, but if we're prone in a certain direction the devil knows this. He always goes for the weakest link in our psychological chain and brings us to despair. James is going to help us here. One way to overcome this problem: when you are encouraged, enjoy it to the full, show it. By doing this more and more and more you minimize the possibility of depression. This is how the Christian life can help us with our emotional problems.

How To Extend The Joy We Feel: Music

James' method is to sing. Why sing? Gratitude, yes, but more than that. It is a way of extending this joy. When the joy comes you immediately think, 'Well, there's got to be some problem. I can't really be this happy.' You look around and you think, 'Ah, I still have this problem', and plummet right back down to depression again. That's why for many of us a burst of joy doesn't last because we just find something to concentrate on that's negative.

What James is saying here is that you can keep extending the joy until you've minimized the possibility of feeling the opposite way. He says that you should sing God's praises. God does the big things. We do the little things. He brings the victory. Then it is up to us and we can determine to a great extent how long the joy lasts. 'Let him sing' is James' way of saying, 'If you're encouraged, show it.' By nurturing the joy God gives, it can become yet a greater joy.

God wants his people to be encouraged

There's a second reason he wants us to sing. God wants his people to be encouraged. If things are bad and getting worse all the time, you can talk yourself into believing that this is what God wants. But what he wants for you is a state of joy. And singing is a way of accepting and dignifying the encouragement that he has given you. If God does something for you and you just say, 'No thanks', that's an insult to him rejecting the joy.

There's a third reason you should sing. That is because Satan wants you to be sad. Peace and joy are the opposites of the way the devil wants you to feel. When you're sad, the devil is glad. When you see cause for joy say, 'This is what God has done for me. Oh, how kind God is to do this!' And the devil will flee. Do not give room to the devil by looking at any imperfection you've got or at any circumstance that the devil would make you gaze at. But thank God for what he has done. And show it by singing.

The Greek word here is *psalleto*. The Authorised Version says, 'Let him sing psalms.' That's one reason there are those who think that's the only thing we should ever sing in worship. But let's look at the Greek word here. The NIV simply says, 'Let him sing songs of praise.' The NASV says 'sing praises'. The Geneva Bible just says, 'Is any merry? Let him sing.'

Making melody

My greatest joy comes from reading the Psalms. But we must be fair here. Had James meant an Old Testament psalm he would have said so. He would have used the verb *ado*, which means 'to sing' and the word *psalmos*, 'psalms'. And even apart from the Greek, obviously there's a difference between songs and hymns and psalms because Paul said in Ephesians 5:19, 'Speaking to yourselves in psalms and hymns and spiritual songs'. The same is true in Colossians 3:16: 'in psalms and hymns and spiritual songs'. James uses a word that doesn't literally mean 'to sing psalms', but 'to touch'. It's physical. It means 'to pluck strings with your fingers', a word that depicts non-verbal praise.

The word 'read' or 'reading' is found in the Bible 81 times. Any word that appears that much in the Bible – that's a lot. But when it comes to singing, the words 'sing' or 'sang' or 'sung' or 'singers' are in the Bible 190 times. Words like 'psaltery', 'music', 'cymbals', 'sackbut', 'cornet', 'trumpet', 'harp' or 'instruments', are in the Bible over 260 times. This is non-verbal, playing or singing. It's making melody, a joyful noise unto the Lord, coming before his presence with singing. It is showing you are happy by singing, by music, by making melody. And it's most certainly a clear proof that God isn't against music or musical instruments in church.

The devil hates music

Back in the Reformation one of the things that separated the Lutheran wing of the Reformation from the reformed was that the reformed largely said, 'We will not have musical instruments in the church.' They sang psalms and at best used a tuning fork. But Luther wanted music. He loved organs and any kind of instrument. So when it comes to that issue I'm not very reformed. I'm a Lutheran. Here was a man, Martin Luther, who wanted to use all the arts in the service, in the worship of God. Listen to this quotation from Martin Luther: 'The devil is a sad spirit and makes people sad. Hence he cannot bear cheerfulness and therefore gets as far off from music as possible and never stays where men are singing, especially spiritual songs.' Don't forget how King Saul, when he was depressed, would send for David to play on the harp and the evil spirit would depart.

The powerful witness of singing

There's yet another reason we should sing. We should sing with vibrance, with vigour, with joy, because that is our witness to those who come in. When a church is vibrant with singing – I mean in volume and with a sense of joy – it puts the sinner under conviction. I could give you testimony after testimony of people who've been converted who said it began with the singing. We all know about the Welsh Revival and how God used the singing. They just sang and people were converted. There wasn't much preaching. Singing. The spirit was contagious and it took its effect in lost men.

I want to make three or four observations with regard to singing. The first is this: it is a sign of culture as much as it is a sign of spirituality that we sing nothing but the old hymns. We should admit that when we do this. There are those who want to sing the same old hymns – the old ones that predate 1900 or even 1800 – and they think it's a sign of spirituality. Now it might be. But it is much more a sign of culture and your own personal taste. If you were living in Isaac Watts' day chances are you would have been very offended by that innovative man who complained about the singing of the dead psalms. He just didn't like the rut that they were in. And he began to write hymns, and look what we've got.

The second observation is that it is a sign of weak spirituality that more new hymns are not being written. The Wesleyan hymns were born in revival and true revival might well do it again. A lot of things are being written today, however, that are weak in theology. That leads to my third observation. Hymns reflect how deep our understanding, our theology is. In 1 Corinthians 14:15 Paul said, 'I will sing with the spirit, and I will sing with the understanding also.' We are caught between a rock and a hard place, in a sense, because so many of the things that are being written today are superficial. The tendency is simply to dismiss them all and to stick with Isaac Watts. I think that would be a mistake.

[*Isn't it wonderful that the climate has changed in the last 15 years since this sermon was preached? God has begun to answer prayer, that God would raise up a Charles Wesley in our day.*]

Finally, we should be careful of being in any kind of a rut and avoid the extremes.

So why sing? If you enjoy what God has done and is doing, show it. This fits in with everything else James has said. 'A man may say, Thou hast faith, and I have works: shew me thy faith without thy works, and I will shew thee my faith by my works' (2:18). It's not simply what we say. It's what we do, how we do it. The non-verbal level is the smile, the spirit, how you look, your countenance, the friendliness. Things like this matter a lot. And singing is James' method to show you're encouraged. It extends the joy and helps defeat a natural tendency. It makes the devil leave. May we all sing with that joy. It's conducive to the atmosphere in which God converts men and women. God help us to see it.

36

Is Faith Healing Possible?

James 5:14–15

Now we come to the third question by which this final paragraph in the epistle is introduced. 'Is any sick among you?' Here is what you are to do: 'Let him call for the elders of the church; and let them pray over him, anointing him with oil in the name of the Lord: and the prayer of faith shall save the sick, and the Lord shall raise him up; and if he have committed sins, they shall be forgiven him.'

There Is No Promise Of Exemption From Sickness

It's not surprising that a congregation of any size would include somebody in it that is sick. Any group in the world would have its proportion of those who are unwell at any one time. Because as 'the rain falls on the just and the unjust, the sun shines on the just and the unjust' (Mt. 5:45), the fact that a person is a Christian doesn't make him exempt from being sick. There's no promise in the gospel that a Christian, who becomes such by grace, will be without any physical impediment. Because all men must die.

We are given eternal life in Jesus Christ, but the Bible shows that there is a two-fold redemption: redemption of the soul which comes through faith and redemption of the body to those who have believed. They will be raised on the last day and they will live for ever with God. The Christian, in the meantime, will physically die. Only Jesus Christ was without sin. He was the perfect lamb without spot and blemish. As for the person of Jesus, he would not have died a natural death, because the Bible says, 'The wages of sin is death' (Rom. 6:23). Jesus did not sin. Jesus was killed. And what brought about the death of Jesus was that he was 'smitten of God' (Isa. 53:4). God did it.

Adam died because he sinned. We are in Adam. 'All have sinned, and come short of the glory of God' (Rom. 3:23). 'The wages of sin is death.' All of us will die, whether by accident, car crash, or some disease. We pray for those who are unwell, but there comes a time when there's nothing that can be done. One's time has come. I just call them to your attention. Men like David Brainerd and Robert Murray McCheyne were godly men who were taken early in life, in their late twenties. And Paul had his 'thorn in the flesh' (2 Cor. 12:7). We don't know what that was, and as long as we don't know, we can all project and pretend that Paul would understand 'me'. There's something to be said for the fact that we don't know. Whatever it was, we do know that Paul said, 'Three times I prayed that it might depart' (v. 8). And it didn't. So we must remember that not only do we know that there are godly people who have physical problems and have died at an early age, but we know of some ungodly people who seem to have excellent health.

Reasons To Seek Health

However, there were two definite convictions of the early church brought out by James. One is that the fact that Jesus went to heaven to be seated at the right hand of God did not imply that his healing ministry was over.

The other conviction of the early church, not as often looked into, was that the life of godliness was profitable for health. It shouldn't surprise you, for it was an apparent conviction.

Fitness of body and soul

In Timothy Paul says, 'Bodily exercise profiteth little' (1 Tim. 4:8). He's referring to your body and what bodily exercise can do. But he went on to say, 'Godliness is profitable unto all things, having promise of the life that now is' – which has to do with the body – 'and of that which is to come' which has to do with the soul and the life to come. As the life of godliness was profitable for health it was conversely true that the life of disobedience invited trouble, even physical trouble.

We've had it preached to us many times that the way of godliness is the way of peace and joy. But godliness is profitable also for health. We know of exceptions to everything that I'm going to be saying. And we shouldn't be deterred by it.

When James raises the question: 'Is any sick among you?' he brings into operation his assumption that Jesus still heals. James did not want the matter of faith healing to die out. We know from what Paul said to the Corinthians that sickness is sometimes traceable to ungodly living. In 1 Corinthians 11 when the apostle upbraided the Corinthians for not discerning the Lord's body and for their abuse of the Lord's Supper he actually said, 'For this cause many are sickly among you, and many sleep' (v. 30). Some had, as it were, a premature call to be with the Lord. 'But some,' he said, 'are sickly among you.' There's no way we can avoid that connection between sickness and disobedience to the Lord.

Sickness Is Not Always Caused By Sin

This belief that sickness is sometimes traceable to ungodly living was in James' mind because in verse 15 he says, 'The prayer of faith shall save the sick, and the Lord shall raise him up; and if he have committed sins, they shall be forgiven him.' He says 'if ', because it shows that sin may not be the cause. It doesn't follow that if you're sick it means you've been ungodly. Great comfort there. But he did say, 'if he have committed sins', because it shows that at the same time it might be disobedience that has precipitated, by God's will, this state of being unwell.

Throughout this epistle he has pointed out the worldly-mindedness of these Christians. It wouldn't surprise James if such flagrant disobedience to the Lord resulted in sickness. Paul said he knew why the Corinthians were like that. But James isn't saying, 'I know there are some among you that are sick.' No, he just says, 'Is there?' He wasn't making any accusations. He was reaching out a hand perhaps, recognizing that sickness is God's means sometimes of bringing a person back to the Lord. 'For such a person may not only be healed outwardly', he says, 'but inwardly.' So if there is any sick, you too can be prayed for. Don't say, 'I know why I'm ill. God has brought this. I haven't been as I ought to be.' James is effectively saying, 'Come. Call for the elders of the church. Let them pray for you with oil in the name of the Lord and you'll be raised up. And if you've committed sins they'll be forgiven.' The healing ministry of Jesus is not abolished, and godliness contains the prospect of health.

It's a pity then, in the light of what James is saying, if the Christian lives with physical ailments all the time and dismisses these prospects. If all that James has said up to now is relevant, applicable for the twentieth century, if it is still true that to be a friend of the world is to make God your enemy (Jas. 4:4) – if we still believe that, are we coming to the place in James' epistle where we just say, 'We've been with you up to now but take the scissors and cut this out'? No, let's keep following him.

What the 'higher critics' believe

I wish I didn't have to say that some claim that this sort of thing has been abolished. They come up with the idea there's not a word of Scripture for this – that, when the closing of the canon of Scripture came, that ended anything like this. I call them deists in evangelical dress. Though they claim to have a high view of Scripture they turn right round and repudiate it. An evangelical deist is little better than a liberal who thinks he can decide what in Scripture is true. There are those who have such a high view of Scripture, supposedly, and who turn right round and say that a verse like this isn't applicable today. We must not only believe this book, my fellow Christian, but we must believe that Jesus Christ is 'the same yesterday, and today, and for ever' (Heb. 13:8). Who can deny that God might be pleased to surprise you and institute this very ministry in your church? This generation has witnessed more of this than some of us are aware. And many of us don't want to look into this.

What James really means

My background is Nazarene. They had anointing with oil from time to time, and there was common knowledge of people being healed. When I was a child I was ill with something very serious and my father just brought in some people to pray for me. They anointed me with oil. And they say that within hours I was raised up. No explanation for it. God did it. This shouldn't surprise us. I only ask, why should the Pentecostals and other groups have the exclusive franchise on this enterprise?

Look carefully at this word of encouragement. 'Is any sick?' Any. God is no respecter of persons. The Greek word *asthenei* means any bodily weakness. But notice how he puts it: 'Is any sick among you?' This limits it to the believing community. This is not a word of exhortation for us to go out and heal people in the street. This is something for the church. He's appealing to each of them directly to stimulate their own faith.

The Healing Ministry In The Church

But now notice this important point. Here comes the onus on all of you. He says, 'Is any sick among you? Let him call for the elders of the church.' He doesn't address the elders and say, 'You elders, look around for the sick people. Go to them.' Many of us prefer the luxury of complaining to actually having the healing take place. If you are ill, if you've got any ailment and you believe this book, don't blame anybody, you take the initiative.

Who are the elders of the church? The Greek word is *presbuteros*. Obviously we get the word 'presbyterian' from that. It's found 180 times in the Bible. In the Old Testament, by which I mean the Septuagint, the Greek translation of the Hebrew, it's there 119 times. It's seen 61 times in the New Testament. In the Old Testament it simply meant 'old man'. It's interesting that Proverbs 20:29 says, 'The glory of young men is their strength: and the beauty of old men is the grey head.' 'Old man' here is *presbuteros*. Why they didn't translate it 'elder' I don't know, but there it is. It just means 'old man'. And this meaning is carried over into the New Testament. For example, Paul said to Timothy, 'Rebuke not an elder' – old man – 'but intreat him as a father.' And he went on to say, 'the elder women' – that's the feminine form of the same word – 'as mothers' (1 Tim. 5:1, 2). In fact, 1 Peter 5:5 says, 'Ye younger, submit yourselves unto the elder', 'the older men'.

In Jewish history this term developed and 'the elder' was a term that eventually meant not just an old man necessarily, but a man of dignity. One Hebrew tradition said that it was an old man who wore a beard. We know that Moses chose 70 elders (Num. 11:16), and this became the model for the Sanhedrin which had 70 elders. The Sanhedrin that crucified Jesus and gave so much trouble to the early church had 70 elders. Chances are, they were all old men, but imperceptibly across the generations of Israel it developed that it didn't have to be an old man but just a man of distinction.

In the New Testament we have the term 'elder' 61 times. We've got to look at them and narrow them down before we can get to the meaning in James. In the four gospels, you find it 25 times. But every time it refers to Jewish leaders. You have twelve references in Revelation, such as 'the four-and-twenty elders' (4:10), and it takes on a rather different meaning there. In the book of Acts the term comes up 18 times. Eight of those refer to Jewish leaders.

The first time we find the mention of an elder in the New Testament in a Christian context is in Acts 11:30 and it says, 'Which also they did, and

sent it to the elders by the hands of Barnabas and Saul.' But there is no hint
at all if it means 'old men' or what. But we do know in Acts 14:23 that
they ordained elders. From the way this is worded by Luke we don't
know if they set aside older men or if certain men were graced with the
title 'elder' because they were prayed for like this. Throughout the book
of Acts, when we see the term 'elder', we have no way of knowing
whether it means 'old man' or if it had become a title of distinction. What
we do know is that in Acts 20:28 all the elders of Ephesus were instructed
to be 'overseers', *episkopos*. We get the word 'episcopacy' from that and it
is usually translated 'bishop'. So in Acts 20 where the elders were made
overseers you have no distinction between bishop and elder.

A bishop did not have to be an old man, because Timothy was a
bishop and Paul said, 'Let no man despise thy youth' (1 Tim. 4:12).
First an old man, then a man of distinction, then 'elder' and 'bishop'
are used interchangeably, and then 'bishop' doesn't have to be an old
man. What we have here is a progression of Christian usage. You
could say that the Old Testament tradition was Christianized. The old
man became a man of dignity, then the bishop became a young man.
You've got here 'bishop' and 'elder' being used interchangeably, with
'bishop' apparently meaning what Paul meant by the elder who had
the gift of leadership and preaching.

The Role Of Elders

What about the elder who did not have the gift of leadership and
teaching? He was a godly man in the church who had everybody's
respect. There's no hint that it was an elected position, but rather a
position of respect. James, by 'elders of the church', did not mean only
those whose gift of leadership and preaching had been sanctioned by
being set apart, nor was he referring to a particular office in the church
to which some had been elected or appointed. For that did not exist in
the New Testament. He meant any minister of the gospel but equally
all mature, godly men whose self-authenticating witness caused the
Christian to know that here was a man you would readily ask to call
upon God.

By the way, I would say that any deacon who doesn't fulfil the role
of an elder is not qualified to be a deacon. There should be no
difference. For as for spirituality there is no hint that a minister should
be more godly than a deacon, so the difference between a minister and
a deacon is not a difference with regard to grace but a difference in gift.

This is why every deacon is, in a sense, an elder. In James' sense there is no doubt this is implied. Many of you are godly men of maturity and you've got a self-authenticating testimony. You should therefore be called for by the sick.

To review this section: the sick are to take the initiative. That seems to be all that the sick person is required to do insofar as his own act of faith is concerned. The rest is up to the elders who do the praying. Obviously if that sick person had all the faith that was needed he could just pray for himself, but he just had enough faith to go on to send for the elders to come.

What does James say should happen when the elders come? He says, 'Let them pray.' The sick person now has done all that was required for him to do. It doesn't mean he's not going to bow his head and be praying, but obviously the onus is on the elders from this point on. It says, 'Let them pray.' They don't come there to counsel. They're not coming there to say, 'You don't look that bad to me. Cheer up. I don't think you're really that sick.' James knows that this is no time for psychology or counselling or teaching or fellowship or even singing. He is saying, 'You're there to do one thing. You're to pray.' The reason you pray is because you recognize you've got to go outside yourself. God must step in.

The elders should be present

How is this praying done? James gives three things. The first is that they pray over him. The second, they anoint with oil. And third, this is done in the name of the Lord. Look at the manner of the praying. He says, 'Let them pray over him.' That's exactly what the Greek says. So it indicates that the elders are actually present. If it just said, 'Pray for him', then they could be ten miles away. But he wants to make sure that they're there. Not that they couldn't carry on prayer ten miles away. Look at the account where the centurion came to Jesus and said, 'You don't have to come to me. Say the word and my servant will be healed.' And Jesus marvelled at his faith and, lo and behold, we're told that the servant was healed that very hour (Mt. 8:5–13). So that can happen and you don't have to be there for a prayer to be answered.

But if you're going to take James seriously here's what he says: the elders should pray over him. He wants an immediate physical contact and it suggests that they gather around the person who is sick, who remains passive. They're praying for him, yes, but he says, 'Pray over him.' We don't want to try to outdo James and try to figure out why and say, 'I don't think we have to do that.' But let us, in childlike biblical simplicity, take him seriously.

Nor do I know why he would require the anointing of the oil. You say, 'What would he need oil for? Surely God can heal without oil.' He can. Jesus did. But we also know that in Mark 6 when Jesus sent out the Twelve it says in verse 13, 'They cast out many devils, and anointed with oil many that were sick, and healed them.' So even when Jesus was there the Twelve went out and anointed with oil. That is what James is continuing. This is nothing novel.

The oil is a symbol of the Holy Spirit

The oil is a symbol, like the bread and the wine of the eucharist. We don't believe that there's anything sacramental about the bread and the wine. The same with the oil. You don't pray for the oil. We are only following our Lord when we come to the Lord's table. 'This do in remembrance of me' (Lk. 22:19). What we do know is that the bread and the wine are visual symbols. They look a bit like the body and blood of Christ visually. So with the oil. It's a visual, tangible reminder of the Spirit and his power to heal.

James asked for the oil and we shouldn't argue with him. In any case, it's not the oil that will do the healing. The prayer of faith shall do it. It's not the bread and the wine that makes the difference when we observe the Lord's Table, it's discerning the Lord's body. There is an analogy between the Lord's table and this praying for the sick. The kind of oil is irrelevant. We must avoid superstition. I knew of a man in America who seemed serious when he said that he had an oil that was imported from Israel with certain spices in it, and he said that every time he used it the person was healed. But that's superstition. It's whatever oil is convenient. In Israel it was olive oil. But the kind of oil is not important.

Some say that the oil here is simply a sign meaning medicine. We do know that in those days, and even to the present time, oil could be used for medicinal purposes. I would accept that. We should most certainly avail ourselves of medicine. If oil was medicine, then medicine ought to be used today. Let no one think that you ought to do away with medicine. In any case, it is clearly not the oil nor any medicine in this particular case. What will make the difference is the prayer of faith.

Finally, James says you do this 'in the name of the Lord'. He means the Lord Jesus Christ. Elders are in the role of ambassadors. They don't come in their own name. As an ambassador from Britain in another country speaks in the name of Her Majesty the Queen, so do elders in the name of

His Majesty King Jesus who is now at the right hand of God. They come in the name of the Lord and they pray in the name of the Lord. Any prayer that bypasses the name of Jesus will not only be ineffectual but arrogant and full of unbelief. For it is the Lord who heals.

James calls us back to a biblical simplicity. That's the issue. The question is, do we really believe the Bible? And do we really believe that Jesus Christ is the same yesterday, today and for ever?

37

What is the Prayer of Faith?

James 5:15

'The prayer of faith' is one of the better-known phrases from the epistle of James. And it is found only here in the Bible. It's in the context of the three questions that James puts as he comes to the final section of this epistle. 'Is any sick among you? Let him call for the elders of the church; and let them pray over him, anointing him with oil in the name of the Lord: and the prayer of faith shall save the sick' (vv. 13–15).

In bringing this latter question into the epistle James wanted to continue the healing ministry of Jesus. And he brought into this an apostolic assumption that there was a certain connection between godly living and your own health – a neglected theme.

It Is The Prayer Of Faith That Heals

The main thing is that it is not the oil that heals, but the prayer of faith. This is an intriguing, fascinating expression. How wonderful it would be if we were to see it in operation. What does James mean? 'The prayer of faith.' We could deduce from this that where there is no prayer of faith there will be no healing, and that obviously not all praying is done in faith. I think we could justifiably raise the question: is it really true that there is such a thing as prayer that is not the prayer of faith? I think we would have to say that it's possible to pray and not pray in faith.

The Greek language clearly says 'the prayer of faith'. The NIV and the NASV and the New English Bible all say 'prayer offered in faith'. But the RSV and the Authorised Version stick to the Greek 'the prayer of faith', using the definite article. Obviously it is a prayer offered in faith, but to say merely that it's 'prayer offered in faith' is to dilute and diminish what James is after.

There are examples right in this epistle of not praying in faith. In chapter 4 James says, 'Ye ask, and receive not, because ye ask amiss, that ye may consume it upon your lusts' (v. 3). The person who made that prayer might have said, 'I prayed in faith', but obviously something went wrong because the prayer wasn't answered. But there's the drawing nigh to God. James 4:8: 'Draw nigh to God, and he will draw nigh to you.' That is certainly praying in faith in some sense. Your relationship with Jesus Christ is what is involved in drawing nigh to God. For it is a simultaneous moving away from the world. But that is something quite apart from putting a specific request or wish to God. Then you have chapter 5 verse 13. 'Is any among you afflicted? let him pray.' I don't think you could call that the prayer of faith. It is simply waiting on God. It could be called, in a sense, 'faith in prayer'.

No, James is on to something that is quite apart from other kinds of praying. When he said, 'Is any among you afflicted? let him pray', the word for prayer there is simply 'coming to God' or 'approaching God'. But then when he says, 'Is any sick among you? let him call for the elders of the church; and let them pray over him', he calls it 'the prayer of faith'. He uses a different word here for the word 'prayer'. Whereas in verse 13 it was simply coming to God, drawing nigh to God, the word he uses here is *euche*. It means a specific request. It is used in various instances in the New Testament. It's the word Paul used in Acts 26 when Agrippa said to Paul, 'Almost thou persuadest me to be a Christian.' And Paul said, 'I would to God' – the same word here – 'that not only thou, but also all that hear me this day, were both almost, and altogether such as I am' (vv. 28–29). The same word is used by Paul again in Romans 9:3. He said, 'I could wish that myself were accursed from Christ ...' It was a wish or request. So we're not talking about drawing nigh to God or waiting on God or pouring your heart out to God. James is talking about a specific desire that is combined with the measure of faith required to produce the results.

Four Kinds Of Prayer

We could summarize the four kinds of prayer that we've seen in James already.

Prayers in the flesh

First, we have the ill-posed prayer request: 'Ye ask, and receive not, because ye ask amiss.' We could call that 'faith of the flesh'. The person may say he has faith. Maybe you say, 'I prayed believing and nothing happened.' Sometimes faith is man-centred even though you may be a godly person. Your specific request is something that comes from you. (Paul Tillich used to talk about faith being 'ultimate concern'. That's a man-centred faith. It's not properly to be graced with the title 'faith'.) And yet fleshly faith can characterize Christians. Who hasn't put a request to the Lord that you thought you were asking for in faith but it wasn't answered? It wasn't faith in the sense James is after.

Drawing close to God

As for drawing nigh to God, it's a simultaneous moving away from the world. There is faith involved. It certainly pleases God. We could even say that it is a faith that achieves results, that is honoured to the extent that God draws nigh to you. That is a verse that largely refers to what Richard Sibbes called 'the returning backslider'. 'Draw nigh to God, and he will draw nigh to you.' But that is not the prayer of faith.

Waiting on God

And then there is this waiting on God in the face of affliction. 'Is any among you afflicted? Let him pray.' That is dignifying our trial. That pleases God. It achieves maturity. And it's wonderful. We need to exemplify this. But that is not, in my opinion, the prayer of faith. For James is talking about a specific request or wish that is granted, not by coincidence, but immediately by the Lord. The specific wish or desire could be for yourself or for another person. There's nothing in Scripture that I know of that suggests you cannot pray the prayer of faith for yourself. After all, in the first chapter of James he says, 'If any of you lack wisdom, let him ask of God ... but let him ask in faith nothing wavering' (vv. 5, 6).

The prayer of faith

But James now doesn't say, 'Pray in faith', as he did in chapter one. He says, 'the prayer of faith'. I think it may be significant that the only time we have this expression in the Bible is in the context of praying for another person. It is legitimate to pray for yourself 'in faith'. We could perhaps say that any answered prayer presupposes that in some sense a prayer of faith was offered. But there is surely a difference between praying 'in faith' and 'the prayer of faith'.

Three things emerge when we look at this verse: 'The prayer of faith shall save the sick.'

- First, it is a prayer for another person.
- Secondly, it's another person with an urgent need – 'sick'. The Greek word shows how urgent it is by the very fact that James didn't just say, 'heal the sick' but 'save the sick'. It shows that they were in bad shape.
- Thirdly, it seems to be a prayer that is only prayed once, a one-off thing.

When we said that we should ask for wisdom and ask in faith the thing is, we can keep doing that, can't we? We can repeat that prayer. Perhaps if I didn't have faith yesterday, maybe I'll have faith today. But when it comes to calling the elders of the church, obviously this is not something you're going to do four or five times a day or every day. You're not going to keep sending them back saying, 'Well, you didn't do it yesterday, try it again today. If nothing happens today, come back tomorrow.' We might do that for ourselves. We could keep praying. But obviously, in this case, it is a prayer prayed once. And that separates it from any other kind of praying.

The prayer of faith then, according to James, is not offered by the sick person but by the elders of the church. 'Let them pray.' Let him call for them, and let them pray. If he had the faith he wouldn't have to send for them. He could just pray for himself and nobody would know about it. His faith is honoured to the extent that he initiates the whole process. The actual prayer of faith is offered, by someone other than the sick person.

When Paul prayed for himself three times that the thorn in the flesh might be removed, it just shows that Paul didn't pray the prayer of faith. My friend, O.S. Hawkins, in Florida told me he was in Oklahoma and went to a meeting where there was a faith healer who was speaking. He said the auditorium was packed with ten thousand people and this faith healer had the arrogance to say that if the apostle Paul knew what he knew, then he would not have had the problem with the thorn in the flesh. Doesn't that just make you angry? Obviously Paul prayed sincerely. Whether Paul called in others it is not known. We don't even know if it was a sickness. I'm glad we don't. What is known is that Paul prayed three times and after the third time of ineffectual praying he packed it in. He just took God's word: 'My grace is sufficient for thee' (2 Cor. 12:9).

It's interesting here that James says, 'Let him call for the elders' – plural – 'of the church.' That means two or more should be present. Why two or more? It could be because Jesus said, 'Where two or three are gathered together in my name ...' (Mt. 18:20).

The Danger Of Spiritual Pride

I also think there's another reason why two or more are called. I think Jesus would say, 'Where two or three are gathered ...' because if two or more pray and the prayer is answered there will always be a doubt which one had the prayer of faith. I think that's the way God wants it, that no one knows for sure who prayed the prayer of faith. The elder might be tempted to the worst kind of pride in the world, spiritual pride. But if two or more pray and healing does occur the temptation to pride is lessened. So James says, 'Call for the elders'. It is partly a preventive measure against pride. Who among us can pray 'the prayer of faith' and keep quiet about it? I'd at least have to tell my wife. This is the way we are, isn't it? There's safety in numbers in this case. A person may be given a special grace to pray the prayer of faith. If so he should be clothed with many layers of humility lest this be abused.

So what stands out? Where the prayer of faith is, there is healing. Therefore there's such a thing as a prayer or wish that is not of faith. There may be an ardent wish, a vehement desire, and it may be from a godly person but not be joined with true faith. I'm reminded of Paul's verse: 'Whatsoever is not of faith is sin' (Rom. 14:23). You may want to say, 'If the prayer is not joined by faith is it sin?' We must be careful here, but the way I would put it is not that it is sinful, but it is still a case where unbelief was not utterly abolished. It's not a case of wilful sin, much less wanting to consume it on your lusts like in James 4:3. Nonetheless it is where an element of unbelief militates against the quantity of faith that is required in this case.

Perfect Faith

Only the Lord Jesus Christ had perfect faith and got every request through. What about that time when the Bible says, 'He did not many mighty works there because of their unbelief' (Mt. 13:58)? The answer is that it was their unbelief. He refused to cast his pearl before the swine. He just backed off. It wasn't that he couldn't. There's not a single case in the New Testament in which Jesus tried and failed. Jesus said to Peter, 'I know you're going to deny me but I have prayed for you that your faith fail not' (Lk. 22:32). Our Lord's prayer was answered. Jesus said, 'I will pray the Father, and he shall give you another Comforter' (Jn. 14:16). That was answered. He said in John 17, 'I pray not for the world, but for them which thou hast given me.' This is another reason I know I cannot lose my salvation.

It was this concept that the apostle Paul said was good enough to live by. The first part of Galatians 2:20 is well known. The latter part is not as well known. 'I am crucified with Christ: nevertheless I live; yet not I, but Christ liveth in me.' That's as far as most people ever get. It goes on to say, 'The life which I now live in the flesh I live by the faith of the Son of God, who loved me, and gave himself for me.' Paul lived by Christ's faith. And obviously there are some things for which Christ doesn't intercede. I am certain that when the word came back to Paul: 'My grace is sufficient for thee', and the Lord Jesus didn't put that request through, that didn't mean that Paul said, 'Well, I'm just going to quit then.' No, he said, 'I continue to live by the faith of the Son of God. He knows what I need and if he doesn't put it through it's all right. I live by his faith. He knows.'

The prayer of faith is when our wish coincides with God's will

The prayer of faith takes place, then, when there is a simultaneous coinciding of the believer's faith and God's will. We must bring in 1 John 5:14–15: 'This is the confidence that we have in him, that, if we ask any thing according to his will, he heareth us: and if we know that he hear us, whatsoever we ask, we know that we have the petitions that we desired of him.' It is not a case of manipulating God or of changing God's mind or of nudging the arm of providence. I believe the prayer of faith is a momentary participation in the very will of God, in the faith of Jesus Christ which lies behind the whole matter.

You have the same thing in Romans 8 which refers to the intercessory prayer of the Spirit. Paul says, 'The Spirit also helpeth our infirmities: for we know not what we should pray for as we ought: but the Spirit itself maketh intercession for us with groanings which cannot be uttered' (v. 20). The reason Jude in verse 20 could talk about praying in the Spirit is because there is such a thing as participating in the intercessory prayer of the Spirit. When your prayer and the Spirit's intercession coincide, that is the prayer of faith. The wonderful thing, by the way, regarding the Spirit's prayer and our Lord's faith is that praying goes right on even if we don't know what it is. Paul called it 'groanings which cannot be uttered.'

James told us to do this. Are you sick? Your duty is to send for the elders of the church. In simplicity they anoint with oil 'in the name of the Lord'. This is not just a perfunctory phrase here. Had the Lord been physically present you know it would have been answered. So the elders stand in the place of Christ but never in their own name.

If one prays the prayer of faith will he know it? I would have thought that he would and yet I want to say, not necessarily. But it is more likely that he will know that he is praying that prayer. We may point out verses like this: Jesus said, 'And all things, whatsoever ye shall ask in prayer, believing, ye shall receive' (Mt. 21:22). This suggests you know consciously whether you really are believing. And so in Mark 11:24: 'Therefore I say unto you, What things soever ye desire, when ye pray, believe that ye receive them' – that they're already there – 'and ye shall have them.' When that kind of faith is given which, interestingly enough, Jesus called 'the faith of God' (Mk. 11:22) – I know the Authorised Version says, 'faith *in* God' (and I don't know why they were afraid to translate it exactly as it is: 'the faith of God') – that's where you just know you have a hold on God. In my experience this is not done very often..

I must give you a caution here. I speak with some experience, rather painfully. There are people who really think that they have this faith and they're sincere. My mother died when she was forty-three years old. She had a stroke and for eight weeks she lay helplessly in bed and my father had different ones come in and anoint her. Seven different times she was prayed for and anointed with oil and among those one or two people said, 'She's going to be healed.' One used the expression – and I don't mean to make fun – 'I've prayed through', and that made us feel good. But the last one that 'prayed through' was two weeks before she died. The only proof that the prayer of faith was prayed is the end result, and not any conscious feeling that yes, this is going to be. And yet I think I would say that it is not impossible that one may anoint and pray and not be so sure even though healing began.

Earthly and heavenly interaction

One other question: this prayer of faith, what really does do it? Is it the prayer of faith or is it the Lord? Because James says two things here, 'The prayer of faith shall save the sick, and the Lord shall raise him up.' Which is it? The prayer of faith does it. But then he goes on to say, 'The Lord does it.' It just shows how the whole of the Bible is consistent, because this is the way it always is. Things occur simultaneously on earth and in heaven. It's true with the very doctrine of justification by faith. What is it that saves and justifies? Is it the Lord or is it us? Romans 5:9 says we're 'justified by his blood', but Romans 3:25 already said we're justified 'through faith in his blood'. It's not one or the other, it's both coming together. And so with the anointing with oil. The prayer of faith does it; the Lord does it. But one without the other will not bring it about. Paul and James are agreed on the nature of faith. God gives the faith.

A further question is, how serious should the illness be? As I already said, this 'prayer of faith shall save the sick'. It implies that one is helpless apart from prayer. It does show a caution not to abuse this verse by calling in the elders of the church when you catch a cold or have a little tickle in your throat. But neither do I think it refers to terminal illness. The Roman Catholics for years have had their doctrine of extreme unction when the person's about dead.

What I would say here is that any serious illness qualifies, especially the illness that keeps one from coping. For the Greek word means 'exhausted'. When James said, 'Is any sick among you?' he used one word which simply meant 'bodily weakness'. But here it's a different word referring to the person who is exhausted. He's come to the end. He can't cope. We ought to take advantage of this verse. It's God's promise. Don't blame the minister or the elders for not coming to you if you are ill. You initiate it. I would encourage this. For we're living in a generation, my fellow Christians, in which the world is seeing nothing of the super-natural. They're seeing the superstitious. They read the astrology charts. They take things like that seriously. The world wants to see that for which there is no natural explanation.

The value of healing in witness

The Greek word 'raise him up' is exactly the same word that is used for the Lord's resurrection. Paul said, 'The Spirit ... that raised up Christ from the dead shall also quicken your mortal bodies' (Rom. 8:11). This healing is no less than a guarantee of our own resurrection. God, in some cases, gives a taste in advance of what he will do later. What a wonderful testimony to the world.

The Question Of Sin And Sickness

In closing it says, 'If he have committed sins, they shall be forgiven.' Thank God for the 'if'. It doesn't follow that sickness is always traceable to sin. James has already referred to Job. The Bible says Job was 'perfect and upright' in his generation. Then came those boils. Some of God's choicest saints are put flat on their backs. Who of us hasn't sinned? We've all sinned. But what James means here is that if it is the case that sickness is a direct result of disobedience (like Jonah's fish), then 'For this cause many are weak and sickly among you' (1 Cor. 11:30).

James isn't throwing out any accusations. It's wonderful to know that the Bible offers salvation and healing for the whole man. It's James' way of saying, 'Look, if it is sin that brought this let him be prayed for and be healed and his sins will be forgiven as well.' He can start all over again and be just like Jonah who said, 'I will pay that that I have vowed. Salvation is of the LORD' (2:9). God gave him another chance.

It could be that this contains an implicit warning for any of us not to play fast and loose with the living of the Christian life. For our bodies are the temple of the Spirit and God can, if he wants to, use something to drive us to prayer. The prayer of faith is something that is not carried out that often. At least, we haven't seen it that often.

Living on the cutting edge of faith

I think our most natural reaction is, 'Well, if we haven't seen it why should we expect it to happen?' But I am more and more aware under God of how we are put in the place of trusting him without a dependence upon any precedent or any collective witness supporting it. We must not be afraid to be on the cutting edge, for that puts us in a position where we are trusting God and not saying, 'It's been done before', and we begin to apologize for this or that. No. If you look at those that God has used in history it has often been those who did what others said was either foolish or hadn't been done before. The whole eleventh chapter of Hebrews relates one unprecedented thing after another. The fact that we're not seeing this or that in our day has nothing to do with it. It's whether we believe the Bible.

38

Confessing Sin to Each Other

James 5:16a

This is one of the more enigmatic verses of this book of James. The Authorised Version chose here, for reasons I do not understand, to translate the Greek word *hamartia* – which every other time is 'sin' – as 'faults'. But the word is 'sins'. 'Confess your sins one to another'. The AV translation here has given rise to some ideas that are not correct.

False Concepts Of Confession

One such idea is that it's all right to confess your faults one to another, but never your sins. It has also given rise to the idea (and there's some truth to the idea but you shouldn't use this text for it) that there are personality blemishes that are not sinful. But that's not what James is talking about.

This verse has become a proof text for certain group therapy meetings and encounter groups where they share with one another. This so-called sharing your weaknesses with one another is supposed to be therapeutic, and it might be. But what is not said perhaps as often as it should be is that sharing your weaknesses with each other can be dynamite, the worst thing in the world. Because if another person discovers a weakness that you've got, especially if it should be sexual, you play into each other's pathology and something can happen that wouldn't have happened if you hadn't done this.

Confessing Sin Put In Context

This is a very threatening verse: confessing your sins to each other. There's nothing about that that makes me feel good. Some people are more open than others. Americans tend to be more open than the British. But when it comes to sin we're all in the same boat. We don't want to be open, do we? Who will be so open as to confess sin? It doesn't say 'to God' here. Of course, it doesn't mean you're not supposed to confess sin to God. 1 John 1:9 talks clearly about confessing your sins to God. But that's not what James said. It's not to a priest although the Roman Catholics would want all confession to be to a priest and a priest only. It clearly says 'to one another'. James is asking for something that hardly comes easily.

Rule number one in dealing with any verse in the Bible is to see it in its context. I think it was G. Campbell Morgan who said that a text without a context is a pretext. If ever there was a verse that we ought not to try to understand out of context it is this one. The context is in this discussion of praying for the sick. It's the third question that James asks as he brings the epistle to its final paragraph. He said, 'Is any sick among you? let him call for the elders of the church; and let them pray over him, anointing him with oil in the name of the Lord: And the prayer of faith shall save the sick, and the Lord shall raise him up; and if he have committed sins, they shall be forgiven him. Confess your sins one to another, and pray one for another, that ye may be healed.' Confession is in the context of sin-related sickness.

Remember that not all illness is caused by sin

The sick are to take the initiative and send for the elders and have them pray for him. 'If he have committed sins.' Not all sickness has sin at the bottom. But then comes 'If he have committed sins'. Not all sickness has sin at the bottom. Paul said to Timothy: 'Drink no longer water, but use a little wine for thy stomach's sake and thine often infirmities' (1 Tim. 5:23). No request there that as he has a little infirmity he should send for the elders. No hint that sin caused it. In Philippians Paul talked about Epaphroditus who fell sick and looked as if he was going to die (2:27). Here was a godly man.

James' epistle is the most Jewish epistle in the Bible. And yet the fact that James would say 'if' shows that, although he is a Jew writing to Jews and understands the Jewish mind, he's been emancipated from this judaistic belief that sin and illness always go together. But our Lord didn't remove that entirely. He could say to the one with the palsy, 'Thy sins be forgiven thee' (Mk. 2:5), implying that Jesus was sanctioning the possibility that in some cases sickness can be the result of sin. Jesus, though, could know what was the cause. In John 9:2 the disciples said, 'Who did sin, this man, or his parents, that he was born blind?' But notice how Jesus answered in this case: 'Neither hath this man sinned, nor his parents: but that the works of God should be made manifest in him' (v. 3). There was, however, this belief in rabbinic thinking. You can read in Nadarim 41:1: 'No sick person is cured of his disease until all his sins are forgiven him.'

The Prayer of Faith For Sin-related Sickness

But James doesn't begin with confession of sin. He begins with the prayer of faith. Now this is significant. Even if illness is traceable to sin, James begins with the prayer of faith which promises instantly both healing of the body and the forgiveness of sins. However, he turns to those who were conscious of sin and he says, 'Confess your sins one to another.' Why does he bother to say this? The sins referred to in verse 16 are directly related to the sin referred to in verse 15. We mustn't forget this. Not only is *hamartia*, the same word for 'sin' used throughout the Bible, used both times, but the continuity is there which shows it. Don't forget that there was no verse enumeration in the original Greek. And the Greek word *oun* is omitted in the Authorised Version. I don't know why. Most other translations include it. It means 'therefore', 'consequently'. And so forgetting verse enumeration and putting the word 'therefore' and remembering that it is 'sin', it would read this way: 'If he has committed sins they shall be forgiven him. Therefore confess your sins one to another.' So you cannot take the verse out of context. The question then is, was this to be a follow-up to the anointing of oil in case the healing didn't come? Or was it that they were to prepare themselves for the elders by confessing their sin? The obvious answer is that when they got this letter they just kept on reading. Or if it was read publicly in the assembly, which is likely, the reader didn't stop at verse 15 and say, 'Okay everybody, we're going to come back next week.' They kept on reading and so, by hearing it read, they were told straightaway that there was a godly obligation implied in sending for the elders.

The prayer of faith comes before confession of sin

In other words, although there was this wonderful promise of healing, James kept them aware of a spiritual obligation. A sick person who would be moved to call for the elders of the church would be conscious of these words: 'Therefore confess your sins one to another.' The onus was on him to repent sooner or later. So he may as well begin doing this now even before sending for the elders. In other words, it's not very likely that any flagrantly disobedient sinner would be so bold as to think that there would be healing without some sense of Christian duty to amend one's ways. The person engaged in wilful sin need not apply. Therefore James doesn't divorce divine healing from godly living.

There's a lot of emphasis today on divine healing, but it is curiously separated from a sense of godliness. You just pray for people and they're supposed to get healed. James will have nothing of that. And yet, having said this, James begins with 'the prayer of faith … and the Lord shall raise him up.' He didn't begin with the confession of sin. Had he had his old Jewish theology working for him, or had he been like so many people who think that everything, when it comes to grace, is conditional upon repentance, then James would have started out by saying, 'Confess your sins one to another and the prayer of faith can be prayed.' But he started with the prayer of faith because God always begins with faith, even to the backslider.

Christianity is primarily and pre-eminently a gospel of grace. As John Newton put it: 'Thy promise is my only plea; with this I venture nigh.' Had James begun with the confession of sin then John Newton couldn't have written a hymn like that or it would have been branded as heresy. John Newton would have said, 'My confession of sin is my plea.' But never is that the case. We begin with faith, with the promise. That's what James has done. God honours faith primarily. It is possible to keep on repenting and never to be any closer to faith.

What The Backslider Should Do

Faith is not only supernatural in its nature, but it is supernatural with reference to its object. Faith always leaves the believer outside himself and focuses upon the object of faith, which is the Lord Jesus Christ. We've all been backsliders to some degree. When a person is a backslider and he wants to come back to God he comes back in faith as though he had not been converted, pleading the merit, the name, the shed blood of Christ and the promise of forgiveness of sins.

Otherwise, the returning backslider will get off on the wrong footing when he begins the Christian life anew. Let's take a backslider who has gone out into deep sin. Maybe he's wandered from the church for weeks or months, maybe years, and he really has made a mess of his life. What often happens is that the returning backslider is so conscious and so ashamed of his sins that he thinks all he must do is stop sinning and that the Christian life is simply to be carried out in nothing but moralistic fashion.

If that's the way the backslider is restored then he's not that much better off. He may not get into as much trouble, but he will have nothing ahead but a life of works. He will be a legalistic Christian, which is exactly what the devil wants. For a legalistic Christian is never a threat to the devil or to the world. He will be so self-righteous that despite his repentance he will live a counter-productive Christian life.

James is rejecting a divine healing that is divorced from godliness, but he's also rejecting the idea that all a returning backslider has to do is to stop his sinning. He takes us straight to the throne of grace. James' procedure is delicately avoiding the pitfalls of what we call antinomianism on the one hand, that is a life of lawlessness, and a moralistic legalism on the other. What is the sick to do? Is he to start confessing sin? No, he is to call for the elders. Because it is the promise of faith alone that is going to do anything.

Over-eager confession

You can confess sin to each other. Do you know this has been tried? People are so anxious to see the Lord work and they use everything that's within their grasp that they can think of. They start confessing sin backwards and forwards and they think, 'Oh, I left one out', and they come back and do another one. This is the way Martin Luther was before he was converted. He would come back to the priest the same day and one confessor said to another priest, 'There he is again. You take him this time. I don't want to hear it.' Luther would think of one more sin. We keep thinking that that's going to do it. So James begins with the promise: 'The prayer of faith will do it and if he has committed sins they'll be forgiven.'

Joy Comes From Living By The Promise

The Christian who has lost joy has ceased to live by the promise. When you don't live by the promise you're going to live by how good you are and how well you are doing and how careful you are to avoid this sin or this temptation. And you become so introspective that you're looking at yourself the whole time and you realize that joy isn't there. It shouldn't surprise you.

You were first converted because you believed the promise. You didn't have any bargaining power with God, did you? You asked for mercy. You asked God to save you for Jesus' sake. And oh, it was wonderful wasn't it – the joy? Just taking God at his word. 'As far as the east is from the west, so far hath he removed our transgressions from us' (Ps. 103:12). The returning backslider, to get that joy, must look to the promise. Remember Hebrews 4:16 was written to Christians: 'Let us therefore come boldly unto the throne of grace, that we may obtain mercy.' You don't ask for mercy if you're pleading any other thing, if you're looking at something in your life. But you're asking for mercy because it's the promise you're pleading. Nobody ever outgrows that and if you try to you become a most miserable person.

A backslider can be restored the wrong way. An acute sense of guilt can be used as a tool of the devil to make that person take refuge in his works and in the fact that he's no longer living such a flagrant, sinful life. And that is where he's getting his joy – by what he's not doing. The devil doesn't want you to live by the righteousness of Christ. If a backslider is restored this way his repentance often is little more than a self-inflicting punishment. He feels so ashamed at what he's done that he just keeps beating himself black and blue, not enjoying what Christ has done.

Even a Christian who is truly converted can get off to the wrong start, especially if he's converted in an atmosphere that embraces a defective theology. He really doesn't understand what living the Christian life is. It can happen to a new Christian or a backslider. The danger is that the restored backslider can come short of true joy because he's more anxious to show repentance than he is to claim the promise through the merit of Christ.

James knows that these Christian Jews had many worldly-minded members, that there were many living counter-productive lives. They were no threat to the devil. As anxious as James is for these Christians to get back on the rails and turn away from the world, he's very careful. He wants their thinking to be right. He doesn't want them to jump out of the frying pan into the fire and go from moral antinomianism to sheer legalism, trading one form of misery in for another.

Healing AND confession

So what about verse 16 then? 'Confess your sins one to another.' Surely James wants them to begin at once confessing their sins. But how? In the light of the promise that the prayer of faith will save the sick. Nothing else will. It doesn't matter how godly you are, how much you have repented, how much you've denied temptation and the devil, the fact remains that if you want to see something take place God must do it. The prayer of faith. The promise that 'the Lord shall raise him up; and if he have committed sins, they shall be forgiven', is the ground of their restoration. For James has made it clear that forgiveness of sins follows the prayer of faith. It's

James' way of saying, 'God is a forgiving God.' Therefore in the light of this promise alone, accept that forgiveness and begin now amending your ways. 'Surely,' James is saying, 'in the light of such mercy you cannot but begin now confessing your sin.'

But why to one another? Why not to God and be done with it? Why not to your minister? It is here we must tread delicately and carefully. We are not forgetful that David in Psalm 51 – David who committed adultery – said, 'Against thee, thee only, have I sinned' (v. 4). That was something between him and God. But James is saying, 'Confess your sins one to another.'

James Envisages A Double Healing

Does James want all Christians to bring the skeletons out of their cupboards? James wants these Christians to admit to each other what is already known in any case. It wasn't the case that someone was going to lay bare all his secrets and spring a surprise. It's not so that those listening could get a vicarious thrill or that some self-righteous person could sit in judgement. For to do that would be casting the pearl before the swine. James envisages a double healing.

We've seen already that there is simultaneous healing of the body and of the soul. But what James sees here is a double healing indeed. Not only of the body, but of the body of Christ. James wants these Christians to admit to each other what is obvious. The proof is this: he has said to them earlier, 'Don't find fault with each other. But now start confessing your sin to each other and pray for one another.' It means to affirm one another in the light of what is now openly admitted.

A change of time

He says, 'Pray for one another that ye *should* be healed.' There's a very interesting contrast. In verse 15 he says, 'The prayer of faith *shall* save the sick.' But in verse 16 he uses a different Greek word and changes the tense. He goes from what shall happen to what should or may happen. The Greek word *iathete* is translated 'healed' here. But in the New Testament this word is used more often for spiritual healing than it is for physical. You can find the word in Matthew 13:15. Here is Jesus quoting from Isaiah: 'This people's heart is waxed gross, and their ears are dull of hearing, and their eyes have they closed; lest at any time they should see with their eyes, and hear with the ears, and should understand with their heart, and should be converted, and I should heal them.' It's talking about a spiritual healing there.

It may be, surmises James, that God will use sickness to bring about a complete healing. So he begins with the sick but then he changes the tense and uses a different word. By doing this he kills two birds with one stone. He goes from the healing of the body to the healing of the body of Christ. He's spreading the invitation to everybody. Having begun with the promise, he now addresses them all, using the issue of sickness as a way of leading them to a wonderful healing indeed. In a word, they confess to each other because they have done so much damage to each other. That's why he says, 'Do it to each other.' And this is why he inserts this phrase: 'Pray for one another.' He said in chapter 4 verse 11, 'Speak not evil one of another, brethren.' But now he says, 'Pray for one another', so that when they should hear a particular person admit a wrong and come forward confessing it, the rest of the body would react with the right response.

What James wants here is a complete healing. By praying for one another you are forgiving one another. Nothing is more hypocritical than praying for the person you don't forgive. James is saying, 'Here's a way to affirm that person who confesses his wrongdoing.'

What an encouraging word this is from James. Faith always leads the believer outside himself to the objective promise. It is faith that pleases God, and faith is the only thing that will move God. Repentance is to follow, but never militating against or competing with beholding the promise. Barriers can be broken down if we admit the sin that has grieved the Spirit and divided the body of Christ. This is why Proverbs 28:13 says, 'He that covereth his sins shall not prosper: but whoso confesseth and forsaketh them shall have mercy.' The sin that James wants us to confess is not a sin that will surprise anybody. The surprise is that we finally admitted it.

39

Effectual Praying

James 5:16b

This is a rather difficult verse to translate, because the literal translation from the Greek is clumsy and sounds redundant. Literally it would be 'a prayer of a righteous man being effectually set in operation avails much'. The Greek states it more strongly, in fact, than the translation can convey. The word 'fervent' in the Authorised Version may not necessarily get across what James means.

Quality Prayers And Quality Pray-ers

Three points are made by James in this verse.

- First, the quality or kind of person who is doing the praying: a righteous man.
- Second, the quality or kind of praying itself is called 'effectual' praying.
- And then the quantity of the answer to that prayer: it avails much.

It's not surprising that James would mention prayer again. He almost has to because he's left us in mid-air. 'Confess your faults one to another, and pray one for another' tells us a lot about the effectual praying James wants us to experience. This not only pulls together the immediate context, but in fact brings together several strands of thought that are seen throughout this epistle concerning prayer. Right at the beginning of this epistle we were plunged into this subject of prayer when James said in chapter one verse 5, 'If any of you lack wisdom, let him ask of God.' He went on to say, 'Let him ask in faith, nothing wavering' (v. 6). He then said that praying with doubting is not going to accomplish anything, but he doesn't say anything more to help us. He saves it for this point.

He also talked about praying when it doesn't do any good, 'Ye ask, and receive not, because ye ask amiss' (4:3). He's going to tell us more about that in this verse. When he said, 'Submit yourselves ... to God' that is a kind of praying, and most certainly when he says, 'Draw nigh to God, and he will draw nigh to you', that is praying (4:7, 8). In chapter 5 he referred to those workers in the field who cried out to the Lord of sabaoth. Their prayers were heard, we're told, but how comforting it must have been to hear this verse: 'The effectual fervent prayer of a righteous man availeth much.'

Quality answers to prayer

It's a verse, then, that not only pulls the immediate context together, but the whole epistle. So that to the one who is asking for wisdom – and who among us hasn't done that – 'the effectual fervent prayer of a righteous man' will produce this wisdom. To the one who has been asking amiss, and to the person who wants to draw nigh to God and wants to know that God is there and feel his presence, here's a great encouragement. The workers out in the fields that had suffered those hardships could also lay hold on a verse like this.

The Prayer Of Faith And The Prayer Of Righteousness

Most certainly there is a connection between the prayer of faith referred to in verse 15 and this effectual praying referred to in verse 16. I think we'll see they are almost the same thing. But there is a difference. The prayer of faith accomplishes exactly what you prayed for. Who would not want the high privilege of praying the prayer of faith? If ever there were a mouth-watering experience at the spiritual level, here it is. None of this business at the end of a prayer: 'Have your own way, Lord.' You don't have to add the redundant PS: 'Your will be done', which largely covers our unbelief as much as it does our desire to please the Lord. It is not possible to pray the prayer of faith and not have the answer.

James' purpose, then, when he comes up with this expression: 'The effectual fervent prayer of a righteous man availeth much' is to do two things. First, to encourage us to pray and to believe that even we could expect great things to come as a consequence of prayer. But he also wants to show an alternative, as it were, to the prayer of faith itself. It is virtually the same thing, but it is cast in a slightly different mould. Why would this be so encouraging? It's a promise to anybody who wants to take James seriously. It's not a promise to the person who has a particular gift. It doesn't say, 'The effectual fervent prayer of the man with the gift of prayer will avail much.' It doesn't say, 'The effectual fervent prayer of a learned man will avail much.' It doesn't say, 'The effectual fervent prayer of a man who has a certain office in the church ...' It doesn't even say, 'The effectual fervent prayer of the person who has been a Christian for a long time avails much.' But it says, 'The effectual praying of a righteous man avails much.'

Two indispensable qualifications to prayer

This brings us to what are two obvious indispensable qualifications: the kind of person praying and the kind of praying. One without the other will render impossible effectual praying. If you ask which is more important: being righteous or praying effectually in order to avail much, I think obviously praying effectually is more important because praying effectually has already guaranteed the answer. But James wants to say something about the type of person praying and there's no way to get around this however much we like to think we might excel in prayer and it makes no difference how we live our lives.

When James talked about the prayer of faith he didn't say anything about the kind of person praying. He didn't mean to lead us to think the not-very-godly could pray that prayer of faith, but neither did he actually say that only the godly could pray the prayer of faith. All we know for certain is that where the prayer of faith is carried out, there is the result. That's a wonderful and yet a daunting thought.

He didn't say that the prayer of repentance or the prayer of thanksgiving or the prayer for godliness or even the prayer of a righteous man would achieve the result when it came to the prayer of faith. It's a simple statement that the prayer of faith will save the sick. But that just seems totally out of reach, so daunting, so intimidating. Have you prayed the prayer of faith in your lifetime? It's an extraordinary thing, this – to pray a prayer and what you pray for is just done like that.

The prayer of faith is the prayer of God

Have you looked at a mountain and said to that mountain, 'Be removed', and it just disappeared? You will say, 'Only God can do that because he is the Creator.' That's exactly right and that is why Jesus said, 'Have the faith of God' (Mk. 11:22). Only God could say, 'Let there be light: and there was light' (Gen. 1:3). And so Jesus said, 'Have faith in God. For verily I say unto you, That whosoever shall say unto this mountain, Be thou removed, and be thou cast into the sea; and shall not doubt in his heart, but shall believe that those things which he saith shall come to pass; he shall have whatsoever he saith' (Mk. 11:22–23).

The prayer of faith that saves the sick requires the intervention of the Creator. God must step in. The sickness that James is talking about would not go away unless God did it. The prayer of faith is a prayer that stands on its own. It is, as it were, an exclusive thing and yet a wonderful promise to claim. But it is so wonderful, it seems utterly out of reach, for who among us has faith like that? And that's why James didn't stop until he had brought many things together in this verse that were left unanswered throughout the epistle.

He started out by saying that the prayer of faith will do it, and then saying that if he has committed sins they will be forgiven. Then he says, 'Therefore confess your sin.' When you see these statements following what James has just said about the prayer of faith, something slightly different emerges: a reference to our relationship with the Lord, our manner and quality of life, our very obedience. As he's moving now to bring up another statement about effectual praying he brings in something about the quality of the person praying.

The prayer of the righteous

Let's look at the two statements. 'The prayer of faith shall save the sick.' 'Effectual fervent prayer ... availeth much.' Now the second statement is not as strong as the first. But in a sense it's more encouraging. The first statement is a categorical statement of a definite fact accomplished. But the second statement is within reach of any of us who want to take James seriously. James is saying that the next best thing to praying the prayer of faith is the effectual praying of a righteous man. You might say that this is better than the first. For there is another implicit promise here. Being a righteous person is obviously very important, and the suggestion is that even the prayer of faith will not be carried out unless it is prayed by a godly man. And yet James didn't say that. He didn't say it because the freedom and sovereignty of God are left intact. God can grant the prayer of faith to anybody. on the other hand, he will not be tied to any level of personal godliness, even the highest level.

But James is making it abundantly clear now that the worldly-minded Christian need not expect to accomplish great things through prayer.

So we look back at Mark 11 where we hear Jesus telling us to have the faith to say to the mountain, 'Be thou removed', and it shall be cast into the sea. He said, 'When ye pray believe that ye receive them, and ye shall have them. And when ye stand praying, forgive' (vv. 24–25). Note the 'And'. We're quite happy to talk about the prayer that accomplishes great things. We're all ears when we hear what it is going to take to increase our faith. We can have a seminar in prayer, in effectual praying, and there will be a lot of interest because every one of us wants to accomplish more in prayer. But we don't like it when we begin to get into it.

The Connection Between Effectual Prayer And Forgiveness

In Jesus' words we see a definite connection between effectual praying and forgiving another person. We may not like this. But we cannot avoid it. For God places our forgiving one another at the very top of the scale.

Do you want to know what the highest level of godliness is? It is not sinless morality, self-denial, suffering, martyrdom, or paying your tithes, which you ought to do. It is not being regular in church attendance or in your Bible reading. It is not even resisting temptation at a sexual level which to you may be the hardest thing in the world to do. But the highest level of godliness is forgiving. As James puts it: 'If ye fulfil the royal law according to the scripture, Thou shalt love thy neighbour as thyself, ye do well' (2:8).

The kind of effectual person

What does James mean here by 'righteous man'? He means two things at once. The first is that he means a justified man. The Greek word is *dikaiou*. He's talking about the person who lives by the righteousness of God, not by his own righteousness. You may say to me, 'You certainly don't believe that James believed what Paul meant by justification by faith alone.' I most certainly do! James believed in imputed righteousness as much as Paul did.

But James is talking not only about a justified man, the man who lives by the righteousness of God, but he's also talking about a man whose obedience has fulfilled imputed righteousness. James had used Abraham's sacrifice of Isaac and Rahab's faithfulness as examples of what he meant by 'justification by works' (2:24). So James means not merely a moral man.

Neither is he talking about a man impervious to temptation, because he's going to say, 'Elijah was a man subject to like passions as we are' (5:17). He means the justified man (or woman) whose life is one of open obedience that is seen before all with a faith demonstrated by works that anybody could see. A 'righteous man' is the person who lives for others and, in particular, forgives others. For he just said, 'Confess your sins one to another, and pray one for another, that ye may be healed.' That is affirming one another. Effectual praying presupposes that we have forgiven everybody. If anyone ever expects to participate in the faith of God at the experimental level he must approach God-likeness. And that means to forgive as God forgave us, for Christ's sake. James had to say it even to these workers in the field who had been maligned, 'Grudge not one against another, brethren, lest ye be condemned', because God is no respecter of persons.

Forgiving one another is something every one of us has got to do, however difficult it may be. Any grudge that you hold militates against effectual praying. You may want to compensate and do something that might sound very righteous when the whole time you're still holding a grudge against somebody and trying to pray effectually. You're just wasting your time. Any feeling that is not God-like towards another person removes the ground for expecting any effectual praying. A sobering thought. This is why there's so little effectual praying. The word 'fervent', in a way, is misleading. It's not that it's a wrong translation, but there are those who think that if you're praying a lot, that's fervent praying. You can feel a fervency and an agony in prayer and think that's what you're doing, but it's not what is meant here.

The kind of effectual praying

What is effectual praying then? The Greek word is *energoumene*. It's the present middle participle. It literally means 'being set into operation'. I have said that if you ask which is more important – the righteous man or the effectual praying – I'd say the effectual praying, because if effectual praying has been set in motion then the answer is inevitable. This is why James saying that it avails much is somewhat redundant, because this operation of effectual praying means that the prayer has got to prevail and achieve its result. James is talking about prayer that is operative, so that I would call it 'the divine machinery which is set in motion'. This means that a person is praying beyond himself now.

This Greek word that is translated 'effectual fervent' was used by Paul when he described to the Thessalonians that which is effectually working in you. He says that you received the word of God 'not as the word of men, but as it is in truth, the word of God, which effectually worketh also in you that believe' (1 Thess. 2:13). That, as Calvinists know, is one of the proof texts for effectual calling or irresistible grace. Because God just does it. It's also the word Paul used in Ephesians chapter one. He said, 'What is the exceeding greatness of his power to us-ward who believe, according to the working of his mighty power, which he wrought in Christ, when he raised him from the dead' (vv. 19–20). When God decided to raise Jesus from the dead do you think anything was going to stop it? No, he just did it. And so in Ephesians 3:20 Paul uses this word again when he talks about 'him that is able to do exceeding abundantly above all that we ask or think, according to the power that worketh in us.'

We're talking about an effectual operation that is beyond ourselves. You cannot work it up. It won't do you any good to start singing songs and clapping hands to start feeling better and say, 'In a minute I really believe we're going to get there.' That's flesh. This is something God does. Once it's set in motion there's no chance of abortion or discontinuance. The mountain will go once this kind of prayer has taken place.

Once a person begins to pray like this it's not random or idle praying. You know what you're doing. It's not communion and yet it is that. It's not agonizing and yet it is that. There is an agony that gets you nowhere. We're talking here about an agony that is God's burden and you know that it is God's the whole time. Therefore you yourself are free of it. It's praying that goes beyond the natural level. There's no worry taking place when this is going on. You don't have to worry about your mind wandering either. It's not a prayer where you're full of anxiety.

Paul said, 'Be careful for nothing' – be anxious for nothing – 'but in every thing by prayer and supplication with thanksgiving let your requests be made known unto God' (Phil. 4:6). James is saying the same thing there. You are almost a spectator. You're participating and yet you know there's unction. There's power. You know it is effectual right at the time. You know it's being heard. There's no anxiety. You know that you are praying in God's will and you're actually being carried consciously into another realm in which time, care and worry are nothing. You know what you're praying for and about. It is intercessory prayer.

I don't want simply to leave it at that, because you could call it intercessory prayer and miss James' meaning. I would prefer to call it a spirit of intercessory prayer by which your personal concern has been overruled by God's concern. You're detached, as it were, from the personal concern. You're simply being an instrument of God. Praying like this is when there is set in operation the very concern of God himself. Not only that, it is praying without doubting. And this picks up the phrase that James started out with when he said, 'If any of you lack wisdom, let him ask of God … but let him ask in faith, nothing wavering … For let not that man' – the man who is doubting – 'think that he shall receive any thing of the Lord' (1:5, 6, 7).

The Wisdom That Comes From Above

One inevitable result when you pray like this is, whatever else you may have asked for, the wisdom that comes only from above will come. James described it in chapter 3 verse 17: 'The wisdom that is from above is first pure, then peaceable, gentle, and easy to be intreated, full of mercy and good fruits, without partiality, and without hypocrisy.' It's the very opposite of the 'earthly, sensual, devilish' wisdom that 'descendeth not from above' (v. 15). Added to this, then, is that feeling of perfect love that casts out fear (1 Jn. 4:18). As we used to sing when I was a boy: '… makes me love everybody'. When you're praying like this you love everybody. You don't have an enemy in the world and you're not threatened by anybody. That wisdom comes from God.

Receiving answers to prayer

Here's what often happens with this. You find yourself putting forward requests that you know will be answered because you know you're not asking amiss. God takes over and the prayer becomes his prayer. You're saying it and feeling it but it hadn't occurred to you to pray about that. God led you to do it. James adds that it accomplishes much. Here is what I mean by redundant. We've already seen that if it's in operation that's what Jesus meant by 'believe that ye receive'. But then he said, 'Ye shall have.' Likewise, James had to finish, 'It availeth much.' Praying like this embodies a wonderful phenomenon. It is its own reward and yet you do see the result. So you enjoy it twice. The praying is wonderful, and then you get to see there's great joy in knowing or seeing it actually happen. By the time we understand what effectual praying is, by the time James says, 'It avails much', it's as though he's saying, 'Surprise, surprise.' You knew it was going to happen, and yet it's wonderful to know that it did happen. 'Believe … have.'

This word translated 'much', the Greek word *polu*, is a superlative word. It's sometimes used as a noun, sometimes as an adjective, sometimes as an adverb. It just means 'great in multitude', 'great in quantity'. The AV just says 'much'. It isn't actually the prayer of faith, and yet it is insofar as its own purpose goes. The only difference between the prayer of faith and effectual praying is that with the prayer of faith you begin with the specific request, with effectual praying you end with the request that is right because you didn't set out to pray it. So with the prayer of faith you guide it. With effectual praying it guides you.

Do we know about this? Let's not be so quick to say, 'I know all about that.' If you really do, then you won't be putting yourself forward like that because you would know that praying like this will prohibit that kind of arrogance. And yet if we haven't experienced it, let's take James seriously. Because if we can begin praying like this then it can be announced: revival is at hand. And don't forget that part about forgiving.

40

Elijah: An Ordinary Man

James 5:17a

This reference to Elijah comes in the context of effectual praying, which is praying without doubting by a righteous man. If the righteous man is one who has fulfilled the imputed righteousness that was given to him because he believed God, this may suggest a level of godliness that seems out of reach of all of us.

James Brings In Elijah's Humanity

It is much the same way we may feel when we think about the great saints in history. Well, James brings in Elijah, about whom every Hebrew Christian knew. But when he brings in Elijah he doesn't do so in terms of Elijah's righteousness but rather his humanity, you could even say his weakness. So that if the idea of effectual praying seems out of reach and the idea that it is a righteous man who engages in effectual praying seems something that disqualifies all of us, James at once comes along to disarm us and makes every one of us feel that effectual praying is even possible for us. So when he brings in Elijah he simply says, 'Elijah was a man subject to like passions as we are.'

What James does, then, is not only to give the Old Testament example of at least one example of effectual praying, but he does so in terms of this man's weakness. James up to now has given two Old Testament examples of people who have fulfilled imputed righteousness, Abraham and Rahab the harlot. James could have brought in countless men and women to show that faith is capable of producing extraordinary things simply by believing God and doing what he tells us to do. 'He that is faithful in that which is least is faithful also in much' (Lk. 16:10). The obedience that Christ wants of every one of us is not out of reach.

I think James brought in Elijah because Elijah was so human. James' source was in 1 Kings chapter 19. We know a lot about Elijah in terms of his effectual praying. But James wants us to think first of all about the man and see the kind of man that God uses. So we can thank God that James begins exactly where he does. God uses ordinary men just like you or me. Or as the NIV translates it: 'Elijah was a man just like us.' The Greek word here is *homoiopathes*. It means being afflicted or affected in the same way as another, to be subject to the same frailties. It's the word that was used in Acts 14:15 when Paul came saying, 'Sirs, why do ye these things? We also are men of like passions with you.' Paul had to say that about himself. Probably the most common pitfall that Christians run into sooner or later is believing that great men were intrinsically better or by nature different and that is why they were great. James just will not let us believe that lie. His proof: Elijah, one of the most wonderful men that ever lived. And yet James focuses on his weakness.

So legendary, though, was Elijah's greatness that he not only had a reputation of his own, Elijah actually gave God a reputation. Because there emerged after Elijah died the saying, 'Where is the Lord God of Elijah?' (2 Kgs. 2:14). Imagine the reputation of God being tied to one man! The most surprised of all that that could happen would be Elijah himself. He was basically a weak, doubting, self-pitying, sulking, pouting, self-righteous man, capable of bitterness deep in his soul. You might say, 'But wait a minute. That's the way Elijah was before God used him. Surely that is the kind of man God begins with. But a man like that must change before God can really use him.' If you have thought like that or if you have said that, you would be wrong.

The wonderful thing that emerges from looking at the account in 1 Kings is that the very event that James has in mind took place after the effectual praying James has in mind. So we cannot say that this is a man who begins like this but gets rid of this problem and then is useful. Now we find what the man was really like after the great victory that was seen on the mount when God came down from heaven with fire and answered Elijah's prayer.

Elijah Was Subject To Depression

The first thing that we see about Elijah is that he was subject to extreme depression. 'He ... went a day's journey ... and sat down under a juniper tree: and he requested for himself that he might die and said, It is enough;

now, O LORD, take away my life; for I am not better than my fathers'
(1 Kgs. 19:4). He actually requested to die.

Have you ever been that low that you actually wanted to die? Have
you ever thought yourself utterly useless and a complete failure? Well, if
you've ever felt like that about yourself, welcome to the club of many
distinguished men. It was said of Job that he cursed the day of his birth
(Job 3:3). Jeremiah did the same thing, 'Cursed be the day wherein I was
born: let not the day wherein my mother bare me be blessed. Cursed be
the man who brought tidings to my father, saying, A man child is born
unto thee' (Jer. 20:14–15). Here we have a case of Elijah, a man of
extreme depression.

Elijah Questioned God's Justice

But not only that. Elijah actually questioned the justice of God in all that
was happening at the moment. He simply said, as the NIV put it, 'LORD, I
have had enough.' It's like saying, 'God, why would you let this go on?'
For here was Elijah claiming that he had had all that he could bear. Have
you ever looked up at heaven and said, 'It's not fair that this should happen
to me'? That was Elijah.

Elijah not only was depressed, not only come to the place where he
actually questioned God's justice, but he showed that he had a
self-righteous streak a mile wide. Amazing this, that God could use
such a self-righteous man. He compared himself to others. He said,
'Take away my life; for I am not better than my fathers.' It is always
self-righteous and judgemental to compare yourself to another person.
And yet who among us hasn't done it? But in saying this Elijah
revealed the most vain kind of ambition. When you read the
biographies of the great saints the biographers usually colour over this
side of men. They want you to see them as heroes and it's very rare to
read a biography of a great man where you get the whole picture.
Great men, on the whole, were men of extreme ambition. And it all
comes out here in the Bible about Elijah. For the Bible doesn't white-
wash the saints. It tells it as it was.

It's sad enough to have an inferiority complex and feel you aren't
worthy to follow a former generation. And that is always wrong because
that's doubting God's power to use you as you are. It betrays that we think
that we have to be qualified in ourselves to be used of God. It shows the
distortion of thinking about God's ways even if we begin to compare
ourselves with somebody else. But Elijah was worse than that. He says,

'I am not better than my fathers.' It's one thing to say, 'I'm not worthy', but what Elijah really wanted slips out. He wanted to be better than anybody who ever lived. He couldn't bear the thought of going down in history just like anybody else. He wanted to stand as the giant and all the other people around to be small men.

Elijah Was Vain

Elijah was a perfectionist. He thought that if he would be used of God he must be better than anybody who had ever come along. It's a classic case of self-pity if ever there was one. Elijah was so vain that he didn't want to be used of God unless he was the best thing ever to come along. He wanted no rival, no competition in history. He was threatened by any precedent. He didn't want anybody to refer to Abraham, Isaac and Jacob. And he wanted to be the last. He didn't really want a successor all that much.

Does this sound like the Elijah that you know about? James says, 'He was a man of like passions', and that means that there's hope for every one of us. We learn from this account in 1 Kings 19 that Elijah wanted to retreat from any kind of responsibility now. We're told that he lay and slept under this broom tree. This is known as the escape syndrome. 'Let somebody else do it. I'm not needed.' Why is it that we retreat? It's our way of avoiding pain, of escaping reality. We'd rather live in a fantasy world. Some people escape by reading books. Some go to the cinema. Some watch television. Some earn money, getting involved in their work in that way. Well, Elijah's way was by sleeping. The real world was too painful for Elijah so he got out of it by sleeping.

I don't know whether I've said anything about Elijah that might possibly overlap with any weakness that you know in yourself, but if you do, don't think less of Elijah but be encouraged. For we're talking about a man that God has already used in an extraordinary way. This should destroy the myth that God can only use a man who has arrived, as it were. Have you wondered this: whether the only man that God uses is the man who has a constant state of elation. Or do you think perhaps it's the person who has attained to virtual sinless perfection who just never has evil thoughts and doesn't know any of the thoughts that you have? You have thoughts and weaknesses and you think, 'That eliminates me from ever being considered.' Well, don't be hard on Elijah or yourself. And don't be angry with God. Because when God used Elijah God used the best he could find. And that's the reason God will use you. You are the best he can find. For there is nobody else. We're all the same.

A Righteous Man Is An Ordinary Man

I repeat: all that we have seen with regard to Elijah came after, not before, the very event James refers to as an example of effectual praying. But you will say, 'I thought James said that it's the effectual fervent prayer of a righteous man that avails much. And surely the man that we see here under the juniper tree is not a righteous man.' But James is telling us that a righteous man is an ordinary man. There's no other kind. For even if Elijah's juniper tree experience came before Mount Carmel it would encourage me. Because that would also mean that God could make something out of us. But, lo and behold, it turns out that the very man God had used already was like that.

If Elijah's success at Mount Carmel had come after the juniper tree experience we might begin to surmise that something had happened to Elijah in the meantime that equipped him. There is reason to believe that, in so far as Mount Carmel was concerned, that made him worse not better. For seeing God answer his prayer at Mount Carmel might actually have made Elijah imagine that he was the greatest. There was Noah, there was Enoch, Abraham, Isaac, Jacob, Moses. Then when you consider what Elijah saw, we find him at rock bottom and he says, 'I'm no better.' His balloon was punctured. God's preparation is his own grace. Our faith is believing in his power, not in ourselves.

The easiest thing in the world is to think that our usefulness to God means that we're able in ourselves. Here we have Elijah now saying, 'Lord, I've had it. I'm no better. Let me die.' You might think that such pouting, such sulking behaviour would have turned God right off. You might think, 'Surely God would throw up his hands in horror that the man he had chosen for such an event as took place on Mount Carmel could turn out like that.' And so you might imagine that God would quietly disown him and let him die in his sleep. But God wasn't threatened by Elijah's pitiful outburst. As the Psalmist put it: 'He knoweth our frame; he remembereth that we are dust' (Ps. 103:14). And Elijah's frame was just like the rest of us. Elijah was the best God could find. God knew what Elijah was when he called him. God knew that the man that he would use at Mount Carmel would later be under the juniper tree wanting to escape reality. God sees the end from the beginning. The wonderful thing is he sees the mistakes you will make but uses you in the meantime.

So while Elijah was sleeping, God was at work. And rather than being turned off, we're told that God sent an angel. We won't know until we get to heaven how many times God despatched an angel in our case. God wasn't mad at Elijah. He sent an angel to him. And he said, 'Arise and eat' (v. 5). Elijah was hungry and so the angel prepared a meal for him. And yet that didn't make any great impression on Elijah.

God always returns to pick us up

God does things like this for us all the time. How many times does he rescue us from an awful situation? How many times does he supply the need right before our eyes? He doesn't make any great impression on us. We just go on. 'Thanks, God. I appreciate that.' Elijah was hungry and he ate. He went right back to sleep. Though he had been wonderfully provided for there's no hint that Elijah was grateful. Would God be put off by such ingratitude? No, the angel came back a second time (v. 7). God always comes the second time. He returns to pick us up and start again. The Lord came to Jonah the second time. As John Newton put it: 'A second look he gave which said, I freely all forgive.' That's the God we serve. That's the way God wants us to forgive. Not by going up to another person and saying, 'I forgive you for what you did to me.' That's the worst thing in the world you can do. The way you forgive another person is by affirming them. And by overlooking anything that they might have done. You act as if you don't even know about it. That's the way God forgives us. He's not saying to us every five minutes, 'You notice I've forgiven you.' No, he shows it. He continues to guide us, to deal with us, supplying our need and making it possible that we can be used again. And so the angel came the second time and said, 'Get up, eat. You've got a journey ahead. The journey's too great for you.' We have a reasonable God who knows what we have to have. He does not ask us to do what we cannot do. He supplies the need that is equal to the task coming up. And we're told that the strength from what Elijah ate lasted as long as Elijah needed it (v. 8).

Our natures are against us but God is for us

But it's not the end with the disclosure of Elijah's weaknesses. We're told that he came to a cave – an unlikely place to see God work. Elijah still had a lot of bitterness inside and he wanted to let God know all about it. Can you imagine such arrogance, such self-pity, such self-righteousness? Look how seriously Elijah was taking himself. Many of us are like that. We take ourselves so seriously. The wonderful thing is that that's the kind of man God uses. It makes us feel so small. There's nothing more humbling and yet nothing more thrilling than to realize we're all just a little spoke in

God's big wheel. We all think ourselves unique, and we are. And yet we're no different when our selfish natures are taken into consideration. Why? That the excellency of the power may be of God and not of us.

God can use us too

Finally one last lesson Elijah was to learn. What we learn from this is that God is not tied to the past or to any precedent or any expectation we may have. 'The LORD passed by, and a great and strong wind rent the mountains, and brake in pieces the rocks before the LORD; but the LORD was not in the wind: and after the wind an earthquake: but the LORD was not in the earthquake: And after the earthquake a fire; but the LORD was not in the fire: and after the fire a still small voice' (vv. 11–12). Elijah was still learning. He had more to do. But slotted right in is the man who was effectual in prayer. And James is saying, 'All right, what about you? That shows you qualify.' For if God can use Elijah he can use anybody.

41

Elijah: Troublemaker of Israel

James 5:17

James brings in Elijah and focuses on an aspect of Elijah's life that, first of all, takes us all by surprise. He says, 'Elijah was a man subject to like passions as we are.' As the NIV put it: 'A man just like us.' By saying that, James removes any obstacle that might come before us to make us think that we're disqualified. It proves furthermore – this is interesting – that a righteous man is not a faultless man. For Elijah had his faults.

God Can Use Anybody To Pray

We have spent time focusing upon Elijah's weakness. When I think that God could use a weak, doubting, sulking, vain man, then I know he can use anybody. There's nothing more encouraging than that. What does James say next? 'Elijah was a man subject to like passions as we are, and he prayed.' This proves that anybody can pray.

Do you sometimes think you can't pray because you're not worthy to pray? James is saying, 'Look at Elijah, a man with faults like that, and he prayed.' Perhaps you might say, 'What a lot of nerve Elijah had to pray. A man like that ought not to be praying.' James said he did. Even the most wicked person can pray.

Just as I am, without one plea
But that Thy blood was shed for me,
And that thou bidd'st me come to Thee,
O Lamb of God I come.

Anybody can pray. We're fools if we don't turn to God.

> *O what peace we often forfeit,*
> *O what needless pain we bear,*
> *All because we do not carry*
> *Everything to God in prayer!*

The Authorised Version and most versions say that Elijah prayed fervently. 'He prayed earnestly.' But the Greek says literally 'He prayed a prayer.'

Effectual praying has nothing to do with the language or eloquence or how many words. The Pharisees thought they were 'heard for their much speaking' (Mt. 6:7). Effectual praying is not necessarily related even to a burden you might feel when you're praying. It's just praying a prayer and knowing that God heard you. You didn't have to shout. It doesn't have to be perfectly right, grammatically correct. A lot of people won't pray in public because they're afraid it won't sound right. But effectual praying is just praying a prayer and knowing that you are heard by God. That's all.

James Tells Us About Elijah's Prayer

James is referring to 1 Kings 17:1 where Elijah first emerges, this great figure of the Old Testament. He comes to Ahab and says, 'As the LORD God of Israel liveth, before whom I stand, there shall not be dew nor rain these years, but according to my word.' Now that's not a prayer, that's a prophecy. When did Elijah pray? If you go by 1 Kings you won't find that he prayed at all that it might not rain. James is the one who told us that.

How did James know? I don't know. Maybe there was an oral tradition. It could be that James knew under inspiration what was exactly right. But James wouldn't have said it if it hadn't been exactly like this. The question is, when did Elijah pray that it might not rain? The answer is, he prayed before he prophesied and had the joy of making a word come alive that he knew was right. Elijah already had the joy of seeing set into operation a prayer that James would call 'effectual prayer'.

That is how we know that Elijah prayed before he prophesied. Because only a fool would have done what Elijah did unless he knew exactly what he was talking about. He went into the presence of the king and make this bold claim: 'As the Lord lives there will be no rain, not even dew, until I say.' He didn't prophesy first and then run to the Lord and say, 'Oh, Lord, did you hear what I did? Bail me out. You've got to do something.' There are times when I'll preach things and I'll say to myself, 'Oh, Lord, help me to forget that I said that. Get me out of this mess.' Because I know what it is to preach in the flesh.

Elijah didn't go to Ahab and make a statement so that he could then manipulate God, saying, 'All right, God, you're going to have to do something.' God never asks us to risk his reputation or ours by foolish speculation. A righteous man doesn't bring God in at the last moment. The righteous man is one who makes a statement because God has witnessed to it first.

There is but one explanation why Elijah could prophesy like this to Ahab. That is that Elijah had touched God and he knew it for God had touched him. In Mark 11 Jesus put it like this: 'What things soever ye desire, when ye pray, believe that ye receive them, and ye shall have them.' The NIV put it: 'Believe that you have received it, and it will be yours' (v. 24). That happened to Elijah. I don't think it happens very often, and yet it ought to happen more than it does. What worries me is that so little of it is known today. And this is part of the reason that the church is in the mess that it is in. The nation is in trouble. The church is to be the salt of the earth and this is a generation in which the Church is not taken seriously by anybody.

Elijah knew exactly what he was doing when he said to Ahab, 'It's not going to rain till I say so', because he had experienced effectual praying. It took no boldness at all, really. It's exactly what Paul did when he was on the ship. It looked as if they were going to be shipwrecked and Paul said, 'There stood by me this night the angel of God, whose I am, and whom I serve, saying, Fear not, Paul; thou must be brought before Caesar: and, lo, God hath given thee all them that sail with thee.' This is when Paul said, 'Wherefore, sirs, be of good cheer: for I believe God, that it shall be even as it was told me' (Acts 27:23–25). That's it. One just knows.

A prophecy that came true

One of the most impressive, moving events I've ever known took place in my home church when I was a boy aged fifteen. Old Dr Tidwell, eighty years old, came and preached for two weeks at my church back in Ashland, Kentucky. And on the last Sunday morning that he preached he used as his text the parable of the man who didn't have the wedding garment and they said, 'Bind him hand and foot, and cast him into outer darkness' (Mt. 22:13). There was great power on the service. Everybody remembers an unusual sense of God's presence.

Dr Tidwell, a mature man who wasn't given to idle comments, said, 'Somebody in this service is getting their last call.' He would not dismiss the service and turned to the pastor and said, 'You dismiss the service.' And the pastor said, 'I won't dismiss the service.' The people just stayed seated and eventually, one by one, they began to leave. My mother happened to be sitting near a young lady aged sixteen who was laughing throughout the service, scoffing and making rude comments out loud as the preacher preached. Finally the girl got up and left as other people did. The next day, 27 hours from the moment old Dr Tidwell made that prophecy: 'Somebody's getting their last call', the same girl was walking down Montgomery Avenue toward 25th Street. On the concrete there was a 'Stop' sign that some kids had turned around so that it was facing the other way. A car driving alongside didn't see the 'Stop' sign and went on through. A car coming down 25th Street at full speed who thought he knew the area careened into the car. It came over on the pavement and Patsy Brown was struck dead instantly.

Having heard my mother's account of things, the news that came out on Monday night had the most sobering and shattering effect on me of any event that I can recall. I didn't tell my parents but I went to my bedroom and I got on my knees and I rededicated my life to God. When Dr Tidwell made that statement nobody thought it would have been a teenager. I always thought church was for grown-ups. I didn't think God took us kids that seriously. And when I knew that she was the one, I remembered how I had talked to my own parents, 'One day I won't have to go to church.' And they would say, 'You're right. You'll have your own home and you can do what you want. But as long as you're under this roof you're going to go to church.' They didn't have any trouble with me after that. I gave my life to God and I was never the same again.

What is it going to take to wake us up? I have a heavy heart when I think of the flippancy among young people. And many parents of teenagers don't even care seemingly whether they go to discos or to Bible study on Friday nights. You may say, 'I don't want to drive them away from church.' The families back in my home church that didn't make their children go are the very ones that lost their children as they came of age. They didn't come back at all. We who had to go are still in the church today. I could name one after another. Two of us are in the ministry. We didn't like to go. You may think you're giving certain mature freedom when you say to your kids, 'You don't have to go.' But you as parents are responsible to God. You will some day watch your children laugh and scoff at you when you can't do anything.

The Test Of A True Prophet

When Elijah said to Ahab, 'It's not going to rain until I say so', there's no indication that King Ahab believed him. Ahab had probably learned to take prophets with a grain of salt. After all, there's a rather simple test of a true prophet: whether or not the prophecy comes true. Ahab didn't care at the moment. There was plenty of time. I suppose the fact that it didn't rain any more that day didn't worry Ahab too much. And the next day was bright and sunny. It still didn't bother Ahab. He thought, 'Well, we've had days like this before.' And after three weeks had gone by there was no rain. But after a month or so somebody came to him and said, 'We haven't had any rain. There hasn't even been any dew on the grass, morning or night.' Then the report came in that the grass was turning brown. The leaves on the trees were withering. It didn't matter at that moment whether Ahab believed Elijah. Elijah believed it. It was effectual praying and Elijah was the only one who knew that from then on meteorological conditions were up to him.

Why do you suppose Elijah prayed like that? God gives us freedom to pray according to our judgement as seems right and fair. We read in 1 Kings 16:30 that Ahab 'did evil in the sight of the LORD above all that were before him'. He had a wife, Jezebel, who was equally as bad, and together they worshipped Baal. Anybody living at the time could see the conditions. Elijah was a man of God. He had to think up what could be done to change things, to reverse the trend. He knew this much was certain: the ministry of God must be rendered credible. The vindication of the word of God was important. So Elijah just came up with this. He prayed that it might not rain. He broke through to the heavens when he prayed that prayer. And he knew he had asked the right thing.

You may say, 'Was this Elijah's own idea or was it God's?' Elijah thought it was his. But the secret work of God lay behind it. Sometimes our keenest desire is really God's will. Sometimes the very thing burning in us is what God is really saying. My own call to the ministry was like this. I wanted to preach so badly I couldn't eat or sleep because I was afraid that the call was from me and I wanted it to be from God. I delayed settling it for that very reason. Elijah prayed like this. It seemed to him that the best thing that could happen was to make Ahab see the danger in the spiritual and moral bankruptcy of the time.

Effectual prayer is unselfish

Elijah believed that conditions must get worse before they could get better. He even put his own security on the line, praying a prayer by which he himself was equally affected. No rain generally meant no rain for Elijah particularly. He found this out shortly when he went to the brook Cherith and it had dried up. Effectual praying is unselfish praying. Elijah couldn't get away with saying, 'Lord, don't let it rain in Israel except where I happen to be at the time.'

I think this provides us with a pretty broad hint. For so much of our praying is a cop-out. We're detached from committed responsibility. We say, 'Deal with all these kids', when we just wouldn't think about getting to know them, understanding what their needs are. Or we say, 'Lord, send in the money for the Organ Fund', when we're not even giving our tithes, much less an offering above them. So effectual praying is not whereby you can be so detached and worry about things just marginally.

This further suggests what James means by a righteous man. It's a man who is personally involved, and this fits the whole book. We know that some of these Christians were social climbers. And James said, 'You're partial.' Impartiality is what makes a righteous man. A righteous man is one who doesn't just say, 'Go be warmed in the fire', but he provides the clothes. He gives. He's not simply the one who is perfectly orthodox and believes there's one God. The devil believes that. The righteous man is one who shows his faith by his works.

Elijah got involved. No rain would affect him as well. God owned Elijah's prayer. He prayed that it might not rain. During the next three and a half years Elijah's prayer was answered. Do you know what? It turned out that Elijah's prayer didn't affect Ahab. Here was Elijah feeling the tension of seeing his prayer answered but a victory not accomplished. But it provided him with an unusual opportunity to demonstrate God's power. It didn't bother Ahab and Jezebel a bit that they continued to worship Baal. They didn't care about true religion. Everybody knew one thing: the land had been without rain. Nobody doubted that. Only Elijah and Ahab knew why. This ought to have been enough to make Ahab repent, but it didn't. It ought to have been enough to make him destroy all the images of Baal, but it didn't. It's like what we read in Revelation 16:11: 'They blasphemed the God of heaven because of their pains and their sores, and repented not of their deeds.'

So Elijah, who should have been proclaimed God's anointed prophet for whom all Israel should be thankful, instead was given a rather unflattering nickname. One day Ahab saw Elijah and said,

'Are you the one that troubles Israel?' (1 Kgs. 18:17). Troublemaker of Israel. That was Elijah's nickname. We never get the nickname we want. The world gives the nickname. Elijah thought, 'No, you're the one that troubles Israel.'

The Frustration Of Answered Prayer Without Victory

God's prophet always gets the blame because he calls a spade a spade. The answer to Elijah's prayer didn't achieve the immediate end because Ahab remained stubborn. But his ministry was given credibility and he had the ear of the seat of power. This is a hard thing to endure: to have God answer your prayer and still not have achieved what you thought the answer to the prayer would achieve. The frustration of answered prayer without any victory can be the most severe test yet.

Elijah was vindicated, and yet he wasn't. It's at a time like this that one proves one's own metal: when God answers your prayer but, instead of the victory that you thought would come as a result, the test is greater. What you do is this: stand back and say, 'Do I believe in God or not? I do believe in him.' And you just wait, for he's still working. Elijah stuck to his guns. Plan A hadn't worked, but he went to a second proposition. He did-n't think this was going to happen. Elijah really thought that a few weeks without any rain would cause Ahab to come running, saying, 'You win. Tell us what to do.'

Plan B hadn't even been thought about, but it turned out to be the most dazzling, thrilling, terrifying moment of that century. Elijah said to Ahab, 'You send throughout all Israel for the prophets of Baal. I want them to be on Mount Carmel. We're going to have a talk.' And the moment had come. Elijah had been taken seriously by Ahab. Elijah put a request to the seat of power and it was honoured. 'Send for the prophets.'

The problem with Britain today is that nobody takes the church seriously. Do you wonder why? Four per cent of Britons attending church, and among that four per cent there's a minimal interest in things spiritual. Nobody is taking the church seriously, and if the people of God do not see him act soon it may well be we will reach the point of no return.

Elijah's time had come. So Ahab sent to all the children of Israel and gathered the prophets together on Mount Carmel. We're told that Elijah had a word from the Lord. He said to these prophets, 'How long halt ye' – waver – 'between two opinions? if the LORD be God, follow him: but if Baal, follow him' (1 Kgs. 18:21). What Elijah did was to seize upon their own insecurity. For he knew that these false prophets were very insecure. Always remember this about anybody who has overthrown his evangelical heritage, who has turned his back upon true religion. He's very insecure. He may sound so certain and secure and learned but he's not. Elijah knew that, and do you know what they said back? Nothing. Because there was nothing they could say. Like Stephen before the Council, 'They were not able to resist the wisdom and the spirit by which he spake' (Acts 6:10).

But they did agree to one thing. They got to talking eventually. Elijah said, 'Look, I'm outnumbered 450 to one. Let's get two bulls. You take one, I'll take one. We'll sacrifice it. I'll call on my God. You call on your god. And whoever answers by fire will be the true God.' And they agreed to that. And Elijah told them to have a go first. We have here one of the most pitiful displays of false religion. Whatever effectual praying is, this isn't it. They started calling on the name of Baal. They were using all kinds of pious tones. They spoke with a tremor in their voice. They tried everything. A lot of people think that the sound of their voice is doing something. Back in the hills of Kentucky we call it 'the holy tone'. But nothing was working.

I never read this passage without almost laughing out loud. You have here one of the funniest, most humorous passages – it's hilarious – with Elijah who was chuckling inside the whole time, only he was afraid they were going to see him. He could hardly contain himself. But he realized it had begun to show and they'd been going at it all morning. It was getting to be about noon. So he told them to try shouting. Then he told them to try shouting louder. Then he said they were not shouting loud enough. 'Perhaps he's talking to somebody and he can only talk to one person at a time. You've got to get his attention and interrupt.' Then he suggested that Baal might be away somewhere or even asleep. They were getting panicky. They started dancing round the altar. They were trying to work it up. And eventually, in desperation, they started cutting themselves and blood was beginning to flow. Finally, Elijah stepped in and tells them, 'All right. You've had your chance.'

The first thing we're told is that Elijah repaired the altar. God didn't need a physical structure to be exactly right for him to come down in power. But it's interesting, isn't it? He took twelve stones according to the number of the tribes of the sons of Jacob. He wanted there to be an unmistakable identification between the God that he was talking to and their own heritage, that they would all know and remember that this was the God of Israel, the ancient God of Isaac and Jacob.

When they got the sacrifice ready he poured water on it, and more water. He wanted to get it so wet that when the fire fell there would be no natural explanation for what was taking place. Now it was time for Elijah actually to pray. A simple prayer. Straightforward. No shouting. No affected tone of voice. He said, 'God of Abraham, Isaac, and of Israel, let it be known this day that thou art God in Israel, and that I am thy servant, and that I have done all these things at thy word. Hear me, O LORD, hear me, that this people may know that thou art the LORD God, and that thou hast turned their heart back again' (1 Kgs. 18:36–37).

Fire that defied a natural explanation

I suspect you could almost hear a pin drop on Mount Carmel. Their hearts were beating faster inside their chests. These pitiful prophets had been humiliated and defeated. Elijah was the only calm soul around. He just prayed. What followed was unprecedented in that generation. For nobody alive had ever seen God's power. They didn't have a clue what it was like. Out of the blue came fire. God's fire.

It defied a natural explanation. Natural fire ascends. This was fire coming down. Whether it had a sound I do not know, like on the Day of Pentecost when there was a rushing mighty wind and there were tongues of fire on each of their heads (Acts 2:2–3). But what we do know is that the fire fell and it consumed the burnt sacrifice, the wood, the stones, the dust, and licked up the water that was in the trench. These men fell on their faces and cried out, 'The LORD, he is the God; the LORD, he is the God' (1 Kgs. 18:39).

You might think that this is going to be the time that Elijah goes round congratulating each one of them. But what happens now prefigures the final judgement of God. Elijah had every one of them slaughtered. As Jesus put it, 'Bind them hand and foot and cast them into outer darkness', like the one who didn't have the wedding garment. Sinner, you will confess that Jesus Christ is Lord sooner or later. It's only a question of when. 'Whosoever was not found written in the book of life was cast into the lake of fire' (Rev. 20:15).

The Supernatural Result Of A Simple Prayer

The interesting thing is that the answer to prayer on Mount Carmel is not the prayer James had in mind. What James talked about is when Elijah prayed that it might not rain. The event, however, would not have taken place if Elijah hadn't prayed the first time that it might not rain. We must begin with conditions as they are. Eventually we'll get to Mount Carmel, but we can never anticipate how it's going to take place. We must be faithful in that which is least so that we prove we can be faithful in that which is much more (Lk. 16:10). There never would have been a Mount Carmel if Elijah had not first prayed years before that it might not rain. Elijah had some of his worst days after the day it stopped raining. He also had some of his best days. They were days of preparation that led to this extraordinary confrontation with the false prophets, this wonderful demonstration of God's power. Praying that it might not rain was being faithful in that which is least. But as each day progressed, the enormity of that prayer became evident.

We don't begin on Mount Carmel, and we don't end there. We don't begin with an audience with the king either. Or with an open confrontation with false prophets. We must prove ourselves faithful in that which is least for we will not be taken seriously until we've had our own secret confrontation with God and prevailed with him and know his anointing is with us.

42

Elijah: Praying the Second Time

James 5:18

James isn't finished with Elijah. So he continues: 'And he prayed again, and the heaven gave rain, and the earth brought forth her fruit.' We know that James brought Elijah in the first time to encourage us, to show us what effectual praying is, to show us what a righteous man is. It's our task now to see why James brought Elijah back into the picture once more. We want to focus mainly on these words: 'He prayed again.' Elijah praying the second time.

Effectual Praying Leads To Repeat Praying

I think the first lesson is simply this: the person who has engaged in effectual prayer once will very likely do it again. We have seen that the prayer of faith is really a one-off prayer. Effectual praying is virtually the same thing, but it is slightly different. For one thing effectual praying can be repeated. Indeed, doing it once almost always means doing it again. You will be so thrilled by having engaged in prayer like this that you will hardly be able to wait to do it again. But Elijah did it again because there was unfinished business in this particular case.

Back in the book of 1 Kings we noticed that when Elijah first entered into Old Testament history it was in this account of going to Ahab and giving a prophecy. The prophecy was: 'It will not rain again. There will be no dew on the earth unless I say so.' And so it stopped raining. It's a bit scary. If Ahab, this wicked king, had been judicious he would have put a bodyguard around Elijah. He would have made sure he had the best medical attention possible in Israel at that time. For Elijah was very important. Because the only hope in the world that it would rain again would be at Elijah's word. So Elijah's very life, at that time, was the world's insurance policy that rain would ever reappear. But Ahab didn't have that kind of attitude towards Elijah. This is typical of the world. The world would like to do away with the church. The world, the flesh, the devil, would keep the church off her knees when, in fact, the only hope of the world is the church on her knees. But Elijah was bound to pray again.

The best thing that was happening at that time in Israel's history was probably unnoticed, but James tells us that Elijah 'prayed again'. It wasn't enough for false religion to be put in its place. For there had to be the emergence of the positive if the world was to survive.

Vindication can be a dangerous thing

Vindication is negative, really. Maybe you want vindication more than anything. But what good comes from it? Is it simply that you can say to another person, 'I told you so'? Or is it that it does something for your own ego? But what does it do for the kingdom of God? It's for this very reason that vindication can be a dangerous thing. How would you handle it were it to happen? This is why few of us know anything about being vindicated. We can't be trusted with it. This is why God says, 'Vengeance is mine; I will repay, saith the Lord' (Rom. 12:19). Elijah was vindicated simply because his concern was not personal. Had it been personal, he could never have been trusted with that extra-ordinary demonstration of God's power on Mount Carmel. He would have just wiped his hands and said to himself, 'Let Ahab and the world perish.' The proof that Elijah could be trusted with vindication and with having been given credibility in the eyes of all the world is in these three words: 'He prayed again.'

Effectual praying means listening to God

Effectual praying is a divine trust and we must follow it wherever it leads us. I don't doubt for a moment that when Elijah prayed the first time that it might not rain, he thought that was his own idea. But the secret will of God and the secret work of the Spirit lay behind it. Indeed we find this out later on if only because we read in 1 Kings 18 that Elijah now was released from this former concern and God said, 'Go, shew thyself unto Ahab; and I will send rain upon the earth' (v. 1).

When Elijah prayed the first time it may have simply been what he thought was the right thing to do. And many times we think our praying is our own idea. That's the freedom God gives to us. We get a particular concern and we just carry through with it. We may not be aware at the time how much God really is behind it. What often happens, though, is that when God does answer our prayer we're vulnerable to feeling self-righteous about it as though: 'It was my idea. Look what I accomplished.' Whenever we feel like that God has a way of humbling us. And he can do it very well. For what we find now is that God is saying, 'This is my idea and now I'm going to send rain.' So when Elijah prayed the next time he knew in advance it wasn't his own idea. He went to Ahab and told him to get up, eat and drink; 'for there is a sound of abundance of rain' (1 Kgs. 18:41). This shows effectual praying in operation. God was in it and Elijah had to listen and obey.

Elijah Had No Doubt That God Was Working

He'd heard from the Lord and he says, 'There is a sound of abundance of rain.' As the NIV put it: 'the sound of a heavy rain.' There was no sound of rain. There wasn't any rain around at all. There wasn't any due. There were no clouds, and yet here goes the prophet Elijah saying to Ahab, 'There is the sound of rain.' But that's what Jesus meant when he said, 'Believe that you have received it and it shall be given to you' (Mk. 11:24). There wasn't the slightest doubt in Elijah's mind that God was working again.

It seems that this time Ahab took Elijah seriously. He didn't the first time, but when Elijah said to Ahab, 'Get up, eat and drink', Ahab did exactly that. The first time he prayed 1 Kings doesn't tell us when it was. But we know now, by correlating James and Elijah, what was going on at about this time in Israel's history. There's no doubt when Elijah prayed the second time. We're told that he went to the top of Mount Carmel and 'cast himself down upon the earth, and put his face between his knees' (1 Kgs. 18:42). I don't know whether any of you have prayed in a position like that. But it doesn't matter – your physical position, your posture. I suppose you could find biblical support for any kind of position: standing, kneeling, sitting, lying on your bed, walking. You can pray riding in the tube, driving in your car.

But here's a man who is sitting cast down with his head between his knees. It's a picture showing a personality, the character of Elijah. He was just being himself. He wasn't trying to imitate anybody. He didn't say, 'I wonder how Jacob did it when he wrestled with the angel? I'll do it just like that.' No, he wasn't worried about any set tradition. There wasn't any precedent for doing it like this. The whole world was waiting for him to pray. Oh that the world would be waiting for the church to get on with

praying. Right now the world would want to destroy the church.
Wouldn't it be wonderful if the world found the church's witness so
credible that it sat on edge saying, 'Pray, pray'? And yet we mustn't wait
for the world to feel like that. They need our prayer now though they
don't know it and though they don't want it or believe it. We must pray
now if only because they don't see us as being credible.

Elijah prayed again. It's an account that can hardly be read without
being brought to tears. Elijah turned to his servant and he said, 'Go up
now, look toward the sea' (v. 43). We know from modern geography in
Israel that the base of Mount Carmel is that modern city of Haifa. The
Mediterranean Sea is right there and so we know from this that Elijah was
telling his servant to go and look toward the Mediterranean Sea. Keep in
mind that it hadn't rained for three and a half years.

Why did Elijah say, 'Look toward the sea'? Elijah thought that when
God would send rain again he would do it according to the course of
nature. He thought it would be natural to expect that vapour would rise
from the sea to form a cloud. Elijah waited. The servant came back.
Nothing. I suspect there was some disappointment. Everything had been
going exactly like clockwork. He prayed the first time and it didn't rain.
Look at the extraordinary demonstration of power on Mount Carmel.
And God had said, 'Go and see Ahab. I'm going to send rain.' So he went
to Ahab and said, 'There's the sound of rain. Just get ready. Go and eat.'
But now the servant came back: 'Nothing.' Was this testing of Elijah's
faith? I think it was.

Effectual praying is done without doubting, knowing you're in the will of
God. Even though you know you are praying in the Spirit, it doesn't mean
that when the answer's there that you're not going to enjoy seeing that.
Elijah wanted to see this happen. We live in the real world. We don't live in
an idealistic world of abstractions. We can pray and know God is hearing us.
But there comes a time when you want to see something happen. It wasn't
enough to go on saying indefinitely, 'It's going to rain.' Elijah wanted to see
it as much as anybody. We have to see something happen before our eyes
eventually to show that there is a God who is hearing prayer.

Elijah wasn't content to know that his prayer was acceptable. He, like
everybody else, was waiting to see a sight that nobody had seen in three
and a half years.

God hides his face sometimes

Elijah just kept his face between his knees. He may have been tempted to
doubt. Sometimes God works in a most definite way day after day after

day and then suddenly hides his face, never giving advance warning. That's what hiding God's face means. He doesn't say, 'Be ready Tuesday afternoon about ten past three. I shall hide myself from you. If you know in advance you can prepare, store up, get everything done you want to.'

You just feel the Lord with you and he's talking to you. Then suddenly he's gone. You begin to ask, 'What went wrong? Did I do something? Maybe I should have done this. Maybe I just thought you were with me. I thought your word was coming alive. I think it was just me.'

Perhaps Elijah went back to the beginning mentally, tracing every step, and nothing happened. He remembers that it used to rain all the time and then he prayed that it might not rain and lo and behold, it stopped raining. Elijah comforted himself a bit. He said, 'Well, that was of God. I don't have to worry about that.' And then he thought about Mount Carmel. He had just cried out to God saying, 'Lord, answer', and God did it. So he knows that God was with him. He knows only God could have done all this. Maybe Elijah took time to reflect on the most recent answer to prayer, to remind himself that God was real and that it wasn't just his imagination that he felt the Lord's presence.

Sometimes God hides his face so that we might take the time to retrace our steps and examine our attitudes and look at events very carefully. It is at times like that that we can sometimes see mistakes we wouldn't have noticed had God not delayed that answer to prayer. Remember this: When God hides his face, the secret operation of the Spirit is still in operation. That never ceases. It is at a time like this that we can undergo mental clarification. Some of life's greatest lessons are learned between answers to prayer.

If Elijah uncovered any need, if he saw anything that was clarified in his mind, if he saw occasion for repentance in his own heart, we're not told. All we're told is that he said to his servant, 'Keep looking toward the sea.' This was apparently the only thing he could do. He just kept his head between his knees. Only God could send the rain. In the earliest church it was normal for there to be continuous remarkable answers to prayer. God was working in this way all the time. They wanted to get into Peter's shadow, just to be in his presence. He'd walk by and people would be healed (Acts 5:15). Peter and John said to the man at the Gate Beautiful, 'Rise up and walk' (Acts 3:6), and he did. We don't know why, but there was a diminishing of that in the second generation. So the epistle of James shows us that it is still 'authentic' Christianity in operation. James is having to show his readers what the Christian faith is and show them something of living by faith.

It could be that because Elijah was seeing so much happen he was beginning to feel just a bit self-righteous. He may have got to the place where he thought that he could just give the nod to God and God would do it. 'Go and look towards the sea. What do you see?' He came back: 'Nothing.' Six times the servant came back: 'Nothing. Blue skies.' Perhaps it was getting a bit embarrassing for the servant. He didn't want to have to come and say this to Elijah again. Perhaps Elijah was getting a bit embarrassed to ask the servant. Perhaps the servant secretly was having second thoughts about Elijah.

Sometimes those who work the closest to any minister can have their own faith shaken when things aren't going smoothly all the time. Elijah waited with his head down. There was nothing more that he could do. Perhaps secretly he was saying, 'Lord, Lord, unless you do something we can't go on.' Perhaps Elijah was a bit embarrassed to say to the servant for the seventh time, 'Go and look again towards the sea.' But he did say it, and the servant went. Who do you suppose was the first to see a definite change in the atmosphere? Not Elijah. It was the servant. I suspect he came charging back, and I suppose Elijah could just sense something. Maybe it was the sound of the servant's footsteps as he came running back. He said, 'There ariseth a little cloud out of the sea, like a man's hand' (1 Kgs. 19:44). Elijah didn't need to know anything else. He knew that the same God who had brought him 'through many dangers, toils and snares' was doing it again. Things were now shaping up. For a sight like that had not been seen in three and a half years. Rain was on the way now. Elijah knew it. So he said to his servant something like, 'You'd better go and see Ahab and tell him to get moving fast because it's going to rain and the water's going to come up and he won't even get his chariot through. Go, go, go.'

There was no doubt what was on the way, so in the meanwhile there appeared all over Israel a most wonderful sight. Black clouds. Everybody was over the moon. People were standing out on the street. I suspect that work shut down all over Israel. Nobody could concentrate. What would normally be a forbidding sight was now the sweetest, most thrilling sight of that generation. The winds came and there it was: one pelting drop after another. Children danced in the streets. People probably went outside and lifted their faces heavenwards to let the water beat down on their faces. Never mind being drenched, rain had come.

What God Starts He Finishes

All this makes me think of when they brought a blind man to Jesus. 'And he took the blind man by the hand, and led him out of the town; and when he had spit on his eyes, and put his hands upon him, he asked him if he saw ought. And he looked up, and said, I see men as trees, walking. After that he put his hands again upon his eyes, and made him look up: and he was restored, and saw every man clearly' (Mk. 8:23–25). What God starts he finishes. When Elijah's servant saw a small cloud Elijah knew that was all that was needed. God would finish it.

Conditions in the church, in the nation, on both sides of the Atlantic are very bleak. Almost nothing seems as it used to be. For all I know, there's an Elijah somewhere who has prayed already that it might not rain. For all I know, what we have seen – or perhaps I should say, what we haven't seen – is God honouring the prayers of somebody somewhere. But I'm sure of this: God has not abandoned his world or his church. Whether there is an Elijah around, I don't know. But there had better be soon. God has singled out every one of us to intercede before his throne. We all need to be praying more than we've been praying. We all need to be more involved than we've been. The church in our day has no credibility in the world. We must pray that God will own our prayers so that some day somebody somewhere can send an undoubted message: 'I do see one thing. Not much. Only a little cloud rising out of the sea about the size of a man's hand.' But it will be a sight that we haven't seen in our generation. By that we will know God will be showing his face again. May he hasten the day.

43

Bringing the Backslider Home

James 5:19–20

We come now to the final sentence of this epistle of James. The theme in this epistle is 'living the Christian life'. We've seen again and again that there is an implicit theme – that of backsliding. In putting this final statement as he does, James is wrapping up the whole epistle if not the immediate context. Now there's a sense in which the epistle was wrapped up in verse 18. But that did not end the epistle because James wasn't finished. He has more to say, and we can be thankful that he comes along with this statement because it is a way of drawing together this underlying theme of backsliding. It shows his real motive in writing this epistle in the first place. And yet we must admit that 'backsliding' is a term James doesn't use. In fact, it's not even a New Testament term. It's an Old Testament term. But there are many synonyms, or at least phrases, that say this same thing.

How James Describes Backsliding

We tend to use this one expression 'backsliding', and yet James has several words for it. For example, in chapter one verse 8 it could be called 'double mindedness'. Or in chapter one verse 14 you could call it a wilful state of temptation. You could even call backsliding being a respecter of persons. Or you could call backsliding faith without works (2:18), or thriving upon gossip – because you love to listen to it or because you want to engage in it. The backslider is one who has bitter envy in his heart (3:14). Or we could simply say that backsliding is being friendly with the world (4:4). Or we could say backsliding is when the Christian takes his life into his own hands like those who said, 'Today or tomorrow we will go to this place, buy and sell, make a little money' (4:13). Or the backslider was certainly depicted when we saw those Christians, those capitalists, who had with-held the just wages of those workers in the field (5:4). In other words, there are many ways backsliding can be described.

James ends the epistle as if to summarize his chief concern for this community of Christian Jews. And I cannot help but think this epistle has definite continuity and order. One evangelical commentary says, 'James is simply a book of pithy sayings. It's like a string of pearls where the string broke and the pearls fell off and you put them back on the string. It wouldn't matter which order you put them in.' But James knew exactly where he was going. He knew what he believed and, whereas it is true I think that James did not have a trained theological mind like the apostle Paul, it is nonetheless a fact that this man James had a radical doctrine of justification by faith alone and writes with a systematic construction of his main themes.

The Implications Of The Doctrine Of Justification By Faith

James was possibly the first epistle of the New Testament to be written. We can't prove that. But I think we must say that no one should ever believe that the doctrine of justification by faith lay hidden until Saul of Tarsus was converted. There is reason to believe that the Christian Jews had theological problems – and the apostle Paul did step in. But I think we could overestimate how much Paul straightened them up, because I think the doctrine was already there.

Where these Jewish Christians needed help was not only in the refinement of the doctrine of justification by faith, but with particular reference to its implications. It's one thing to believe in justification by faith, it's another thing really to believe it and live by it. Paul could say, 'I live by the faith of the Son of God' (Gal. 2:20). Paul tells us that there was a time when he stood alone and he mentions James, our James, but he also mentions Peter and John who were 'pillars'. They were the big men. Paul was a nobody. And he was pointing out to them, 'If what you believe is true why is it that you don't want to be seen with Gentiles? You were doing fine seated alongside myself with Gentiles. Then you saw some Jews coming and up you got and went and sat somewhere else. Now,' says Paul, 'that was wrong.' And so he says, 'I withstood Peter to the face because he was to be blamed' (Gal. 2:11).

He doesn't mention James. But James was there. James gets on to these Christian Jews about being a respecter of persons, just as Paul did with Peter. It could be that James learned from that. Again, we don't know for sure whether Paul and James discussed openly the doctrine of justification by faith. But it wouldn't surprise me. I think we can see from Galatians chapter 2 that James did learn something from Paul with regard to the implications. James was aware that he had something to learn and he needed correcting. We are all affected by our backgrounds. We tend to preach out of our experience even if we say we're not doing it. Because we're human. James knew exactly how to talk to these Christian Jews. He said at one stage, 'In many things we offend all' – we all stumble (3:2). There's nothing self-righteous about James. But he was so clear on this matter of backsliding. Perhaps he saw his own vulnerability. And this helps explain this epistle – especially its ending.

James Addresses Them All As Brothers

For I want us to look now at the spirit of this final exhortation. He addresses them as 'My brothers'. None of us would be defensive if James talked to us like that. It takes great wisdom and grace to be able to rebuke and yet not let the person be defensive when he hears the rebuke. James' way of doing it is to say, 'My brothers'. The Authorised Version simply says 'brethren'. I don't know why they didn't translate the Greek here. It's clearly 'my brothers'. It's a way of saying, 'I regard you all as my own brothers.'

He doesn't address these Jewish Christians in such a way as to say, 'I only mean some of you now.' He doesn't say, 'If any one of them needs this.' He says, 'If any one of you, my brothers.' It's not an address to the super-pious or the invulnerable. He's addressing us all.

Paul said, 'If a man be overtaken in a fault, ye which are spiritual' – those are the only ones that can do it – 'restore such an one in the spirit of meekness' – that's the way you go about it – 'considering thyself, lest thou also be tempted' (Gal. 6:1). For sometimes the very one who tries to help a brother overtaken in a fault is brought down himself, sometimes because he was self-righteous in the way he went about it. True spirituality is embodied in the realization of our own weakness. That keeps us from being self-righteous, judgemental. We're all so prone to this. You might think you're being so righteous when you say, 'I can see the fault in that person.' You ought to realize when you think that that it didn't show any spirituality at all. It's strictly operating at the level of nature.

James' motive here is to promote unity among these Christians. If he had ended this epistle at a certain spot and left them hanging he could have had them quarrelling with each other. They could have said, 'The fact that he ended there shows James is on our side.' Then they would use this epistle to club another person. But James won't let them do that. He's ending the epistle in such a way that he brings them all in together. It's an exhortation that forces them to accept each other. And this took some doing when you consider the kind of problems that he's had to deal with.

James doesn't set himself up as a harsh judge. He doesn't give any one person in that Jewish Christian community a feeling that they're any better than anybody else. The truth is, every one of us needs this word. So he says, 'My brothers'. He doesn't dissociate himself from these Christians. And this is so comforting to us. It's just like our Lord would be. Isn't it amazing how some people think it's so spiritual to separate themselves from certain ones because they just don't toe the line on a certain thing?

James wants to promote unity

Look at the reasons he could have used for doing that. Here were Christians who were lusting, social climbers, worldly-minded. There were those who were gossiping and full of bitterness. I could go on and on. But James says, 'My brothers'. Can we do this? That's the way our Lord was.

The writer of the Hebrews tells us that 'he that sanctifieth' – that's the Lord – 'and they who are sanctified' – that's us – 'are all of one; for which cause he' – that's the Lord – 'is not ashamed to call them' – and us – 'brethren' (2:11). You say, 'These are those who didn't have any personal problems, any spiritual weakness.' Not according to this. It goes on to say that 'he is able to succour them that are tempted' (v. 18) and that our Lord was 'in all points tempted like as we are, yet without sin' (4:15). Jesus didn't demand perfection in order to call us brethren. That absolute separation from a Christian brother is an exceedingly rare thing in the New Testament. You've got a case in 1 Corinthians 5 where there was one person who was bringing disgrace upon the Christian community at large and Paul said, 'Deliver him to Satan.' What worries me is that there are those who are willing to break fellowship with anybody over the slightest bit of worldliness or the slightest bit of doctrinal deviation. We seem to think it's a sign of spirituality.

Look at the problems James had to deal with. You name a problem and that church had it. And at the end he wants to bring them all together. 'My brothers', he says. That's the spirit. He says, 'If any of you do err from the truth …' Despite all he knew about them, that's his appeal. So he moves from the general to the particular. 'If any of you …' I repeat, he didn't say 'any one of them'. Certain ones would have loved it if he had said that. It's likely that the elders of this church, the officers, were the first to see the epistle. They probably looked over it first, read it together before they read it to the congregation. They knew they were going to have to read it aloud. And they knew that James meant them as well, that anybody in the congregation could say, 'Okay, that applies to you too.'

Nobody is above the Word

But there are some who actually think they're above the Word. I've known of ministers who think like that. They just say, 'This is a bit of an exception in my case.' It often happens to the most spiritual type of layman. Because the person who as a layman has grown in grace, begins to feel the Lord's presence, gets overly familiar with the Lord. He says, 'God understands me. I wouldn't recommend that you do this. But God knows it's all right for me.'

We all think we're the exception. James will not let anybody be above the Word. Not even Saul of Tarsus was. After he was converted and a mature man he said, 'I keep under my body, and bring it into subjection: lest that by any means, when I have preached to others, I myself should be a castaway' (1 Cor. 9:27). That was Paul's greatest fear. None of us is above the Word. So this letter was read with fear and trembling. And these elders, for their own souls' sake, had to take it seriously as well as anybody else.

These Christian Jews were capable of wandering, erring. The Greek word is *planethe*. It means 'to go astray'. It's the word Jesus used when he said to the Sadducees, 'Ye do err, not knowing the scriptures, nor the power of God' (Mt. 22:29). It's the word that Paul used in Titus 3:3, where the word is translated 'deceived', 'We ourselves also were sometimes foolish, disobedient, deceived.' It's translated 'going astray' in 1 Peter 2:25. Nobody is exempt.

Should any of us wander from the truth, aren't we glad that James would still call us brothers? Whenever you are tempted to say, 'So and so couldn't be a Christian and do that', I ask you, is that the way you want to be regarded if you should go astray or err? Have you ever wandered? We all have. Who among us does not have a skeleton in our closet? Who among us has not at one time or another known what it is to have faith without works?

Faith Without Works IS Possible, But ...

I think the reason so many people have never understood James is they come to this epistle with an entrenched position and a spirit of fear. I'm sure that was the reason Luther didn't like this book. He was so afraid that it wasn't going to fit in with all he thought the Lord had revealed to him, so he just couldn't look at it carefully. There are many who wouldn't go as far as Luther but they're scared to death just the same and they say, 'James surely wouldn't say this.' But he never does say that faith without works is an impossible situation, because it is possible to have faith without works.

James never said that the Christian who didn't have works is dead. He says, 'Faith without works is dead' (2:20), by which he meant 'useless'. But faith joined by works demonstrates what faith was equally designed for: not only to save you but to save somebody else.

In this final exhortation James is putting into practice what he's trying to get them all to do. It's like our Lord who throughout his ministry said, 'Bless them that curse you ... pray for them which despitefully use you' (Mt. 5:44). And then on the cross Jesus put it into practice. He said, 'Father, forgive them; for they know not what they do' (Lk. 23:34). Throughout this book James is saying, 'Don't be a respecter of persons. Consider the other person.' He has this eloquent statement about mercy transcending judgement (2:13). And he says, 'We're going to be judged by the law of liberty. You don't want to be judged any other way, do you? All right, treat other people like that.'

James ends the epistle treating them like that when he sees what they've done. They've been a disgrace. James at the end accepts them. When we're judgemental we put ourselves in the position of the one who was forgiven and then he wouldn't forgive and God was angry with him for that (Mt. 18:23–35). We've all been forgiven. That leaves us without any excuse when we judge another person. The moment you're tempted to judge another person, stop. Get alone and begin to think of how God has forgiven you. And just keep going. Make a list. And you'll be so overcome you'll think, 'How could I have even thought to feel as I felt?' James had to speak as he did to them and then he ends up saying, 'My brothers, if any of you do err from the truth ...'

Theological Backsliding

Someone will say, 'That's true with regard to behaviour. But the way to know whether a person is a Christian is by whether he maintains the truth.' You want to have that as a little hatchet by which you can get at some person: 'He's just not maintaining the truth. He couldn't believe this and still be a Christian.' James says, 'If any of you do err from the truth ...' There's such a thing as theological backsliding. A person can be a Christian and then for a while embrace an error. Peter had some theological correcting necessary in his own life. It's recorded in the book of Acts.

Chances are, all of us have got a lot of ideas that are just wrong. Theological ideas. We're opinionated. It is possible when you backslide theologically that you're even worse than the devil. At least the devil knows the truth (Jas. 2:19). A Christian can stray from the truth. It's so humbling. Jesus got it right theologically. And we've got a substitute in glory made unto us not only righteousness, sanctification but also wisdom (1 Cor. 1:30). Thus when we err from the truth, thank God it does not render void the wisdom that has been imputed to us. Paul could say, 'If we believe not, yet he abideth faithful' (2 Tim. 2:13).

However, the term 'truth' applies not only to doctrine but to practice. Peter could talk about 'the divine power' giving to us 'all things that pertain unto life and godliness' (2 Pet. 1:3). Paul said to Timothy, 'Thou hast fully known my doctrine, manner of life ...' (2 Tim. 3:10). This practice, in fact, is probably what James has mainly in mind. Because these Christians had been giving in to lust. And he warned them that when you're in a state of lust you're in a dangerous state of temptation. It can bring forth sin, and when sin has finished it brings forth death.

What is needed for a person like this who strays from the truth? James says, 'There's one thing needed: conversion'. 'If any of you do err from the truth, and one convert him ...' Does this tear up your theology? Is conversion only a once for all, never-to-be-repeated experience? Or do we have a verse here that plays into Arminian theology? There are two kinds of Arminians. There's the inconsistent Arminian who denies the doctrine of election but believes in the eternal security of the believer. Then there's the consistent Arminian. He denies both. He doesn't believe in election. He also thinks you can lose your salvation. Those who believe you can lose your salvation use this verse as one of their proof texts.

We begin with the very word itself, the Greek word *epistrepse*. It means 'to turn towards', 'turn around'. It has been translated in a variety of ways. For example in Luke 1:16: 'And many of the children of Israel shall he turn to the Lord', referring to John the Baptist. Peter used the word in Acts 3:19: 'Repent ye therefore, and be converted.' It's used in Matthew 9:22 when the woman who had the issue of blood came up and just wanted to touch the hem of Jesus' garment. We're told that Jesus turned towards her. It's used in Acts 9:40. Peter knelt down to pray with the woman who had just died and he turned himself to the body and said, 'Arise.' And in Revelation 1:12 John said, 'I turned to see the voice.'

You can see that obviously in these cases these people weren't converted. So this Greek word is not necessarily a theological word. The context determines its usage. The NIV translates this verse: 'If one of you should wander from the truth and someone should bring him back ...' It's restoring one to the place where one once was. It's not a reference to the non-Christian being converted. It's not a reference to a Christian who lost his salvation. That's not possible. Anybody who thinks you can lose your salvation betrays that he hasn't seen the glory of the cross of Jesus. What it refers to is the Christian who has strayed but has come to see his error. The turning here is not merely an outward turn, but the Greek word is similar to *epistrama* which means 'to know'. In other words, you are aware of what you are doing. This is what happened to the prodigal son. He came to himself (Lk. 15:17). It's a turning that is not mechanical but a conscious realization.

The backslider cannot see his own folly

James wants us to see that the backslider is not likely to come back of his own accord. He is not likely to see his own folly by himself. A person like this needs special help from the outside. The prodigal son was a different case because he was starved out. He had no choice but to go back home. Sometimes God can do it like that. In the case of Samson, he was left alone. He had no choice but to talk to God. God can bring you to the place where there's nothing to do but look to him.

But these Christian people didn't have the sort of backsliding that was likely to result in economic ruin where they were boxed in. Their backsliding was the sort of thing where it is hard to prove really that they're in real trouble. This is why James has to walk very delicately, and yet he calls a spade a spade. Their backsliding was serious, but not to the point of the kind of scandal that they could really be shown up for what they were. So James says that someone must convert him. It means somebody on the outside is going to come in and help. God uses means. Another person.

Convert Someone

I know there are people who are critical of the phrase: 'So-and-so converted me' or 'I got converted by so-and-so'. James doesn't object to putting it like that. Of course, God does it but he uses others. And so James says, 'Go on, convert him.' James didn't say, 'Faith will do it.' 'Faith without works is dead.' James says, 'You do it. You turn that person around.' It may be like when you lead a person to Christ – that you have to deal with this person. It's not simply reading off a little spiritual slogan in five seconds and saying, 'One, two, three, now you believe.' Some people have been converted like that but not many. Usually you stay with a person and you plead with them. A backslider can be harder to reach and you must plead and stay there. You might stay to the end of the night, pleading with a person, pulling him out of the fire. A brand plucked from the burning (Zech. 3:2).

It's as though James is saying, 'Sort it out among yourselves. You're going to have to help each other.' Perhaps someone from another Christian community, an outsider, might come along, perhaps James' own letter will do it. God can use the power of preaching to do it. But we should not underestimate our own influence on a one-to-one basis. You might be the very one that can help another person.

I was listening to a tape recording recently of Gene Phillips, who was my pastor as I was growing up. He made a powerful impression on me. The Church of the Nazarene in which I was brought up would give an altar call at the end. And sometimes people would go to another person in the same auditorium and just gently say, 'Don't you think you should go forward?' You could pick that to pieces but if you were brought up in that context it's the most natural thing in the world. I heard Dr Phillips on this tape say that he was at a service preaching. He was a visiting evangelist and he noticed a person coming in each night, sitting in a certain place. He said, 'I thought he must be a Christian because he came every night and sat there.' But he said, 'The Lord kept saying to me, "You must go to that person." This particular night I knew I had to do it. I was just shaking to think that I should have to go talk to another person like that. But I did. And it turned out that that very person had just said that day, "I believe I've committed the unpardonable sin. God, if there's hope for me cause Dr Phillips to come to me", and I did and the man was restored.'

I tell that story for a reason. You just never know what another person is secretly hoping you might do. I think this is the chief way James wants us to go about helping a person who is overtaken in a fault. Sometimes a firm line is needed. But always remember: consider yourself, lest you also be tempted. And then, if you should convert someone, look what you do. James says, 'You shall save a soul from death and shall hide a multitude of sins.'

44

The Joy of Bringing the Backslider Home

James 5:19–20

This is our final study from this general epistle of James, and the very last verse of the epistle. 'Let him know, that he which converteth the sinner from the error of his way shall save a soul from death, and shall hide a multitude of sins.' It is James' way of wrapping up the epistle. And it is very interesting how, in the middle of a sentence, he does something which, if you were looking at it strictly at a natural level, is brilliant.

James Targets The Unbeliever, The Backslider And The Brothers

He starts dealing with the backslider in verse 19. What he does is to bring in unobtrusively not only the backslider but he shows the effect that it will have on the sinner. This means not only the backslider but the non-Christian as well as the believer.

The Three Benefits Of Conversion

We've heard the expression 'killing two birds with one stone', but I think we'll see before we're finished that James actually kills three birds with one stone. We have seen that living the Christian life is the general theme. But there is also this implicit concern for the backslider – the Christian who will even go to heaven if he is not restored.

The backslider needs help from outside

James shows that every backslider needs help from outside himself, as it were. It's very unusual and quite infrequent for a backslider, by himself, just to turn around. It can take place through the preaching. But I think James is suggesting here that these Christians who had been quarrelling with each other could sort it out among themselves.

For a backslider to be restored by somebody else in the same congregation, who himself may have his problem, requires very delicate handling. James is hoping that somebody will take the initiative. And yet to do that requires great grace and wisdom. It probably will not take place until somebody has the courage, the honesty, the integrity, to confess a sin to somebody else.

I was pastor of a church once where there were two families who were rivals and they talked about each other. They would sit on opposite sides of the church. And you'd wonder what was going to happen. One had to take the initiative. One day one of them did. He broke down and confessed his own sin. It set off a chain reaction. The other side said, 'It's not you, it's me.' They fell into each other's arms and the Spirit came down and everybody was melted. And lost people were convicted in that very service. This is the kind of thing that James has in mind.

When James says in verse 20, 'Let him know …' it's really a command that if you come forward and take the initiative you should know what you're doing. 'Know this.' The NIV translates it: 'Remember this.' That gets this sense over. Somebody must make the first move. Whoever will volunteer to break the stalemate is going to get a personal word from James.

The Goal Of Christian Living

To break such a stalemate presupposes a high degree of wisdom and a spirituality without any self-righteousness. There are not very many spiritual people who are not self-righteous. And it makes you want to say, 'I don't even want to be like that.' But this is the goal of Christian living: to be spiritual without being self-righteous. However, the backslider is not going to be restored accidentally. Somebody must do it. To do this kind of thing frequently calls for a more delicate operation even than winning the non-Christian to the Lord.

What is James' purpose in singling somebody out? Why should anybody bother to restore another person? Cain asked the question, 'Am I my brother's keeper?' (Gen. 4:9). James says we are. If you do try to restore your brother you're doing that person the greatest possible favour. First of all you're converting him from the error of his ways. You're also going to save him from death. And that's a lot. But there's another benefit: you 'hide a multitude of sins'. Not only are you doing something for that other person, but you're restoring the Christian witness to its credibility. It will be a faith with works.

The impact on witnessing

The underlying cause of all the division and the double mindedness and the worldliness of this Christian community was their failure in evangelism. They gave Christianity a bad name by the very way they went about witnessing. They gave the impression that Christianity is middle class. They only wanted to reach a certain type of person. They were being so defective in their evangelism by trying to discriminate. And it backfired.

But there was a further fall-out from all this: an internal backfire. When we are disobedient to God and what he tells us to do in evangelizing, it backfires on us. The church will be divided. There will be fault-finding. We become introspective and the world laughs. It goes back to our failure to reach the lost with the gospel. Not only did it cause division within the ranks of the believers, but something snapped inside every heart. A condition followed which James calls being double minded. Their thinking processes became fuzzy and nothing was clear to them.

James is appealing to somebody somewhere to step forward and aspire to be the one who restores. You may say, 'How do you know if you're qualified? Where do you begin?' First, you begin with yourself. You don't begin with the other person. You ask yourself if your own witness has resulted in a defective evangelism. You say, 'I'm afraid maybe it has. That means I can't help another person because I've got to get myself straightened out before I can help them.' If you find this has been true about yourself, admit it. Confess it. It's not going to surprise anybody. And that keeps us from being self-righteous when we're trying to help somebody else.

Ask yourself: Am I double minded? Have I become at home with the world? Have I been guilty of taking my life into my own hands? Have I been a gossip? Have I been fault-finding? Go to the person who knows this about you and admit it. Take the initiative. When you do this you will help that other person. You will restore your own credibility in the meantime and make it easy for the other person to say, 'It's me.' It's like the old Negro spiritual put it:

> *It's not my brother, nor my sister,*
> *But it's for me, O Lord,*
> *Standing in the need of prayer.*

Not the preacher. It's the easiest thing in the world to criticize the preacher. Not the deacon. People love to go for the deacons. But it's me, O Lord, standing in the need of prayer. This kind of confession doesn't come as any surprise. The surprise, perhaps, is that you would actually admit it. It is when you get right that you become an effective instrument in restoring the backslider.

God lets us save face

You will never bring the backslider home if you yourself have not forgiven that brother. Don't say, 'If he gets straightened out I'll forgive him.' According to James, you may be the very one to restore him. You say, 'I just couldn't do that.' James would say to you, 'If you don't, who will?' You restore the brother overtaken in a sin when that brother sees that you hold absolutely nothing against him. You may say, 'Does that always work?' No, it doesn't. But you leave that brother knowing in his heart of hearts that you have forgiven him. And you must never underestimate what it can do. For that person very likely already feels ashamed. And he will love you for letting him save face. Isn't it wonderful how God lets us save face?

God lets us save face by overlooking our sin. That's what forgiving sin is. He says, 'I don't even know about it. What sin are you talking about?' When we are that way with another person they can feel it. They can say, 'He doesn't hold anything against me. I can't believe it.' You say, 'Do I go to the person and say, "I forgive you for what you've done"?' No, that's the worst thing in the world. Whenever you say that it shows you haven't forgiven them. You're really wanting to stick the knife in again, saying, 'I forgive you for what you've done to me.' You forgive when you absolutely forget it. That's the way you win a brother. Peter said, 'Love covers a multitude of sins' (1 Pet. 4:8). When you really do forgive it will show.

> *It is a thing most wonderful,*
> *Almost too wonderful to be,*
> *That God's own Son should come from heaven,*
> *And die to save a child like me.*

It's at this point that James manages unobtrusively, in a most wonderful way, to broaden his concern. This is how he kills the second bird with the same stone. He now has both the weak Christian but also the non-Christian in mind. We don't need to look any further at this word 'convert'. The expression is used: 'He which converteth the sinner ...' It's the same Greek word that means 'to turn', 'to bring him back'. But James says it is a person who does the converting. I know people who are so afraid to use language like this: 'I got converted by so-and-so.' Somebody out to be so theologically exact says, 'Don't say that. God did it.' James knows that because he's already said in chapter one, 'Of his own will begat he us with the word of truth' (v. 18). Of course, God does it. But James isn't in a theological straitjacket. He's not afraid to say that one can convert another. It's a hint to us not to be so uptight about how we word things and not to be on the run lest there be somebody opposing us as a theological witch-hunter, always looking for opportunities to say the way we see it.

The point here is that he broadens the concern.

Saving Sinners

He's not only dealing with the weak Christian but he uses a word here that has a double meaning. It's this word *hamartolon*, 'sinner'. How do we know that James could mean the Christian by using the term 'sinner'? James has been addressing them all along as Christians, 'My brothers'. He deals with them as regenerate men. And in James chapter 4 verse 8 he calls them 'sinners'. In chapter 2 he said, 'If ye have respect to persons, ye commit sin' (v. 9). And he said in the end, 'Confess your sins one to another' (5:16). Don't be surprised that James could call a Christian a sinner.

James 5:20 has often been used as an evangelistic text, and it fits very well. There's nothing wrong with that. But I think we must be fair and say that what James has in mind in this verse is that the backslider should be restored so that he may now reach the lost. By 'sinner' he does mean the backslider, but it also means the lost. The New Testament uses this word 'sinner' for Christian and non-Christian alike many times. Paul said to Timothy, 'This is a faithful saying, and worthy of all acceptation, that Christ Jesus came into the world to save sinners; of whom I am chief' (1 Tim. 1:15). Paul was a Christian. That's how he regarded himself. And yet there are times when the term 'sinner' is used to refer to a non-Christian as, for example, in

1 Peter 4:18: 'If the righteous scarcely be saved, where shall the ungodly and the sinner appear?' This is why I say James kills two, no three, birds with one stone.

This double meaning, referring to the backslider but also the non-Christian, is now extended in this verse. And we see three things that will happen to the backslider or to the non-Christian should you convert or turn him around.

Saved From Going The Wrong Way

The first is, you save him from the error of his ways. This word 'error' is the noun of the verb that means 'to go astray'. So it simply shows that the restoration of the backslider, in this case, puts him right on the path where he should have been all along.

If it's theological backsliding it means he will return to 20 / 20 vision. He will see things clearly. If it's moral backsliding it means he will repent and mend his ways. If it's a case of holding a grudge and fault-finding, love will replace this feeling. It will change him from the error of his ways so that on his way to heaven from now on he will walk a straight line. Or to use Richard Sibbes' quaint expression, 'exact walking'. That's what the practising Christian is meant to do. And to the backslider and the non-Christian, it refers to the error of his ways.

Converting the non-Christian causes him to see things that he wasn't able to see up till now. As long as the Christians are all backsliders and are quarrelling among themselves, the non-Christian thinks that it's not going to be any great thing if he doesn't become a Christian. As long as the church is divided and we can't get on with each other, it shouldn't surprise us that we're at a standstill and the world takes no notice. But if the back-slider is restored then the sinner – the non-Christian – begins to see something he hadn't seen before – the lostness of his own condition. And the poor man says, 'I do believe they want to save me now. There must be something in the Christian faith for me.'

And then the rich person, for the first time, sees how serious it is. He sees that he's not being catered to and that's what stirs him. Because the rich man is used to being buttered up in the world. But when he comes into the Christian church and finds that he's treated like everybody else, that's what grips him. He begins to see that he's lost. For the first time the rich and the poor see the responsibility that they have to themselves and that they're going to hell. That is what James means by turning a person around from the error of his ways, the way he had been looking at things.

Saved From Death

But he goes on to say that in doing this 'you shall save a soul from death'. How does this apply to the backslider? This word for 'death' is the same word that was used in chapter one: 'Every man is tempted, when he is drawn away of his own lust, and enticed. Then when lust hath conceived, it bringeth forth sin: and sin, when it is finished, bringeth forth death' (vv. 14–15). We have seen the four possible states: suggestion, temptation, sin, death. No matter how godly you are, you cannot help having an evil suggestion put before you.

Temptation is something else, but even that is not sin. But you are responsible for the temptation. It is the task of every Christian not to be at home with temptation but to fight it and reduce temptation to the level of suggestion. Now temptation, if not brought under control, will give birth to sin. It is this stage three – sin – that many of these Christians had reached and it's obviously what James is worried about. He's worried that stage four will follow: death.

How 'death' is used in the New Testament

What does it mean for the Christian to reach stage four? This is a bit complicated. Death is used in the New Testament in three ways:

- One, spiritual death: that is, the way a person is brought into the world at a natural level. All men by nature are spiritually dead. 'You hath he quickened, who were dead' (Eph. 2:1).
- Second is physical death. We're going to die. Death is the result of sin. 'The wages of sin is death' (Rom. 6:23). God said to Adam, 'On the day you eat of this fruit you will surely die' (Gen. 2:17).
- Third means what is called 'the second death'. Jude's epistle refers to being 'twice dead, plucked up by the roots' (v. 12). In Revelation chapter 20: 'Whosoever was not found written in the book of life was cast into the lake of fire' (v. 15). 'The second death' (v. 14). That's everlasting punishment.

What does 'death' in James 5:20 mean? It's got to be one of these three. With respect to the Christian, it doesn't mean the first type of death because they had no danger of being brought to spiritual death because they were born again. It doesn't refer to the third category, the second death, because these Christians are not going to go to hell. They are saved. 'They shall never perish, neither shall any man pluck them out of my hand' (Jn. 10:28). And even to the disobedient Christian Paul said, 'He shall suffer loss: but he himself shall be saved; yet so as by fire' (1 Cor. 3:15). James himself has said, 'Mercy will triumph against judgement' (2:13).

But the Christian can, by reckless living, hasten his own physical death. We've seen this before. But I do think it is a missing note in the modern church. Paul says to the Corinthians who had abused the Lord's supper, 'For this cause many are weak and sickly among you, and many sleep' – some have already died a premature death, as it were (1 Cor. 11:30). They hastened their own death by the way they lived. And this is what Paul rendered to that abusive Christian in the church of Corinth when he said, 'Deliver such an one unto Satan ... that the spirit may be saved in the day of the Lord Jesus' (1 Cor. 5:5). In this very epistle when James said that the prayer of faith would save the sick he said, 'If he have committed sins ...' (5:15). There's the belief that sin could be the very cause of the sickness. And that was a way of showing that even that would be forgiven.

Rescued from 'death'

When we left our church in Fort Lauderdale different people came to say goodbye and one particular man, whom we had had the joy of leading to the Lord about a year before, looked at me with tears rolling down his cheeks and said, 'You saved my life.' Perhaps you've heard of Christians who have said, 'If the Lord hadn't converted me I wouldn't even be alive today.' This is true of the non-Christian. But even the Christian, as a backslider, can bring about death. This is why Paul said to Timothy that 'bodily exercise profiteth little' which shows now he's talking about the physical – 'but godliness is profitable unto all things, having promise of the life that now is, and of that which is to come' (1 Tim. 4:8). What is James saying? You are going to save the backslider from a premature death. But when it comes to the non-Christian it includes all three meanings of death. First of all, you rescue him from his natural state. He will be quickened who was dead in trespasses and sins. You may well prolong his own life by him becoming a Christian. And third, most of all, you rescue him from going to hell itself.

Saved From Past Sins

I close now with a third benefit: the benefit of bringing a backslider home. It's a benefit of no small proportion. This is why I said that James has killed three birds with one stone. Because by the way he words this last phrase, he shows most wonderfully something else that takes place when you bring the backslider home. He says that not only do you correct 'the error of his way' – you save him from death – but you 'shall hide a multitude of sins.' The Greek word is *kalupse*, 'shall conceal'. They'll not even be known about. Whose sins? Is it the backslider's? Is it the non-Christian's? Could it be the believer who goes about doing this? The answer is, all three of these.

It's a most profound phrase here. As for the newly converted, it goes without saying that what you've done for him would be covering a multitude of sins. All of his sins are washed away to begin with. And you've spared that person a further earthly sorrow. But as for the backslider, you've given him a new beginning. Look at it like this. Paul says, 'We must all appear before the judgement seat of Christ; that every one may receive the things done in his body' – 'body' – 'according to that he hath done, whether it be good or bad' (1 Cor. 5:10). Now the backslider, were he to be snatched out of this world, would go to heaven but he would lose his reward. But by coming home he starts all over. So that at the judgement when he will receive a reward for what he has done in his body – all this changes now.

A whole new person

But that's not all that that means. By bringing the backslider home you have perhaps corrected an area of his life that is so blatant but – it's a strange thing – repentance over one sin will affect other sins. In the same way that defective evangelism ricocheted – it was a chain reaction and all kinds of problems happened as the result of one great defect – so it is when there is repentance with regard to one specific sin. It has a way of having a chain reaction and other things happen. A person even gets nice to live with. People who live with them say, 'You're different. What is it?' It was really a deeper-seated problem that was dealt with, but it affects the whole. This is again what is meant.

Credible witness with much joy

But that's not all. Look what you do for yourself in this. Should you volunteer to be a restorer you've begun to show your faith by your works at long last. By what you are doing you are restoring the Christian witness to credibility in the world. And the joy for having done that is beyond calculation. James began his epistle by saying,

'Count it all joy when ye fall into divers temptations [trials]' (2:2). Suffering, trial – that's your invitation to grow rapidly in grace. And suffering helps expose sins that you didn't know about on the condition that you dignify the trial. This is why you can count it joy.

The Greatest Joy Of All

But now he moves to the greatest joy of all. For the joy of trial leads to the joy of bringing the backslider home. As Paul put it to Timothy, 'Take heed unto thyself' – that's where you begin – 'and unto the doctrine; continue in them: for in doing this thou shalt both save thyself, and them that hear thee' (1 Tim. 4:16). When you begin to restore like this, each doing it according to his own gift, do you realize what is taking place, that that is the very key to your own survival? Because this matter of restoring one another in the spirit of meekness is not an optional thing. You do it or it will backfire on you. We're not really given the choice. We must all volunteer. It's not a matter of saying, 'I hope somebody will step forward.' No, you must do it.

This is the burden of my heart this week when I've been hearing so much idle talk about when we've had a problem with the teenagers. Somebody says, 'Why doesn't somebody do something?' Why don't you do something? I'm tired of hearing everybody say, 'Somebody ought to do something.' It's for all of us to do something. It's our problem. So when you see that there's a problem somewhere and you see a person that is overtaken, you have no choice. Because if you don't do, it it will backfire on you.

The reason James could say, 'Doing this covers a multitude of sins', is because it's not only what you do for the non-Christian and the backslider, it is the key to your own survival. Not only will you save your own soul and others but you will conceal a multitude of sins which inevitably would have been committed were we not so engaged in this task to which we've all been called. That's James. That's his word. Will we listen or will we forget what we've heard and be like the man who just looked at himself in the mirror and then forgot what he looked like (1:23–24)?

Scripture Index